New Mexico

New Mexico

Sharon Niederman

with photographs by the author

The Countryman Press ✳ Woodstock, Vermont

FIRST EDITION

Also by the author

The Santa Fe & Taos Book: Great Destinations

Return to Abo

A Quilt of Words: Diaries, Letters & Original Accounts of Life in the Southwest 1860–1960

We welcome your comments and suggestions. Please contact Explorer's Guide Editor, The Countryman Press, P.O. Box 748, Woodstock, Vermont 05091, or e-mail countrymanpress@wwnorton.com.

First Edition

ISBN 978-0-88150-657-0

Maps by Mapping Specialists, © 2009 The Countryman Press
Book design by Bodenweber Design
Text composition by PerfecType, Nashville, TN
Cover photograph © Kerrick James
Interior photographs by the author unless otherwise indicated

Published by The Countryman Press, P.O. Box 748, Woodstock, Vermont 05091

Distributed by W. W. Norton & Company, Inc., 500 Fifth Avenue, New York, NY 10110

Printed in the United States of America

10 9 8 7 6 5 4 3 2 1

For Irma Bailey and all who love the adventure of the road

EXPLORE WITH US!

New Mexico: An Explorer's Guide is broken down into sections representing different areas of the state. Because of the state's size, most of these geographic sections are subdivided into "mini-chapters" for easy navigation. Each chapter opens with a general introduction touching on the history and highlights of the area, and then continues with information on destinations, accommodations, and restaurants that guide you to the best of New Mexico.

I offer independent venues almost exclusively, for two reasons. Most readers are familiar with franchise food and lodgings. More importantly, independent businesses are less known and more capable of delivering an authentic New Mexican experience. I have done my best to share with you my knowledge of the state based on two decades of traveling and writing about its unique cuisine, venerable history, diverse cultures and customs, architecture, and natural beauty. I have tried to show you my favorite places and to give you the kind of honesty I would appreciate in getting to know a place.

Guidance lists the entities such as chambers of commerce, visitor centers, and public land managers that you can refer to for information on the area.

Getting There tells you the best routes to take and what means of transportation are available to get you there. **Getting Around** lists means of public transportation or shuttles where they are available.

Medical Emergency lists hospitals and/or clinics. Dialing 911 is also an option at all times.

To See lists attractions and points of interest you may want to visit, including museums, historic sites, scenic drives, and more.

To Do features key activities available in each area.

Lodging will give you ideas of where to find unique and consistently good places to stay, even in more remote areas.

Where to Eat lists venues that serve dependably good food. There are two categories here, *Dining Out*, the better restaurants, and *Eating Out*, the more casual options. Please let us know if the food or service is up to the standard we expect—places do change hands and have off nights.

Entertainment gives suggestions on theater, music, and relaxing in the evening.

Selective Shopping points you in the right direction for shopping, particularly for wares that are characteristic of a place.

Special Events is a month-by-month compendium of the most important annual events and festivals in each community.

KEY TO SYMBOLS

⚭ The wedding rings symbol appears beside facilities that frequently serve as venues for weddings and civil unions.

⚑ The special-value symbol appears next to lodgings and restaurants that combine high quality and moderate prices.

⚘ The kids-alert symbol appears next to lodgings, restaurants, activities, and shops of special appeal to youngsters.

🐾 The dog-paw symbol appears next to lodgings that accept pets (usually with a reservation and deposit) as of press time.

♿ The wheelchair symbol appears next to lodgings, restaurants, and attractions that are partially or fully handicapped accessible.

"ⁱ" This symbol appears next to cafes and lodgings that have Wi-Fi.

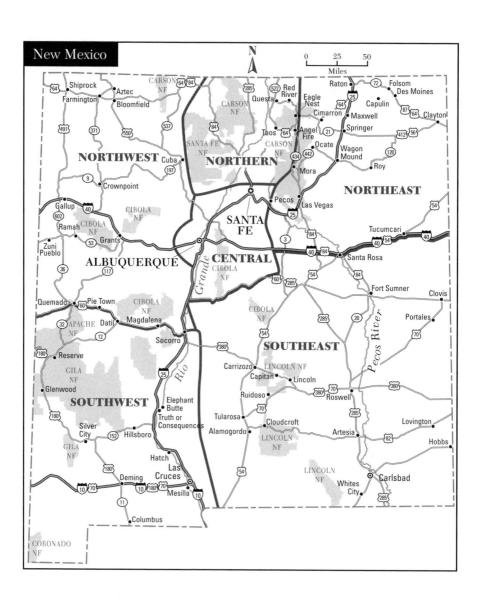

New Mexico

N

0 25 50
Miles

Shiprock
64
Aztec
Farmington
Bloomfield
491
371
550
537

CARSON NF
64 84
285
CARSON NF
84
SANTA FE NF
Cuba
NORTHERN
197
NORTHWEST

9
Crownpoint

Gallup
40
602
CIBOLA NF
Ramah
CIBOLA NF
53
Grants
Zuni Pueblo
36
ALBUQUERQUE
117

Quemado
60
Pie Town
CIBOLA NF
32
APACHE NF
Datil
Magdalena
12
Socorro
180
Reserve
GILA NF
Glenwood
25
SOUTHWEST
Elephant Butte
Truth or Consequences
Silver City
152
Hillsboro
180
GILA NF
Hatch
Deming
Las Cruces
10
70
180
70
10
11
Mesilla
10
Columbus

CORONADO NF

Taos
64
Angel Fire
CARSON NF
434
442
21
Ocate
Wagon Mound
Mora
Roy
Pecos
Las Vegas
25

SANTA FE
3
84
40
84
Santa Rosa
CENTRAL
CIBOLA NF
60
285
285
20
CIBOLA NF
54

SOUTHEAST
Carrizozo
LINCOLN NF
Capitan
Lincoln
Ruidoso
70
Tularosa
70
Cloudcroft
Alamogordo
LINCOLN NF
54

Raton
72
Folsom
Des Moines
Questa
Red River
522
Eagle Nest
64
25
Capulin
Cimarron
Maxwell
87
64
Clayton
Springer
412
56
120

NORTHEAST

54
40
Tucumcari
54
40
40

Fort Sumner
Clovis

Portales
70

Pecos River

380
Roswell
285
Lovington
Artesia
82
Hobbs

LINCOLN NF
Whites City
Carlsbad
285

CONTENTS

HOW TO USE THIS GUIDE

WHAT YOU REALLY NEED TO KNOW ABOUT EXPLORING NEW MEXICO

The first time I saw New Mexico was on a road trip with a school buddy in 1972. We drove down I-25 from Boulder where I was attending graduate school at the University of Colorado. It was nighttime when we crossed Raton Pass into northern New Mexico. I had never seen so much empty space, and the expanse made me nervous.

"Why are there no people or lights out there? What's wrong?" I asked my friend.

A Colorado native, she laughed.

A few years back, I was showing my cousin around northern New Mexico. We drove from Albuquerque to Ojo Caliente Hot Springs.

She was visiting from New Jersey, the most populous state. As we turned out of Española onto the road north, she looked at me and asked,

"Where are you taking me? This is the middle of nowhere!"

Now it was my turn to laugh. "No," I replied. "The middle of nowhere is the gas station in Vaughn where the wind is always blowing."

To paraphrase Governor Lew Wallace, who presided over the state during the tumultuous Lincoln County War era, "Calculations based on experience elsewhere do not work in New Mexico." Governor Wallace, who hailed from Indiana, made that observation from his vantage point in the Palace of the Governors in Santa Fe, while writing his classic, *Ben Hur*, and attempting to bring Billy the Kid to justice.

It is a simplistic, yet useful truth to note that one's greatest strength is also one's greatest weakness. That truism may also be applied to entities such as a state. While New Mexico is not exactly the land of *mañana*, it remains the land of *poco tiempe*, or "pretty soon," just as it was originally characterized by the writer Charles L. Lummis in 1893.

The good news first: New Mexico is one place, perhaps the only place, in the United States where its oldest cultures continue to live on. They have cohabited and adapted to the impacts of outsiders—including 21st-century urbanization—for centuries, and they continue to practice their languages, religions, and life

TAOS PUEBLO IS THE PLACE TO FIND GENUINE MICACEOUS POTTERY.

ways regardless. The 19 Indian pueblos (each a sovereign nation), the Navajo and Apache nations, Hispanic villages, and ranching towns with homesteader legacies persist, against all odds, precariously, in New Mexico. The Indian ruins and mission churches, the graveyards and wealth of vernacular architecture are no more than a short trip down the road from virtually anyplace in the state. Somehow New Mexico absorbs whatever enters it and makes it "New Mexican."

Speaking of roads, despite the fact that New Mexico was, and is, crisscrossed by many of the great trails across the continent—the north-south Camino Real Aldente from Mexico City to the furthest reach of New Spain, Santa Fe; the east-west Santa Fe Trail trade route from Independence, Missouri, to Santa Fe; Route 66 from Chicago to Los Angeles; and the first paved intercontinental highway, the Ocean to Ocean Highway, US 60 (each bringing goods, ideas, visitors, colonizers, and eventual residents)—somehow the state remains remote and somewhat "off the map." Today, even if traveling on the north-south interstate, I-25, or the east-west interstate, I-40, or any of the state roads that meander through the quadrants between, traces of the old roads remain, if one's imagination is open to a bit of a reconstruction process. Many of the sites named in this book will assist that process.

And that itself is a source of good news: New Mexico's cuisine, festivals, arts, ancient customs, and history remain accessible, constant, and exciting. Consequently, the exotic, what one hungers for in planning a trip to a foreign land, may be experienced here by the explorer without so much as a visa, while granting a deeper understanding of the United States.

On the other hand, everything is a trade-off. While authenticity is available, New Mexico remains in its own time frame, with one foot planted in yesterday and the other not really serious about getting to tomorrow. Ironically, it may be the Indians, with their franchise on gaming, and the Las Vegas–style resorts they have built around their casinos, which have become most skilled at offering the level of hospitality world travelers expect.

In addition, you may not find roads marked very well, or you may receive instructions such as, "turn left at the dip, then right at the big cottonwood," so it is essential you travel well armed with detailed maps. Anyone can get lost, so bring water and don't let your gas tank go below half-full. And the altitude really can get to you, so be sure to allow yourself to adjust before you take that hike up Wheeler Peak.

Despite recent population booms from Las Vegas to Las Cruces, outsiders still may not find the efficiency, public transportation, speed of service, and promptly returned messages they are accustomed to. Hours posted do not always align with hours kept. New Mexico was the 47th state admitted to the Union, in 1912. Everything really does move more slowly here in the land of mañana. Perhaps mañana is not the most accurate term, but being aware that everything takes longer than expected is probably a good idea to adopt if you don't want to raise your blood pressure. Even, maybe especially, in expensive Santa Fe, there is such a rapid turnover of employees that you are likely to encounter service people who are neither well trained nor well informed. If you are prone to frustration on such matters, it is probably best to book a lodging that provides experienced concierge service.

Therefore, it is always a good idea to call a planned destination ahead of time. Do not assume that it will be open or that it even still exists. Every effort has been made to assure the reliability of establishments, but there is no guarantee that it has not gone out of business or moved.

If you love the outdoors, it is all here: hiking, fishing, skiing, and birding. The beauty of the night skies; the fun of discovery in ghost towns; the power inherent in the great ruins of Chaco Canyon or the Gila Cliff Dwellings; the back road adventure of a finding a café serving real home cooking; the freedom of driving an open two-lane without billboards under a huge wide-open sky. There is a tremendously varied terrain, from high desert to forest to river and lake. One lifetime is simply not enough to do it all.

GETTING AROUND

The truth is that if you want to see New Mexico, you are best off driving. Otherwise, you will be at the mercy of slow and sporadic to nonexistent public transportation. So for the greatest freedom and safety, you need to bring or rent a car.

Amtrak runs one train each day from Raton to Albuquerque and back again, with stops in Las Vegas and Lamy. The train heads west to Gallup after Albuquerque. If you have time, this is a wonderful way to travel.

Albuquerque bus service continues to improve.

Shuttles from the Sunport in Albuquerque run to Santa Fe and Taos. See those cities for specific information.

Some smaller towns have cab service, but not all. It's best to call the numbers in the Guidance section to check before you go.

WHEN TO COME

There really is no bad time to come to New Mexico, no real "off-season." It is up to you to plan your visit to coincide with your interests, which may be skiing Taos in winter or attending the Santa Fe Indian Market in summer or the Albuquerque Balloon Fiesta in fall. You can be sure that if you are planning to come during a highly popular event, however, that lodging rates will be higher, and advance reservation times will be longer. The advantage to a perceived "off-season" time, say October–November in northern New Mexico, or January–February in southern New Mexico, is, of course, less competition for rooms and tables. You will have the place more to yourself. The beauty of the place is always present, and there are always plenty of sights to see and events to attend.

A FEW INTERESTING FACTS

While New Mexico remains the fifth largest state in land area, it still boasts a population of well under 2 million. Most of that is centered in the biggest cities: Albuquerque, Rio Rancho, Santa Fe, and Las Cruces.

The state bird is the roadrunner; the state plant is the yucca; and the state cookie is the bizcochito, an anise-flavored shortbread. The state question is: "Red or Green?"

The visitor's most frequently asked question might be: "Which is hotter, red or green?" but there is no way to generalize that. It is amazing how different

REJUVENATION AWAITS AT OJO CALIENTE HOT SPRINGS.

establishments can take the same basic ingredients—chile, garlic, salt—and vary their flavors. When in doubt, ask for a small taste before you order, or ask for your chile on the side.

I might also nominate, if I were ever asked, a State Pastry, which would be the sopaipilla, an adaptation of the Indian fry bread, a crispy, chewy, and light donutlike pillow that is eaten with honey and doubles as dessert and bread.

If you are wondering about the terms referring to the cuisine, New Mexican food is quite different from Mexican food, but you may find the terms used interchangeably in names and conversation. However, in this book, unless specified otherwise, eating establishments are serving the distinct New Mexican cuisine.

The holiday season brings displays of lights that are actually candles in paper bags full of sand. In the northern part of the state they are called *farolitos,* and in Albuquerque and south, they are called luminarias.

A FEW KEY DATES IN NEW MEXICO HISTORY

1598–Juan de Oñate establishes the first permanent settlement at San Juan Pueblo

1640–Francisco Coronado searches for the Seven Cities of Cibola through New Mexico

OLD-TIME RODEO AT THE COLFAX COUNTY FAIR.

1680–Pueblo Revolt drives Spanish governors and Franciscan fathers out of New Mexico

1821–Mexico gains control of New Mexico and Santa Fe Trail opens

1856–Stephen Kearney's "Army of the West" gains peaceful occupation of New Mexico for the United States

1879–Railroad arrives

1912–New Mexico becomes the 47th state

1926–US Route 66 goes through New Mexico

1945–The atom bomb is successfully tested at Trinity Site

IMPORTANT PHONE NUMBERS AND WEB SITES

Emergency (911)

To report drunk or dangerous driving (on your mobile phone): #DWI

New Mexico road conditions: 1-800-432-4269; www.nmroads.com

Indian Pueblo Cultural Center: 1-800-766-4405; www.indianpueblo.org

New Mexico State Parks: 1-888-NMPARKS; www.nmparks.com

www.skinewmexico.com

www.nmjeeptours.com

www.nmparks.com

www.countyfairgrounds.net/newmexico

www.newmexico.org

www.newmexicoscenicbyways.org

www.newmexicorvparksandcampgrounds.org

www.wildlife.state.nm.us/recreation/fishing

Information on accessibility: www.nmged.org

To purchase a $20 bargain pass to museums and state monuments: www.newmexicoculture.org

For information on mom-and-pop motels: www.motelguide.com

AREA CODES

New Mexico is in transition between a single area code, 505, and the addition of a 575 area code for areas outside Albuquerque and Santa Fe. This designation is still in flux, so if one code does not work, please try the other.

PUEBLO ETIQUETTE

When visiting a pueblo, think of your visit as if you were an invited guest in someone's home.

• Inquire ahead of time about visitor's hours. Remember that some pueblos are closed to outsiders on certain days for religious activities.

• Drive slowly.

• Never bring drugs or alcoholic beverages to a pueblo.

• For your comfort, bring along folding chairs to watch the dances from.

• Do not walk into or onto a kiva (ceremonial structure, sometimes, but not always, circular).

- Follow the tour leader and remember that homes, kivas, and ceremonies are not open to non-pueblo visitors. However, if you are invited into someone's home to eat, it is considered impolite to refuse. (It is also considered polite to eat and leave promptly so others can enter and eat.)
- Do not step on or cross the plaza or area where dances are being performed —instead, walk on the perimeter.
- Applause is not appropriate at dances.
- No photography, recordings, or sketching is permitted, in general, at events open to the public. Observe each pueblo's regulations on use of cameras, tape recorders, and drawing. If you want to photograph a pueblo resident, ask permission first and give a donation to the family. In some cases, such as Taos Pueblo, it is possible to purchase a photography permit.
- Any publication or public use of information about pueblo activities must receive prior approval from the tribal government.
- No pets are allowed.
- Questions about ceremonies, dances, and rituals are considered rude.
- When entering a structure, such as a church, observe the same protocols as you would in any sacred building.

OTHER MATTERS—AND A FEW CAUTIONS

Rapid temperature changes are the norm. The thermometer may vary by 40 degrees or more from day to night. Therefore, always dress in layers, and be prepared for sudden weather changes. Weather warnings should always be heeded. In summer, dry arroyos (ditches) and roads can flood very rapidly from an afternoon thunderstorm. Every year, it seems, hikers set out to climb La Luz Trail in summer and end up with hypothermia. The sun here really is stronger.

Always wear sunscreen, hat, sunglasses, and take more water than you think you will need, as well as a few energy bars, just in case. Be alert for weather changes. A snowstorm may come up suddenly just while you are planning to drive over Glorieta Pass. It's better to wait it out, even if you have to adjust your plans.

You may have heard about cases of bubonic plague and hanta virus occurring here, but unless you are handling rodent feces or have contact with infected rodents, there is no need to worry.

SMOKING
New Mexico is a smoke-free state.

CELL PHONES
Only hands-free devices are permitted while driving in Santa Fe, Albuquerque, and Taos.

PRICE CODES

Dining

Inexpensive	Up to $15
Moderate	$15–40
Expensive	$40–65
Very Expensive	Over $65

CONTACT ME

I would like to hear from you. If you liked a place you found in this book, or if you found it did not work out for you as you had hoped, I want to know. If you have suggestions you would like to see included in future editions, I would like to hear them. Please contact me directly or though the publisher.

My Web site is www.sharonniederman.com. Please visit it for additional travel information and articles.

MY THANKS

I want to thank my wonderful publisher, The Countryman Press, and their great staff, including my editorial director, Kermit Hummel, managing editor, Jennifer Thompson, and production coordinator, Julie Nelson. They are a joy to work with in every way, and their support, openness, skill, and professionalism are the best a writer could hope for—as is their ability to produce beautiful books. Thanks to Kim Grant for her guidance, and to Megan Mayo for her research assistance. Thanks to my writing friends for their examples of dedication and perseverance, their everlasting wisdom and kindness: Miriam Sagan, Demetria Martinez, Sallie Bingham, and always, to my mentors, Max and Pat Evans, and to V. B. Price, whose generous sharing of inspiration and wisdom over the years has helped many dreams come true. Thanks also to dear friends Irma Bailey, Karen Schmidt, Lynda Parker, Irene Clurman, Lynn Hamrick, Dr. Sigalit Hoffman, Cynthia Prelo-Riedlinger, Tom and Paula Murphy, and Jack and Monica Ingemells for their enthusiastic encouragement of my projects, always. The reunion with my best high school girlfriends, Lois Frischling, Pat McCall Martens, and Nancy Wolfe Wiley was a magical gift that arrived at exactly the right time. Big thanks and hugs to my wonderful husband, Charles Henry, who provided me with writing schedules, dark chocolate, and popcorn; fed me grilled cheese and green chile sandwiches; ground the coffee beans; brewed the tea; and reassured me through a long, cold winter that this book would get done.

And even though he can't read this, I want to acknowledge the comforting presence of Trooper, my English springer spaniel, who was beside me every day during the writing of this book.

I love you all, and I couldn't do it without you.

Sharon Niederman
Raton, New Mexico

Central New Mexico: Rio Grande Country

WEST OF ALBUQUERQUE:
RIO RANCHO, BERNALILLO,
PLACITAS, CORRALES,
JEMEZ SPRINGS

EAST OF ALBUQUERQUE: BELEN,
MORIARTY, MOUNTAINAIR, MADRID,
CERRILLOS

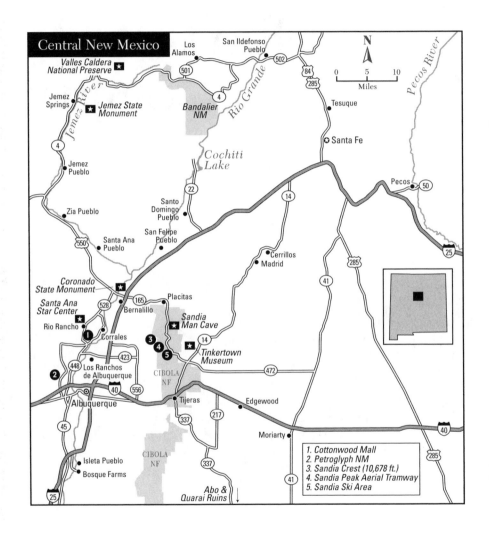

Central New Mexico

Valles Caldera
National Preserve ★

Los
Alamos

San Ildefonso
Pueblo

501

502

84

285

N

0   5   10
Miles

Pecos River

Jemez
Springs

Jemez River

Jemez State
Monument ★

Bandalier
NM

4

Rio Grande

Tesuque

4

Jemez
Pueblo

Cochiti
Lake

Santa Fe

Zia Pueblo

22

Santo
Domingo
Pueblo

14

Pecos

50

San Felipe
Pueblo

550

Santa Ana
Pueblo

Cerrillos
Madrid

285

25

Coronado
State Monument ★

Placitas

41

Santa Ana
Star Center ★

528

165

Bernalillo

Rio Rancho

Sandia
Man Cave ★

Corrales

1

3

4

14

423

5

Tinkertown
Museum ★

2

448

Los Ranchos
de Albuquerque

CIBOLA
NF

472

40

556

Albuquerque

Tijeras

Edgewood

45

337

217

Moriarty

40

285

CIBOLA
NF

337

Isleta Pueblo

Bosque Farms

25

Abo &
Quarai Ruins

41

1. Cottonwood Mall
2. Petroglyph NM
3. Sandia Crest (10,678 ft.)
4. Sandia Peak Aerial Tramway
5. Sandia Ski Area

WEST AND EAST OF ALBUQUERQUE

The Rio Grande Valley surrounding Albuquerque is rich with overlays of Spanish and Native American history. Here markers of the earliest Spanish settlements in New Mexico coexist with Native American arts and ceremonies of these ancient cultures of the Rio Grande pueblos. Here too are communities of the Manzano Mountains, characterized by homesteading roots that extend into today's multigenerational ranching families. The cherished practice of winemaking, dating in Sandoval County to the 1620s, is continued in several local wineries and celebrated each Labor Day weekend at the Bernalillo Wine Festival. Small farming still thrives in much of the region, and farmers' markets bursting with fresh local produce are crowded each summer with small growers selling their organic vegetables, jams, cheese, and garlic.

This is a region fascinating for the multiple layers of history that may be experienced at the crossroads of the major trails that converge here, in particular, the Camino Real—the north-south colonial Royal Road between Mexico City and Santa Fe that followed the Rio Grande—and the original 1926 Route 66 alignment that ran more or less north to south, as well as the post-1937 Route 66 east-west alignment.

This is the land of the Turquoise Trail National Scenic Byway, a colorful back road to Santa Fe that links the East Mountains to the old mining towns of Golden, Madrid, and Cerrillos. To the west is the Jemez Mountain National Scenic Byway that courses through the glorious red rock country of Jemez Pueblo.

Although the Rio Grande Valley area has grown and urbanized tremendously during recent decades, the values of small-town life and independence, of religious faith and practices, prevails and endures—sustained by generations that continue to live in the same place and in much the same ways as previous generations.

The traveler will find an abundance of recreational opportunities in easy reach: snow sports, camping, golfing, hiking, fishing, and enjoyment of nature are part of the way of life here.

The presence of a half-dozen Indian pueblos makes Bernalillo and Sandoval counties unique. Here ancient cultures continue to live and practice traditional ways. Many of these Indian tribes have recently opened splendid resorts offering luxurious dining, accommodations, and gaming.

Even as the outside world continues to make its presence known, there remains something about this place that keeps it suspended in its own time and keeps its own sense of itself strong. Many are attracted to that very quality, but living with it may prove something of a challenge if you are accustomed to a fast-paced urban lifestyle.

As with much of the rest of New Mexico, don't think you will change it, or that it has any desire to change. If you love it, you live with it on its terms, not on yours. The place will go on maintaining its own soul long after visitors leave and current residents pass into history. The spirit of the place is as strong as an enormous cottonwood tree in the bosque that has watched change come and go yet remains deeply rooted in the *acequia* that nourishes its thick bark, profuse leaves, and multistoried branches.

Enjoy your stay, and may the place nourish you and yours as well.

West of Albuquerque

GUIDANCE **Corrales Visitor Center** (505-350-3955; 505-897-0502, www .visitcorrales.com), 4324 Corrales Rd., Corrales. Open Mon.–Fri. 8–5.

Rio Rancho Chamber of Commerce and Visitor Center (505-892-1533; www.rrchamber.org), 4001 Southern Blvd. SE, Rio Rancho. Open Mon.–Fri. 8–5.

JAVA JUNCTION IN MADRID IS THE PLACE FOR GREAT COFFEE ON THE TURQUOISE TRAIL.

Rio Rancho Convention and Visitors Bureau (1-888-746-7262; 505-891-7258; www.rioranchonm.org), 4011 Barbara Loop, Ste. 208, Rio Rancho. Open Mon.–Fri. 8–5.

Sandoval County Visitor Center (1-800-252-0191; 505-867-8687; www.sandovalcounty.org), 243 Camino del Pueblo, Bernalillo.

Walatowa Visitor Center (505-834-7235; 1-877-733-5687; www.jemezpueblo.org), 7413 NM 4, Jemez Pueblo. Fifty-five miles northwest of Albuquerque on US 550, north on NM 4. Open daily 9–5.

GETTING THERE Please see *Getting There* in "Albuquerque: The Duke City."

MEDICAL EMERGENCY **Lovelace Westside Hospital** (505-727-2000), 10501 Golf Course Rd. NW, Rio Rancho.

University of New Mexico Hospital (505-272-2411), 2211 Lomas Blvd. NE, Albuquerque.

Presbyterian Family Healthcare (505-864-5454), 609 S. Christopher Rd., Belen.

McLeod Medical Center (505-832-4434) 1108 Rt. 66 SW, Moriarty.

✳ To See

TOWNS **Jemez Springs.** A tiny, picturesque community due north of Jemez Pueblo, this village is primarily dedicated to the service of tourists, with several bed and breakfasts, hot springs, and a few galleries.

Corrales. An agricultural community of small Hispanic, French, Basque, and Italian farmers through the 19th and 20th centuries, Corrales is today an exclusive village of pricey homes and beautiful horses, shaded by gracious old cottonwoods. Interesting galleries and boutiques make this pretty town worth a prowl.

Bernalillo. One of the first areas settled by the Spanish, this is where Coronado is said to have spent the winter of 1540–41, which was at the time the site of an Indian pueblo. Markedly Catholic, it is inhabited by many descendants of the old Spanish families. Traditions, such as the mid-August Matachines dances performed annually in the streets in honor of the patron saint, San Lorenzo, involve much of the village. Because of its proximity to Albuquerque, but well on the way to Santa Fe, Bernalillo is in the process of sprucing itself up, refurbishing its buildings even as new condos and homes appear on the edges of town. Yoga studios, galleries, and boutiques now grace the main street. Still, just beyond that main street, snug little houses with carefully tended rosebushes remain very private residences. If you are not an old-timer here, you will feel like a visitor who just dropped in and ought not overstay her welcome.

Placitas. A bedroom community of both Albuquerque and Santa Fe, this town is populated mainly by those who prefer to stay off the beaten track, enjoy their unbelievable views and their privacy, and have the money to afford to do just that.

THE MYSTERIOUS MATACHINES DANCES HAVE BEEN PERFORMED EVERY AUGUST FOR MORE THAN 350 YEARS IN BERNALILLO.

Rio Rancho. Not too terribly long ago, Rio Rancho was inhabited largely by coyotes and rattlesnakes, with retirement acreage staked out and a small population of brave retirees from the East Coast hanging in there. Growth accelerated with the arrival of Intel, and Rio Rancho has for years remained New Mexico's fastest-growing city, the one that has actually fueled Albuquerque's boom. It now boasts its own Cottonwood Shopping Mall and nearly every chain store and restaurant found across America. And it is still growing, as all the new homes going up along NM 550 testify. Where will the water come from? We shall see.

MUSEUMS **J & R Vintage Auto Museum** (505-867-2881), NM 528, a half mile south of US 550, Rio Rancho. Open Mon.–Sat. 1–5, Sun. 10–5. Nov.–Apr. closed Sun. Founder Gab Joiner is a vintage car collector and restorer whose collection just got too big to store at home. The more than 60 restored classic cars and trucks on display, including Packards, Buick Roadsters, and so many more, are all for sale. There's a huge gift shop with die-cast toys, books, and memorabilia. If you don't have an auto nut in your clan, you may have to become one yourself when you see this. $6, $5 seniors, $3 children 6–12, under 6 free.

Casa San Ysidro (505-898-3915), 973 Old Church Rd., Corrales. Open Wed.–Fri., tours at 9:30 and 3, Sun. 3. Reservations are required. As a branch of the

Albuquerque Museum, the Guitierrez/Minge casa houses rare and exquisite New Mexican rugs, textiles, furniture, and art. The Ward Alan Minge family painstakingly and authentically restored this 18th–19th century rancho, down to matching the original wall colors, as a labor of love. $4 adults, $3 seniors, $2 children.

DeLavy House (505-867-2755), Edmunds Rd., Bernalillo. West of Coronado State Monument and east of Santa Ana Star Casino. Watch closely the north side of US 550 for the Sandoval County Historical Society sign. The former home of local artist Edmond DeLavy, now the home of the historical society and its archives and photo collection, this is often the site of lectures and community meetings. Call for hours.

HISTORIC LANDMARKS, PLACES, AND SITES **Coronado State Monument** (505-980-8256), I-25 exit 242, US 550 west 1.7 miles. Wed.–Mon. 8:30–5. Closed Tues. The 77-year-old visitor center and small museum, designed by Santa Fe–style architect John Gaw Meem, houses the recently restored ancient kiva paintings of Kuaua, which exude a kind of sacredness and grant insight into the roots of Native American art. Here you can walk the grounds of pueblo ruins on the 0.2-mile self-guided trail. As you take in the expansive view overlooking the Rio Grande and Sandias, especially impressive at sunset when the mountains turn "watermelon" red, imagine yourself as an ancient tribesperson or perhaps one of the first conquistadors, said to have spent the winter of 1540–41 on this spot. The ramada-covered tables are perfect for a picnic anytime. $3. Call for RV and camping availability.

San Ysidro Church (505-898-1779), 5005 Corrales Rd., Corrales. Call for hours. This lovingly restored 1875 village church with twin bell towers and pitched tin roof serves as a venue for community events, acoustic and chamber music concerts, lectures, and festivals. The Corrales Historic Society cares for this treasure.

Jemez State Monument (505-829-3530), 43 miles north of Bernalillo, NM 4, 1 mile north of Jemez Springs. Open daily Wed.–Mon. 8:30–5. Closed Tues. Beneath stunning mesas, the dramatic ruins of the 14th-century Towa pueblo and the Spanish mission ruins of the church of San Jose de los Jemez that dates to the 17th century tell an unmistakable story of the history of this place. Jemez Springs on NM 4. $3, 16 and under free.

Petroglyph National Monument (505-899-0205), 4735 Unser Blvd., Rio Rancho. West from Albuquerque on I-40 to exit 154, north 3 miles to Western Trail, go left and follow signs. Open daily 8–5. Closed Thanksgiving, Christmas, and New Year's Day. From the Unser Blvd. Visitor Center, get maps to the prehistoric rock art trails on West Mesa volcanic escarpment. The monument has over 20,000 examples of indigenous rock art, including animals, birds, insects, and geometric designs such as the spiral. This is a sacred landscape to Native Americans. All trails are a short drive from the visitor center. Boca Negra Canyon is 2 miles north of the visitor center and has three self-guided trails. All are easy walks. Do bring water, stay on the trail, keep your pets leashed, and beware of rattlesnakes. $1 weekdays, $2 weekends.

Soda Dam (no phone). Two miles north of Jemez Springs on NM 4 is a 300-foot natural dam made of mineral deposits.

East of Albuquerque

GUIDANCE **Belen Chamber of Commerce/Visitor Center** (505-864-8091; www.belenchamber.com), 712 Dalies Ave., Belen.

East Mountain Chamber of Commerce (505-281-1999), Cedar Crest.

Mountainair Chamber of Commerce (505-847-2795; www.mountainair chamber.com), Mountainair.

Turquoise Trail Association (www.turquoisetrail.org).

Valencia County Chamber of Commerce (505-352-3596; www.loslunasnm .gov/chamber), 3447 Lambros, Los Lunas. Open Mon.–Fri. 8–5.

✳ To See

TOWNS **Moriarty.** Contrary to popular legend, there is no relationship between the name of this town and a character created by Arthur Conan Doyle, though the Sherlock Holmes Society was known to gather here annually. This small crossroads town, once the supply center for Estancia Valley dry-land farmers, still retains much of its Route 66 character in its main street architecture. It was

THE MORADA IS THE CENTER OF THE SPIRITUAL LIFE OF THE PENITENTE BROTHERHOOD.

named for Michael Moriarty, a young health-seeker from Iowa who arrived in 1887 and did indeed find relief for his rheumatism under the sunny skies. Corn, alfalfa, pinto beans, and pumpkins are grown nearby.

Madrid. Through its incarnations as a 20th-century coal mining town, an abandoned ghost town that was once entirely for sale, and, from the 1970s onward, a magnet for hippies and artists who moved into the abandoned miners' homes and subsequently turned them into pricey real estate, galleries, and cafes, Madrid makes an enjoyable and worthwhile stop along the Turquoise Trail. The more than thirty galleries are lively and varied. It has always been known for its especially lovely Christmas lights.

Cerrillos. Mining town, abandoned Western film set, ghost town—Cerrillos melds all these identities into a place so quiet it is almost spooky, yet it has its own irresistible allure for artists, photographers, and wanderers. The streets, where the only being you are likely to see is a lazy dog parked in the road, seem about to reveal their secrets any moment. For conversation, walk into Mary's Bar, where you are likely to find the locals hanging out.

Belen is a town that grew up with the railroad, and it still serves as a switching station for as many as 300 Burlington Northern Santa Fe trains every day. The main attraction here is the Belen Harvey House Museum beside the railroad tracks.

Mountainair, formerly "the pinto bean capital of the world," located along US 60, the "slow road" or two-lane across New Mexico, is actually at the geographic center of the state. As the headquarters of the Salinas Pueblos National Monument and the home of the Pueblo Deco Shaffer Hotel, with some of New Mexico's most interesting folk art created by jack-of-all trades Pop Shaffer in the early 20th century, it harkens back to its homesteading and ranching roots. New waves of artists continue to move here and call it home.

MUSEUMS **Belen Harvey House Museum** (505-861-0581), 104 N. First St., Belen. Open Tues.–Sat. 12:30–3:30. Closed Sun.–Mon., major holidays. Sitting beside the railroad tracks, this museum was originally a Fred Harvey Co. dining room, from 1908 to 1939. The collections relate to the history of the area and primarily to Santa Fe railroad history. Free.

Los Lunas Museum of Heritage & Arts (505-352-7720), 251 Main St. SE, Los Lunas. Open Tues.–Fri. noon–5, Sat. 10–5. Closed Sun.–Mon. This brand new museum concentrates on the heritage and families of the region with exhibits on founding families, the Civil War in New Mexico, educational exhibits for teachers, and a Genealogy Resource Center. Free.

 Tinkertown Museum (505-281-5233; www.tinkertown.com), 121 Sandia Crest Rd., Cedar Crest. I-40 east, exit north at exit 175, NM 14 north 6 miles, left on NM 536. Tinkertown is 1.5 miles on your left. Open daily Apr. 1–Nov. 1, 9–6. Guaranteed—you will never find another museum like this one. "I did all this while you were watching TV," folk artist Ross Ward said of his carving, which amounts to a 22-room collection of miniature animated scenes of Americana. Prediction: in years to come, this environmental folk artist and his work will be discovered and acclaimed as simply amazing. $3, $2.50 seniors, $1 children 4–16, under 4 free.

U.S. Southwest Soaring Museum (505-832-9222; www.swsoaringmuseum .org), 918 E. Old Hwy. 66, Moriarty. Exit 197 from I-40, 30 miles east of Albuquerque. Open daily 9–4. Antique sailplanes, hang gliders, and a history of soaring from the 1920s to the present make this an interesting stop. The collection of 96 model gliders in miniature is most appealing. Call for admission prices.

Old Coal Mine Museum and Engine House Theater (505-438-3780), 2846 NM 14, Madrid. Open daily, weather permitting. Call for hours and fees. Located on 3 acres filled with vintage vehicles and other remnants of the days when this was a working coal mining town, the museum itself houses Engine 767, the most complete nonoperating steam locomotive in the United States. During the summer, it serves as a theater for weekend melodramas. Also on view are the coal mineshaft and original mining headquarters.

HISTORIC LANDMARKS, PLACES, AND SITES Eaves Movie Ranch (505-474-3045; www.eavesmovieranch.com), 14 miles from Santa Fe via NM 14, west on NM 45 (Bonanza Creek Rd.). Call for hours. If this movie set looks familiar, don't be surprised. Many gunfights have been staged here, so you've likely seen the place in a Western or two. Daily tours, parties, and events are offered, and large groups may book staged gunfights.

Salinas Pueblo Missions National Monument (505-847-2585), visitor center is on US 60 in Mountainair, one block west of NM 55. Open daily. Closed Thanksgiving, Christmas, and New Year's Day. This monument is composed of three separate pueblo ruins located within a 50-mile radius, with impressive ruins of Spanish mission churches built on these sites. Call each site for specific hours: **Abo** (505-847-2400), **Gran Quivira** (505-847-2770), and **Quarai** (505-847-2290). Free.

Tome Hill (no phone), from Albuquerque, south on NM 47; pass Peralta and Los Lunas, then left on Tome Hill Rd. to Tome Hill. This landform is a Camino Real landmark and Good Friday pilgrimage site. Witness New Mexico's Calvario, as marked by crosses on top of the hill. The main path to the top, the South Trail, begins at Tome Hill Park at the intersection of La Entrada—the sculpture designating the three cultures, Native, Spanish, and homesteader, who have resided here—and the Rio del Oro Loop roads. The climb is steep and strenuous.

Mystery Rock (505-841-0705), west of Los Lunas on NM 6 about 15 miles at the base of Mystery Mountain. One of the area's most curious "unsolved mysteries," this rock with the Ten Commandments carved into it has long been a source of intrigue. Who put it here? No one knows for sure. Stout shoes and good knees are required for the short scramble to view the rock close up.

Sandia Tramway (505-856-7325), 10 Tramway Loop NE, Albuquerque. From I-25, exit 234 at Tramway Rd., follow it east 6 miles to Sandia Peak Tramway. Open Memorial Day–Labor Day 9–9, Labor Day–Memorial Day 9–8, Balloon Fiesta Oct. first Sat.–second Sun. 9–9. Billed as "the world's longest aerial tramway," a ride, or flight as it is called, carries visitors in a dramatic ride from the desert to the crest of the mountain for 2.7 miles through four of the earth's six biozones and astounding views of the rugged mountainside, its rocky outcroppings, and canyons. Atop the crest is the Four Seasons Visitor Center, open May–Nov., as well as restaurants and a gift shop. $17.50 adults; $15 seniors, teens 13–20, and military; $10 children 5–12; under 5 free.

Kasha-Katuwe Tent Rocks National Monument (505-761-8700), I-25 north, exit 259, follow signs to Forest Rd. 266. Open daily Apr.–Oct. 7–7, Nov.–Mar. 8–5. One of the newer national monuments, it is comanaged by the BLM and Cochiti Pueblo. Hike the hoodoos, the conelike structures that are unique in New Mexico. These magical-looking rock formations, the result of volcanic activity, are like giant sand castles. The 2-mile Cave Loop Trail is easy, while the steep 1.5-mile Canyon Trail is rated difficult. If you do one high desert hike in New Mexico, come on up here. $5.

✳ To Do

BICYCLING **Manzano Meander** (no phone) is a 55-mile round-trip from Four Hills Shopping Center in Albuquerque over NM 333 (Old Route 66) 7 miles to Tijeras. At the intersection of NM 337 go right up to Cedro Canyon, the roughest part of the trip, then coast down to Chilili, an old Spanish land grant village. Be careful, though, because there isn't much in the way of shoulder along NM 337.

ABO RUINS AT SALINAS PUEBLO NATIONAL MONUMENT.

NATIVE AMERICAN PUEBLOS

For the most up-to-date information on pueblo dances and feast days, contact the Indian Pueblo Cultural Center (505-843-7270; www.indianpueblo .org). Christmas Eve Midnight Mass, Christmas Day, New Year's Day, King's Day (January 6), Easter, and Thanksgiving are customary times for dances to be performed, and the public is welcome.

Jemez Pueblo (505-834-7235), 7413 NM 4, Pueblo of Jemez. Fifty-five miles northwest of Albuquerque, north to US 550 then to San Ysidro, north on NM 4. Feast days: November 12, December 12, Christmas Day, New Year's Day, January 6, Easter. See **Walatowa Visitor Center** under *Guidance*. For authentic dances, the opportunity to purchase fine pottery from the makers, and a warm welcome, Jemez Pueblo makes a wonderful introduction to the Indian way of life.

Isleta Pueblo (505-869-3111), from Albuquerque, I-25 south to exit 215 or take NM 47 to intersection with NM 147, go left, cross the river to the pueblo. While you can drive through the pueblo and visit the historic Church

HORNO BREAD BAKING IS DEMONSTRATED AT JEMEZ PUEBLO'S WALATOWA CENTER.

of San Augustine and buy oven bread, roasted blue corn meal, and chile from various homes with signs offering them for sale, Isleta (which means "little island") also offers the sophisticated side of golfing, gaming, nightlife, and dining. Feast days: January 6, August 28, September 4.

Sandia Pueblo (505-867-3317), 12 miles north of Albuquerque off I-25. Perhaps best known for its business enterprises, this pueblo of approximately 4,000 people has entered the 21st century with panache and now operates the grand new Sandia Resort & Casino (open 24 hours) with several fine restaurants, a high-end spa, the Bien Mur Indian Market (where pottery and fine hand-crafted jewelry are sold), and Sandia Lakes Recreation Area. Feast days: January 6, June 13.

Santa Ana Pueblo (505-867-3301), the ancient site of this Keresan village along the Jemez River is reserved for ceremonial functions and open to visitors only during certain annual celebrations. Today the pueblo is known for its various enterprises, including the magnificent Hyatt Tamaya Resort & Spa and the Santa Ana Star Casino west of Bernalillo on US 550. Feast days: June 29, July 26.

Zia Pueblo (505-867-3304), a village of about 700 off US 550 about 15 miles west of Bernalillo, gave New Mexico its symbol, the Zia sun sign. The village was abandoned and then repopulated after the 19th century. Many of those who live here are superb potters and painters. Feast day: August 15.

San Felipe Pueblo (505-867-3381) is known for its annual Corn Dance on May 1, a celebration that includes the sale of food, pottery, and jewelry, but perhaps better known for its Casino Hollywood, only 32 miles north of Albuquerque at exit 252 off I-25. Feast day: May 1.

Cochiti Pueblo (505-465-2244), population about 800, is due south of Santa Fe off I-25 and overlooks the Rio Grande. Storyteller pottery figures originated here with Cochiti potter Helen Cordero, and drums are another specialty of the pueblo. Feast day: July 14.

Santo Domingo Pueblo (505-465-2214) holds a complex and moving Corn Dance each year on August 4. Artist Georgia O'Keeffe is quoted as saying that witnessing the Corn Dance was one of the great experiences of her life. Several hundred dancers moving rhythmically on the plaza, the sounds of their shells and bells, and the drums and singing, make this an unforgettable event. A big carnival of wares from all over (but be sure what you are buying is authentic and handmade—if the price is too good to be true, it probably isn't) and native foods makes this a fine day to be here. Feast day: August 4.

HIKING THE HOODOOS AT TENT ROCKS.

Straight and Easy (no phone) is a perfectly good workout on a perfectly flat road from Moriarty south on NM 41 to Estancia 17 miles, or if you are feeling strong, you can pedal all the way to Willard for another 13 miles. You'll find lots of big skies, fields, and farms along the way.

BIRDING See Manzano Mountains State Park under *Green Space*.

Corrales Bosque Nature Preserve (505-897-0502). Birding, hiking, horseback riding, and walking along a quiet and unspoiled stretch of dirt trails shaded by giant cottonwoods along the Rio Grande. Free.

BOATING Cochiti Lake. See *Wind Surfing*.

CAMPING See *Camping and Cabins* under *Lodging*.

FARMERS' MARKETS Corrales Growers Market (505-898-6336), next to the post office on Corrales Rd., Corrales. Open Apr. 22–Oct. 28, Sun. 9–noon, Wed. 4–7. A bustling lively market with the highest quality, and priciest, produce. Neighbors meet up here over coffee and breakfast burritos.

Bernalillo Growers Market (505-867-9054), 282 Camino del Pueblo, Bernalillo. Open July 6–Oct. 26, Fri. 4–7. It's likely you will encounter growers from San Felipe Pueblo at this market.

Cedar Crest Farmers & Arts Market (505-514-6981), 12127 N. NM 14, Cedar Crest. Open June 27–Oct., Wed. 3–6. Get there early for the best selection.

FISHING **Isleta Lakes Recreational Complex** (505-877-0370), 13 miles south of Albuquerque on I-25, exit 215. Fish peacefully from the shores of two beautiful lakes. Open daily 6 AM–8 PM spring–summer, 7–5 fall–winter. Lakes stocked with channel catfish in warm weather and rainbow trout in fall and winter. There are also 50 full-service RV hookups. New Mexico fishing license is not required. Limit five fish per adult. $15, $3 children 11 and under.

Sandia Lakes Recreation Area (505-897-3971), Sandia Pueblo, on NM 313. Three lakes here are stocked with rainbow trout during the cooler months and channel catfish during the summer. New Mexico fishing license is not required. This area has been closed for some time for renovations. Call for reopening information.

Zia Lake (505-867-3304), Zia Pueblo, south of San Ysidro on US 550. A tribal permit is required to fish here for bass, catfish, and trout. Gas motors are not allowed.

✎ **Shady Lakes** (505-898-2568), I-25, exit Tramway Blvd. to NM 313 for 2 miles. The place known as Shady Lakes is a pleasant area with small lakes that in summer are covered with water lilies and can, for a small fee, provide every child with the opportunity to catch a fish. New Mexico fishing license is not required. Call for fees and hours.

GOLF **Isleta Eagle Championship Golf Course** (505-848-1900), 13 miles south of Albuquerque, exit 215. Open daily. This 27-hole native desert–style course offers play around three scenic lakes and the Rio Grande. Fees for 18 holes, including cart, $45–55.

Twin Warriors Golf Course (505-771-6155) Hyatt Tamaya Resort, 1300 Tuyuna Trail, Santa Ana Pueblo. This is the ultimate, an 18-hole high desert championship course where play takes place around 20 ancient cultural sites. The setting provides a truly magical experience. $60–145, depending on time of year; $55–79 New Mexico residents.

Santa Ana Golf Course (505-867-9464), Santa Ana Pueblo, is the naturally landscaped sister course of Twin Warriors. Golf around eight crystal-blue lakes, framed by three mountain ranges. $49–59.

Chamisa Country Club (505-896-5017), 500 Country Club Dr. SE, Rio Rancho. Rio Rancho 1 and Rio Rancho 2 courses, designed by Lee Trevino, provide a total of 27 holes for all skill levels. $20–28.

HIKING **Battleship Rock** (no phone) along the Jemez Mountain Trail is an easy 2-mile, extremely popular hike to the river, accessed at Battleship Rock turnout on NM 4, 5 miles north of Jemez Springs.

Las Conchas Trail (505-829-3535) provides moderate forested hiking along the east fork of the Jemez River.

Red Canyon/Ox Canyon Trail, Manzano Mountains. This moderate 5.5-mile trail through Red Canyon is easily accessed. Go left in the town of Manzano along NM 337. The shady trail, good for mountain biking, too, is populated with alligator junipers and New Mexico swallowtail butterflies in summer. This is another of my favorite area hikes.

Sandia Crest Trail, Sandia Mountains. This 27-mile trail along the top, with incredible views, is easy to moderate. Sandia Peak provides a convenient access point.

Tree Springs Trail, I-40 to NM 14 (exit 175), go north, take NM 536, the Crest Rd., is one of the prettiest hikes on the east side of the Sandias, with wild primroses blooming May–June and a green, wildflower-filled landscape completely different from the desert vegetation of the west side of the mountain. It's a moderate 3-mile climb to the top, where you can connect with the Sandia Crest Trail. $3.

10K Trail, Cedar Crest. Take NM 536, the Crest Road, to the trailhead, to access this moderate 7-mile hike along a 10,000-foot contour.

HORSEBACK RIDING **The Stables at Tamaya** (505-771-6037), Hyatt Regency Tamaya Resort & Spa, 1300 Tuyuna Tr., Santa Ana. A unique way to experience Pueblo backcountry is with experienced native instructors and trail guides. Journey peacefully on horseback through cottonwoods along the Rio Grande and Jemez rivers on twice-daily trail rides. Carriage rides, pony rides, and riding lessons are also available. Non-resort guests are welcome. $80 individual, $60 each in a group.

HOT SPRINGS **Giggling Springs Hot Springs** (505-829-9175), Jemez Springs. Open Wed.–Sun. 11–5. This lovely spot across the road from the Laughing Lizard is a hot spring pool next to the Jemez River. An intimate location with a sweet cabin where you can take a break, relax, and enjoy fruit smoothies and herbal teas. $15 per hour per person, $35 day pass.

Jemez Springs Bath House (505-829-3303 or 1-866-204-8303), 062 Jemez Springs Plaza, Jemez Springs. Call for hours. Built from 1870 to 1878, this bathhouse and gift shop is fed by a rich mineralized spring and retains its Victorian feeling. Individual private soaking tubs, massage and spa treatments available. $10 for 30-minute soak.

MOUNTAIN BIKING See **Las Huertas Canyon** under *Green Space* for a creekside moderate to difficult ride toward the Sandias, and **Red Canyon**, under *Hiking*, in the Manzano Mountains is a favorite moderate 5.5-mile trail ride.

Also see **Turquoise Trail** under *Scenic Drives* and **East Fork** of the Jemez, under *Snow Sports—Cross-Country Skiing*, plus **Petroglyph National Monument** (see *Historic Landmarks, Places, and Sites*) offers easy packed dirt cruises.

See **Sandia Peak Ski Area** under *Snow Sports—Downhill Skiing*. Lift open June 2–Labor Day. In the summer, you can bring your bike up the mountain on the tram and find 30 miles of easy, moderate, and difficult trails graded like ski runs. You can ride the chairlift at the ski area to King of the Mountain, a black diamond (or difficult) trail, to Golden Eagle, marked green (or moderate), and descend King of the Mountain for a trail marked blue (or easy). Rentals are available at the top and bottom of the lift.

Corrales Rio Grande Bosque makes a delightful, easy, mostly level ride, or walk, for 12 miles. Follow NM 425 (Corrales Rd.) through Corrales; at Mockingbird Ln. go left until you reach the bosque.

SCENIC DRIVES For more information on NM Scenic Byways, call 1-800-733-6396, ext. 24371.

Salt Missions Trail. From Albuquerque, take I-40 east to Moriarty, south on NM 333 at Moriarty, follow NM 41, US 60, NM 513, 55, 337, and 131 for a total of 140 miles to travel the entire length of the trail and see all three ruins: Abo, Quarai, and Gran Quivira, with their Indian pueblos and 17th-century Franciscan mission churches, through the Manzano and Cibola National Forests en route. Abo is 9 miles west of Mountainair on US 60, and Quarai is 8 miles north of Mountainair on NM 55. Gran Quivira is a longer drive, 39 miles south of Mountainair on NM 55.

Turquoise Trail National Scenic Byway is the back road between Albuquerque and Santa Fe. Take I-25 to the Cedar Crest exit, go north on NM 536, then follow NM 14 for 48 miles through mining ghost towns of Golden and Madrid, now more of an arts town than a ghost town, and Cerrillos, then on into Santa Fe. The route gets its name from local turquoise mines. The serpentine, up-and-down two-lane carries you past the Ortiz Mountains to the right, with views of the Sangre de Cristos up ahead and the Jemez Mountains to the left. Allow a good day to take your time and explore and shoot photos, perhaps have dinner in Santa Fe, then loop back down I-25 to Albuquerque.

Jemez Mountain Trail National Scenic Byway. From Albuquerque, the length of this trail runs 163 miles. Take I-25 north to US 550, go northwest on 550 to San Ysidro, then right on NM 4. Along the way take in the Walatowa Visitor Center—where across the road and beneath the red rocks, ladies may be selling bowls of chile, Indian tacos, and oven pies—Pueblo of Jemez; Jemez Springs; Jemez State Monument; past Battleship Rock, Soda Dam, and La Cueva; past the Valle Caldera, Bandelier National Monument, and on into Los Alamos. This is a great way to see a huge amount in one day. You can loop back around to Albuquerque via Santa Fe on I-25 for a quicker return trip.

Corrales Road. The pretty two-lane, 6.7-mile road that winds along NM 448 through the Village of Corrales shows off the beauty of this rural community squeezed between busy Rio Rancho and Albuquerque (be sure to drive slowly, to savor and to avoid a ticket). Fruit orchards, horses grazing beside adobe homes, and expansive views of the Sandia Mountains speak of a less-harried time and insist you slow down, if only just to get a good look.

Abo Pass Trail connects the Salt Missions Trail and the Camino Real for 31 miles along NM 47 and US 60. It is a journey through big open skies and the empty loneliness of the Old—and older—West, and a time to speculate how life used to be. You can imagine riding it on horseback or by wagon and appreciate the modern comforts of air-conditioning and motorized vehicles.

Sandia Crest Scenic Byway, I-40 east to Tijeras exit, north on NM 14, then to Sandia Crest on NM 536 for 13.6 miles. The drive up is beautiful and green, with many hiking trails along the way, but once at the top of the crest, you can see 100 miles in all directions. This is a favorite destination of first-time visitors, where friends and relatives introduce them to Albuquerque. Over a half million people drive to the 10,687-foot crest annually, and another quarter million ride the Sandia Tramway.

SNOW SPORTS—CROSS-COUNTRY SKIING **La Cueva** (1-800-252-0191), NM 4 east for Redondo Campground, Los Griegos area, and west of La Cueva on NM 126 and Valle San Antonio Rd. to Upper San Antonio Canyon.

East Fork of the Jemez River is mostly level through the Santa Fe National Forest, with plenty of ponderosa pine and the glorious silence of a landscape in deep winter. You'll find the trailhead 10 miles north of La Cueva. This trail also works for mountain biking.

SNOW SPORTS—DOWNHILL SKIING **Sandia Peak Ski Area** (505-587-8977), I-40 east to Cedar Crest exit 175, north on NM 14, left on NM 536 for 6 miles to ski area. Or take the Sandia Peak Ariel Tram at 10 Tramway Loop NE, Albuquerque. Open daily Dec. 19–Jan. 6, 9–4; Wed.–Sun. and holidays Jan. 10–Mar. 11, 9–4. Thirty trails are serviced by four chairlifts. The area has a children's lift, some of the longest cruising terrain in the state, snow sports school, ski rental shop, and café. Skiers and snowboarders need to rent equipment at the base if taking the tram, or drive up. There are no rentals at the lift. $45 all-day lift, $52 tram and lift.

SPAS **Tamaya Mist Spa & Salon,** Hyatt Regency Tamaya. Inspired by the prehistoric journey of their people, the spa offers various pathways to rejuvenation and healing through salt scrubs, herbal wraps, expert massage, and facials. Pricey and worth the price.

Green Reed Spa, Sandia Resort & Casino. Total pampering waits in this fullservice spa amid the soothing sounds of waterfalls, with body treatments that incorporate indigenous healing plants, such as the green reed found in the bosque for the Green Reed Polish and clay from the desert for the Clay Body Wrap.

SPECTATOR SPORTS **New Mexico Scorpions** (505-881-7825), Santa Ana Star Center, 3100 Civic Centre Dr., Rio Rancho. Mid-Oct.–mid-Mar. Expect exciting pro hockey action from the 2006–7 Southwest Division Champions. $11.50–40.

WIND SURFING **Cochiti Lake** (505-465-0307). Fifty miles north of Albuquerque, west of I-25 at Santo Domingo exit. Wind surfing on this no-wake lake with paved boat ramp and campground is popular Apr.–Oct.

WINERIES **Anasazi Fields Winery** (505-867-3062), Camino de Peublitos Rd. at the western edge of Placitas. Open Wed.–Sun. noon–5 or by appointment. This winery has made a name for itself by featuring dry, not sweet, fruit wines of apricot, peach, plum, wild cherry, and New Mexico raspberry.

Milagro Vineyards (505-898-3998), 985 W. Ella, Corrales. Tours of vineyards and winery, as well as tasting room hours by appointment only. "Handcrafted Vine to Wine" is the slogan of this boutique winery, dedicated to making wine from grapes grown in New Mexico. Small quantities of Merlot, Zinfandel, and Chardonnay are aged in French oak.

Ponderosa Valley Vineyards (505-834-7487), 3171 NM 290, Ponderosa. Tasting room open Tues.–Sat. 10–5, Sun. noon–5. With grapes planted in 1976 in the Ponderosa Valley of the Jemez Mountains, proprietors Henry and Mary Street produce award-winning Riesling, as well as Pinot Noir, Viognier, and more.

Corrales Winery (505-898-5165), 6275 Corrales Rd., Corrales. Tasting room open Wed.–Sun. noon–5. Specializing in producing unique flavors of small batch New Mexico wines grown from New Mexico grapes, this winery is set beside its own vineyard. They especially recommend their Muscat Canelli dessert wine.

Milagro Winery (505-898-3996), 985 W. Ella, Corrales. Open by appointment. Handcrafted, small batch wines are aged in French oak to showcase the New Mexico *terroir* at this boutique winery, where pet pigs roam the vineyards.

✳ Green Space

Cibola National Forest, Mountainair District (505-847-2990). District Office two blocks north of US 60 in Mountainair. Office open Mon.–Fri. 8–4. Six developed campgrounds and 100 miles of hiking and horse trails are found, mainly in the Manzano Mountains, within an hour to a two-and-a-half-hour drive from Albuquerque, east on I-40, and south at Tijeras exit. Two of the most popular camping areas are at Tajique, and Fourth of July Canyon is famous for its flaming red fall color. Roads and campgrounds are frequently closed during winter months, so be sure to call the above number before venturing out. Free.

Sandia Ranger District (505-281-3304), visitor center at Sandia Crest. Open 8–4:30. Closed Sat.–Sun. and during the winter. Hiking, mountain biking, cross-country skiing best accessed by driving the Crest Road, NM 536 to Sandia Crest, or taking the Sandia Peak Aerial Tram. Day use only. $3.

Manzano Mountains State Park (505-847-2820). Campsites. Northwest of Mountanair on NM 55 or about an hour south of Albuquerque on I-40 east, then south at Tijeras exit. Open Apr. 1–Oct. 31, 7:30–sunset. Birds love this place. Take the opportunity to spot 200 species, including mountain bluebirds, hummingbirds, jays, and hawks. There is also trout fishing in Manzano Lake. $6 per vehicle; $10–18 camping.

Fenton Lake State Park, 33 miles northwest of San Ysidro via NM 4, then left at La Cueva on NM 126. Open 6 AM–9 PM summers, 7–7 winters. Ponderosa pines sweep down to the shore of this pretty small 28-acre lake that is stocked with rainbows and has a natural population of German brown trout. Only small rowboats and canoes are allowed. There are 40 developed campsites, some with hookups. $3, $7 camping.

Ortiz Mountain Educational Preserve (505-428-1684). Open Mar.–Nov. There are 1,350 acres through the Ortiz peaks outside Madrid that allow for a moderate hike to 9,000-foot Placer Peak. Many worthwhile outdoors activities are scheduled here, including a bat watch, lecture tours, geology, and plant life studies. Call for schedules.

WILDLIFE REFUGES AND AREAS **Ladd S. Gordon Waterfowl Complex** (505-864-9187), 4 miles north of Bernardo on NM 116. Over 5,000 acres along the Rio Grande are divided into several different units where wildlife viewing, fishing, and hunting in season take place at this state managed waterfowl area.

Sevilleta National Wildlife Refuge (505-864-4021), 20 miles north of Socorro off I-25 at exit 169. Headquarters is located on the west side of I-25. This Chihuahuan desert ecosystem research center refuge hosts an annual open house with guided tours in October only. Special educational tours may be arranged.

Wildlife West Nature Park (505-281-765), I-40 east, exit 187. Open daily summer 10–6, winter noon–4 or by appointment. This is an interactive 122-acre wildlife park where rescued critters like coyotes, cougars, bobcats, mountain lions, and wolves may be observed in their natural habitats. An easy walk. $5, $4 children over five, under five free.

Las Huertas Canyon (no phone). Continue on NM 165 through Placitas and up the mountain 7 miles. This narrow scenic drive up through the rugged Sandia foothills often offers the running water of Las Huertas Creek, and there are several nice places to camp and fish. In the evening, you have a good possibility of sighting bear. I have seen them here, so keep alert and keep food locked up unless you plan on sharing your picnic with them. Las Huertas Canyon makes a moderate-difficult 15-mile mountain bike trail. Free.

✳ Lodging

BED & BREAKFASTS **Hacienda Vargas B&B Inn** (1-800-261-0006 or 505-867-9115; www.hacienda vargas.com), 1431 NM 313, Algodones. Saturated with history, the seven rooms here, part of a 17th-century hacienda, each with private entrance, compose the only bed and breakfast actually located on the Camino Real in New Mexico. Sweet dreams will be yours within the serenity of thick adobe walls, and you will be greeted in the morning with the house special, pumpkin pancakes with roasted piñon nuts. You'll be ready for a day of exploring in either Albuquerque or Santa Fe. $89–189.

Elaine's, A Bed & Breakfast (1-800-821-3092 or 505-281-2467; www.elainesbnb.com), 72 Snowline Estates, Cedar Crest. Elaine O'Neal has been providing hospitality in the East Mountains for so long, she must be doing something right. You can be sure you will be well taken care of here in this five-room rural setting, with hot tub and handicap access. Elaine's also offers golf packages. $99–149.

Blue Horse B&B (1-877-258-4677 or 505-771-9055; www.bluehorse bandb.com), 300 Camino de Las Huertas, Placitas. Utterly adobe, utterly Southwest, utterly situated to maximize the glorious sunsets, stars, and mesas up in Placitas, the Blue Horse promises privacy and the deep quiet that promotes deep rest in any of its three rooms. Gather around the kiva fireplace to unwind and enjoy breakfasts of Swedish pancakes, crepes, waffles, and omelets. You deserve this! $99–129.

Casa de Koshare (1-877-729-8100 or 505-898-4500; www.casadekoshare .com), 122 Ashley Ln. NW, Corrales. The koshares are the sacred clowns of the Indian dances, and this delightful B&B goes all the way with the Native

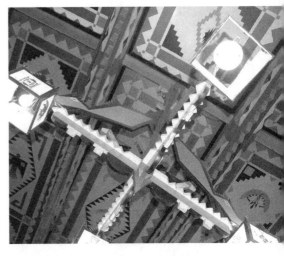

HOMESTEADER AND JACK-OF-ALL-TRADES POP SHAFFER DESIGNED HIS OWN BRAND OF PUEBLO DECO ART FOR THE DINING ROOM CEILING OF HIS MOUNTAINAIR HOTEL.

THOUGH HE NEVER CALLED HIMSELF AN ARTIST, POP SHAFFER'S GATE IN MOUNTAINAIR IS REGARDED AS ONE OF NEW MEXICO'S FOLK ART TREASURES.

American–Southwestern theme, with a Storyteller Suite and a Warrior Room among their four accommodations. It's a little piece of heaven here, with breakfast catered to your needs and appetite and panoramic views of the Sandia Mountains and city lights from the garden patio. Discounts for extended stays are offered. $139–99.

Chocolate Turtle B&B (1-877-298-1800 or 505-898-1800; www.chocolate turtlebb.com), 1098 W. Meadowlark Ln., Corrales. Four charming and colorful Southwest-style rooms, big picture views of the Sandias, free Wi-Fi and 24-hour complimentary snacks, plus a huge delicious breakfast served on the covered portal in season makes this an appealing alternative for the business traveler who is simply tired of hotel living. $65–120.

Dancing Bear (1-800-422-3271 or 505-829-3336), 314 San Diego Dr., Jemez Springs. For a quick getaway or a surprise celebration or just some restorative R&R, this four-room luxurious bed and breakfast will surely fill the bill. It's a great place to take quiet walks, visit the hot springs, and then lounge in front of the massive fireplace in the great room with two-story cathedral windows overlooking the Jemez River, where you are snug against the canyon mesa. $80–130.

Casa Blanca Guest House and Garden Cottage (505-829-3579), 17521 NM 4, Jemez Springs. Known for exquisite gardens, with a riverfront terrace and grandmother cottonwoods on the premises, this lodging is classically New Mexico, with thick vigas (ceiling beams) and kiva fireplace in the guest house, which sleeps four and has a kitchenette. The cottage, where you can hear the Jemez River lull you to sleep, rents for $110 a

night and sleeps two. The advantage here is that you can walk to town. $150–170.

Shaffer Hotel (505-847-2888 or 1-888-595-2888; www.shafferhotel .com), 103 Main St., Mountainair. This art deco vintage hotel, a New Mexico treasure built by blacksmith, jack of all trades, and folk artist Clem "Pop" Shaffer in 1923, has been recently remodeled, offering five rooms with shared bath, three suites and double suites for families, and ten rooms with private baths, all done in period furniture. The rooms are not large, but they are adequate. The café on the premises has been up and down, much like the ownership of this hotel. All in all, this is probably your best base site for exploring the nearby ruins. $79–225.

HOTELS, RESORTS, AND LODGES

Isleta Casino & Resort (505-869-3111), 13 miles south of Albuquerque, exit 215 to NM 47. Known for its gaming, golf, fishing, camping, dining, and entertainment, this is a great place just to come and play. There's even the Isleta Fun Connection, which has you covered on bowling, billiards, and arcade games. The big names headline here. Country stars that have recently appeared on this stage include Willie Nelson, Alan Jackson, and Randy Travis. Whatever your taste buds are craving, you can find it here in one of the five restaurants, from the well-priced Tiwa Steakhouse, serving a full menu, to the Ma-Tu-Ey Buffet, the Triple 7 Sports Bar, Dauber's Grill, and Chile Ristra Café & Deli. There's always something happening here.

Sandia Resort & Casino (505-796-7500), 30 Rainbow Rd. NE,

Albuquerque. Following a recent multi-million-dollar expansion, Sandia Resort has emerged as a posh new seven-story hotel. It has 228 Southwest-style spacious rooms with Ernest Thompson–designed furnishings. The four restaurants are the Council Room Steakhouse; the rooftop Bien Shur, featuring New American Cuisine (overseen by well-known chef Jim White); a deli; and a buffet. The resort also boasts a fitness center, salon, upscale spa, the Green Reed, plus a championship golf course. The likes of Trisha Yearwood, the Gipsy Kings, Lyle Lovett, and Harry Connick Jr. appeared recently in the Sandia Amphitheater, and the lounge has live entertainment nightly until midnight. $109–260.

Hyatt Regency Tamaya Resort & Spa (505-867-1234; www.tamaya .hyatt.com), 1300 Tuyuna Trail, Santa Ana. Convenient to Santa Fe as well as Albuquerque, the Hyatt Tamaya works just as well as a secluded self-contained resort with the Sandias as backdrop. It has 350 rooms, many with private balconies; a fabulous spa; Twin Warriors Golf; the Rio Grande Lounge, with live entertainment; two restaurants; a knockout art collection; demonstrations of bread baking and other arts—all in an exquisite pueblo-style setting that qualifies it as a "cultural resort." You might find it worth the big bucks for the best money can buy. In the works are "Dude Ranch" packages, which include horseback riding in Santa Ana lands. Golf and spa specials and packages are available. $250–800.

THE FIREPLACE AT HYATT TAMAYA IS A COZY PLACE TO RELAX.

BIKE RIDING IN THE SHADOW OF THE SANDIAS AT HYATT TAMAYA ON SANTA ANA PUEBLO LAND.

Elk Mountain Lodge (1-800-875-2859 or 505-829-3159; www.elk mountainlodge.cc), 38690 NM 126, La Cueva, just west of junction of NM 4 and NM 126. If you are seeking a romantic getaway that offers convenience to hiking, cross-country skiing, and fishing in the heart of the Jemez Mountains, this four-room, comfy rustic log lodge is the place. Candlelit in-room whirlpool spa helps to soothe exercised muscles, and a simple continental breakfast is included. A café and general store are just across the way. $109–179.

CABINS AND CAMPING See *State Parks* under *Green Space* for camping.

Coronado RV Park (505-980-8256), US 550 next to Coronado State Monument. Open year-round. Tenting Mar. 1–Oct. 1 only. No discounts for tents. No reservations are the policy at this serene 23-hookup RV park, popular due to its views overlooking the bosque and the splendid northwest view of the Sandias. $22.

Trails End RV Park (505-829-4072), NM 126, La Cueva. Open May 15–Oct. 30. Weekly and monthly only, 20 and older only, preapproved pets are OK, advanced reservations only for these 10 full hookup sites located in old growth ponderosa pine close to all the outdoor recreational opportunities of the Santa Fe National Forest along the Jemez.

✳ Where to Eat

DINING OUT Luna Mansion (505-865-7333), 110 W. Main St., Los Lunas. Open for dinner Wed.–Sun. This grand 1821 historic mansion, an architectural anomaly of Southern plantation–style architecture, built of adobe with Ionic white columns spanning two stories, is a local institution that holds much of the area's history. It is reputedly quite haunted—among other sitings, many report seeing a ghostly figure of a woman in the rocking chair on the landing. The second-story bar, with its vintage family photos of the Luna and Otero families, is a divine place to have a drink. The food served here, however, is at best uneven, and the service can be slow, especially on Valentine's Day or other holidays; it's a favorite romantic place to go and can be quite crowded. Best to order steak or pasta, and the green chile stew is very tasty. Moderate.

Prairie Star (505-867-3327), 288 Prairie Star Rd., Santa Ana. Dinner only. Open 5–9 Sun.–Thurs., 5–10 Fri.–Sat. A special-occasion restaurant with everything you could want in the way of atmosphere and service, Prairie Star is located in an elegant 1920s adobe home. Chef Heath van Riper combines imaginative flavors in ways that allow the ingredients to chime together without confusion. The second-floor lounge shows off the Sandias, and the soft lighting and New Mexico art on the walls sets the stage for a special evening. Under management of the Santa Ana Pueblo, the Prairie Star's menu features upscale Southwest-based (not dominated) cuisine, including the very best game, fresh fish, and steaks. Bring someone you want to impress here. The food is exquisite, as good as the best, and the setting is suitable for marriage proposals. Expensive–Very Expensive.

Corn Maiden (505-867-1234), Hyatt Tamaya Resort, 1300 Tuyana Tr., Santa Ana Pueblo. I-25 exit 242, US 550 to Tamaya Blvd., 1.5 miles to the resort. Dinner only, Tues.–Sat. 5:30–10. This, the Tamaya's upscale restaurant, presents the signature rotisserie, more than you can possibly eat, of an assortment of gigantic skewers of meat, fish, sausage, and chicken, each flavored with its own delectable marinade. Very Expensive.

Consetta's, the Green Restaurant (505-829-4455), 16351 NM 4, Jemez Springs. Open Wed.–Sun., lunch 11–2:30, dinner 5–9:30. Live music Sun. evening and Wi-Fi. Proof that vegans and vegetarians need not sacrifice, this environmentally conscious and lovely little spot with views of the red rock canyon began life as an Italian restaurant and morphed, through the interests of its owners, into a delightful eatery that serves sustainable seafood as well as herbs and vegetables grown in their own organic garden. Beer and local wines from nearby Ponderosa Winery and renewable energy sources make this a special place. Eggplant Parmesan, chicken Florentine Panini, apple raisin cobbler, caramel chocolate brownie, and pizza, pizza, pizza—it's all good. Moderate.

EATING OUT ✿ Banana Leaf Asian Grill (505-892-6119), 355 NM 528 SE, Rio Rancho. Open daily. Lunch, dinner. Serving what many believe is the best Asian food in the area, this small family-run café has been a hit ever since it opened not five years ago with its Thai, Vietnamese, and

Chinese food, which are all delicious and well spiced. Go for the Thai. Curries and wraps are fresh and flavorful. And it has a surprisingly cool interior, considering the strip mall location. Inexpensive.

Noda's Japanese Cuisine (505-891-4378), 2704 Southern Blvd., #13, Rio Rancho. Lunch Tues.–Fri. 11:30–2, dinner Tues.–Sat. 6–9. Closed Sun.–Mon. If the sushi wasn't the best and the Japanese the most authentic you will find in the metro area, I wouldn't recommend Noda's because it can be challenging to find it the first time. Guaranteed—you will rave about this serene, unpretentious place for a long time to come. Order anything! It's all great. A little secret: you can order your own menu for a party ahead of time. What a birthday present for your favorite sushi lover! Moderate.

The Merc at Placitas (505-867-8661), NM 165, Homestead Village, Placitas. A grocery store and deli, and a local hangout selling beer, wine, and spirits; the high point of the week is the 4 PM wine tasting on Friday. Call for hours.

Mine Shaft Tavern (505-473-0743), 2846 NM 14, Madrid. Open daily. Lunch, dinner. Sun.–Thurs. 11:30–9, dinner 'til 8:30; Fri.–Sat. 11:30–midnight, dinner 'til 10. Long a biker hangout and fallen into somewhat seedy and sinister times, the Mine Shaft, constructed in 1946 as a coal company town saloon with a 40-foot-long lodgepole pine bar, has new ownership and is cleaning up its act. The menu is far from simple burgers and now offers oysters Rockefeller and such Californicated entrees as sake steamed salmon and carrot-ginger soup, in addition to T-bone steaks and roast chicken. If you

haven't been to the Mine Shaft, you haven't been to Madrid. Live entertainment weekends. Moderate.

El Comedor de Anayas (505-832-4442), 1009 W. Hwy. 66, Moriarty. Open daily 6:30 AM–9 PM. Breakfast, lunch, dinner. You can tell this place is a Route 66 icon by the twirling, multi-colored neon ball sign. From the old-timer ranchers and farmers who meet here for their morning coffee klatch to the families who stop in for dinner, all enjoy the homey atmosphere and home-cooked Mexican food served up in healthy portions. Chile rellenos and sopaipillas rate highly, and the green chile is not to be scoffed at. When in Moriarty, you won't find a better place to dine. Inexpensive.

Mama Lisa's Ghost Town Kitchen–No Pity Café (505-473-1172), 2859 NM 14, Madrid. Mama Lisa's is the kind of roadside stop you dream about. Offering "good food that's good for you," Mama bakes everything, including her breads, rolls, red chile chocolate cake, and apple walnut strudel, fresh, by hand, daily. The barbeque brisket sandwich with chipotle sauce is a marvel worth the drive on its own. Absolutely so casual and laid-back, you might think you've time-traveled back to 1968. Call for days and hours. Inexpensive.

Mary's Bar, Main St., Cerrillos. It may look closed on the outside, but inside is the 120-year-old building built by Mary Mora's father. Bartender and befriender of movie stars (here on shooting schedules), 90-something Mary holds forth, pours forth, and remains the town historian and storyteller. Inexpensive.

Perea's Restaurant & Tijuana Bar (505-898-2442), 4590 Corrales Rd.,

Corrales. Open Mon.–Sat. 11:30–2. Lunch only. This ancient building was constructed of terrones, blocks of mud cut from the river. The original construction is displayed inside. You can't eat the history; however, you certainly can eat the green chile enchiladas and the chicken enchilada casserole. Yum! Inexpensive.

Teofilo's (505-865-5511), 144 Main St., Los Lunas, across from the Luna Mansion. Lunch, dinner. Closed Mon. This simple, welcoming 1912 adobe home serves some of the best, most consistent New Mexican food anywhere. The yeasted hot sopaipillas are little pillows of heaven when slathered with honey, and the red chile is superb. There's no better place for Sunday lunch, and the patio is lovely in warm weather. Who needs Santa Fe? This is the real deal. Inexpensive.

Bombay Grill (505-899-6900), 3600 NM 528 NE, Rio Rancho. Open daily. Lunch, dinner. When the craving for Indian food hits, do not resist; go directly to Bombay Grill, one of the easier places to find in Rio Rancho on the west side, by heading up the hill from the intersection of Alameda Blvd. and Coors Rd. and looking to your left. An upscale-feeling dining establishment with an ongoing slide show of Indian scenes flashing on the wall and an interior waterfall, its food is as close to perfectly spiced, prepared, and served as possible. Curries

YOU MAY RUN INTO A MOVIE STAR OR A SALTY OLD MINER AT MARY'S BAR IN CERRILLOS.

are scrumptious, and the lamb dishes are highly recommended. Chicken masala is hard to resist. The lunch buffet is one of the great deals in town. Moderate.

Flying Star Café (505-938-4717), 10700 Corrales Rd., Corrales. Open daily 6 AM–11 PM, Fri.–Sat. 6 AM– 11:30 PM. Located just north of Alameda Blvd. in front of the Bosque Trail, this is the perfect place to meet friends. Drop in for a late-night snack of key lime pie, a morning latte and blueberry scone, or just a bowl of soup and a sandwich, anytime. Home-made egg salad and chicken salad, and the grilled beef and chile sand-wich are favorites. Daily specials can be mighty fine and tend to run out early, but salads can be skimpy. Burg-ers and fries, vegetarian fare—they have it all. But the tab can become surprisingly pricy with pie at $4.99 a slice. Moderate.

Santa Ana Café (505-867-1234), Hyatt Tamaya Resort, 1300 Tuyuna Tr., Santa Ana. Open daily 6:30 AM– 10 PM. Breakfast, lunch, dinner. A fine place to enjoy a Sunday brunch or Friday evening prime rib buffet, and a place to try interesting lighter fare, like fish and salads, with a native twist the rest of the time. Moderate– Expensive.

Los Ojos Restaurant & Saloon (505-829-3547), Jemez Springs.

TRY THE FAMOUS JEMEZ BURGER AT LOS OJOS RESTAURANT & SALOON IN JEMEZ SPRINGS.

Despite the relatively new addition of an outdoor patio, nothing could be better than the dark, woody interior of this classic Western bar. Go for the "Famous Jemez Burger" or, on weekend nights, the prime rib special. There are always folks shooting pool. Count on waitresses with attitude and characters with plenty of tales at the bar. This is the place to warm up with a hot bowl of chile after a day cross-country skiing or exploring Bandelier National Monument up north. Inexpensive.

Range Café (505-867-1700), 925 Camino del Pueblo, Bernalillo. Open daily 7:30 AM–9:30 PM. With live music on weekends; casual, consistent home cooking served in huge portions (like meat loaf and mashed potatoes and chicken-fried steak); plus excellent pancakes, huevos rancheros, and divine desserts, with their trademark "Death by Lemon"; no wonder this is a great gathering spot. Expect to wait in line for Sunday breakfast. Inexpensive–Moderate.

✳ Entertainment

Engine House Theater (505-438-3780), 2814 NM 14, Madrid. Open weekends Memorial Day–Columbus Day. Hiss and boo at three melodramas each season in the only venue with a steam engine on stage. Call for ticket prices.

✐ **Wildlife West: Chuckwagon** Sat. 6–10, June 30–Sept. 1, with BBQ feast followed by vintage Western swing music.

THE RANGE CAFÉ IN BERNALILLO IS THE PLACE TO HEAR LIVE MUSIC ON WEEKENDS, WATCH THE GAME, OR JUST HANG OUT.

MADRID IS LOADED WITH COLORFUL GALLERIES.

Sandia and Isleta Pueblos offer big-name entertainment; popular comedians, musicians, and performers; as well as those who were big "back in the day." See listings under *Hotels, Resorts, and Lodges.*

Santa Ana Star Centre (505-891-7300), 3001 Civic Centre, Rio Rancho. Find a busy schedule of sports events, car shows, concerts, ice shows, and much more at this brand new facility.

✳ Selective Shopping

Jackalope (505-867-9813), 834 W. US 550, #44, Bernalillo. Open daily 9–7. An international import bazaar with pottery, rugs, ethnic folk art, antique teak chests from India, silver candlesticks from Mexico, puppets from Bali, and home and garden products from everywhere. This is the perfect place to shop for gifts for yourself or everyone you know. Not

cheap, but not expensive, either. Shop carefully for the best deals.

Walatowa Visitor Center See *Guidance.*

Bien Mur Indian Market Center (505-821-5400), 100 Bien Mur Dr. NE. I-25 exit 234 east on Tramway Rd. Open Mon.–Sat. 9–5:30, Sun. 11–5. For high quality, guaranteed authentic Indian jewelry, rugs, pottery, baskets, and turquoise and silver jewelry, this is an excellent place to shop. You are sure to find something you simply must have at a fair price.

Abo Trading Company (505-847-0390), 101 E. Broadway, Mountainair. Find 4,500 square feet of value-priced Mexican imports where you least expect to, in a refurbished mercantile building at the intersection of NM 55 and US 60. This shop has well-chosen, handcrafted, one-of-a-kind rustic furniture, dishes, textiles, wall art, and housewares that can go a long way toward giving your home a Southwest feel. The proprietor says that people drive down from Santa Fe for the bargains. Call for hours.

Just Imagine Gallery & Coffee House (505-281-9611), 488 E. NM 66, Tijeras. Some of the prettiest dresses may be found at Just Imagine —dresses in a feminine, Victorian-gypsy style that may have been popular in the 1960s do not look at all dated here. The shop also has beautiful jewelry and well-selected home and garden pieces. This is also the site of the new-juried **Tijeras Open-Air Arts Market,** weekends May–Oct. 10–5, a delightful way to spend a summer afternoon, with live music and dance.

Johnsons of Madrid (505-438-3780), 2846 NM 14, Madrid. In a town with 30 galleries, the Johnsons remain the first and oldest. They feature regional textiles, fiber arts, photography, and fine art.

✳ Special Events

May: Memorial Day Weekend, Jemez Pueblo, **Red Rocks Arts & Crafts Festival.**

June–July: **Music at the Ballpark** (505-471-1054), Madrid. Concerts all summer long. **Wildlife West** (505-281-7655), Edgewood. Third weekend in June, **Bluegrass Weekend** with bands, vendors, workshops, zoo tours. Chuckwagon BBQ and Western swing music.

August: **La Fiesta de San Lorenzo** (505-867-5252), Bernalillo. Traditionally held Aug. 9–10 to honor the town's patron saint, the fiesta features the ancient Matachines Dances, performed in the streets.

September: Labor Day Weekend, **Bernalillo Wine Festival.** Also in September, visit the **Manzano Hawk Watch Migration Site** (505-255-7622; www.hawkwatch.org), 1420 Carlisle Blvd. SE, Ste. 206, Albuquerque. Join Hawk Watch for raptor counts March and April in the Sandias, and September and October in the Manzanos, at Capilla Peak, off FR 245, near Manzano, in Cibola National Forest. Assist with the raptor count and learn about the migrating birds of prey from interpretive rangers on-site.

October: **Corrales Harvest Festival** (505-350-3955), Corrales. Music, hayrides, produce, and storytelling. Also **National Pinto Bean Festival** (505-384-2418), Moriarty.

December: **Christmas in Madrid** (505-471-1054), annual community open house, parade. **Christmas at Kuaua** (505-867-5351), Coronado State Monument, Dec. 20, 5:30–8:30, with luminarias, Pueblo and Spanish dancing. Free. **Farolito Tour** (505-829-3530) Jemez State Monument, 5–8, Pueblo dances and music, plus 1,500 farolitos light up ancient Giusewa Pueblo ruins. Free.

Albuquerque and Beyond

ALBUQUERQUE: THE DUKE CITY

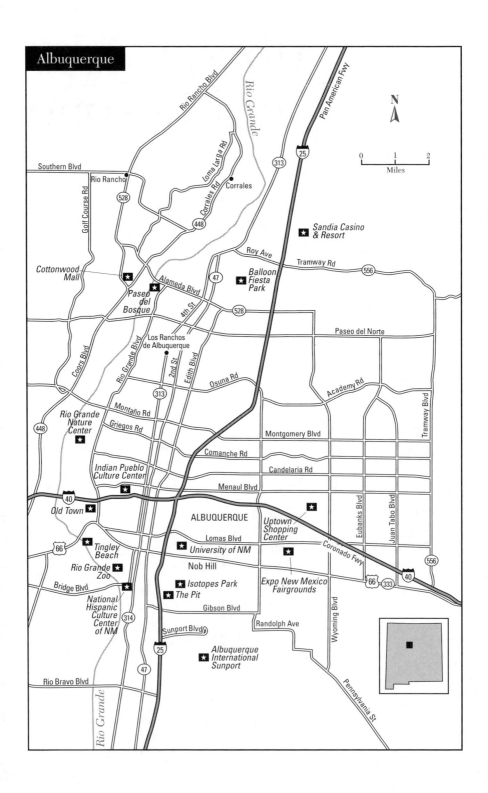

Albuquerque

Rio Rancho Blvd

Rio Grande

Pan American Fwy

N

0   1   2
Miles

313

25

Southern Blvd

Rio Rancho

528

Corrales Rd

Loma Larga Rd

Corrales

448

Sandia Casino & Resort ★

Golf Course Rd

Roy Ave

Tramway Rd

556

Cottonwood Mall ★

Alameda Blvd

47

Balloon Fiesta Park ★

Paseo del Bosque ★

4th St

528

Paseo del Norte

Los Ranchos de Albuquerque

Coors Blvd

Rio Grande Blvd

2nd St

Edith Blvd

Osuna Rd

Academy Rd

313

Montaño Rd

448

Rio Grande Nature Center ★

Griegos Rd

Montgomery Blvd

Tramway Blvd

Comanche Rd

Indian Pueblo Culture Center ★

Candelaria Rd

Menaul Blvd

40

Old Town ★

ALBUQUERQUE

Uptown Shopping Center ★

Eubanks Blvd

Juan Tabo Blvd

66

Tingley Beach ★

Lomas Blvd

University of NM ★

Coronado Fwy

556

Rio Grande Zoo ★

Nob Hill

★

40

Bridge Blvd

Isotopes Park ★
The Pit ★

Expo New Mexico Fairgrounds

66

333

National Hispanic Culture Center of NM ★

314

Gibson Blvd

Randolph Ave

Wyoming Blvd

Sunport Blvd

25

47

Albuquerque International Sunport ★

Rio Bravo Blvd

Pennsylvania St

Rio Grande

ALBUQUERQUE: THE DUKE CITY

A bout 10 years ago there emerged a movement to change the spelling of Albuquerque. Some wanted to restore the missing *r*, so the city's name would be spelled "Alburquerque," like its Spanish forebear, the original Duke of Alburquerque. Although that idea never took hold, there is no arguing that Albuquerque, New Mexico, takes great pride in its Spanish heritage.

There were as many as 40 Indian pueblos in the province of Tiguex (t-gway) existing in the Rio Grande Valley at the time of the Spanish conquest. The city was founded by a determined band of families through a land grant from the Spanish crown. They settled in the Old Town area and left a legacy of a Spanish identity that has endured, through subsequent waves of immigration, to the present.

Today's Albuquerque, with a population of 1 million, boasts a rainbow of Italian, Chinese, Indian, Japanese, Mexican, African American, Thai, Vietnamese, and Native American communities, families, and neighborhoods. These various ethnic identities continue to find expression in festivals, places of worship, restaurants, and shops that give the city much of its vitality.

Centrally located within New Mexico at the crossroads of east-west I-40 and north-south I-25, Albuquerque is fairly easy to navigate as it is divided into quadrants, with Central Ave., or Old Route 66, dividing the city into its north and south sides. Route 66 neon lights up the night along Central, the boulevard that extends through the core of the city and where the University of New Mexico, Nob Hill, Presbyterian Hospital, Downtown, and Old Town may be found. Broadway is the street that divides the city into its east and west sides. (One helpful navigational tool: the Sandia Mountains are to the east, while the volcanoes and the river are to the west.) The Rio Grande meanders through the length of the city north to south, providing a 15-mile greenbelt and a much-loved running, walking, and bike path that serves as an urban park.

Albuquerque is in the midst of a dynamic, seemingly unstoppable growth spurt. It is a transformation that began with the arrival of Intel and a critical mass of newcomers that expanded its life as a small town where mom-and-pop businesses served each other to a magnetic relocation site for people and business. Headlining the exciting growth are the development of Mesa del Sol, a live-work "smart" community on the south end of town, and the green renovation of a downtown beauty, the 1939 La Posada Hotel, once the proud possession of New Mexico native Conrad Hilton. An optimistic opening date for the hotel is late 2008.

The city is a mecca for young creatives, Web- and arts-savvy, educated, and energetic young folks who bring rich "cultural capital" that is finally being appreciated. Many are quite entrepreneurial and enterprising, and they find the diversity and openness, as well as the cultural richness of the town, to their liking. Religious and lifestyle freedom and toleration are givens, and alternative, artistic, and unconventional lifestyles coexist comfortably beside cowboy and blue-collar values. It is as if the positive side of the code of the West, particularly respect for individuality, as well as an appreciation for community, has taken hold here.

Albuquerque retains distinct neighborhoods well worth exploring, although they may require a bit of initial navigation to find: Nob Hill, a walking district packed with small shops and cafés; Downtown with its movie theater and bars, generally considered the "entertainment district"; the University of New Mexico with its prototypical southwest architecture; Huning Highlands, a stronghold of Victorian homes; and Old Town and the North and South Valleys, each with their agrarian traditions, which hold on to their particular flavors and compounds of history, architecture, commerce, and cuisine. What we think of as the North

ENJOYING A SPRINGTIME ICE CREAM CONE ON OLD TOWN PLAZA.

Valley actually was a group of independent farming villages until after WW II.

Up and coming neighborhoods, those taking shape by re-creating themselves right now, include EDO, short for "east of downtown," which includes the stretch of Central between the university down to the railroad underpass; Sawmill, in the hopping area of 12th and Mountain in walking distance of the Old Town museums; and the area on the eastern fringe of Nob Hill between Carlisle and San Mateo.

A walk or bicycle ride through these neighborhoods yields a feeling for the city that is impossible to obtain from from driving through along the freeway, where the view appears initially to be only of mundane urban sprawl.

Route 66, the mother road, winds east to west through the city like a ribbon of neon, granting Central Avenue a nostalgic heart. From original Route 66 motels to restored historic gas stations now adapted as popular watering holes, it retains its sense as a destination for travelers and explorers, even as they mingle with the descendants of eight and 12 generations of families who have lived in the same community

The Rio Grande divides Albuquerque from its high-tech neighbor to the west, Rio Rancho, home of Intel Corporation's largest computer chip plant as well as the attendant service businesses, suburbs, stores, and shopping centers (loaded with national chain restaurants) this giant has spawned.

Albuquerque is waking up to itself and appreciating its human and natural resources. The city continues to interpret itself and its culture in a wider way, with the National Hispanic Cultural Center of New Mexico, the expanded Museum of Art and History, and the Museum of Natural History and Science; intelligent and emerging galleries of significance; and a growing diversity of shopping, dining, learning, and entertainment venues. It is that feeling of ongoing growth, of being in the midst of change, that prevails in the city at the moment, like a brisk spring wind, even as neighborhoods battle to save landmarks that preserve the city's unique past.

In addition, the appearance of major Indian gaming resorts nearby at Isleta, San Felipe, Santa Ana, Sandia, and Laguna Pueblo's Route 66 Casino are venues that have attracted top entertainment in recent years. The growth of the film industry and the development of Mesa del Sol to the south are additional elements of opportunity. Climate is another advantage. With 360 days of sunshine, as well as four distinct seasons, Albuquerque appeals to those who appreciate easy access to outdoor activities.

The only note of concern in the midst of all this good news is water. This is the high desert after all, and the question of where the water will come from to support all the growth is one that is asked continually. However, conservation efforts are paying off, and hope is held for the Chama River diversion project to satisfy the needs of a thirsty metropolis.

All of this adds up to the fact that Albuquerque is in the process of articulating its own unique identity, even as it emerges as a cultural, as well as a legal, medical, and educational capital separate from Santa Fe. Albuquerque is still a city that is coming of age and still deciding its identity—sunbelt metropolis, oasis of multicultural tradition, dusty Western outpost, military base; it is a mixture of all of these.

As it loses a bit of its old New Mexico edge with the influx of new people, money, ideas, and education, it gains in sophistication and talent. While it continuously becomes more like everyplace else, there is something within it, perhaps the centuries of indigenous, then Spanish colonial, pioneer spirit, that refuse to be deleted from the city's cultural memory. It is not, nor will it ever be, completely prettied-up or smoothed out. It continues to be a magnet for entrepreneurs, immigrants, artists, retirees, and especially for those with hopes of making it in the West.

To find out what is happening, check out www.dukecityfix.com, www.kunm.org, or look at calendars in the *Weekly Alibi* and *Venue* or the Friday entertainment section of the *Albuquerque Journal*.

GUIDANCE **Albuquerque Chamber of Commerce** (505-764-3700), 115 Gold SW, Ste. 201, Albuquerque.

Albuquerque Convention & Visitors Bureau (1-800-733-9918; 505-842-9918), 20 First Plaza, Ste. 601, Albuquerque.

Albuquerque Hispano Chamber of Commerce (1-800-754-4620; 505-842-9003), 1309 Fourth St. SW, Albuquerque.

Key Numbers: 311 in town brings listings of cultural happenings; 505-768-3556 out of town; www.cabq.gov/crs.

GETTING THERE *By car:* Albuquerque lies at the crossroads of I-25 and I-40.

By bus: **Greyhound Bus** (1-800-231-2222) and **Grey Line and TNM&O Coaches** (505-243-7992), 420 First St. SW.

By air: Many major airlines, including United, Southwest, Continental, and Delta, fly to the **Albuquerque International Sunport** (505-244-7700), 2200 Sunport Blvd. SE.

By train: **Amtrak** (1-800-872-7245) brings passengers to Albuquerque daily from Chicago and Los Angeles. The **Alvarado Transportation Center** at First and Central, or 214 First St. SW, downtown is the terminal for both bus and train passengers.

GETTING AROUND Public transportation has improved greatly in recent years, and the **Abq Ride** (505-243-7433) now includes a public bus system known as Rapid Ride that extends through an 11-mile corridor along Central Ave. and promises to deliver you 11 minutes between each stop. Fare is $1, and it can get you most places you want to go. **Rapid Ride** operates 6 AM–9 PM daily, and 6–3 AM during the summer. Pick up schedules at the Alvarado Transportation Center, 100 First St. SW. The **New Mexico Rail Runner Express** (505-245-RAIL; www.nmrailrunner.com), which stops here also, goes south to Belen and north to Bernalillo, with Santa Fe stops scheduled to begin in 2008. Fares are $1 per zone, each way. Schedules vary with seasons and special events. **Albuquerque Cab** (505-883-4888) and **Yellow Cab Co.** (505-243-7777) operate 24-hour service.

HOT-AIR BALLOONS FLOAT OVER THE RIO GRANDE YEAR-ROUND.

WHEN TO COME The Albuquerque International Balloon Fiesta, held the first two weeks of October, is the city's premier event.

MEDICAL EMERGENCY Heart Hospital of New Mexico (505-724-2375), 504 Elm St. NE, Albuquerque.

University of New Mexico Hospital (505-272-2111), 2211 Lomas Blvd. NE, Albuquerque.

Presbyterian Hospital (505-841-1234), 1100 Central Ave. SE, Albuquerque.

✳ To See

MUSEUMS Albuquerque Museum of Art & History (505-242-4600), 2000 Mountain Road NW, Albuquerque. Open Tues.–Sun. 9–5, 9–8 Fri. Closed Mon. and city holidays. This premier city museum features art of the southwest, vintage Albuquerque, four centuries of Rio Grande Valley history, a sculpture garden, café, museum shop, and walking tours, as well as major traveling exhibitions. $4 adults, $2 seniors, $1 children 4–12, under 4 free. Free Sun. 9–1 and first Wed. each month.

Anderson-Abruzzo Albuquerque International Balloon Museum (505-768-6020), 9201 Balloon Museum Dr. NE Albuqueque, Balloon Fiesta Park. Open Tues.–Sun. 9–4. Closed Mon. Named for pioneering Albuquerque balloonists Maxie Anderson and Ben Abruzzo, who completed the first manned crossing of the Atlantic Ocean in 1978, this museum has exhibits that highlight the development of hot-air and gas balloons in military, science, aerospace research, and for recreation. $4 adults, $2 seniors, $1, children 4–12, under 4 free.

National Hispanic Cultural Center of New Mexico (505-246-2261), 1701 Fourth St. SW, Albuquerque. Open Tues.–Sun. 10–5. Closed Mon. This glorious facility has blossomed into a center for music, dance, theater, and exhibits of art of the contemporary Hispanic world. Special community events such as Dia de los Muertos and Cinco de Mayo are celebrated here as well. La Fonda del Bosque is the on-site restaurant, and la Tiendita, the gift shop, has a good selection of books on related subjects. $3 adults, $2 seniors, under 16 free. Free Sun.

◊ **New Mexico Museum of Natural History and Science** (505-841-2800), 1801 Mountain Rd. NW, Albuquerque. Open daily 9–5. Closed Thanksgiving, Christmas, and nonholiday Mon. in Jan. and Sept. With a live volcano, huge dinosaurs, hands-on exhibits, natural history of New Mexico, a café, and an entertaining gift shop, this museum is guaranteed fun for the whole family. Starry Nights programs are given many Friday nights at the Planetarium. Lockheed

NEW MEXICO MUSEUM OF NATURAL HISTORY AND SCIENCE APPEALS TO KIDS OF ALL AGES.

✍ ALBUQUERQUE BIOLOGICAL PARK

(311 or 505-768-2000). Open daily 9–5, Sat.–Sun. 9–6 in summer. Closed Jan. 1, Thanksgiving, Christmas. This complex consists of an aquarium, botanic garden, and zoo (as described below), and the Tingley Beach fishing lakes, (see under *To Do—Fishing* and *Green Space*). $7 adults 13–64, $3 seniors and ages 3–12. Combo tickets, with admission to aquarium, garden, and zoo, sold Tues.–Sun. before noon, $12 adults and bargain rates for children. Tickets entitle participants to ride the Rio Line train between the aquarium and the zoo, and the Thunderbird Express, a loop around the zoo.

Albuquerque Aquarium (505-764-6200), 2601 Central Ave. NW, Albuquerque. Exhibits trace Rio Grande from the Rockies to the Gulf Coast, with saltwater fish, invertebrates, and habitats of the Gulf of Mexico. There is a shark tank, reef fish, turtles. Summer concerts Thurs. nights June–Aug. 7. See above for rates.

Rio Grande Botanic Garden (505-768-2000), 2601 Central Ave. NW, Albuquerque. Open Mon.–Fri. 9–5, Sat.–Sun. 9–6. Conservatory exhibits xeric plants of desert and Mediterranean climates, formal walled gardens, medicinal plants, Children's Fantasy Garden, Heritage Farm, and a Japanese garden. The PNM Butterfly Pavilion is open summers. Summer concerts are held Thurs. nights June–mid-Aug. at 7, and holiday light festival is open evenings during Dec. See above for rates.

Rio Grande Zoological Park (505-764-6200), 903 10th St. SW, Albuquerque. More than 1,000 animals are shown in their natural habitats. The 64 acres includes elephants, rhinos, giraffes, gorillas, wolves, polar bears, big cats, seals, tigers, amphibians, and reptiles. Zoo Music Concerts June–July, Fri. at 7. See above for rates.

Martin DynaTheater shows hourly 10–5 daily. $7 adults, $6 seniors, $4 children 3–17, under 3 free.

Rattlesnake Museum and Gift Shop (505-242-6569), 202 San Felipe NW, Albuquerque. Open Mon.–Sat. 10–6, Sun. 12–5. In Old Town you will find the largest exhibit of rattlesnake species, art, and artifacts in the world. $3.50 adults, $3 seniors and children.

Maxwell Museum of Anthropology (505-277-4405), University of New Mexico, Albuquerque. Open Tues.–Fri. 9–4., Sat. 10–4. Closed Sun. With over 10 million items in its collection, the Maxwell is considered one of the leading anthropological museums in the United States. Free.

Gallery 516 (505-242-1445), 516 Central Ave. SW, Albuquerque. This "museum-style" gallery is two floors of ambitious, adventurous, and notable national, local, and regional work. Somewhat avant-garde, it remains intelligent and accessible.

Turquoise Museum (505-247-8650), 2107 Central Avenue NW, Albuquerque. Open Mon.–Sat. 10–5. Closed Sun. Exhibits from 60 turquoise mines around the world, as well as the geology, mythology, and history of turquoise, plus lapidary room and gift shop, make this an irresistible stop. $4 adults, $3 age 7–17 and seniors, six and under free.

Indian Pueblo Cultural Center (505-843-7270), 2401 12th St. NW, Albuquerque. Open daily 9–5:30. There is no better place to learn about New Mexico's 19 pueblos than this museum, which is owned and operated by the pueblos themselves. Browse the extensive gift shop that features authentic jewelry and Indian arts, plus books, music, and videos on tribal life. The Pueblo Harvest Café & Bakery serves Native American cuisine. The café is currently undergoing a big upgrade and renovation. You can enjoy dance and artist demonstrations every weekend for the price of admission. Two permanent exhibits showcase history, culture, and artistic traditions of New Mexico's 19 pueblos. In addition, you may view exhibits of contemporary artists of painting, sculpture, and pottery. $4 adults, $3 seniors, $1 students, under five free.

Unser Racing Museum (505-341-1776), 1776 Montano NW, Los Ranchos de Albuquerque. Open daily 10–4. Four generations of racecars, antique cars, winning pace cars, and uniforms that display the racing accomplishments of the Unser family. This museum recently received a $1.5 million cash injection from the state, so look for great things to come. $8.

National Museum of Nuclear Science and History (505-245-2137), Eubank and Southern Blvd., Albuquerque. Open daily 9–5. Closed Jan. 1, Easter, Thanksgiving, and Christmas. This museum is a resource for nuclear science, with exhibits, artifacts, and documentaries telling the story of the atomic age and its pioneers, as well as many related scientific topics. Call for rates.

New Mexico Holocaust and Intolerance Museum and Study Center (505-247-0606), 415 Central Ave. NW, Albuquerque. Open Tues.–Sat. 10–6:30. Closed Sun. and Mon. At press time, this museum is planning to move to a nearby location downtown. Donation.

✂ **Explora** (505-224-8323), 1701 Mountain Rd. NW, Albuquerque. Open Mon.–Sat. 10–6, Sun. noon–6. This is a science center where families can explore science, technology, and art through interactive activities and 250 hands-on exhibits. $7 adults, $5 seniors, $3 children 1–11.

✂ ♿ **Rio Grande Nature Center** (505-344-7240), 2901 Candelaria NW, Albuquerque. Open daily 8–5. This small museum (really, an expanded visitor center) provides information on the flora and fauna of the bosque, as well as blinds for viewing waterfowl. It is a major entryway to the bike and walking paths of Rio Grande Valley State Park. Educational events and festivals are held throughout the year here. $2.

HISTORIC LANDMARKS, PLACES, AND SITES **Harwood Art Center** (505-242-6367), 1114 Seventh St. NW, Albuquerque. Open Mon.–Fri. 10–4 and by appointment. This 1925 Methodist girls' boarding school was refurbished as a community arts center, and the Art School at Harwood now offers an impressive

KIDS GET HANDS-ON FUN AT EXPLORA.

calendar of arts classes, yoga, and dance. With five galleries and 45 artists' studios, the place is an artists' haven with frequent exhibitions and many shows of new work.

San Felipe de Neri Catholic Church (505-243-4628), 2005 N. Plaza St. NW, Albuquerque. Open daily. Museum open Mon.–Sat. 10–4. Founded in 1706 and in almost continuous use for 300 years, this Old Town landmark maintains a strong community today. Mass is held in English and Spanish. Free.

Old Town Albuquerque (505-243-3215), south of I-25 near Rio Grande Blvd., or I-25 to Rio Grande Blvd. exit, then south. Or take Central Ave. west. The original site of Albuquerque, Old Town is a must-see for visitors who will enjoy museums, shops, restaurants, a traditional plaza, and Southwestern architecture.

Sandia Man Cave (no phone), NM 165, 5 miles southeast of Placitas. Rumored to be a hoax dreamed up by members of the University of New Mexico anthropology department, this cave in the Sandia Mountains is reputed to be the site holding evidence of ancient man. It has, by and large, been discredited as an ancient site.

Ernie Pyle Memorial Branch Library (505-256-2065), 900 Girard SE. Open Tues.–Sat. 10–6, Wed. 11–7. Closed Sun.–Mon. This modest little house in southeast Albuquerque, once the home of WW II correspondent and pioneer

American journalist Ernie Pyle, who was killed in action, is a cozy, beloved neighborhood library with Pyle memorabilia.

✳ To Do

Check www.itsatrip.org for the latest sports activities in and around the city.

AMUSEMENT PARKS **Cliff's Amusement Park** (505-881-9373; www.cliffs amusementpark.com), 4800 Osuna NE, Albuquerque. Roller coasters, water park, arcade, rides, and more rides: Cliff's is Albuquerque's answer to Disneyland.

BICYCLING Contact the **NM Touring Society** (505-237-9700; www.nmts.org) for events.

The **City of Albuquerque** (311; www.cabq.gov/bike) provides maps for its many interconnecting bike paths.

Rio Grande Valley State Park has the 16-mile, practically level, Paseo del Bosque bike path through the bosque and parallel to the Rio Grande. (See *Green Space*.)

MARIACHIS SERENADE IN OLD TOWN PLAZA.

BIKING ALONG THE PASEO DEL BOSQUE TRAIL.

CLIMBING **Stone Age Climbing Gym** (505-341-2016), 4201 Yale NE. Climbing school, group events, and guided climbs in the Sandias.

FARMERS' MARKETS Saturday mornings 7–noon, early July–late Oct.

Albuquerque Downtown Market (505-480-6943), Eighth and Central, Robinson Park.

Albuquerque Growers' Market (505-869-2369), Central and Louisiana, behind Ta Lin World Market.

Village of Los Ranchos Growers' Market (505-890-2799), Los Ranchos City Hall, 6718 Rio Grande Blvd. NW.

FISHING **Tingley Ponds.** For generations preceding the polio scare of the 1950s, Tingley Beach was a popular swimming spot for Albuquerqueans. Recently restored as a fishing area with snack bar and train service running between here and the Biopark, Tingley Ponds is a good place to walk as well as fish for stockers. Boats and bike rentals are available Memorial Day–Labor Day.

GOLF **The Championship Golf Course at the University of New Mexico** (505-277-4546), 3601 University Blvd. SE, Albuquerque. I-25 south to Rio Bravo exit, go left and continue half a mile. Open year-round, weather permitting. Soft spikes and collared shirts are required at this highly regarded, 18-hole public course known as UNM South or "the Monster." It has been ranked among the Top 25 public courses and boasts rolling fairways, panoramic views of the city, and undulating greens with a three-hole beginner course and driving range. $39–49.

University of New Mexico North Course (505-277-4146), corner of Tucker and Yale NE. Play a midday nine holes on midcity greens shaded by tall trees. The perimeter of the course is also a popular walking and jogging path, adding up to 4 miles once around. $18–20.

Arroyo del Oso Golf Course (505-884-7505), 7001 Osuna Rd. NE. Named for the Bear Canyon Arroyo where it is located, the sloping topography of the 27-hole course makes it best suited to intermediate-advanced players. $21–27.

HIKING **Elena Gallegos Park** (505-452-5200), 7100 Tramway Blvd. NE. This vast mountain park offers a variety of trails, plus panoramic views of the city. Trails permit hiking, biking, and horseback riding. This is a nice place for a summer evening picnic. Free.

Juan Tabo Campground (505-281-3304), 10 miles northeast of Albuquerque at NM 556 and FR 333. Open year-round. 22 picnic sites. $3.

La Luz Trail (505-346-3100). The trailhead is at the end of FR 444, or you can access the trail from Juan Tabo Campground. This 15-mile challenging round-trip hike to Sandia Crest over switchbacks is only for the very in-shape. Still, it is *the* Albuquerque hike. The trail goes through four life zones and rises over 3,000 feet to an altitude of 10,500 feet. As they say, you can always take the tram down. Some prefer to take the tram up and down. Travel well prepared for rapid weather change. Every summer, someone hikes up on a hot August afternoon, then gets hypothermia when the temperature falls 40 degrees and a hailstorm comes in. Free.

HORSEBACK RIDING **Del Sol Equestrian Center** (505-873-0888), 6715 Islet Blvd. SW. Horse boarding and lessons.

Flying Horse Riding Academy (505-822-8473), 9500 Wilshire Blvd. NE. Horse boarding and lessons.

HORSE RACING **The Downs at Albuquerque** (505-266-5555), Expo New Mexico, 300 San Pedro NE. Open daily 10–"late." Racing in season, with year-round simulcasting and slot machines providing excitement, as does the Fri. night Jockey Club all-you-can-eat prime rib special for $10.95. Slated to be moved to Moriarty.

ICE SKATING ✿ **Outpost Ice Arena** (505-856-7594), 9530 Tramway Blvd. NE. Open daily. Lessons, public sessions, and group events are scheduled. Call for more information. $9. Skate rental $3.

*ROLLER-SKATING **Roller King** (505-299-4494; www.rollerkingabq.com), 400 Paisano NE. Northeast corner of I-40 and Juan Tabo. Open daily. Call for specific events and hours. Price includes skate rental. $7.75.

*SKATEBOARDING **Los Altos Municipal Skate Park** (505-857-8640), 10140 Lomas, west of Eubank, east of Easterday. Open daily, sunrise–sunset. Considered "the fastest skate park in the West," Los Altos demands that you wear a helmet. Free.

SPECTATOR SPORTS **Albuquerque Isotopes Baseball Club** (505-924-2255), 1601 Avenida Cesar Chavez, at intersection of University Blvd. SE. Take I-25 to Avenida Cesar Chavez, go east. The farm team for the Florida Marlins, the Isotopes are a Triple-A member of the Pacific Coast League. The new Isotopes Stadium is a classic ballpark and has an abundance of dining and treat opportunities. Take me out to the ball game! $6–24.

UNM Lobos and Lady Lobos Basketball (505-925-LOBO), corner of Avenida Cesar Chavez and University Blvd. SE. Both the men's and ladies' teams play throughout the season in the Pit, or University Arena, a stadium that slopes 37 feet down toward the floor, where 18,000 fans dressed in Lobo red enjoy intimidating visiting teams and giving the Lobos their home court advantage. $12–27.

A GLORIOUS AUTUMN AFTERNOON RIDE THROUGH THE BOSQUE NEAR CORRALES.

WALKING TOURS Walk Albuquerque (505-344-9742; www.walkalbuquerque .org) has plans for several self-guided walking tours in neighborhoods all over town. **Albuquerque Museum** (505-242-4600) offers walking tours of Old Town.

WINERIES Anderson Valley Vineyards (505-344-7266), 4920 Rio Grande Blvd. NW, Albuquerque. Tasting room hours Wed.–Sun. noon–5. One of the first contemporary vineyards in New Mexico, founded in 1973, featuring Red Chile Cabernet and Balloon Blush, as specialties.

Casa Rondena Winery (505-344-5911), 733 Chavez Road NW, Albuquerque. Tasting room hours Wed.–Sat., 10–6, Sun. noon–6. Winemaker John Calvin has created a splendid Tuscan estate in Albuquerque's North Valley to frame his award-winning creations.

Gruet Winery (505-821-0055), 8400 Pan American Freeway, Albuquerque. Proprietors are the Gruet family. Tasting room hours Mon.–Fri. 10–5, Sat. noon–5, closed Sun. Fine sparkling wine and still wines like Pinot Noir and Chardonnay.

St. Clair Winery (505-243-9916), 901 Rio Grande Blvd. NW, Albuquerque. Tasting room hours Mon.–Thurs. 11–9, Fri.–Sat. 11–10, Sun. noon–9. A sixth-generation winery, with its original location in Deming, its Albuquerque Old

CASA RONDENA WINE TASTING ROOM IN THE NORTH VALLEY.

Town location is a bistro with a spacious outdoor patio, fine service, and excellent food, with the wines used as menu ingredients.

Tierra Encantada Vineyards and Winery (505-764-9463), 1872 Five Points Rd. SW, Albuquerque. Tasting room hours Fri.–Sun. noon–5, or by appointment. Located in the heart of the South Valley, a centuries-old agricultural region. Syrah, Viognier, and Cabernet Sauvignon are created by winemaker Jim Dowling.

✳ Green Space

Rio Grande Valley State Park (505-344-7240), 2901 Candelaria NW, Albuquerque. Open daily 8–5. Visitor center open daily 10–5. Closed Thanksgiving, Christmas, and New Year's Day. Two easy approximately 1-mile trails through the center; a 3-acre observation pond with waterfowl, turtles, and dragonflies; demonstration gardens; wetlands; and interpretive nature trails make this a friendly place to explore the river, forest, and riparian environment. It is a migratory bird sanctuary that sponsors many events to celebrate the inhabitants. In addition, it provides access to the paved walking and bike path that extends 15 miles through the city along the bosque, or cottonwood forest. $3.

Tingley Ponds (505-764-6200), 1800 Tingley Dr. Open daily, sunrise to sunset. Opened during the 1930s, the city's Tingley Beach was a popular place to swim, until the polio epidemic scare shut it down. In recent years, Tingley Ponds have been restored as 18 acres of pond and wetlands that are stocked and open to public fishing. Free.

PARKS Roosevelt Park. Coal and Spruce SE. A lovely, large, unfenced off-leash dog park. Bring your own water. For a complete list of all off-leash parks, go to www.abqdog.com.

Hyder Park. In the beautiful southeast at the corner of Richmond and Santa Monica SE is a beloved neighborhood park with mature shade trees, benches, and walking and running paths.

Tiguex Park. 1800 Mountain Rd. NW. With shady old cedar trees and gently rolling paths, this Old Town green space between the Albuquerque Museum and the Museum of Natural History makes a nice respite where you can get some fresh air and sunshine and stretch your legs.

✳ Lodging

BED & BREAKFASTS, MOTELS, AND HOTELS Old Town Bed & Breakfast (505-764-9144; www.inn-new-mexico.com), 707 17th St. NW, Albuquerque. For convenience and comfort, this B&B is ideal. Though only two rooms are available, either one will afford a sense of well-being. The place is ideally situated for walking explorations of the Old Town area and museum visits. Breakfasts, such as whole-grain pancakes and New Mexican quiche, served with fresh fruit, are wholesome and taste homemade. $85–120.

"¶" ⌖ Los Poblanos Inn and Cultural Center (505-344-9297; www.lospoblanos.com), 4803 Rio Grande Blvd. NW, Albuquerque. For a sense of the expansive history of Albuquerque, a stay in this John Gaw

Meem–designed masterpiece of classic Territorial Revival architecture overlooking fields of lavender and an organic farm will be a memorable one. The beauty of the former Simms estate has been preserved with reverence by the current owners, the Rembes, and every detail of the property evokes its rich past. For an extra-special stay, consider the Girard Guest House, a two-room casita decorated with Mexican folk art. Eight different lodgings are available. Breakfast is a grand affair, prepared with seasonal local produce and eggs directly from Los Poblanos Organics. Throw in free Wi-Fi, complimentary *New York Times,* and concierge service, and you have the premier Albuquerque lodging experience. $145–265.

Sarabande Bed & Breakfast (1-888-506-4923 or 505-345-4923; www .sarabandebb.com), 5637 Rio Grande Blvd. NW, Albuquerque. For a charming North Valley retreat, you couldn't do better than Sarabande, named for the rose that grows in its courtyard. *Quiet, gracious* and *relaxing* are all words that well apply to the mood you will find here. $99–179.

&. "T" ✆ **Hotel Blue** (505-924-2400; www.thehotelblue.com), 717 Central Ave. NW, Albuquerque. Definitely the place to stay Downtown, Hotel Blue is a fairly recently renovation of tasteful midcentury modern design with a hip ambience. The place provides unexpected attention to details and is both business and family-

CRANES WINTER IN ALBUQUERQUE'S OPEN SPACES.

friendly. They brag on their state-of-the-art mattresses and attention to guest comfort. You can walk anywhere Downtown from here, and you can catch a bus anywhere else you might want to go. There's a buffet breakfast bar to get you going, plus a 24-hour coffee room. $77.

Hiway House (505-268-3971), 3200 Central Ave. SE, Albuquerque. If you're craving a taste of the old road, that is Old Route 66, consider this vintage remnant of what was a classic Southwest motel chain once owned by Ramada Inn founder Del Webb. You'll be in the proximity to Nob Hill, with plentiful dining and shopping choices, walking distance to the University of New Mexico, and close to the Sunport. It is set back a bit from Central Ave., so you'll have a bit of protection from traffic noise. Not a bad place at all for those who want a road experience. $28–58.

✳ Where to Eat

DINING OUT **El Pinto** (505-898-1777), 10500 Fourth St. NW. Open Mon.–Thurs. 11–9; Fri.–Sat. 11–10; Sun. 10:30–9. When you want to impress your out-of-town guests with Mexican food that isn't too hot and take them to a really nice place for dinner, El Pinto, at the north end of the North Valley, is where to go. Spicy salsa, chips, splashy margaritas on the patio, and barbeque ribs on the side go well with the enchiladas and chile rellenos. Moderate.

Vernon's Hidden Valley Steakhouse (505-341-0831), 6855 Fourth St. NW. Dinner only. Open 5–9 Thurs.–Sat., 5–8 Sun. You've got to walk through the wine shop, knock, and give the password ("Joe sent me") to be admitted to this speakeasy-style

backroom steakhouse with piano bar panache. Dark and romantic as you want it to be, Vernon's is the place for relaxing with a drink and a good steak after a workweek or for celebrating an anniversary. The service is impeccable, and the classic American food is beautifully prepared and delicious. Vernon's is for serious red meat eaters only, whether you crave a slab of New York steak or Colorado lamb chops. The sides are luscious, too, especially the creamed spinach and mac and cheese. Chocolate mousse pie for dessert, anyone? Expensive.

Artichoke Café (505-243-0200), 424 Central Ave. SE. Dinner nightly, lunch Mon.–Fri. Closed Sun. For over two decades, Pat and Terry Keene have set the standard for fine dining in Albuquerque. The simplest dishes here—steamed artichoke, roast chicken, and salmon of the day—are always well prepared and beautifully presented, with just the right seasoning, intriguing sauce, and side dishes. The restaurant seats 120 but feels more intimate. When excellent service is a must, the Artichoke will do the job and do it right. Expensive.

Le Café Miche (505-299-6088), 143 Wyoming Blvd. NE. Open for lunch Mon.–Fri. 11–1:30; dinner nightly 5–9, except Sun. and Mon. Chef Klaus has long put his personal touch on his country French restaurant, and it remains a success among businesspeople out for lunch and all of Albuquerque for fine holiday meals or special dinners. Start with pan seared foie gras or house-smoked duck, and move on to stuffed quail or lamb shank with garlic mashed potatoes. The adjoining wine bar is very special, with many greats by the glass and live music Thurs.–Sat. at 7. Plenty of

THAT'S NOT CHAING MAI. IT'S A BUDDHIST NEW YEAR CELEBRATION AT AN ALBUQUERQUE TEMPLE.

special events, like wine dinners and cooking classes, make this a good place to know. You just don't expect to find a place like this in a strip mall next to a motorcycle dealership. Expensive.

Scalo Northern Italian Grill (505-255-8781), 3500 Central SE. Dinner daily, lunch Mon.–Sat. White linen on the table, crispy fresh bread to dip in flavorful olive oil, pasta perfectly prepared, and a nice glass of wine. Scalo remains, after 20 years, one of the city's top addresses for a business lunch or birthday celebration. The wine list has over 300 selections, there's a full bar that is a chic hangout on its own, and there's live jazz two nights a week. Expensive.

Antiquity (505-247-3545), 112 Romero St. NW. Lamb roasting on the grill greets you as you enter this cozy warren of an Old Town hideaway that is charming in all seasons. Get your reservations early. There is always a fresh fish special; fresh lobster and scallops; five delicious cuts of steak, including Chateaubriand for two with béarnaise sauce; and the French onion soup is the best. Wine by the glass is most reasonable. All in all, a good value. Expensive.

Le Crêpe Michel (505-242-1251), 400 San Felipe NW. Open Mon.–Sat. Closed Sun. Lunch, dinner. The founder holds a PhD in anthropology, but more to the point, year after year she turns out absolutely authentic crêpes and quiche in this enduringly charming spot that is down a winding back alley in Old Town. Take a seat close to the fireplace and enjoy. Pâté and imported cheese, chicken and mushroom crêpes, filet de boeuf, and crêpe au chocolate for dessert. It can be a bit chilly on a cold night, so

bring a wrap. Reservations are essential. Moderate.

Yanni's (505-268-9250), 3109 Central NE. Open Mon.–Thurs. 11–10; Fri.–Sat. 11–11; Sun. noon–9. The wildly popular Yanni's and its fashionable Opa Bar is a popular Nob Hill hangout and watering hole, as well as a power lunch spot. All the typical Greek specialties are served here, and they serve an especially good vegetable moussaka. Beware of long waits, however, even if you have a reservation. Moderate.

EATING OUT ♨ Route 66 Malt Shop and Grill (505-242-7866), 1720 Central Ave. SW. Hours uncertain. Best to call first. Housed in a former Route 66 Horn gas station, this little retro joint serves the best blue cheese–green chile cheeseburgers in the city. House-made root beer (voted one of 10 best in United States), fantastic Frito pies, fresh-squeezed limeade, Coke floats, and what more do you want? Chocolate malts, of course. Proprietors, the "mom and pop," Eric Szeman and Diane Avila do everything in their power to make sure you have a wonderful time and a great lunch. They elevate lunch counter food to new levels. Inexpensive.

Frontier Restaurant (505-266-0550), 2400 Central Ave. SE. Located across Central from UNM, open daily 24 hours, the Frontier is an Albuquerque institution. Known for their gigantic cinnamon rolls, fresh-squeezed orange juice, green chile–smothered huevos rancheros, and soft chicken tacos, as well as their home-made tortillas, the bustling Frontier serves as social scene and study hall in addition to restaurant. Try the Frontier burger, with hickory smoke sauce, thousand-island dressing, and onion. Blindfold an Albuquerquean, and that person will be able to tell what dish came from the Frontier. However, folks have complained in recent times that prices are going up too far. Inexpensive.

Monte Carlo Steakhouse (505-836-9886), 3916 Central SW. Open Mon.–Sat. Closed Sun. Lunch and dinner. Enter through the liquor store, and then step down into the deep, dim hideaway replete with bar, red leather booths, and 1970s-era kitsch, even Elvis on velvet. Daily specials, Thurs.–Fri. evening prime rib special is a great deal, steak dinners with mounds of French fries, swell Greek salads, and the best baklava in town for dessert. The chummy, clubby atmosphere makes you want to order another bloody Mary and sit out a hot July afternoon. The place is full of characters that may or may not slightly resemble those you've seen on *The Sopranos*. This place was recently featured on the Food Network. Moderate.

Il Vicino Wood Oven Pizza and Brewery (505-266-7855), 3403 Central SE. Open daily. Lunch, dinner. The closest you can get to an Italian trattoria in New Mexico. The dozen varieties of crispy, thin-crust pizza turned out in the wood-fired ovens here are perennially excellent, and when savored with a fresh spinach salad, certainly one of the best budget dining experiences in Nob Hill. Other locations as well. Panini and baked lasagna are also worth trying. Microbrews add to the experience. It's generally busy here and a tad rowdy, in a good way. This one is the original, and it still has the buzz.

Siam Café (505-883-7334), 5500 San Mateo NE #101. Open Mon.–Sat. 11–9. Others come and go, and we give them all a try. Still we return here for authentic Thai food at unbelievable prices, including an under-$5 lunch buffet. But get there early for the full selection! Green curry, drunken noodles, pad Thai, and hot and sour chicken soup—a family favorite of ours—are all consistent and served with aplomb. Just about every dish on the menu can be ordered vegetarian. I have been to cooking school in Thailand, and the food here is indistinguishable from the real thing. Inexpensive.

Blake's Lotaburger (www.lotaburger .com). Open daily. Lunch, dinner. This New Mexico fast food chain, with 76 outlets throughout the states, serves the Lotaburger special with fries that half the town runs on. Characters in Tony Hillerman's novels pack Lotaburgers with them when they go out to solve mysteries. Once you try it, you will be hooked. Several serve grand breakfast burritos as well. As a word of caution, the Lotaburger on Rio Grande in Old Town can be slow during busy lunchtimes; however, the Lotaburger at 6210 Fourth St. in the North Valley (505-345-0402) is open 24 hours to serve you whenever the craving hits. Inexpensive.

Calico Café (505-890-9150), 6855 Fourth St. NW. Open daily. Breakfast, lunch, dinner. This is a great place to meet a friend for lunch or bring the family for Sunday brunch, with Mexican and American selections. The portions are big enough to split. Try the French toast with brandy peach sauce, green chile cheese grits, huevos rancheros—and we dare you to make it past the bakery pastry shop empty-handed. The sticky buns are irresistible. The menu also features homey dishes like chicken fried steak, pot roast, and meat loaf, all with real mashed potatoes, of course. The atmosphere is friendly, the décor is contemporary-Western, and the staff aims to please. The enclosed patio is great for a summer supper out, and you can sometimes catch live informal local acts on weekend nights. There's plenty of parking, and there's a wine shop and antiques shop housed in the same building. Moderate.

I Love Sushi Teppan Grill (505-883-3618), 6001 San Mateo NE, Ste. F4. Open Mon.–Sat. Closed Sun. Lunch, dinner. The Japanese food artists will dazzle you as they turn your dinner preparation into a performance at the grill. And you can't beat the sushi. Prices here are very reasonable, and the presentation is always impressive. Beer and wine, too.

Sushi King Sushi & Noodles (505-842-5099), 118 Central SW. Open daily. Lunch, dinner. Open late Fri.–Sat. For après-cinema sushi or noodle soup, you'll love this place with its urban feel and superb tastes. And they have beer and wine. Moderate.

🍴 **India Palace** (505-271-5009), 4410 Wyoming Blvd. NE. Open daily. Lunch, dinner. When craving a taste of India, spoil yourself with curry, chai, naan, and saag paneer at this scrumptious, all-you-can-eat lunch buffet, every day, 11:30–1:30, for under $10. You won't be interested in dinner. Many Indian restaurants in Albuquerque are good, but this one is the best, and quite respectably appointed. Moderate.

🍴 **Tomato Café Gourmet Italian Food Bar** (505-821-9300), 5901 Wyoming Blvd. NE. Open daily.

Lunch, dinner. Yes, it is a buffet, and yes, it is a bargain. But the food doesn't taste like buffet food. Unlimited handcrafted pizza; pasta with a choice of homemade sauces, like roasted tomato garlic; giant meatballs; garlicky green beans; minestrone soup; fresh salad; spinach and ricotta ravioli; and much more make this a fine place to bring teenagers with bottomless stomachs, or just yourself and your honey after a workout at the gym when you just can't stand to cook or don't have time to put a real meal on the table. You'll spend less than if you shopped and cooked yourself. Moderate.

Middle East Bakery (505-883-4537), 5017 Menaul Blvd. NE. Get your hummus and baba ghanoush fix here along with fresh-baked pita bread, stuffed grape leaves, and halvah. When a place has been in business as long as this one, you know they must be doing something right. Save room for baklava for dessert. Inexpensive.

Cheese & Coffee Café (505-883-1226), 2679 Louisiana NE. Open Mon.–Sat. Lunch. This is the quintessential lunch stop, a deli with giant sandwiches, salads almost too big to be believed, and a New York–ish bustle generated by working folk and shoppers. The salad trio is hard to pass up. Chicken salad is the best. Inexpensive.

66 Diner (505-247-1421), 1405 Central Ave. Open Mon.–Thurs. 11–11; Fri. 11 AM–midnight; Sat. 8 AM–midnight; Sun. 8 AM–10 PM. Perhaps the best chicken-fried steak in town, with real mashed potatoes and pie for dessert. Definitely worth the carbs. The Route 66 motif is in your face, and it is definitely fun here. Inexpensive.

Owl Café (505-291-4900), 800 Eubank Blvd. NE. Open Mon.– Thurs. 7–10; Fri.–Sat. 7–11. Closed Sun. The city cousin of the San Antonio original, this Owl, which is quite recognizable from the highway, has a comfy 1950s atmosphere and serves a different all-you-can-eat special nightly for under $6, like the famous burger and fries or spaghetti and meatballs. The menu lists just about every homey dish you remember from childhood. Nostalgia all the way. Inexpensive.

Mr. Powdrell's (505-345-8086), 5209 Fourth St. NW. Open daily. Lunch, dinner. Mr. Powdrell, who hailed from Louisiana, brought barbeque to Albuquerque from Texas 50 years ago, and today his family carries on the business, serving his scrumptious, tender slow-smoked meats with just-right sweet-hot-tangy sauce, fresh cole slaw, and sweet potato pie. The location is a pleasant old North Valley home. Moderate.

Sunshine Café (505-242-1499), 1134 Mountain Rd. NW. Open Mon. –Thurs. 6:30 AM–8 PM; Fri. 6:30 AM– 9 PM; Sat. 8 AM–9 PM, Sun. 8 AM– 2 PM. In a food genre that seems to be popping up everywhere in town, let's call it "gourmet comfort food," the Sunshine is serving the best and the brightest, with a swell Cobb salad; sandwiches of house-roasted meats including roast turkey with chipotle cranberry aioli; potpie du jour; and many-flavored paninis, like balsamic marinated portobello and roasted red pepper pesto on focaccia. For breakfast try their version of biscuits and gravy: green chile and white cheddar scone with house smoked ham smothered in bechamel sauce. Dinner specials to go cater to the very busy. Moderate.

Quarters BBQ (505-843-7505), 801 Yale Blvd. SE. Open Mon.–Sat. Closed Sun. Lunch, dinner. When there is an argument about where to get the best barbeque in Albuquerque, many old-timers are likely to bet on the Quarters. It's dark and rowdy, being somewhat of a university hangout, and people bring their children here generation after generation. Both the original and the uptown Quarters have some of the best wine and beer selections in town at their liquor shops. Inexpensive.

BREWPUBS AND WINE BARS Kelley's Brew Pub (505-262-2739), 3200 Central Ave. SE. On summer nights, it sometimes seems the entire town is sipping a brew on Kelley's Nob Hill patio, and it just may be. In other towns, a place like Kelley's might just be a college hangout, but this establishment rises above that designation. This historic building, the 1939 Jones Motor Co., was renovated to keep its Route 66 feel, and the food is surprisingly good, especially the green chile stew and the Albuquerque Turkey, with house-roasted turkey, green chile, and cheese. With over 20 in-house brews on tap, no wonder this place is always hopping. Inexpensive.

Zinc Wine Bar & Bistro (505-254-9462), 3009 Central Ave. NE. Open daily. Lunch and dinner 'til 11. Sun. brunch only. Wine cellar open 5 PM– 1 AM nightly, closed Sun. The chic upscale restaurant is on the main floor and mezzanine, but the real hangout is the wine bar downstairs, where you may purchase wine flights and enough interesting bar food to keep you going. You could be in Seattle, or even Paris. The new American cuisine has interesting twists, like portobello-crusted Alaskan halibut, and the veal Oscar with asparagus is quite good, as is the burger with steak frites. And the live entertainment is top-notch. Expensive.

CAFÉS ⁰₁⁰ **Flying Star** (505-344-6714; www.flyingstarcafe.com), 4026 Rio Grande Blvd. NW; (505-244-8099), 723 Silver SW. The Bernsteins started on a shoestring, and now they run a tidy chain of locally owned, wildly popular cafés all over town, each a different style. The newer ones, like the one on Eight and Silver downtown, and in Bernallilo, are stunning. Their baked goods are out of sight, particularly the towering key lime pie, carrot cake, or strawberry-rhubarb pie. The burgers and fries are excellent, and the daily lunch and dinner specials go quickly. They brag that everything is made from scratch, and you will pay a little more for that. Their motto, "You're never far from a Flying Star," becomes truer every day. Moderate.

⁰₁⁰ **Satellite Coffee** (505-254-3880), 2300 Central Ave. SE. Several locations around the city. If you long for a quieter place to check your e-mail, sip a latte, study, or read the paper, ease on into one of these Flying Star siblings, where you can also grab just a little bite to eat and a comfy easy chair. Wi-Fi hot spot, for sure. Moderate.

Java Joe's (505-765-1514), 906 Park SW. If your tastes hanker to a bygone era—shall we say the 1960s?—and

DOWNTOWN FLYING STAR CAFÉ.

TEN FAVORITE MEXICAN RESTAURANTS

El Patio (505-268-4245), 142 Harvard Dr. SE. Open daily. Lunch, dinner. This beloved university area restaurant has been serving the same reliably fluffy light sopaipillas and savory green chile chicken enchiladas for over 30 years. How pleasant to sip an ice tea on the shady, well-trodden patio on a hot summer day and taste the flavors of New Mexico. In fall, when the chile crop comes in, the green is over-the-top with heat. No matter how many others come and go, this place remains a top favorite. Inexpensive.

Barelas Coffee House (505-843-7577), 1502 Fourth St. SW. Open daily. Breakfast, lunch. If they ever made a movie about Albuquerque, they'd have to use this downtown neighborhood standby as a location. Politicos and TV celebrities come here to mingle with the working folk. You never know whom you'll run into. It's best known for its thick, burning red chile and delectable slow-baked carne adovada, but the huevos rancheros are not to be missed. For serious chile lovers and those who swear they know their chile. Try to come at off hours, or be prepared to wait in line. Then you'll have your choice of seating, including the pocket-sized enclosed patio. It's a short walk to the National Hispanic Cultural Center from here. Inexpensive.

Mac's La Sierra Restaurant (505-836-1212), 6217 Central Ave. NW. Open daily. Breakfast, lunch, dinner. If you can find a better deal than Mac's red enchiladas with steak fingers for $3.95, by all means go for it. Admittedly, it's a bit shabby in here. Battered Naugahyde booths, dim lighting, neighbors who've been eating here for an eternity, waitresses always in a hurry hoisting trays of nothing fancy but plain old reliable tasty Mexican food, and you've got yourself an authentic experience on the far end of Old Route 66. By the time you finish eating here, you'll feel like one of the gang. Inexpensive.

Garcia's Kitchen (505-842-0273), 1736 Central SW. Don't start your East Coast friends out on the red chile here. Only experienced chile eaters need apply to Andy Garcia's tables. It takes a true chile addict to ooh and ahh over the roasty green chile stew served with homemade fresh tortilla, and you can easily become addicted to the brisket tacos and the carnitas breakfast. You've just gotta have it! Of the many Garcias around town, the one on Central near Old Town, with its carnival décor, is probably the best. But we each have our favorite.

Casa Grande (505-243-2519), 2424 Central SW. Open daily. Breakfast, lunch, dinner. Many say the Casa serves the best red chile in town, and it's a point that's hard to argue. Clearly, it is brewed from red chile pods, not powder, and it is dynamite with a kick. The Red Special, served weekdays, of red chile enchiladas, beans, and rice, may be the best under-$5 lunch around. Gringo food is served here, too, on daily specials, and mariachis serenade Sunday mornings after church.

Casa de Benevidez (505-897-7493), 8032 N. Fourth St. NW. With its exquisite green patio, waterfall, fountains, and full bar, Casa B's is a longtime favorite of North Valley residents. HOME OF THE SOPAIPILLA BURGER, reads the marquee, but that doesn't really describe the experience. The side café, geared to takeout, is a popular morning hangout and serves up a contender for the best breakfast burrito, with chorizo. The fajitas are among the best, too. It's a bit pricey for Mexican food, but the portions are immense. A nice place to take the folks for dinner or a special occasion. Moderate–Expensive.

Gardunos of Mexico (505-898-2772), 8806 N. Fourth St. NW. Open daily. Lunch and dinner. All half-dozen Gardunos locations are lovely, with an upscale mood and a happy cantina feeling, but the one on N. Fourth St. in the North Valley remains a favorite. Happy hour is Mon.–Fri. 3–6, with complimentary appetizers 4–6. Expect fine service, but the taste and quality of the food sometimes depends on who is cooking that night. You can make a meal of the *favoritos* platter, sort of a Mexican pupu platter of miniature flautas, tacos, and other tasty appetizers. But you can compose your own combination plate, depending on how hungry you are. The green chile caldillo is always good, and the sizzling fajitas platter is reliable. Sun. brunch, which begins at 11 and goes all day, is a feast that will leave you feeling stuffed and happy. Moderate.

Duran's Pharmacy (505-247-4141), 1815 Central Ave. NW. Open Mon.–Sat. 10–5. Weave your way through the cosmetics and household goods to the back, where you will find a line waiting for a seat at the legendary lunch counter or on the patio, or for one of the half-dozen tables, to taste the tortilla soup and what is likely the most delicious fresh tortilla, hot off the grill and doused in butter. Portions are immense, so unless you are famished, be prepared to share. Inexpensive.

Charlie's Front Door and Back Door (595-294-3130), 8224 Menaul NE. Serving a winning margarita along with old-fashioned traditional Mexican cooking that includes side dishes rarely found outside Grandma's kitchen, this is a favorite haunt of Albuquerque old-timers, who, believing they have found the best, have no need to experiment with new restaurants. The cozy step-down bar with its big black booths feels like the 1970s for sure. Charlie's carnitas were recently voted Albuquerque's best. And they are tender and tasty when served with red chile blue corn enchiladas. Moderate.

Casa de Ruiz Church Street Café (505-247-8522), 2111 Church St., Old Town. Open Sun.–Wed. 8–4; Thurs.– Sat. 8–8. Claiming to be located in the oldest building in Old Town, dating to the 1700s, the Church Street Café does for sure serve delicious Mexican food prepared from family recipes. In addition, there are sandwiches, salads, wine, and beer.

you love good coffee and great scones, by all means come on down to this Downtown hangout, where live folk and jazz transpire over much of the weekend. Scruffiness encouraged, tattoos, while not required, are omnipresent, and the bagels and lox are just fine, thanks. Homemade soup and great egg salad are available daily. Inexpensive.

GROCERIES **Moses Kountry** (505-898-9763), 7115 Fourth St. NW. There is good reason why Mrs. Bertha Moses, well into her 80s, has a rose petal complexion. She has been running her health food store for a half-century and using her products to become beautiful inside and out. The selection of natural cosmetics and beauty products is beyond compare, and the staff is most knowledgeable and helpful. Bulk groceries and organic frozen foods fill out the selection.

La Montanita Co-op (505-242-8800), 2400 Rio Grande Blvd. NW. Nob Hill location, too. Pay $15 a year to join, and you support a member-run food co-op that is a small supermarket featuring organic and

sustainably produced edibles. The take-out deli is a bit strange, but if you are a vegan or a vegetarian, you'll think you can't live without this place. Your membership fee entitles you to a rebate at the end of the year and certain specials, too. Shop here and feel good about where you're spending your money.

Trader Joe's (505-796-0311), 8928 Holly Ave. NE (off Paseo del Pueblo Norte). Albuquerque really became a city the day Trader Joe's opened its doors. The snacks and nuts, prepared salads, and take-out meals; the bargain wines; and the variety of frozen foods make this the favorite place to have fun while spending the weekly grocery budget. Every reason to look good in the kitchen is here, and a stop here is essential for party planning.

Whole Foods (505-856-0474), 5815 Wyoming Blvd. NE. The concept of grocery shopping as entertainment has come to Albuquerque with a glorious Whole Foods. Expensive, for sure, but the fish is delivered daily and the produce is the most beautiful around. The cheese and wine sections, as well as the bakery, make this a worthwhile stop. Free beer and wine tastings Fri.–Sat. 4–6.

TaLin Market World Food Fare (505-268-5206), 230 Louisiana Blvd. SE. The most exotic grocery shopping experience in town, with aisles dedicated to India, Thailand, China, and the Caribbean. If you can't find the ingredient you're looking for, it probably doesn't exist. The produce and fresh fish sections are also geared to cooks of Asian cuisine. The store offers bargain prices, and there's a café and cooking lessons. What more could a foodie want?

CHOCOLATE, COFFEE, AND TEA

Theobroma Chocolatier (505-247-0848), 319 Central NW. Come here when you want the good stuff, the very best quality chocolate, in interesting thematic shapes, like footballs and chocolate heart-shaped boxes, or tastes, like chocolate covered ginger. The dark chocolate is sinfully luscious and creamy and irresistible. As if that weren't enough, Theobroma also serves Taos Cow ice cream that is well worth driving around town for.

Candy Lady (505-243-6239), 524 Romero St. NW. Notorious for her "back room" selection of adult, erotic, anatomic chocolates, the Candy Lady excels at imported candies, chocolate-dipped strawberries and apricots, truffles, turtles, and all manner of confections, plus sugar-free varieties. Plus, she has 21 varieties of fudge in her Old Town shop.

Buffett's Candies (505-265-7731), 7001 Lomas Blvd. NE. You know you've arrived when you see the big candy cane out front. Buffett's chocolates, especially those with piñon nuts, have been making New Mexicans smile for a long, long time.

New Mexico Tea Company (505-962-2137), 1131 Mountain Rd. NW. This tiny shop is packed with several dozen elegantly arrayed varieties of fine imported teas, as well as New Mexico–grown organic herbals and medicinals. Shopping here is a most pleasant experience, where you can you can deepen your tea experience and knowledge.

Whiting Coffee Co. (505-344-9144), 3700 Osuna Rd. NE. It's worth a drive to this strip mall for the finest fresh-roasted coffee beans, six original blends, a fine selection of loose teas, brewing devices, imported spices, chocolates, and cookies.

PET GOURMET AND BOUTIQUE

Three Dog Bakery (505-294-2300), 9821 Montgomery NE. Organic dog biscuits, fancy and fanciful doggie pastries and birthday cakes, doggie wear, and Wednesday night "Yappy Hour" make this a popular stop for pets and their human companions.

Bow Wow Blues (505-341-4484), 3845 Rio Grande Blvd. NW. Doggie specialties in nutrition and fashion, as well as pet home décor, ceramics, and art, are for sale here. Small-dog lovers and owners will be especially delighted with the varieties of doggie bling.

Clark's Pet Emporium (505-268-5977), 4914 Lomas Blvd. NE. This fine local pet shop has been catering to its clientele with the best in bird, fish, dog, and cat supplies for many years. They stock everything you could possibly need, provide personal attention, and all in a store that is definitely not a big box.

DOGGIE DAYCARE Canine Country Club and Feline Inn (505-898-0725), 7327 Fourth St. NW. Both you and your beloved pet will be treated well here, whether your pup is in for grooming, boarding, or "doggie day care."

BAKERIES Le Chantilly Bakery & Café (505-293-7057), 8216 Menaul NE. Croissants, brioche, cheese sticks, and napoleons are the order of the day here at this classic French bakery.

Great Harvest Bread Co. (505-293-8277), 11200 Montgomery NE. Folks drive from all over town to stock up on the hearty, whole grain breads that Great Harvest turns out in delectable varieties. They will also sell you packages of their Montana stone ground red wheat for your own baking.

Golden Crown Panaderia (505-243-2424), 1103 Mountain Rd. NW. Home of the green chile cheese bread, this longtime neighborhood favorite can supply your dinner party with a bread sculpture of a turtle or armadillo, or a turkey for your Thanksgiving. Empanadas, biscochitos, New Mexican wedding cookies, and other local favorite sweets fill the display cases. And you can lunch on their beloved "bakery-style" pizza, sandwiches, and latte at the in-house café. Featured in *Gourmet* magazine.

TLC Bakery (505-344-0449), 3700 Osuna Rd. NE. Pick up your challah, chile cheese rolls, rye bread, sweet rolls, and whatever else you might crave at this no-frills, walk-right-in, old-fashioned bakery. Something about it makes the experience of a "loaf of bread" extraordinary.

WINE SHOPS Jubilation Wine & Spirits (505-255-4404), 3512 Lomas Blvd. NE. This is the best wine shop in town, with an in-depth selection

that will tempt you to try a new one. Emphasis is on service, and it is fun to shop here. Wine tastings bring in knowledgeable instructors.

Quarters Discount Liquors (505-247-0579), 801 Yale Blvd. SE. This place has a wide array of imported beers in stock. Other locations, too.

Kelly's Liquors (505-296-7815), 2226 Wyoming Blvd. NE. A huge selection of wines, beers, and liquors at discount prices makes this a good stop before a dinner party. Other locations in the North Valley and Rio Rancho, too.

✳ Entertainment

Journal Pavilion (505-246-8742; www.journalpavilion.com), Bobby Foster Rd. I-25 to Rio Bravo exit or S. University Blvd. The big name acts show up here every summer. The venue is enormous. Take your time leaving, as traffic tends to pile up.

Popejoy Hall (505-925-5858; www .unmtickets.com). University of New Mexico's Popejoy Hall, with 2,000 seats, is the city's premier stage venue for the New Mexico Symphony and big-stage road show musicals. The university offers a regular schedule of theater events. Several other smaller theater spaces are in this building as well, including Keller Hall for classical music performances, Rodey Theater for smaller theater pieces, and the Experimental Theater.

South Broadway Cultural Center (505-281-4492), 1025 Broadway SE. A library, exhibition space, and beautiful small theater space, the cultural center is a stage for live theater and touring world music acts.

Outpost Performance Space (505-268-0044), 210 Yale Blvd. SE. This simple intimate space is the place to come and hear a variety of live music, including jazz, folk, world music, local acts, and touring companies, as well as spoken word.

Tricklock Theater Company (505-254-8393), 1705 Mesa Vista NE. Now the resident theater company of the University of New Mexico, Tricklock is a solid and intelligent group of young theater people who perform exciting, new, and experimental work and tour internationally.

The Cell (505-766-9412; www.fusion abq.org), 700 First St. NW. The FUSION Theatre Company is a top-notch provocative new theater that competes well with any other form of entertainment out there. Expect that chances will be taken and boundaries will be stretched.

KiMo Theater (505-768-3522), 423 Central Ave. NW. Originally built in 1927 as a movie palace in the flamboyant Pueblo Deco style, which used Indian ornamentation on art deco, the restored landmark KiMo is worth a visit on its own or to see a performance. Go upstairs to see the Van Hassler murals.

Vortex Theater (505-247-8600), 2004½ Central SE. For decades, the Vortex has given a home to the offbeat, the avant-garde, the kind of theater designed to provoke and make you think.

CLASSIC PUEBLO DECO KIMO THEATER DOWNTOWN IS HOME TO SYMPHONY CONCERTS.

Albuquerque Little Theater (505-242-4750), 224 San Pasqual Ave. SW. One of the oldest ongoing community theaters in the country, the Little Theater continues to draw an audience of dedicated and loyal followers, typically to a playbill of conventional, established theater favorites, usually very well done. There's a strong children's theater program here as well.

Adobe Theater (505-898-9222), 9813 Fourth St. NW. A dedicated band of theater lovers produce consistently high-quality performances in this tiny out-of-the way stage.

✳ Selective Shopping

Albuquerque Flea Market (505-222-9766), 300 San Pedro SE, Expo New Mexico. With acres upon acres of booths to survey, you can find everything and anything from bargains on CDs, blankets, pots and pans, and everything you didn't know you needed, from sets of long-handled iced-tea spoons to handmade soaps to calico cat cookie jars. You're bound to go home with a sack full of something you just love, feeling very proud of yourself for all the money you saved.

The Man's Hat Shop (505-247-9605), 511 Central Ave. NW. Over a half-century in business, with well-earned high marks in service and quality, this Downtown landmark has a great selection of hats from Panama to Stetson for the man in your life.

PeaceCraft (505-255-5229), 3215 Central NE. You can do good by spending money in Nob Hill, if you shop at PeaceCraft, a store that sells handmade clothing, household utensils, Fair Trade coffee and nuts, and all manner of colorful imported goods that profit the makers directly.

Dan's Boots & Saddles (505-345-2220), 6903 Fourth St. NW. Even the real cowboys shop here, but if all you want to do is find the right pair of jeans, Western shirt, boots, or hat, by all means get yourself to this store that's been selling feed and saddles since 1938. Hint: they have fantastic sales, if you hit it right!

The Palms Trading Co. (1-800-748-1656), 1504 Lomas Blvd. NW. Stop in here, near Old Town, for deals on handmade Indian jewelry, antique Indian pots, and all other manner of Native American wares. You may not find the absolute top-of-the-line, but you are bound to find something you like. This is a good place to shop for gifts.

Mariposa Gallery (505-268-6828), 3500 Central Ave. SE. The finest, most adventurous, and well made in crafts, many by local artisans, grace the walls and shelves of this long-established gallery, including glass, jewelry, sculpture, pottery, and ceramics, in all price ranges. If you are looking for an unusual gift for yourself or someone else, have a look here.

Martha's Body Bueno/Seventh Goddess (505-265-1122), 3901 Central Ave. NE. A Nob Hill pioneer, in 1975 Martha Doester created her own line of environmentally conscious, biodegradable bath and body products of pure ingredients. The shop recently changed hands, but the offerings are still high quality, with a well-selected assortment of other brands. Lacy underthings, jewelry, and cards round out the stock and make a visit here fun—whether you come solo or with a close friend. Even though she sold the store to a new owner, Martha's products are still available.

SHOPPING CENTERS Abq Uptown,
Louisiana and Indian School NE.
Albuquerque's long-awaited 25,000-
square-foot shopping center has
quickly become the favorite place to
shop. It is designed to keep you walking outdoors between upscale retail-
ers Coldwater Creek, Anthropologie,
Chico's, Pottery Barn, Williams-
Sonoma, the Apple Store, and so
many other desirable national chains.
Here you have every opportunity to
be fashionable and really spend some
money. For a break, try the Elephant
Bar, which is a fine and reasonable
restaurant in addition to being a bar.

Nob Hill Shopping Center, corner
of Carlisle and Central SE. Built in
1937, this vintage shopping center
was the first "mall" constructed west
of the Mississippi. Today the art deco
center houses an engaging variety of
galleries, chic home furnishings
stores, a shoe store, a paper store,
jewelry shops, a trendy salon, La
Montanita Food Co-op, a bar, and a
restaurant. There's free parking one
block south of the center.

**VINTAGE AND RECYCLED Buffalo
Exchange New and Recycled
Fashion** (505-262-0098), 3005
Central Ave. NE. If you are stylish,
trendy, or want to be, you can trade in
wardrobe items you are tired of and
cash in on the huge supply of both
men's and women's fashions and
accessories that fill the racks at Buffalo Exchange. Both styles and sizes
appear geared to the university set.

My Best Friend's Closet (505-298-
4099), 7915 Menaul Blvd. NE. An
in-depth assortment of seasonally
well-chosen, gently worn, generally
reasonably priced apparel is available
here, sold on consignment. From

sportswear and sweaters to evening-
wear, bargains abound.

**INDEPENDENT AND USED BOOK-
STORES Page One** (505-294-2026),
11018 Montgomery Blvd. NE. Albuquerque's oldest independent bookstore, now with café and Wi-Fi, can
be a bit confusing to navigate, as used
and new books are mixed on the
shelves together. The store offers a
good selection of local newspapers
from all over and a huge magazine
assortment as well. Toys, best-sellers,
cards, computer aids, and just about
everything else the savvy reader could
want are all here. For fun, take a look
at Page One Too (505-294-5623), the
sibling used and antiquarian bookstore, across the street.

Bookworks (505-344-8139), 4022
Rio Grande Blvd. NW. Specializing in
children's books, service, and the latest in current events books, plus a
schedule of book signings to fill anyone's calendar, Bookworks has managed to survive and thrive in a city
that has lost too many independent
bookstores to count. The North Valley
loves to browse here, then meet friends
in the adjacent Flying Star Café.

Title Wave Books (505-294-9495),
1408 Eubank Blvd. NE. Somehow
Title Wave keeps rolling along with an
intelligent selection of used books
that is both wide and deep. This is
that rare bookstore where you will
find just what you are looking for as
well as the next big thing that you had
no idea you were interested in, until
you spotted it here.

Newsland Bookstore (505-242-
0694), 2112 Central Ave. SE. Whether
you're in search of the Santa Fe
papers or the *New York Times,* a 'zine,
or *Popular Mechanics,* chances are

CASAS GRANDE POTTERY MAY BE FOUND IN OLD TOWN GALLERIES.

good that among the hundreds of publications, you'll find what you're after here.

Bookstop (505-268-8898), 118 Tulane SE. With an in-depth selection of browsable used, fine, and rare books, the venerable Bookstop, despite its recent relocation, retains an intellectual book-lover's air.

✳ Special Events

Check 311 or the local paper for information on the monthly Friday evening **Artscrawl** (505-244-0362; www.artscrawlabq.org), where various gallery districts open their doors.

January: **Revolutions International Theater Festival** (505-246-2261), National Hispanic Cultural Center, 1701 Fourth St. SW.

March: **Rio Grande Arts and Crafts Festival—Spring Show,** Expo New Mexico. **National Fiery Foods and BBQ Show** (www.fieryfoods.com), Sandia Resort and Casino, I-25 and Tramway Blvd.

April: **Gathering of Nations Powwow** (505-836-2810), the Pit, University of New Mexico. **Albuquerque Isotopes** baseball games (505-924-2255; ww.albuquerquebaseball.com), Isotopes Park, Apr.–Sept.

May: **Cinco de Mayo** Concert Celebration (505-246-2261), National Hispanic Cultural Center, 1701 Fourth St. SW.

June: **Festival Flamenco Internacional de Albuquerque** (505-277-1855; www.nationalinstituteof flamenco.org). **NM Arts and Crafts Fair,** June 16– July 28. **Sizzlin'Summerfest** offers musical themes each Saturday night in Civic Plaza Downtown.

July: **Mariachi Spectacular Showcase** (505-255-1501), call for location.

BUNNIES TAKE THE PRIZE AT THE STATE FAIR JUNIOR LIVESTOCK AUCTION.

Duke City Shootout (505-768-3270), various venues. Short scripts are shot and screened around Albuquerque July 25–Aug. 2.

September: **New Mexico Wine Festival** (505-867-3311), 370 Camino del Pueblo, Bernalillo, Labor Day Weekend. **New Mexico State Fair** (505-265-1791), Expo New Mexico, held for 21 days each September. Livestock, home arts, Indian and Hispanic arts, food, midway with rides. The fair celebrates all things New Mexican.

October: **Albuquerque International Balloon Fiesta** (1-888-422-7277; www.balloonfiesta.com), Balloon Fiesta Park, I-25 and Alameda NE. Held the first two weeks of October, this is the world's largest hot-air balloon gathering, with as many as 800 balloons from all over the world, including special shapes, lifting off each weekend morning in mass ascensions. Balloon glows, special shapes rodeo, fireworks, gigantic midway.

November: **Dia de los Muertos** (505-246-2261), National Hispanic Cultural Center, 1701 Fourth St. SW. **Weems Gallery Artfest** (505-293-6133), Expo New Mexico, 300 San Pedro NE.

December: **River of Lights** (505-764-6200), Rio Grande Botanical Garden, Nov. 24–Dec. 29.

North Central New Mexico: Georgia O'Keeffe Country

TAOS AND THE ENCHANTED
CIRCLE: TAOS, QUESTA, RED RIVER,
ANGEL FIRE, TAOS SKI VALLEY,
ARROYO SECO

HIGH ROAD COUNTRY: CHIMAYO,
TRUCHAS, CORDOVA, PEÑASCO,
DIXON

RIO CHAMA COUNTRY: ABIQUIU,
ESPAÑOLA, TIERRA AMARILLA,
LOS OJOS

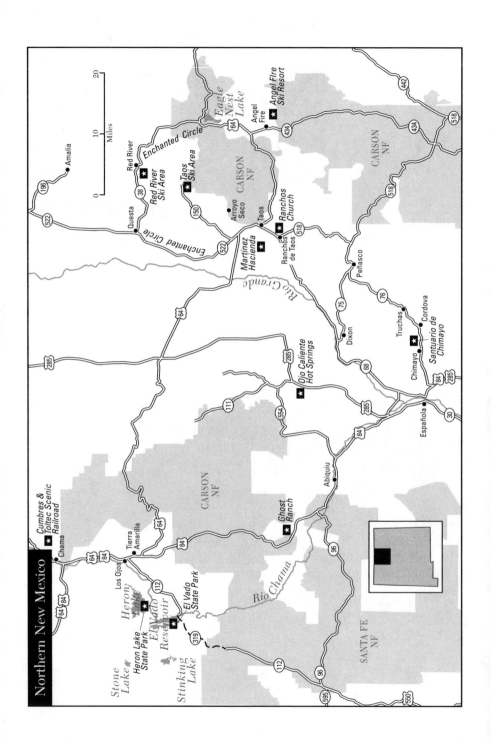

Northern New Mexico

Stone Lake

Heron Lake
Heron Lake State Park

El Vado
Reschoir

Stinking Lake

El Vado State Park

Rio Chama

Los Ojos

Tierra Amarilla

Chama

Cumbres & Toltec Scenic Railroad

CARSON NF

Ghost Ranch

Abiquiu

Española

SANTA FE NF

Ojo Caliente Hot Springs

Dixon

Chimayo

Santuario de Chimayo

Cordova

Truchas

Peñasco

Ranchos de Taos

Ranchos Church

Martinez Hacienda

Rio Grande

Taos

Arroyo Seco

Taos Ski Area

Enchanted Circle

Questa

Red River Ski Area

Red River

Amalia

Angel Fire

Angel Fire Ski Resort

Eagle Nest Lake

CARSON NF

CARSON NF

Miles
0   10   20

INTRODUCTION

There is something about northern New Mexico that speaks to our deepest, most heartfelt mythical image of the state. Perhaps it is the adobe houses shaded by grandmother cottonwoods, the scent of piñon smoke, or the figures of saints hand-painted on the altars of High Road mission churches. Then there is the rush of water through an ancient *acequia,* the sight of snow on Taos Mountain, the curve of the buttress on the Ranchos Church, the rhythms of drum and rattle at an Indian dance, the wind-sculpted red rocks of Abiquiu . . .

Whatever it is, northern New Mexico is where our love for this place finds its home at last. We catch our breath around every bend in the road as we wind through the Rio Grande canyon on the way up to Taos or follow the Rio Chama northward. We never get tired of it, and we are always glad to see it again. Perhaps we learned this love by looking at the paintings of the Cinco Pintores and the Taos Moderns, those who were captivated by the northern New Mexico light and spent their lives seeking it among the people who lived in the old way.

Here is where the four seasons unfurl themselves most deliciously, from the stillness of a snow-covered landscape overlooking the Mora Valley, to the green bursting forth from Velarde apple orchards, to the busy summer season in Santa Fe, with rainbows stretching across the sky, to, as writer John Nichols titled one of his books, "the last beautiful days of autumn" in Taos.

The changing seasons renew the enduring traditions, as each season brings its own: clearing the *acequias* in spring; planting, harvesting, and selling at the farmers' markets; fly-fishing for trout; chopping wood for winter; and once again retreating to the warmth of the fire, and the simple pleasure of a pot of beans and chile on the stove.

Northern New Mexico reminds us that this is, for many here, still a sustainable way of life, one in harmony with the land, where one eats what one grows and warms oneself by the direct labor of one's own hands. The crafts of weaving and carving are more than decorative, they are life essentials. Take away the asphalt and the television satellite dishes, and the High Road, along with many mountain villages of New Mexico, has changed very little in the past three or four centuries.

This section of the state offers much variety: retreat at artist Georgia O'Keeffe's Ghost Ranch, visit traditional weavers at Chimayo or Los Ojos, enjoy artists' studio tours during the fall at Dixon and Abiquiu, attend the Santa Fe Opera, and immerse yourself in all the cultural events of that extraordinary city.

To facilitate your travel and allow you to focus on the delights of each area, think of it in three geographic sections: Taos and the Enchanted Circle Country of Questa, Red River, and Angel Fire; High Road Country of Chimayo, Truchas, Cordova, Peñasco, and Dixon; and the Rio Chama Country of Española, Abiquiu, Tierra Amarilla, Los Ojos and Chama, Ojo Caliente, and El Rito. US 84/285 parallels the course of the Rio Chama north to the Colorado border.

TAOS AND THE ENCHANTED CIRCLE: TAOS, QUESTA, RED RIVER, ANGEL FIRE, TAOS SKI VALLEY, ARROYO SECO

Warning: the incomparable beauty and magic of the Taos area may change your life. Taos Mountain is famous for doing that—as well as bringing out the dreams and creativity you have been yearning to express. Add a wealth of art, history, Native American and Hispanic culture, fine dining, and outdoor activities of hiking, skiing, rafting, and fishing for the sum of a destination with four-season appeal. You are guaranteed to love this region whenever you visit—and may it be soon.

GUIDANCE Angel Fire Visitor Center (575-377-6555), Centro Plaza on NM 34 (Mountain View Blvd.), Angel Fire.

Red River Visitor Center (1-877-754-1708; www.redrivernewmex.com), Red River Convention Center.

Village of Taos Ski Valley Chamber of Commerce (505-776-1413; www.taos skivalley.com).

Taos County Chamber of Commerce (575-758-3873; www.taoschamber.com), 1139 Paseo del Pueblo Sur, Taos.

MEDICAL EMERGENCY St. Vincent Regional Medical Center (505-983-3361), 455 St. Michael's Dr., Santa Fe.

Los Alamos Medical Center (505-662-4201), 3917 West Rd., Los Alamos.

Holy Cross Hospital (505-758-8883), 1397 Weimer Rd., Taos.

Española Hospital (505-753-7111), 1010 Spruce St., Española.

GETTING THERE From Santa Fe, go north on NM 68. It's a slow 67 miles to Taos. From Taos, take NM 522 north, about 25 minutes, to Questa and the Enchanted Circle. Also from Taos, take NM 150 to Taos Ski Valley, a half-hour drive.

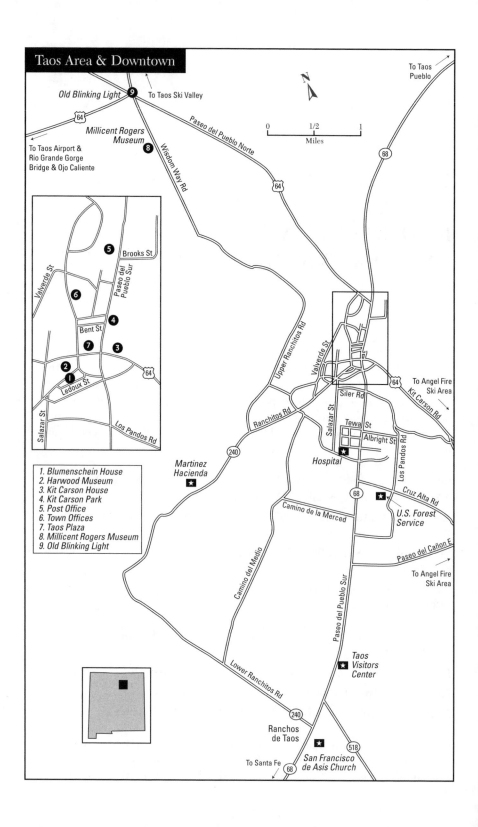

Taos Area & Downtown

Old Blinking Light ⑨ → To Taos Ski Valley

To Taos Pueblo

⑥④ 64

Millicent Rogers Museum ⑧

To Taos Airport &
Rio Grande Gorge
Bridge & Ojo Caliente

Paseo del Pueblo Norte

Wisdom Way Rd

N

0   1/2   1
Miles

68

64

⑤ Brooks St

Valverde St

Paseo del Pueblo Sur

⑥

④

Bent St

⑦ ③

② ①

Ledoux St

Salazar St

Los Pandos Rd

64

Upper Ranchitos Rd

Valverde St

Siler Rd

64

To Angel Fire
Ski Area

Kit Carson Rd

Salazar St

Tewa St

Albright St

★

Hospital

Los Pandos Rd

Cruz Alta Rd

Ranchitos Rd

240

Martinez Hacienda
★

68

★

U.S. Forest Service

Camino de la Merced

Paseo del Cañon E

To Angel Fire
Ski Area

1. Blumenschein House
2. Harwood Museum
3. Kit Carson House
4. Kit Carson Park
5. Post Office
6. Town Offices
7. Taos Plaza
8. Millicent Rogers Museum
9. Old Blinking Light

Camino del Medio

Paseo del Pueblo Sur

Taos Visitors Center ★

Lower Ranchitos Rd

240

Ranchos de Taos ★

518

To Santa Fe
68

San Francisco de Asis Church

❋ To See

TOWNS **Taos.** The legendary town of artists and the home of multi-storied ancient 800-year-old Taos Pueblo has a magnetism and mystique like nowhere else. Established in 1615 as a northern outpost of New Spain, it was the site of the annual autumn rendezvous and trade fair of mountain men who hunted and trapped. The town itself is a historical composite of three parts: Ranchos de Taos on the south, Don Fernando de Taos in the central part of town radiating out from the Plaza, and Taos Pueblo. Eventually, these three sections grew together to form a unit we think of today as Greater Taos. In addition to its arts, Taos is also known as the home and habitat of legendary, larger-than-life characters like Kit Carson, Padre Martinez, Mabel Dodge Lujan, and D. H. and Frieda Lawrence.

Questa. The drive north of Taos to Questa along NM 522 passes several interesting potential explorations: the sweeping valley of Arroyo Hondo; the D. H. Lawrence Ranch, now owned by University of New Mexico; and Lama Mountain, where the Lama Foundation—an ecumenical retreat center founded in the 1960s that offers workshops on ecology, personal growth, and spirituality—still survives. The Lawrence Ranch, originally known as the Kiowa Ranch, was given to Frieda Lawrence by Mabel Dodge Luann in exchange for the original manuscript of D. H. Lawrence's *Sons and Lovers*. Questa was for many years

PRAYER FLAGS WAVE OVER THE RIO GRANDE GORGE ATOP LAMA MOUNTAIN.

primarily a mining community where molybdenum, an agent used for hardening steel, reigned, but it is now home to a combination of artists, organic growers, escapees from urban life, and traditional Hispanic families. It was founded in 1829.

Red River. A family resort town created for fun, with a ski area, plenty of lodging, cafés, and shopping, and what many New Mexicans believe is a "Texas" flavor. At 8,750 feet, it is the highest town in the state. Founded in 1892 by homesteaders; prospectors followed suit and found their way to the settlement. The Red River takes on its color after rains due to the high mineral content.

Angel Fire. A town of many second-home condominiums and rentals with a resort at the center, yet also with a solid community of year-round citizens. It is a good place to stay and play year-round. It was the fall meeting grounds of the Utes and took its name from the Indian "breath of spirits," later Christianized by Franciscan friars to "breath of angels."

Taos Ski Valley. New Mexico's newest town, located in the old mining area of Twinings, it is the state's premier ski resort. Summer activities are scheduled along with winter fun, which, as of March 2008, includes snowboarding.

Arroyo Seco. This pretty little village on the road to Taos Ski Valley has cafés, shops, and a historic church.

MUSEUMS **Millicent Rogers Museum** (575-758-2462; www.millicentrogers .org), 1504 Millicent Rogers Rd., Taos. Four miles north of Taos off NM 522. Turn left on Millicent Rogers Road and follow museum signs. Open Tues.–Sun. Nov.–Mar. 10–5. Closed Mon., Easter, Thanksgiving, Christmas, New Year's. This outstanding private museum was founded in 1953 by relatives of Millicent Rogers, a model, heiress, and socialite who moved to Taos in 1947. Her love of regional architecture and Indian and Spanish colonial art, including Penitente Brotherhood artifacts, inspired an extensive collection of jewelry, textiles, basketry, pottery, and paintings. Here find one of the most important collections of black pottery by San Ildefonso artist Maria Martinez and her family. A trip here makes a great immersion into the art of the region. $7 adults, $6 seniors and students. Group rates available. Fantastic (and pricey) gift shop.

Harwood Museum of Art (575-758-9826), 238 Ledoux St., Taos. Open Tues.– Sat. 10–5, Sun. noon–5. Closed Mon. and holidays. Here is a treasury of Taos art, housed in an exemplary 19th-century Spanish-Pueblo adobe structure. Founded in 1923, the Harwood contains the work of the artists who made Taos famous: Victor Higgins, Ernest Blumenschein, Andrew Dasburg, and Patrocinio Barela, as well as that of contemporary artists like Larry Bell, and Fritz Scholder, Anita Rodriguez and Melissa Zink. Of special note is the Agnes Martin Gallery, where seven canvasses of the nation's most acclaimed minimalist and Taos resident, Martin, hang for contemplation in a light-filled chamber. $6 adults.

Kit Carson Home and Museum (575-758-4613), 113 E. Kit Carson Rd., Taos. Open daily 9–6. Closed Thanksgiving, Christmas, New Year's, and Easter. Famed mountain man and Indian scout Kit Carson and his wife, Josepha, lived in this 12-room adobe for a quarter-century. It is authentically furnished, and guides in period costume give tours. Next door is the Carson House Shop, an excellent showcase of Indian and folk art, jewelry, Christmas ornaments, and the work of Taos artist Valerie Graves. $5 adults, $4 seniors, $3 teens, $2 children, under 6 free, $12 families.

Governor Bent House (575-758-2376), 177-A Bent St., Taos. Open daily 10–5. Prominent citizen Charles Bent was appointed first U.S. governor of the New Mexico territory. He was killed on this spot during a local revolt in 1847. $2 adults, $1 8–15, under 8 free.

Ernest L. Blumenschein Home (575-758-0505), 222 Ledoux St., Taos. Open summer 9–5 daily; call for winter hours. Taos Society of Artists founders Ernest and Mary Greene Blumenschein lived and worked in this 1797 Spanish colonial adobe. Recently restored, the house appears much as it did in their day, with the original colors and artwork brought back to life. $6 adults, $3 under 16, $15 families.

Taos Art Museum & Fechin House (575-758-2690), 227 Paseo del Pueblo Norte. Open summer Wed.–Sun. 10–5; winter Wed.–Sun. 10–4. A Russian-style adobe home designed by artist Nicolai Fechin features his woodwork, paintings, collection of Asian and Russian art, plus many fine works by Taos school painters. $6 adults, $3 ages 6–16, free under 6; local residents free on Sun.

FOLK LIFE FESTIVAL AT THE MILLICENT ROGERS MUSEUM.

HISTORIC LANDMARKS, PLACES, AND SITES Kit Carson Cemetery (no phone), Kit Carson Park. History makes strange bedfellows. That is why you will find, by strolling through this historic cemetery in the center of town, the graves of characters such as Mabel Dodge Lujan, Padre Martinez, and Kit Carson all within a stone's throw of each other.

Martinez Hacienda (575-758-1000), Ranchitos Rd., Taos. Two miles south of plaza on NM 240 or 4 miles west of Ranchos de Taos on NM 240. Open daily 9–5 summer; call for winter hours. If you want to see what a real 19th-century hacienda looks like, come here and experience the fortresslike restored building designed to keep out Comanche and Apache raiders. Exhibits explain trade on the Camino Real and Spanish colonial culture of New Mexico. It is furnished authentically, and you are likely to come upon demonstrations of quilting, colcha embroidery, weaving, and other traditional crafts. $6 adults, $3 6–16, $15 families.

Rio Grande Gorge Bridge (no phone), at intersection of NM 68 and NM 150 (Taos Ski Valley Rd.), go left 17 miles on US 64. Completed in 1965, at 650 feet above the Rio Grande, this bridge is the nation's second-highest span: 2,000 feet from rim to rim across the gorge. The winding Rio Grande below and view of the Taos Plateau is a look into the deep heart of New Mexico. From this height, river rafters on the Taos Box look like tiny specs. Hang on to your hat! The wind always blows hard up here. Free.

Vietnam Veterans Memorial State Park (575-377-6900), 24 miles east of Taos on US 64, Angel Fire. Visitor center open daily 9–5. Chapel open daily, 24 hours. Established in 1971 by Dr. Victor Westphall to honor his son, David, killed in Vietnam in 1968, this is the only state park in the country dedicated as a Vietnam Veterans Memorial. The 6,000-square-foot visitor center offers informative and deeply touching videos, exhibits, and memorabilia. Architect Ted Luna designed it with the idea "such that no person entering it could leave with quite the same attitude toward peace and war." Free.

San Francisco de Asis Church ("Ranchos Church") (575-758-2754), Ranchos de Taos. Four miles south of Taos on NM 68. Open Mon.–Sat. 9–4. The most frequently painted and photographed church in the United States was built sometime between 1776 and 1813. Its massive adobe walls change appearance with the changing light. $3 to see video and Mystery Paintings in Parish Hall.

Taos Pueblo (575-758-1028), 2 miles north of Taos off NM 68. Feast days: Sept. 29–30, San Geronimo. Open daily 9–5. Closed during private Pueblo events. Pueblo may be closed during Feb.–Mar. and Aug. Taos was well established long before Europe emerged from the Dark Ages, and the ancestors of today's people have been in this area for a thousand years. About 150 live on the Pueblo full time, and about 2,000 are living on Taos Pueblo lands. This is the only living American Indian community that is both a UNESCO World Heritage Site and a National Historic Landmark. The present Pueblo has been occupied since about A.D. 1450. To honor their traditions, there is still no indoor plumbing or electricity at the Pueblo. The Rio Pueblo, running from the sacred Blue Lake in the Sangre de Cristo Mountains, courses through the Pueblo. The Feast of San Geronimo is a highlight of the year, as is Christmas Eve. Pueblo artists are

SAN FRANCISCO DE ASIS IS PERHAPS BETTER KNOWN AS "THE RANCHOS CHURCH."

known for their micaceous, gold-flecked pottery, which is sold on the Pueblo. Entrance fees include a guided tour. It is appropriate to tip your guide. $10 adults, $5 seniors and students, under 12 free. $5 per camera. Parties of 10 or more, $8 per person.

Picuris Pueblo (575-587-1099), NM 75 at MM 13, Peñasco. Attractions at this tiny Pueblo on the High Road to Taos include a museum, the ancient Pot Creek Pueblo site, and historic restored church. The Pueblo is known for its golden-flecked mica pottery. The haunting Matachine Dances are performed here Dec. 24–25.

Pot Creek Cultural Site (575-587-1099). Nine miles from Taos on NM 518. Open late June–early Sept. Wed.–Sun. An easy 1-mile trail leads to a reconstructed pueblo that includes a ceremonial kiva. This site was inhabited by the Ancestral Pueblo people between A.D. 1100 and A.D. 1300. Many pots were found here when the Spanish arrived, hence the name. Free.

✳ To Do

BICYCLING **US 64 between Taos and Angel Fire.** An approximately 25-mile ride through narrow Taos Canyon (which can be backed up with traffic) and over

ANNETTE IS THE EXPERT ON RED CHILE. FIND HER ON THE OUTSKIRTS OF TAOS PUEBLO.

9,100-foot Palo Flechado Pass. Several hairpin turns before you come down into Angel Fire as you travel around the mountain.

CLIMBING Mallette Park, Red River. At the west end of town three blocks from Main St. is a granite face fitted with anchors and bolts.

FARMERS' MARKETS Taos Farmers Market (575-758-3982), in back of the county courthouse at Civic Plaza. May–Oct., Sat. 7–noon. Northern New Mexico and southern Colorado growers from the San Luis Valley sell the most remarkable array of produce, baked goods, flowers, preserves, bath products, and beans.

FISHING Costilla Creek/Valle Vidal. Open July 1–Dec. 31. Catch and release of the native Rio Grande cutthroat.

Latir Lakes. It takes a moderate 4-mile hike—at least—to reach the nine glacier lakes that form the Latirs, which hold trophy cutthroats. The views and the wildflowers make it a worthwhile trek. The Latirs are the headwaters of the Rio Costilla.

Rio Grande. The confluence of the Rio Grande and Red rivers near Questa and just below John Dunn Bridge in Arroyo Hondo.

Rio Hondo. Parallels NM 150 from Arroyo Hondo up to Taos Ski Valley.

GHOST TOWNS **Elizabethtown,** 4 miles north of Eagle Nest on NM 38. The first incorporated town in NM in 1868, E-town, named for a founder's daughter, was a boom-and-bust gold mining settlement. The ruins of several buildings and the cemetery survive. It now is home to the **Elizabethtown Museum,** and your best chance for finding it open is on weekends during the summer.

GOLFING **Angel Fire Golf Course** (575-377-3055), Angel Fire Resort. Usually open mid-May–mid-Oct. You can golf in an absolutely gorgeous setting up here. At 8,600 feet, this is one of the highest and most lushly wooded regulation courses in the world. It's an 18-hole, par-72 course. $50–65.

Red Eagle Golf Course (575-754-6569), Red River. At 8,800 feet, this 18-hole, par-72 course is even higher than Angel Fire. It's located in between the two towns. $30–45.

Taos Country Club (575-758-7300), 54 Golf Course Dr., Ranchos de Taos. Open year-round, weather permitting. Tee times are required and take up to a seven-day advance reservation. Open to the public at 7,000 feet, this is a forgiving desert course of 18 holes. $53–65.

NATIVE CUTTHROATS ROVE THE RIO COSTILLA.

HIKING **Williams Lake.** The trailhead is above Taos Ski Valley, past the Bavari-
an Restaurant about 1.3 miles. The best time to go on this classic Taos hike,
rated moderate, is during July–Aug., when the wildflowers are at their peak. Plan
for 4 miles on a well-marked trail, at an altitude of 11,450 feet to Williams Lake
at the base of Wheeler Peak.

HORSEBACK RIDING **Taos Indian Horse Ranch** (575-758-3212), Miller Rd. on
Taos Pueblo, Taos. Horseback rides, sleigh rides, cookouts, Indian storytellers,
and Taos Mountain music. Reservations required.

Cieneguilla Stables (575-751-2815), 13 miles south of Taos Visitor Center on
east side of NM 68, near Pilar. Custom rides or ride to the miner's cabin Rio
Grande Gorge canyon country.

MOUNTAIN BIKING For detailed information, visit the BLM Pilar Visitor Center
(575-751-4899) 15 miles south of Taos on NM 68 or the BLM Taos office (575-
758-8851) on Cruz Alta Rd.

Rio Grande Gorge West Rim Trail, the Rio Grande Gorge Rest Area at
US 64. An easy 9-mile one-way trip with great rewards. Check out the Rio
Grande Gorge from the bridge south to NM 567.

Wild Rivers Recreation Area, 35 miles north of Taos on NM 378 east of
Cerro. From the 6-mile Rinconada Loop Trail and the 5-mile Red River Fault
Trail to the 2-mile Red River Fault Trail, this trailhead offers rides from easy
to difficult. Maps are at the Wild Rivers Visitor Center or any BLM office.
$3 day use.

RIVER RAFTING The **Taos Box** and the **Racecourse** are two of the most popular white-water stretches on the Upper Rio Grande. If the runoff is good, you
can be on the river from May through July. Adrenaline is the name of the game.
Be prepared for class IV rapids.

SCENIC DRIVES **Enchanted Circle Scenic Byway** (1-800-733-6396, ext.
42371). US 64 and NM 522 and 38. Setting out from Taos, the Enchanted Circle
links the communities of Angel Fire and Eagle Nest, circling Wheeler Peak, the
state's highest mountain. Return to Taos via Bobcat Pass through Red River and
Questa. The best time to do the 84-mile Enchanted Circle is when the aspens
are turning, usually the last weekend in September, but it's beautiful any time at
all. The road takes you over Bobcat Pass, with its 9,820-foot summit, so named
for the many bobcats that lived there. This was once all part of the Maxwell
Land Grant, the largest private holding in the western hemisphere during the
19th century.

High Road to Taos (no phone). Pick up the High Road by driving north on
NM 68 out of Santa Fe through Española. Go right at NM 76 and continue
on through the towns of Chimayo, Truchas, Ojo Sarco, Peñasco, and on to Taos
on NM 75. Cordova is a jog to the right between Chimayo and Truchas. This is a
scenic drive any time of year, during a golden fall, a green spring, or a snowy
winter, but always be alert to weather reports and fast-changing weather what-

ever the season. Pack a picnic, binoculars, camera, and fishing gear, and bring your hiking boots and plenty of layers of outdoors wear. Each village has its historic Spanish colonial church, and each village lives much as it has for centuries, making them almost living history museums. This is a tour through New Mexico history, and really, the best way to experience it. The soaring Sangre de Cristo Mountains offer views like you've never encountered. There are shops, cafés, roadside stands, and historic churches to investigate along the way. Depending on your pace, this can be an all-day trip.

River Road to Taos. From Española, continue north on NM 68 for 47 miles to Taos. The road follows the course of the Rio Grande and swoops past the green agricultural villages of Alcalde and Velarde, then Embudo, then past the landmark Ranchos Church in Ranchos de Taos. In summer and fall, fruit stands along the way are filled with the new harvest—tomatoes, local apples, cider, plums, pears squash, melons, and preserves. From late May on through midsummer, you are likely to see river rafters down below. It's fun to stop at the little store and café in Pilar, aka the Pilar Yacht Club, where rafters put in. If you have time and inclination, you can turn right on NM 76 toward Dixon and take the remaining High Road to Taos through Peñasco, Ojo Sarco, and on into Taos along NM 76-75.

RAFTING THE RIO GRANDE BELOW PILAR.

Wild Rivers Back Country Byway (1-800-733-6396, ext. 42371), 26 miles north of Taos, goes west on NM 378 off NM 522, north of Questa. This is a phenomenal 13-mile ride that parallels the Rio Grande and Red rivers along NM 378, with access to Wild Rivers Recreation Area north of Taos. Scenic over-looks above the Rio Grande Gorge into the canyon will have you in a state of wonder. You must return the same way you drove in. A word of caution: If you are thinking of hiking down to the river, be prepared for a Grand Canyon–Bright Angel Trail–style return—in other words, the hike up and back is only for those in shape, wearing good hiking boots. While it is not a difficult hike, it is extreme-ly steep and seems to become longer with every step. And there are no mules to come rescue you.

SKIING **Angel Fire Resort** (575-377-6401), 22 miles east of Taos via US 64 and NM 434. Known as a "cruiser's mountain" with long, well-groomed trails, up to 3.5 miles, Angel Fire is a comfortable place for beginning and intermediate skiers. The waits are not more than 5–10 minutes even in the busiest times. Snowmaking capabilities guarantee 2,000 vertical feet. Tubing, polar coaster, cross-country skiing, ski school, and snowboarding. The Nordic Center has 10 miles of groomed cross-country ski trails with three loops from easy to moderate to more difficult. With over 3,000 beds, this is one of the most affordable lodg-ing bases in the state. $50.

Red River Ski Area (505-754-2382). Claiming to offer the best value among Rocky Mountain ski areas, Red River caters to juniors, teens, small children, and families. There's tubing, snowboarding, and a well-respected ski school. You can enjoy excellent skiing on the 10,350-foot mountain, which rises from the middle of town toward the Old Western mining sites of the 1800s. High in the southern Rockies, skiers tackle 57 powder-covered runs. Gaining popularity is the "Moon Star Mining Camp," where the family can ski to a replica of the Moon Star Mine of the 1890s.

Taos Ski Valley (1-866-986-7336), north of Taos on NM 150. The news is out: TSV has finally abandoned its long-standing policy against them and now allows snowboards. Ten chairlifts; a vertical drop of 2,612 feet; challenging runs; and 110 downhill runs, over half of which are advanced; eye-popping views; moguls galore; rentals of everything you will need; and over 300 inches of snow annually make this ski area what many consider the premier skiing experience in the state. While it attracts experts, it does accommodate novices and intermediates as well. $65.

SNOWMOBILING **Carson National Forest.** Access from Angel Fire tour from Forest Rd. 76 or the Elliot Barker Trail on Palo Flechado Pass.

Red River. Greenie Peak and Midnight Meadow are north of town.

SNOWSHOEING See **Angel Fire, Taos, Red River,** and **Enchanted Forest** ski areas for snowshoeing fun. Many trails are located in the Carson National Forest as well, which are often shared with cross-country skiers and snowmobilers.

Elizabethtown. Summer. Jeep ride, then hike to Placer Creek to prospect pan in the creek. By reservation only. Full-day excursion $50.

✳ Lodging

BED AND BREAKFASTS, MOTELS, AND HOTELS ♿ **Casa Europa** (575-758-9798), 840 Upper Ranchitos Rd., Taos. For a true Taos getaway, this 18th-century adobe lodge—which contains the oldest door in Taos, stunning views of Taos Mountain from a pastoral valley setting, and all the New Mexico romance of cottonwoods and kiva fireplaces—is simply the best. Hosts Joe and Lisa provide a scrumptious breakfast of juice, fruit, yogurt, scones, and interesting egg dishes; fresh-baked goodies for after-noon tea; and they see to your every comfort without being intrusive. The rooms are furnished in European period and Southwestern décor, but it all goes together. Whether you are contemplating a ski vacation or an anniversary celebration, this is a good choice. $125–185.

♿ **Mabel Dodge Luhan House** (575-751-9686), 240 Morada Ln., Taos. Set on 5 acres at the edge of the Taos Pueblo, this rambling three-story, 22-room adobe hacienda was the property of Mabel Dodge Luhan, the

THERE'S A BIG FRENCH BRASS BED AT CASA EUROPA B&B.

arts patron who arrived in Taos in 1918, married a Taos Pueblo man, Tony Lujan, then proceeded to import artists like Georgia O'Keeffe and D. H. Lawrence to town for their first taste of New Mexico. Intellectuals and luminaries like Carl Jung, Aldous Huxley, and Willa Cather all visited here. Following Mabel's death, it was purchased by Dennis Hopper, who lived in it during the filming of *Easy Rider*. You can soak it all up with a stay in this meticulously furnished and decorated B&B that is romantic to the core. $95–220.

♦ **Sun God Lodge** (575-758-3162), 919 Paseo del Pueblo Sur, Taos. Almost too good to be true, the Sun God is a real bargain find. The 53 rooms are decorated in Southwest style, and with colorful tile accenting the rustic Taos wood furniture, it never feels cut-rate. It is quiet despite its location on a busy strip mall across from Wal-Mart. Still, it is best to ask for a room toward the back. $59–79.

Dobson House (575-776-5738), 1.3 miles north of Taos, El Prado. Do call for directions—dirt roads out here are not marked and, in some cases, not reliable. You may want an escort to get there the first time, and by all means arrive before dark. Built on the principles of the nearby eco-friendly and totally sustainable earth ships, Dobson House is a solar-powered modern adobe castle at 7,000 feet, perched on a 100-foot hill on 25 acres beside the Rio Grande Gorge. This puts you at eye level with hawks in flight. Each of the two suites has its own private patio surrounded by a bottle garden. The tile work, artwork, and spectacular stairway, all of which were built by Joan and John Dobson, are guaranteed to change your ideas

about interior design forever. The breakfasts, hospitality, and gardens (in summer) are lovely. The place has justifiably been hailed in the national media as an eco-resort. Neither pets nor children under 14 are accepted. $118–140.

♦ & **Inn on the Rio** (575-758-7199; www.innontherio.com), 910 Kit Carson Rd., Taos. Brilliant flower gardens and brightly painted flowers adorn this charmingly renovated 22-room 1950s-style motor court inn with heated outdoor swimming pool and hot tub, all beautifully tended. The breakfast of quiche, lemon poppy seed cake, and other hearty dishes prepared and served by hostess Julie and host Robert are rich enough to spoil you. The inn is worth the press it gets as a choice comfortable destination. $99.

& **Taos Inn** (575-758-2233; www.taosinn.com), 125 Paseo del Pueblo Norte, Taos. Stay here and you'll be signing the same guest register as Greta Garbo, Thornton Wilder, and D. H. Lawrence. Each of the 37 guest rooms in this National Historic Landmark property has a distinct personality—most have a pueblo fireplace. Taos-style antique furniture and several rooms open onto the balcony overlooking the lobby. Despite its historic past and the renovations of the early 1980s, it still feels a bit dark and dreary. And there is the risk of noise from the Adobe Bar disturbing your rest. $70–250.

Taos Mountain Lodge (575-776-2229), Taos Ski Valley. Located on a south-facing mountainside, Taos Mountain Lodge has 10 condominium split-level A-frame suites that hold four to six. Eight have a fireplace. All are tastefully decorated in Southwest décor. Indoor and outdoor whirpools can be a blessing after skiing. Here you are completely surrounded by the Carson National Forest, with only a seven-minute trip to the lift. $144.

Angel Fire Resort (575-377-6401), Angel Fire. With 157 rooms, Angel Fire Resort is by far the biggest lodging establishment in town. The décor is contemporary Southwestern, and the ski area is right outside the window. The inn has two restaurants, a lounge, and an indoor pool and hot tub. It is quite comfortable. $99–220.

CAMPING See **Carson National Forest,** in the sidebar later in the chapter, where you can camp virtually anywhere.

Roadrunner RV Resort (575-754-2286), Main St., Red River. Open May 1–Sept. 15. A large campground has everything you need, including almost 100 full hookups, tennis court, and playground. $35.

Questa Lodge (575-586-0300), Questa. Open May–Oct. On the Red River, only a quarter mile off NM 522, there is a motel and RV park with 26 full-service hookups, five cabins, and tent sites. $30 RV site; $180 cabin (three nights).

✳ Where to Eat

DINING OUT Roasted Clove (575-377-0636), 48 Angel Fire Rd., Angel Fire. Open daily 5–close. Closed Tues. Dinner only. Reservations strongly recommended. Whether you've spent the day on the slopes or want to finish your aspen tour with an evening of pampering, this is the place. Not just another high-end restaurant, Roasted Clove serves its coconut shrimp appetizers, chicken in pesto cream, scallops sautéed in Dijon mustard and cream over linguine, and all the other creative and well-prepared dishes with flair and care. The lovely Mediterranean-style setting elevates the surroundings to suit the cuisine. Expensive–Very Expensive.

Apple Tree (575-758-1900), 123 Bent St., Taos. Open daily. Serving lunch, dinner, and Sunday brunch. Located in a romantic Victorian house, the Apple Tree is a Taos classic that serves a convivial candlelit dinner with impeccable service and superb food in a country inn atmosphere. The menu is a creative combination of Mexican, Continental, East Indian, and New Mexican–influenced dishes. Two favorite entrees are the grilled mango chicken enchiladas and the barbecued duck fajitas with chipotle raspberry sauce. The grilled tiger shrimp enchilada is a famous lunch dish. Try the chocolate pecan pie for dessert. The eggs Benedict are a Sunday extravaganza. Expensive.

Trading Post Café (575-758-5089), 4179 NM 68, Ranchos de Taos. Lunch, dinner. Closed Sun., Christmas, and New Year's. Located in the former favorite general store and meeting place in town; there is no better place to meet on a chilly winter night than in front of the fireplace or at the counter. Order a glass of fine wine and peruse the extensive menu that includes salads, fish, pastas, soups, roast duck, chicken Vesuvio, paella, and an astounding number of daily specials. In warm weather, try the patio. This is the spot for casual sophistication. Moderate–Expensive.

Doc Martin's (575-758-1977), 125 Paseo del Pueblo Norte (in the Taos Inn), Taos. Open daily. Lunch, dinner.

The home of beloved Taos physician T. P. Martin from the 1890s to the early 1940s is now one of the top people-watching spots in town. Dinner entrees include Colorado lamb and piñon-crusted salmon with nacho chile pesto, and a favorite dessert is Aztec mousse flavored with Kahlúa. The wine list has earned the *Wine Spectator* Award of Excellence many times. Expensive.

Lambert's of Taos (575-758-1009), 309 Paseo del Pueblo Sur, Taos. Open daily. Dinner. If you crave a memorable splurge, and perhaps one of the finest dinners you will ever set a fork into, make a reservation here. It will feel like a bargain despite the tab. House special pepper crusted lamb loin with red wine demi-glace, medallions of beef tenderloin with blue cheese mashed potatoes, and pistachio crusted chicken breast with roasted shallot sherry sauce are a few of the luscious options. The menu changes seasonally, and the wine list is considered the most complete and intriguing in a town of fine wine lists. Expensive–Very Expensive.

EATING OUT Zebadiah's (575-377-6538), 3431 Mountainview Blvd., Angel Fire. Open daily. Lunch, dinner. This big pub serves up Mexican food, steaks, and decent salads at reasonable prices. It may remind you of your college hangout, but there's no problem feeding a hungry family after a day of skiing. There's a game room and a big screen TV, too. Inexpensive–Moderate.

Shotgun Willie's (575-754-6505), 403 Main St., Red River. Homemade barbeque by the pound, hand-breaded catfish, and New Mexican cuisine hearty enough to appease any starving skier. Looking, as it does, like a small shack of a place, you might be tempted to pass Shotgun Willie's by. Don't make that mistake. The sibling of **Willie's Smokehouse,** Angel Fire, this place serves by far the best barbeque (and remember, there are a lot of Texans in Red River) and the fattest breakfast burritos, and the paper plates don't hurt a bit. Inexpensive.

Graham's Grille (575-751-1350), 106 Paseo del Pueblo Norte, Taos. Open Mon.–Sat. Lunch, dinner. Closed Sun. Sonoma's loss is Taos' gain. Restaurateurs Lesley and Peter Fay have given us a hip (in a good way), stylish eatery in the old JCPenney space just off the Plaza that accomplishes the seemingly miraculous: food with flair at an affordable price. They are doing a deservedly brisk business with locals and take-out orders. The crab-corn chowder, applewood-smoked BLT, and the signature creamy, dreamy mac and cheese with bacon and green chile are mouthwatering. The lamb with fresh mint is divine. Everything is cooked and served with care. This could be my current favorite Taos restaurant. Within a year of opening, it earned a "Best of Taos" Award. Inexpensive.

Taos Diner (575-758-2374), 908 Paseo del Pueblo Norte, Taos. Open Mon.–Sat. Closed Sun. Breakfast, lunch. Nothing chichi here. Just good old American fare, freshly prepared, and lots of it. It's quite lively at peak lunch and breakfast hours. Inexpensive.

Bravo (575-758-8100), 1358 Paseo del Pueblo Sur, Taos. Open Mon.–Sat. Lunch, dinner. Closed Sun. With a fantastic wine collection, deli atmosphere, and freshly prepared buffet selections, this is where locals love to congregate for lunch. But things slow down a bit in the evening, and customers move from the bar to a little table for a meal of sweet potato fries, crab cake, and Asian salad finished off with Bourbon pecan pie. The food here is combination of California, Mediterranean, and home-style European. Moderate.

The Bean (575-758-5123), 1033 Paseo del Pueblo Sur, Taos. Open daily. Still serving the best java in town, with a full array of fresh-baked pastries. Try to resist the sticky buns or the blueberry muffins. When you're really hungry for breakfast, go for the huevos rancheros or breakfast burrito. The place is bare bones, but the folks are friendly and the food can't be beat. Inexpensive.

Café Tazza (575-758-8706), 122 Kit Carson Rd., Taos. Open daily. Call for hours. This lovably funky place has been here forever it seems, and hopefully will remain as it is just as long. Definitely the place for people watching and a latte, or, when it's warmer, take your Taos Cow ice cream and journey out to the patio. You never know whom you'll run into! Live music and spoken word events Fri.–Sat. evenings. Inexpensive.

Orlando's (575-751-1450), 1.8 miles north of plaza on left, off Paseo del Pueblo Norte, 114 Don Juan Valdez Ln., Taos. Open Mon.–Sat. 10:30–3, 5–9. Closed Sun. and Christmas. From its humble beginnings as a hot dog cart on the Plaza, Orlando's mother's authentic northern New Mexico recipes, minus the lard, is what you'll get here in this colorful Mexican-looking café decorated with folk art. Try the chile bowl "with everything" or the Frito pie. Summer dining on the patio is a joy, day or night, but avoid peak

times to avoid the crowds. If you can save room, try the homemade carrot cake. Inexpensive.

Taos Pizza Out Back (575-758-3112), 712 Paseo del Pueblo Norte, Taos. Open daily 11–10. Closed Thanksgiving, Christmas. You may think you've had the best pizza, but this really is the best. You may have to hunt a bit to find it—it really is out back—but you'll remember where it is and what it is—a funky, hip, wood-warm busy spot. It specializes in "Taos-style gourmet pizza" lovingly made to order from organic Colorado wheat. I love the Florentine with chicken, garlic, and herbs sautéed in white wine. A slice of pizza with a salad will satisfy most appetites. Inexpensive.

Taos Cow Ice Cream Scoop **Café & Deli** (575-776-5640), 485 NM 150, Arroyo Seco. Open daily 7–7. You might think you're in a time warp here with the longhairs and Rastafarians, but we all know a good thing when we see it. If you're an ice cream lover, head up the Taos Ski Valley Road to the ice creamery that has the creamiest, most exquisite all-natural and rBGH-free ice cream you've ever tasted, in delectable seasonal flavors like peach and lavender, and the chocolate variations will win your heart. Fresh-roasted organic Fair Trade coffee and Wi-Fi, too.

Tim's Stray Dog Cantina (575-776-2894), 105 Sutton Pl., Taos Ski Valley. Open daily 8–9 winter, 11–9 summer. This is absolutely the place for a lively, if not rowdy, après-ski libation. Plenty of big portions of standard American fare are awaiting. Inexpensive.

The Hole Thing Donut Shop (575-754-2342), 601 W. Main St., Red River. Open daily 7–2. Breakfast and lunch. If you're a sucker for fresh homemade donuts, with or without bacon and eggs, you'll get up early and hightail it over here. It's the real thing, for sure. Inexpensive.

✳ Entertainment

Sagebrush Inn (575-758-2254), 1508 Paseo del Pueblo Sur, Taos. Live music most nights at 9, with some of the best local country and western performers and dancing.

Best Western Kachina Lodge (575-758-2275), 413 Paso del Pueblo Norte, Taos. Local bands play here weekend nights.

Taos Inn (505-758-2233; www.taos inn.com), 125 Paseo Del Pueblo Norte, Taos. Long considered "Taos' living room," there is live entertainment here most nights in the Adobe Bar to accompany your margarita. The place can get elbow-to-elbow on weekend evenings. In warmer weather, the street-side patio is divine.

Caffe Tazza (575-758-8706), 122 Kit Carson Rd., Taos, often has live poetry and spoken word performances, on Fri.–Sat.

Eske's Brew Pub (575-758-1517), 106 Desgeorges Ln., Taos, is still the best place to relax with a microbrew.

Taos Center for the Arts (575-758-2052; www.taoscenterforthearts.org), 145 Paseo del Pueblo Norte, Taos. The Taos Community Auditorium here is a venue for music, theater, film, and concerts of all varieties.

Don Fernando de Taos Hotel (575-758-2444), 1005 Paseo del Pueblo Sur, Taos. Live music and karaoke sound off at the Hideaway Lounge, and complimentary appetizers are served during happy hour Mon.–Fri. 4–6.

El Taoseno Restaurant and Lounge (575-758-4142), 819 Paseo del Pueblo Sur, Taos. If you want to mingle with the locals, hang out here on a Friday night. One of them might ask you for a turn on the big dance floor.

Bull O'The Woods (575-754-2593), 401 E. Main St., Red River. Live

GAMING

In addition to serving as venues for Las Vegas–style gaming and dining, Indian-run casinos are popular venues for celebrity performers.

Camel Rock Casino (1-800-GO-CAMEL), 10 minutes north of Santa Fe on US 84/285. Run by Tesuque Pueblo, Camel Rock offers slots, blackjack, bingo, roulette, and a restaurant.

Cities of Gold Casino (1-800-455-3313), 15 miles north of Santa Fe on US 84/285. Cities of Gold is run by Pojoaque (po-ah-kay) Pueblo and has more than 700 slot machines, plus an extravagant 24-hour buffet spread.

Ohkay Casino (1-877-829-2865), just north of Española on US 84/285. Operated by Ohkay Owingeh (formerly San Juan) Pueblo, this casino is known for its breakfast buffet, lounge, and new 100-room hotel.

Taos Mountain Casino (575-737-0777), Taos Pueblo. This is the only non-smoking casino in the state, offering slots but no bingo.

ARROYO SECO GENERAL STORE HAS JUST ABOUT EVERYTHING.

music nightly at 9. Dancing, too. This *is* the nightlife scene in Red River. It's a historic bar with shuffleboard, pool, and karaoke.

Alley Cantina (575-758-2121), 121 Teresina Ln., Taos. Said to be Taos' oldest building, the place is haunted by crowds of tourists and locals who dance into the late hours to the live music every night. Happy hour is a terrific bargain.

✳ Selective Shopping

Arroyo Seco Mercantile (575-776-8806), 488 NM 150, Arroyo Seco. Anyone who loves to shop will adore this 1895 general store stocked with vintage textiles, quilts, toys, gifts, books, and garden ornaments.

Clay & Fiber Gallery (575-758-8093), 201 Paseo del Pueblo Sur, Taos. An excellent selection of textiles, ceramics, jewelry, glass, and sculpture by contemporary artisans makes this a fascinating stop.

Fenix Gallery (575-758-9120), 228-B N. Pueblo Rd., Taos. Intriguing displays of contemporary-verging-on-cutting-edge sculpture, painting, mixed media, and the work of many of the area's best known artists, including Bea Mandelman, Alyce Frank, Earl Stroh, and Suzanne Wiggin.

La Lana (575-758-9631), 136 Paseo del Pueblo Norte, Taos, is stocked with warm and colorful hand-woven and hand-knit items: shawls, coats, sweaters, and jackets. They also sell unusual yarn to inspire your own creations.

Market Contemporary Crafts (575-758-3195), 125 Kit Carson Rd., Taos. For more than 30 years, the ample market has been showcasing the finest in contemporary pottery, kitchenware, and jewelry while featuring the crafts of Colorado and New Mexico artisans. Whether you purchase a mug or a five-quart oven-to-table casserole dish, you will enjoy it for many years.

Moby Dickens Bookshop (575-758-3050), 124-A Bent St., Taos. Moby Dickens is one of the very best independent bookstores anywhere. In addition to a brilliantly selected two floors of books for browsing, the upstairs has a section devoted to the rare and out of print.

Overland Fine Sheepskin & Leather (575-758-8820), 3 miles north of Taos off Paseo del Pueblo Norte. Shearling coats to get you through the coldest winters, fine Italian leather coats, fringed and embroidered suede outfits, hats, slippers, mittens, and more. Of course it's pricey, but think of it as an investment. I do. This is my favorite store! The mid-winter sales, around Valentine's Day, are phenomenal.

Parks Gallery (575-751-0343), 127 Bent St., Taos. In a town of superlative galleries, this one stands out with

EACH PONY ON THE VENERABLE CAROUSEL KNOWN AS TIO VIVO WAS DECORATED BY A WELL-KNOWN TAOS ARTIST.

its eye-opening contemporary painting, photography, sculpture, prints, and jewelry. Melissa Zink, one of my favorite New Mexico artists, is represented here.

Steppin'Out (575-758-4487), 120 Bent St., Taos. Two floors of fine leather goods, including many, many shoes you will want, plus belts and handbags. The high-end waterproof boots turn bad weather into an opportunity for chic. My favorite shoe store! But save your allowance before you go.

🖊 **Tiovivo** (575-751-3456), 226 Ranchitos Rd., Taos. *Tiovivo* means "your old uncle," or, in Taos, the name refers to a venerable carousel that is taken out on special occasions. This shop is a kids' dream come true, with rooms full of toys from kites to stuffed animals to games for all ages.

FaFa's Furniture & Fine Arts (575-758-8898), 105 Camino de la Placita, Taos, is a showcase of mid-century modern and retro knockoff furniture to give your décor a big boost. Find luxurious leathers and Italian imports to grace your home.

HIGH ROAD COUNTRY: CHIMAYO, TRUCHAS, CORDOVA, PEÑASCO, DIXON

Take away the satellite dishes and asphalt, and you might think you've fallen into an 18th-century mountain village. Very little has changed here over the centuries. Many descendants of original settlers still farm and live sustainably, getting by with bartering, cutting their own wood, hunting, and fishing on the land granted their ancestors by the Spanish crown. The ancient crafts of woodcarving and weaving still thrive here, along with the tried-and-true way of life. Isolated in small villages within high mountain ranges, the people are polite but not overly friendly to outsiders. The mission churches of Truchas and Chimayo are not to be missed.

GETTING THERE From Santa Fe, take US 68 north to Española. From Española, go right on NM 76 on up the High Road to Chimayo.

✳ To See

TOWNS **Chimayo.** Ten miles east of Española on NM 76. The name comes from the Tewa Indian, meaning, "good flaking stone." The village, founded near here in the early days of the Spanish Reconquest in 1692, is famous as the home of El Santuario de Nuestro Senor de Esquipalas, commonly called El Santuario, known for its healing dirt, miraculous cures, and as a Good Friday pilgrimage site. The nearby shrine dedicated to Santo Nino de Atocha is also considered holy. There is a local "belief" that says Santo Nino must have his shoes replaced as he wears them out going around the village at night performing good deeds. The Plaza del Cerro is the only original fortified plaza in the southwest.

Truchas. Eighteen miles northeast of Española on NM 76. Known as the place where the movie *The Milagro Beanfield War*—based on the novel set in Taos by John Nichols—was filmed; it is named for the Rio de Truchas, "trout river," nearby. Set in the high Sangre de Cristos, it is the quintessential isolated High Road village, sprinkled with galleries, with an active morada, the home of the

WHAT'S AN ARTISTS' STUDIO TOUR WITHOUT HOME-COOKED NEW MEXICAN FOOD?

Penitente Brotherhood. Warning: packs of untended dogs roam the streets. And those who live here are not really crazy about those who do not.

Cordova. Fourteen miles east of Española on NM 76, 1 mile south of NM 76. Traditional woodcarving is the essence of this village's soul. It's what everyone does. The Cordoba style is unpainted aspen and cedar. You can walk into anyone's studio and find exquisite tree of life, Noah's ark, nativities, and santos you need to take home.

Peñasco. Two miles SE of Picuris Pueblo on NM 75. This is probably the largest village on the High Road, where you can find an ATM, a couple of cafés, and gas. Families have lived here for generations, and everyone is either related to or certainly knows everyone else. Much of the life of the town still revolves around barter and living off the land.

Dixon. Twenty miles northeast of Española, 2 miles east of NM 68. Named for the town's first schoolteacher, this village on the Embudo River has an idyllic appeal. With its Victorian architecture intermixed with adobe homes, it is a cozy community of artists, old-timers, and agricultural folk, who appear to share a vision of neighborliness. There's a sweet co-op grocery store in the middle of town next to the library where you can pick up supplies and a great cup of coffee.

✳ To Do

BALLOONING **Eske's Air Adventures/Paradise Balloons** (575-751-6098), El Prado, offers valley and Rio Grande Gorge balloon flights year-round. Each includes an hour aloft and a champagne brunch. Ultralight flights are also available. $250.

CAMPING AND FISHING See **Carson National Forest** in the sidebar later in the chapter.

MOUNTAIN BIKING **Carson National Forest** trails off US 64 will take you all the way to Angel Fire.

Rio Chiquito, a long forest service road off NM 518 that connects with Garcia peaks, is a favorite of families and includes beaver ponds and good picnicking.

Picuris Peak, access off NM 518, is an intermediate-to-difficult route with a steep grade and a great view.

UNIQUE ADVENTURES **The Tower at El Bosque Garlic Farm** (575-579-4288), Dixon. Stan and Rosemary Crawford have built an interesting life in rural New Mexico. The author and former president of the Santa Fe Farmers Market and his wife bring their garlic and fresh produce to sell in town Tues. and Sat. Now they have constructed "The Tower," a guest house on their farm, where guests are free to forage for vegetables and flowers during the growing season. Hiking, biking, kayaking, and skiing are all nearby. Two-night minimum. $85.

WINERIES AND WINE SHOPS **Black Mesa Winery** (1-800-852-6372), 1502 NM 68, Velarde. Open Mon.–Sat. 10–6, Sun. noon–6. Jerry and Lynda Bird live

HIGH ROAD CHURCHES

The hand-carved and painted altar screens and *santos* (saints) found in the High Road Spanish colonial churches represent some of the most striking examples of folk art found in New Mexico. A *retablo* is a two-dimensional santo, while a *bulto* is three-dimensional. Those who created them are known as *santeros.* Many remain anonymous or nearly so.

Santa Cruz de la Canada, Santa Cruz. NM 76, 3 miles north of Española. One of the most venerable High Road churches, located in a community founded by Governor De Vargas in 1695.

El Santuario de Chimayo (575-351-4889), 25 miles northeast of Santa Fe on US 84/285 to Española. Turn east on NM 76. Follow signs to Chimayo. The site of this chapel, known as the "Lourdes of America" for its "healing dirt," is believed to be a healing place of Pueblo Indians. It was built in 1813–16 by Bernardo Abeyta, who constructed the Santuario to commemorate the remarkable healing he received here. A variation of the legend says there was a cross that was taken from here that kept returning, and on the spot where it returned, Abeyta built the church. Pilgrims arrive with prayers for healing all year long, but on Good Friday it becomes a pilgrimage destination for thousands who walk here.

Nuestra Senora de Sagrada Rosario (no phone), Truchas. Constructed around 1805, this beautiful church is not often open. It may be appreciated from the outside, however, or perhaps you will be lucky and find it unlocked.

San Jose de Gracia de Las Trampas (575-531-4360), NM 76, 40 miles northeast of Santa Fe. Open daily 8–5 in summer. Considered one of the most beautiful, if not the most perfectly beautiful and best-preserved, Spanish colonial churches in New Mexico, it was constructed between 1760 and 1780. If you arrive and find the church locked, ask at one of the gift shops on the plaza for the person who keeps the key, or call the parish number above to arrange a tour. Donations accepted.

on the road to Taos in fruit country where grapes have been cultivated for centuries. Their most interesting wine is probably their Black Beauty, a chocolate-flavored dessert wine, but their Viognier, Antelope, and several others, especially their big reds fermented in oak barrels, are superb.

La Chiripada Winery (575-579-4437), 3 miles east of NM 68 on NM 580, Dixon. Open Mon.–Sat. 10–6, Sun. noon–6. At 6,100 feet, this is the highest commercial vineyard in the United States. Hearty grapes: two Pinot Noir hybrids, for example, ripen into intense flavor right here. A signature favorite is the Primavera, a blend of Riesling and French hybrids.

BLACK MESA WINERY TASTING ROOM.

Vivac Winery (575-579-4441), Dixon. Twenty-five miles south of Taos at the intersection of NM 75 and US 68. Open Mon.–Sat. 10–6, Sun. noon–6. A showy place with an adobe tasting room built by the owners, colorful flower beds, colorful art, jewelry, and hand-painted chocolates. The wines are interesting, too. Their V. Series represents their highest quality reserve blends and best varietals.

Kokoman Fine Wines & Liquors (575-455-2219), NM 84/285, Pojoaque. Twelve miles north of Santa Fe. An exceptional selection of 2,500 wines, 161 tequilas, and 400 beers are sold here at very competitive prices. A well-informed staff will assist you in your selection.

✳ Lodging

BED AND BREAKFASTS **Hacienda Rancho de Chimayo** (575-351-2222), Chimayo, 25 miles north of Santa Fe off NM 76. A converted rural hacienda owned by the Jaramillos is your home away from home. Seven guest rooms with Spanish-Victorian flair, all with fireplaces and some with balconies. And it's right across the street from Rancho de Chimayo. $79–105.

☉ **Rancho Manzana** (575-351-2227), 24 miles northeast of Santa Fe off NM 76. This establishment is a working four-acre farm known especially for the lavender and apples watered by an ancient acequia. The lodging is a 2-foot thick adobe dating to the 18th century. Gourmet full breakfasts are served outdoors under the grape arbor, weather permitting. There's a hot tub and outdoor pond for dipping, and a separate garden cottage in addition to the two guest rooms in the adobe. It doesn't get any more romantic than this, folks. $75–115.

☘ **Rancho del Llano** (505-689-2347), Truchas. This three-bedroom guest house also offers a comfortable stall where your pony can bed down. With so much beautiful mountain and valley trail riding through piñons and meadows, with glorious scenic overlooks, this is a place where you can get as close as you like to nature. $85–125.

✴ Where to Eat

DINING OUT Rancho de Chimayo (575-351-4444), NM 520, Chimayo. Open daily. Lunch, dinner. Closed Mon. Nov.–May. After experiencing the "holy dirt" of the Santuario, try some of the "holy chile" served here at the epitome of New Mexico dining. Despite anything disparaging said about the food (and locals can sometimes become overly picky), it is consistently good here. Just try not to fall in love as you sip a margarita by the fireplace on a chilly winter afternoon. And if you have only one New Mexico classic restaurant to sample, do not miss this beauty. The chile is on the mild side, but that does not detract from its tastiness. This beautiful adobe ranch house has been in the Jaramillo family since the 1880s. With its wooden floors, whitewashed walls, vigas, and terraced patio, you couldn't be anywhere but northern New Mexico. Try the crispy nachos; the sopaipilla stuffed with beef, beans, and rice; and the Chimayo chicken, with flan for dessert. Moderate.

EATING OUT ☙ **Sugar Nymphs** (575-587-0311), 15046 NM 75, Peñasco.

Hours are uncertain. Serves lunch and dinner. Here's a gourmet experience where you least expect to find one. Fresh-baked bread and homemade mushroom soup, pizza, and calzones made to order. Interesting combinations of wholesome contemporary American flavors are put together by a San Francisco–trained chef. Save room for the chocolate-pecan pie. This tiny spot adjacent to the El Puente Theater, with its occasional live performances, has been discovered by foodies from *Gourmet* and *Sunset*. Inexpensive–Moderate.

Embudo Station (575-852-4707), NM 68 between Taos and Santa Fe at Embudo. Hours are variable. Closed Nov.–Apr. Lunch and dinner. During the 1880s, this pretty site beside the Rio Grande was home to the narrow-gauge Chile Line railroad. It is also the place where explorer John Wesley Powell measured the flow of the Rio Grande. The patio under the giant cottonwoods is one of the loveliest in New Mexico. Embudo Station was the first brewpub in the area, and it is still known for its fine microbrews, some flavored with chile. They are just right with the slow-smoked meats and trout grilled lovingly in a stone smokehouse. Heaping plates of fries, smoked brisket sandwiches, superb black bean soup, and a Greek salad the gods would approve of give you a mandate to cross the rickety-looking bridge and stop. Be sure to check hours first! Moderate.

Sugar's BBQ & Burger (575-852-0604), 1799 NM 68, Embudo. Open Mon. and Wed.–Sun. 11–6. Closed Tues. Lunch, dinner. When you need a quick, tasty lunch stop, come to this unpretentious little drive-in that has a national reputation for its delectable smoked ribs and a phenomenal Sugar Burger. Inexpensive.

✷ Selective Shopping

Ojo Sarco Pottery (575-689-2354), Ojo Sarco. Open daily 10–5. Durable and beautiful premade or custom-ordered dinner- and serving-ware that blend with just about any décor are created here.

High Road Marketplace Artists' Co-Op & Gallery (575-351-1078), directly west of Santuario at Chimayo on Chimayo Plaza. Traditional and contemporary arts and crafts by more than 70 northern New Mexico artists, from whimsical sage dolls to tinwork to fine woodcarving, are found in this nonprofit community outlet.

Galeria Ortega and Ortega's Weaving Shop (575-351-2288), NM 520 at NM 76, Chimayo. Authentic 100 percent woolen blankets, rugs, coats, vests, and purses are hand-woven here in the traditional Chimayo weaving style. You can watch Andrew Ortega, a seventh-generation weaver, at work in his studio. Southwest books and snacks are available as well.

Theresa's Art Gallery and Studio (575-753-4698), NM 76, Santa Cruz. Open daily 8–8. Local folk, Jewish, and Indian art, angels, tinwork, retablos, pottery, kachinas, and more make this a worthwhile stop.

RIO CHAMA COUNTRY: ABIQUIU, ESPAÑOLA, TIERRA AMARILLA, LOS OJOS

I f you love the paintings of Georgia O'Keeffe, in this region you can see the landscapes and the wind-sculpted red rocks that inspired her iconic work. Outside of Española, known for its culture of cruising low-riders, much of the area is occupied by ranchers and villagers with a complex history of Native American and Hispanic relationships. These folks maintain a great sense of pride in their heritage. Faith and tradition guide the way. Ghost Ranch makes a wonderful base for hiking and sight-seeing. The weavers at Tierra Wools, who work with wool grown by Churro sheep, the breed originally brought by the Spanish, make Los Ojos a model of renewed sustainability.

GETTING THERE From Santa Fe, take US 68 north. Continue through Española, turn on US 84/285, and continue north.

GUIDANCE Chama Valley Chamber of Commerce (575-756-2306).

Española Valley Chamber of Commerce (575-753-2831), 710 Oñate, Española.

Oñate Monument & Visitors Center (575-852-4639). Open daily Mon.–Fri. 9–5. Exhibits of local culture and traditions as well as Hispanic and Pueblo farming traditions. It is also a venue for live events.

✳ To See

TOWNS Abiquiu (ab-eh-q). Famed as the haunt and home of 20th-century America's best-known woman artist, Georgia O'Keeffe, Abiquiu was founded as a Spanish land grant community and became the home of people known as *genizaros*, or detribalized Indians who lost their tribal identity through warfare and captivity. Here they were Christianized and given full citizenship by the Spanish Crown. Abiquiu residents were given a 16,000-acre land grant for grazing and timber. In 1829 it became the trailhead for the Old Spanish Trail linking

1,200 miles between Santa Fe and Los Angeles. Along with the magnificent beauty of its landscape, which has attracted the rich and famous, including several from the Hollywood set, the descendants of the original settlers remain fiercely proud people who continue to practice their traditions, including a contemporary revival of the Penitente brotherhood.

Española. Known as the territory of the low-riders, those who cruise the streets slowly in their elaborately altered and colorfully painted automobiles, Española is a crossroads and jumping off point to both the River Road and the High Road to Taos. According to local lore, the name means "Spanish woman," with local tradition referring to a woman who worked in a restaurant here and was known to railroad workers.

Tierra Amarilla means "yellow earth," a name common to all the native people who lived here and used the yellow pigment for pottery. It is the county seat of Rio Arriba County. It gained notoriety in 1967 for the courthouse raid led by Reyes Lopez Tijerina.

Los Ojos. A tiny community, which, during the 1960s, experienced a revival of traditional, sustainable ways through the raising of Churro sheep and the restoration of the Rio Grande weaving tradition. You'll want to visit **Tierra**

RIO CHAMA AT SUNSET.

WEAVINGS IN THE RIO GRANDE STYLE ARE AVAILABLE AT TIERRA WOOLS IN LOS OJOS.

Wools (575-558-7231), 91 Main St., and the weaving co-op there. You can watch the weavers and, if your timing is right, observe the hand dying of the yarn.

MUSEUMS Florence Hawley Ellis Museum of Anthropology (575-685-4333), Ghost Ranch Conference Center, Abiquiu. US 84, 35 miles northwest of Española. Open summer Tues.–Sat. 9–5, Sun.–Mon. 1–5; winter Tues.–Sat. 9–5. Named for a pioneer anthropologist, this museum specializes in excavated materials from the Ghost Ranch Gallina digs. The Gallina culture of northern New Mexico was rooted in the people who left Mesa Verde and Chaco Canyon during a drought around A.D. 1200. The adjacent **Ruth Hall Museum of Paleontology** displays a copy of the diminutive Coelophysis dinosaur skeleton, the official state fossil. $4 adults, $1 children and seniors.

✒ **Ghost Ranch Piedra Lumbre Education and Visitor Center** (575-685-4312), US 84 between MM 225 and 226, just north of Ghost Ranch. Open daily Mar.–Oct. 9–5; Nov.–Feb. Sat.–Sun. only Nov.–Feb. Exhibits of Georgia O'Keeffe, paleontology, archaeology, geology, and the Old Spanish Trail, as well as the Jicarilla Apache. Free.

Ghost Ranch Conference Center (575-685-4333; www.ghostranch.org), Abiquiu. Forty miles northwest of Española on US 84. Classes and seminars in photography, writing, pottery, silversmithing, tin punching, history, health, and spirituality are offered year-round at this 21,000-acre retreat center in the heart of O'Keeffe's red rock country. Operated by the Presbyterian Church, rustic Ghost Ranch is a center of diversity. Upgraded accommodations are being planned and constructed. It is possible to stay and camp there, and there are very special intermediate hiking trails, including Kitchen Mesa and Chimney Rock, that go through expansive desert landscape with clear views of forever. There is also a Ghost Ranch center in Santa Fe, where many Elderhostel events take place.

Georgia O'Keeffe's Home and Studio (575-685-4539), Abiquiu. Mar. 16–late Nov., Tues. and Thurs.–Fri. 9:30–3:30. Small group tours are available here by reservation only. $23.

Pedernal means "Flint Mountain" and is where the ancient people hunted that valuable stone. "God told me that if I painted it often enough, He would give it to me," said the painter Georgia O'Keeffe. She made the imposing peak hers, regardless of who holds the deed.

Echo Amphitheater, 18 miles north of Abiquiu on US 84, is a remarkable natural sandstone amphitheater-shaped formation where echoes really resound. Find a few campsites here and a short, easy hiking trail.

Los Brazos means "the arms" and refers primarily to the tributaries of the Rio Brazos. However, as you drive north on US 84, look to the right as you approach Chama to see striking cliffs of sheer Precambrian quartzite, popular with climbers.

Dar Al-Islam (575-685-4515), above Ghost Ranch. Off CR 155 at Sign 42A. Built by the world's foremost adobe architect, Hassan Fathy, this is an authentic mosque that hosts the Annual North American Muslim Pow-Wow in June.

Monastery of Christ in the Desert (no phone; www.christdesert.org), west on US 84 past Ghost Ranch Visitor's Center. Left on Forest Service Rd. 151. A 13-mile winding dirt road leads to monastery grounds. A Japanese monk designed the primitive rock-and-adobe church of this remote Benedictine monastery along the Chama River. It is possible to make a retreat here by contacting the guestmaster. You will have the opportunity to take part in the life of the monks during prayers and meals. $40.

✳ To Do

BOATING **El Vado Lake State Park** (575-588-7247), near Chama, has ramps, camping, and waterskiing, plus kokanee salmon fishing waters.

Heron Lake State Park (575-588-7470) is a popular sailing lake set in a ponderosa pine forest. Cross-country skiing, fishing, camping, and hiking. Since it is a restricted no-wake lake, it is ideal for canoeing and kayaking as well. During Apr.–Nov. contact Stone House Rentals (575-588-7274) for boats and canoes, and kokanee salmon fishing waters.

CROSS-COUNTRY SKIING Cumbres Pass north of Chama is a popular cross-country spot where people pull their vehicles off the road and break their own trails.

FISHING Abiquiu Lake (575-685-4371; 575-685-4433), 65 miles northwest of Santa Fe on US 84/285; turn on NM 96. Open year-round. This large, scenic reservoir behind Abiquiu Dam offers a little of everything. Kokanee salmon fishing is fine, and, if you bring your own equipment, windsurfing, waterskiing, and canoeing are all doable. RV and tent sites here, too.

Canijlon Lakes. From El Rito take NM 554 to NM 129 for approximately 16 miles to these gems of small lakes for some of the best trout fishing on the Carson National Forest. Also nearby, check out Trout Lakes and Hidden Lake. The best access to Trout Lakes is off US 84 above Tierra Amarilla; go right at Cebolla for about 2 miles.

HIKING Ghost Ranch has four popular hikes: Chimney Rock, between easy and moderate as it climbs about 600 feet, about two hours, with a stunning view of the Piedra Lumbre Basin; Box Canyon, the easiest, about 4 miles, across the arroyo in back of the main property, with a bit of rock scrambling en route;

CHIMNEY ROCK IS ONE OF SEVERAL OUTSTANDING HIKES AT GHOST RANCH.

Kitchen Mesa, the most challenging at 5 miles; and the Piedra Lumbre Hike, beyond the WETLANDS sign off the main road to the left, through the bosque and over a suspension bridge crossing Canjilon Creek for a 3-mile round-trip gentle hike to the Ghost Ranch Piedre Lumbre Visitor Center. You can get maps and details at the visitor office, where you must sign in.

HOT SPRINGS **Ojo Caliente Mineral Springs** (575-583-2233), 50 Los Banos Dr., Ojo Caliente. Open daily. Closed Christmas. The reason to come to Ojo Caliente is to visit the hot springs, stay at the lodge, and relax. The quality and composition of these geothermally heated waters is said to be equal to that found in the finest European spas. Ojo has been getting progressively more expensive as improvements have been made, but it is still a bargain compared with taking the waters in Santa Fe. It is much cheaper, and less crowded, during the week. Ask about Tues. specials, local bargain rates, and winter specials. A half-dozen pools of varying temperature and mineral composition are guaranteed to relax you, and there are private tubs, too. Massage is available on the premises. You can sweat out your toxins with the Milagro wrap. $16–33. There is also an easy 4-mile round-trip hike. See *Lodging*.

THE GEOTHERMALLY HEATED HOT SPRINGS AT OJO CALIENTE RANK WITH THE WATERS FOUND AT THE BEST SPAS IN EUROPE.

ALL ABOARD FOR THE CUMBRES AND TOLTEC NARROW-GAUGE RAILROAD IN CHAMA.

SNOWMOBILING **Cumbres Pass** (no phone). Snowmobiles are given free reign and parking areas along NM 17 across the 64 miles of the 10,222-foot pass that borders Colorado in the Rio Grande National Forest. Be sure to travel well prepared, with maps, supplies, and water. Folks do get lost out here.

🚂 **TRAIN RIDES Cumbres and Toltec Scenic Railroad** (1-800-286-2737; www.cumbrestoltec.com), Chama. Open daily May 26–Oct. 14. This narrow-gauge steam-powered railroad runs 64 miles along 10,015 Cumbres Pass between Chama and Antonito, Colorado. Built over 125 years ago by the Denver & Rio Grande Railway to carry the products of mining and timber out of the region. The fare includes an all-you-can-eat hot lunch at the stagecoach town of Osier, Colorado, along the route. Hamburgers, hot dogs, hot turkey, soup, and salad bar are on the buffet. Make reservations well in advance. Autumn color tours are especially sought after. A special Cinder Bear three-hour ride designed with children in mind runs during the summer months. $62–76 adults, $31–38 children 2–11. Parlor car $115–129.

✳ Guides, Outfitters, and Rentals

FLY-FISHING **Don Wolfley** (575-588-9653), Heron Lake.

Dos Amigos Anglers (575-377-6226).

Los Rios Anglers (1-800-748-1707).

Carson National Forest (575-758-6200), 208 Cruz Alta Rd., Taos. Stop in here for maps and guidance when planning a trip on this 1.5-million-acre national forest. You can find any kind of seasonal recreation you seek: snowshoeing; snowmobiling; jeeping; hiking on 330 miles of trails (which in winter become cross-country skiing trails); fishing in 400 miles of cold-water mountain streams for rainbow, brown, and Rio Grande cutthroat trout; and you can camp virtually anywhere, in a designated campground or outside one, if you prefer. The forest elevation ranges from 6,000 feet to the 13,161-foot Wheeler Peak, the state's highest. Plus, there are 86,193 acres of wilderness, limited to foot and horseback travel, including the Wheeler Peak and Latir Wilderness areas. Black bear, mountain lion, and bighorn sheep roam the old-growth forests, as do fox, deer, beaver, and smaller animals. In other words, the Carson is an outdoor paradise. Like the Gila National Forest in southwestern New Mexico, you could spend a lifetime exploring it.
Tres Piedras Ranger District (575-758-8678)
El Rito Ranger District (575-581-4554)

High Country Anglers (575-376-9220), with Orvis Guide of the Year, Doc Thompson.

CLIMBING, SKIING, HIKING, AND PADDLING **Taos Mountain Outfitters** (575-758-9292), 114 S. Plaza, Taos.
Cottam's Ski Shops (575-758-2822), 303 Paseo del Pueblo Norte, Taos.
Mountain Sports (575-377-3490), NM 434, Angel Fire.
Bumps! Ski Shop (575-377-3146), N. Angel Fire Rd., Angel Fire.

RIVER RAFTING **Known World Guide Service** (1-800-983-7756).
Far Flung Adventures (1-800-359-2627), El Prado.
Los Rios River Runners (575-776-8854), Taos.
Native Sons Adventures (575-758-9342).

CROSS-COUNTRY SKIING **Miller's Crossing** (575-754-2374), Red River.
Angel Fire Excursions (575-377-2799; www.cti-excursions.com), Angel Fire.
Bobcat Adventures (575-754-2769), Red River.

SNOWMOBILING AND JEEPING **Fast Eddie's** (575-754-3103), Red River.
Bitter Creek Guest Ranch (575-754-2587), Red River. Jeeps, snowmobiles, tours, and rentals, plus rustic cabins.

✳ Green Space

Resting in the River Organic Farm & Natural Products (575-685-4364), Abiquiu. Certified organic medicinal herbs are grown according to "Spiritual Agriculture." Farm tours and retreats are scheduled by reservation ($10) at this organic farm operated by movie star Marsha Mason, where fine herbal products are also sold.

PARKS Kit Carson Memorial Park (575-758-8234), central Taos. This park is the site of the historic cemetery, walking paths, and a playground on its 22 acres of green space in the middle of town.

Rio Grande Gorge Park (no phone). Includes shelter and campgrounds along the road by the river. Beautiful!

✳ Lodging

BED AND BREAKFASTS, MOTELS

Branding Iron Motel & Restaurant (575-756-2162), 1151 W. Main St., Chama. Open May–Oct. This is as clean and serviceable motel as you are likely to find. It's nothing special, but it is comfortable enough, and you will be happy to have a reservation here during railroad season. $85.

Las Parras de Abiquiu B&B (575-685-4200), Abiquiu. This casita along the Chama River has two sweet bedrooms, El Jardin and El Pedernal, and breakfast includes fixings from the organic garden. Tranquility promised. $125.

Abiquiu Inn (575-685-4378), US 84. Abiquiu Southwest style par excellence in a gracious lodge with a restaurant and gallery. Seven casitas have fireplaces and kitchens. $80–130.

🦌 ♿ **Elkhorn Lodge and Cafe** (575-756-2105), Rt. 1, Chama. A 50-year-old lodge on the bank of the Rio Chama has 22 rooms and 11 cabins. The café serves a decent breakfast and has a fine outdoor patio, and you can fish from the Rio Chama out back on their 10 acres. $45–69.

LODGES AND RANCHES Ojo Caliente Mineral Springs (575-588-2233; 1-800-222-9162), 50 Los Banos Drive, Ojo Caliente. Remodeling is a continual state of affairs here, and several of the older cabins have recently received a renovation. Not so the antique lodge, which remains darkly and drearily the same—basic, cramped, and old-fashioned, with a drafty feeling. Oddly, there is something comforting in all that, as well as the benefit to staying here with spa soak included in your bill. You can warm yourself by the lobby fireplace or sun yourself in a rocker on the front porch. And Artesian Café down the hall serves wholesome, healthy breakfast, lunch, and dinner, with decent salads and fresh fish on the menu. $99–115.

🐟 **Corkins Lodge** (575-588-7261), Chama. A very special place, suitable for family reunions and other special gatherings. Located in the Chama Valley on 700 acres at the foot of the Brazos Cliffs, there is no more beautiful setting. Guests may fish along a private 2.5-mile stretch of the Brazos River. $165–185.

Cooper's El Vado Ranch (575-588-7354), Tierra Amarilla. On the Chama River below El Vado Lake. The state record brown trout resides in the grocery store here, which tells you something. Two-night minimum required during peak season; three nights on holiday weekends. Ten comfortable log cabins on 100 acres make this an outdoors lover's getaway. El Vado is the put-in site for river rafters on the Chama, which in season gets Class II and III rapids. $96.

CABINS AND CAMPING Brazos Lodge & Rentals (575-588-7707), 15 miles southeast of Chama in the Brazos Canyon on NM 512. Here find a lodge, about a dozen cabins of whatever size you need to suit your group, as well as condos with a minimum two-night stay. Three-night minimum during holidays. No pets. $90–200.

Stone House Lodge (575-588-7274). Off NM 84, go west on NM 95 for 14 miles. Lodge is 3 miles west of Heron Dam. The location is perfection—right between El Vado and Heron Lake State Parks. The cabins are properly rustic; however, the Stone House itself holds up to 20 people. RV hookups are here as well. And you can rent a boat, stock up at the grocery store, fill your propane tank, or engage a professional fishing guide. Snowmobilers can head out on 300 miles of trails, and cross-country skiers can take off to the backcountry. Cabins $80–275, Stone House $450.

Rio Chama RV Park (575-756-2303), two blocks north of depot on NM 17 toward Alamosa, Chama. Located along the Rio Chama, this RV park with full hookups and electric is walking distance to downtown

Chama and the railroad depot. RV site $22–36, tent site $14.

Sky Mountain Resort RV Park (575-756-1100), 2743 S. US 84/64, Chama. With unobstructed views of the Rio Chama on 10 acres are 46 sites with full hookups. $25–35.

✳ Where to Eat

DINING OUT El Paragua (575-685-4829), 603 Santa Cruz Rd., or NM 76 just to the right of NM 68. Open daily, lunch and dinner, 11–9. Like visiting your favorite old aunt, this dark, very Spanish institution continues to serve consistently fine New Mexican and mesquite-grilled meals. If you can get past the scrumptious carne adovada, chile rellenos, and chimichanga, there's the garlic shrimp in butter. If you can find better chips and salsa, go for it! Moderate.

EATING OUT Bode's General Store (575-685-4422), 1919 US 84. Open daily 6 AM–8 PM. Breakfast, lunch. This is no ordinary gas station. Trader Martin Bode arrived in Abiquiu at least a century ago, and his family still operates the place, which is a combination pit stop, bakery, grocery store, hardware store, and gift shop. Where else can you spot a monk from Christ in the Desert Monastery buying a shovel while you are eating a fresh-baked cinnamon roll or Frito pie and reading the Sunday *New York Times*? Inexpensive.

El Parasol (575-753-8852), 602 NM 76, Española. You could spot actress Diane Keaton munching on an out-of-sight chicken guacamole taco at this drive-in, on one of the picnic benches along with the local Sikhs and low-riders. Don't miss this cultural mix. Inexpensive.

El Farolito (575-756-2229), 1212 Main St., El Rito. The reason to drive on NM 15 to El Rito is to dine at this darling New Mexican eatery with eight tables. They might serve my favorite green chile in all of New Mexico. Inexpensive.

Foster Hotel Bar Restaurant (575-756-2384), 393 S. Terrace Ave., Chama. Open daily. Breakfast, lunch, dinner. Okay, so it's not the Ritz. The big old woodstove in the middle of the café puts out the heat, and that's just fine when the temperature is eight below and streets are lined with 3-foot snowdrifts. Standard American fare is offered. Breakfast is probably the best meal. It's cozy, it's warm and friendly,

and you can go next door to the bar after you've eaten (or before). Inexpensive.

The Diner (575-758-3441), US 64/285. Hours uncertain. If you simply must try the best Frito pie in the land, continue north of Ojo Caliente to Tres Piedras to this one remaining Valentine Diner, circa 1936, in New Mexico. Or you can approach from Taos on NM 64, past the Rio Grande Gorge Bridge and what is known as the "Earthship Landing Zone," where you will see a scattered neighborhood of off-the-grid earthships constructed of recycled tires and tin cans, across the sagebrush mesa. Inexpensive.

OFF-THE-GRID "EARTHSHIPS" SIT ON THE SAGEBRUSH MESA OUTSIDE TAOS.

✳ Entertainment

High Country Lounge (575-756-2384), 2289 S. NM 17, Chama. Order a steak and take in the live country music on weekends. You might hear a dead-ringer for Patsy Cline, who once performed at the Grand Ole Opry! This cowboy bar is the place to go for an evening in Chama.

✳ Selective Shopping

Trackside Emporium "The Railfan Store" (575-756-1848), 611 Terrace, Chama. Everything railroad—books, magazines, guides, model trains, videos, and railroad items "for the serious railfan."

Tin Moon Gallery (575-685-4829), 1 Bode's Court, Abiquiu. Located directly across US 84 from Bode's at the entrance to Abiquiu, this adorable gallery has handmade jewelry, tinwork, pottery, and works on paper that will make you exclaim with the overused, but certainly apt word, "Charming!"

✳ Special Events

January: **Taos Winter Wine Festival** (575-758-3873), last two weeks. Wine and food events, seminars, grand tastings in Taos and Taos Ski Valley.

June: **Taos Solar Music Festival** (www.solarmusicfest.com), Kit Carson Park, last weekend. It rocks, with demos of sustainable energy projects as well as bands like Los Lobos plus

TRADITIONAL SPANISH DANCES.

the new music. **Toast of Taos** (575-751-5811), late June–early July. Golf tournament, gallery tours, wine dinners, and art auctions. **Taos School of Music Summer Chamber Music Festival** (575-776-2388), mid-June–mid-Aug.

July: **Taos Pueblo Pow-wow,** second weekend. **Eight Northern Indian Pueblos** (575-747-1593; www.eight northernpueblos.com), second weekend, at Ohkay-Owengeh (formerly San Juan) Pueblo, 26 miles north of Santa Fe off US 68. Annual sale and exhibit of Indian art, pottery, and jewelry.

August: **Music from Angel Fire** (575-377-3233). Internationally known musicians perform classical in concerts all over northern New Mexico. $18–23, with some complimentary performances.

September: **High Road Art Tour** (1-866-343-5381; www.highroadnew

mexico.com), last two weekends, 10–5. **San Geronimo Day, Taos Fall Arts Festival** (575-758-3873). **Taos Mountain Film Festival** (575-751-3658) is a blaze of adventure films.

October: **Taos Wool Festival** (1-888-909-9665), Kit Carson Park, Taos, first weekend. A celebration of the animals, textiles, fiber arts, and a gathering of the fiber people that retains its folksy feel. **Annual Abiquiu Studio Art Tour** (www.abiquiustudiotour .org), Columbus Day Weekend.

November: **Taos Balloon Fiesta. Dixon Art Studio Tour** (www.dixon arts.org), first weekend. Over 50 area artists open their studios in a grand gala of arts and crafts.

December: **Yuletide in Taos** (575-758-3873), all month. Farolitos, tree lighting, open studios on LeDoux St., and lovely festivities of the season.

Santa Fe and Beyond

SANTA FE, TESUQUE, LOS ALAMOS, LA CIENAGA, GALISTEO

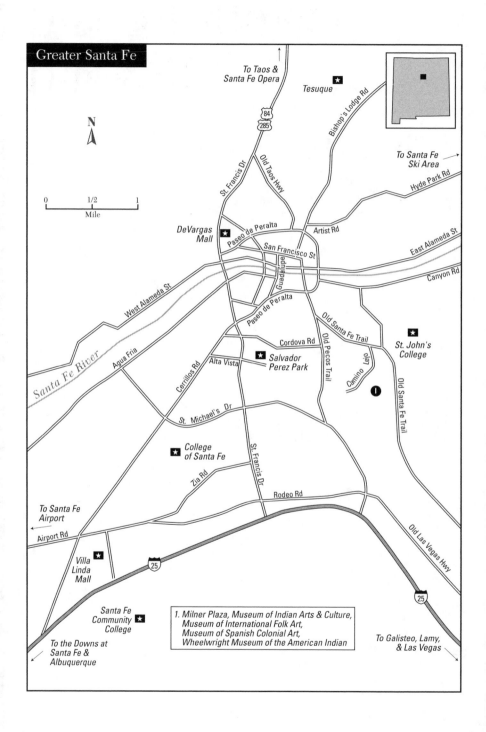

Greater Santa Fe

To Taos &
Santa Fe Opera

Tesuque ★

Bishop's Lodge Rd

N

84
285

To Santa Fe
Ski Area

St. Francis Dr

Old Taos Hwy

Hyde Park Rd

0   1/2   1
Mile

DeVargas ★
Mall

Paseo de Peralta

Artist Rd

San Francisco St

East Alameda St

Guadalupe

Canyon Rd

West Alameda St

Paseo de Peralta

Old Santa Fe Trail

St. John's ★
College

Santa Fe River

Agua Fria

Cordova Rd

Old Pecos Trail

Camino Lejo

Aqua Fria

Cerrillos Rd

Alta Vista

Salvador ★
Perez Park

Old Santa Fe Trail

❶

St. Michael's Dr

College ★
of Santa Fe

St. Francis Dr

Zia Rd

Rodeo Rd

To Santa Fe
Airport

Old Las Vegas Hwy

Airport Rd

25

25

Villa ★
Linda
Mall

Santa Fe ★
Community
College

1. Milner Plaza, Museum of Indian Arts & Culture,
   Museum of International Folk Art,
   Museum of Spanish Colonial Art,
   Wheelwright Museum of the American Indian

To Galisteo, Lamy,
& Las Vegas

To the Downs at
Santa Fe &
Albuquerque

SANTA FE, TESUQUE, LOS ALAMOS, LA CIENAGA, GALISTEO

Santa Fe. The very sound of the name conjures visions of blazing sunsets, ancient adobe buildings, romantic patios, colorful fiestas, and shopping beyond compare. This "City Different" is, after all, the oldest capital city in the United States, founded in 1610. This City of Holy Faith sits at the foot of the Sangre de Cristos, the Blood of Christ Mountains, at 7,000 feet. In fact, this city is so intriguing that it consistently places in the top three favorite U.S. travel destinations.

What distinguishes Santa Fe from other American cities are its flat-roofed, wood-beamed adobe houses and public buildings. This "Santa Fe Style" of architecture is called Pueblo Revival. The style was inspired by one building: the Museum of Fine Arts, a 1917 structure that still stands just off the Plaza, modeled originally on San Estevan Mission at Acoma Pueblo. This signature building style was subsequently enforced by city ordinance and the town fathers with the foresight, a century ago, to understand the city's mission was to attract tourists. The scale and the use of natural materials both capture and communicate the ancient essence of this place.

Stroll up Canyon Road and browse the dozens of galleries that give the city a reputation as one of the nation's top art markets, then over to Camino del Monte Sol and Acequia Madre, on the path of the annual Christmas Eve farolito walk. These streets were made famous by the many artists who once lived and worked there during the first part of the 20th century, and whose work still hangs in the Museum of Fine Arts and sells for six and seven figures in the better galleries. One of the best remembered, Will Shuster, created Zozobra, also known as "Old Man Gloom," a giant effigy that is burned at Santa Fe Fiestas every September as the season changes, in a joyous communal celebration.

And there is truth to the mystique. There is nothing like sipping a margarita on Sena Plaza when the gardens are in bloom, or brunching at Geronimo, or walking into the Santa Fe Opera, or maxing out your credit cards on Canyon Road.

It is also true that there is no such thing as a "bargain" in Santa Fe. There is no real off-season, not in a city that receives over a million visitors a year and where

ART IS EVERYWHERE ON CANYON ROAD.

retail space is reputedly higher per square foot than on Madison Avenue in Manhattan. Finding a good value, not falling into a "tourist trap," is the best you can
hope.

For just when you thought prices couldn't go any higher, they do. This is a
city where, quite honestly, price has severed its connection with value. Be assured
that every entry presented here for your consideration has been screened for
value.

To receive the best selection, it is necessary to make reservations well in advance, particularly if you are interested in experiencing one of the well-known
events, like Indian Market. Even though Santa Fe charm has been packaged and
commercialized, some say "Disney-fied," it remains irresistibly charming
nonetheless.

It is true that if you have to ask the price of something, you probably can't
afford it. No longer are there casual artists' studios on Canyon Road. Gypsy Alley
is strictly high-rent and upscale these days. The artists who once might have
set up shop here have likely moved to Albuquerque or Truth or Consequences
because they can't afford the rent. There are no shoe shops or drugstores on the
plaza anymore, only expensive boutiques and galleries, and local people have
been driven farther and farther from the center of town.

If you are so charmed that you want to move here, as so many are by the looks of the sprawling developments south and east of town, keep in mind that a substantial trust fund, pension, or reliable alimony check will help you live in the style to which you would like to become accustomed.

There is no real industry, and the biggest employers are state government and public education, or the tourist business. As in many other places, and probably more so here, it is who you know, or more likely, to whom you are related, not what you know, that will get you a job.

It is not like anyplace else in New Mexico; Santa Fe is a world of its own. What other small city, with a population under 75,000, has this old-world feel, this vast historic legacy, and this concentration of culture—opera, classical music, museums, galleries—as well as shopping opportunities?

Although it is located in New Mexico, Santa Fe does not think of itself as particularly Mexican. Many of the longtime locals and those descended from old families regard themselves as "Spanish," and they are quite sensitive on this point. However, the presence of recent immigrants from Mexico is obvious when you look at who is providing service in this tourist economy and when you drive out Cerrillos Rd. and see all the restaurants and businesses catering to Mexican people.

The Railyard District off Guadalupe St. and Paseo de Peralta is in the process of creating itself as an entertainment, dining, and shopping area, anchored by the year-round Farmers Market and multiplex cinema. As of press time, we hear of several popular local cafés that are relocating here, and the area is slated as Santa Fe's newest star on the map.

Because of the annual explosion of cultural events, and because so many people come to Santa Fe to experience them, there are many more such opportunities listed in the "To Do" section than you will find in other chapters.

Friday nights are the customary time for gallery openings, when in summer, especially, Canyon Road is crowded with strollers out to see what's new.

To keep up or find out what's going on, check the *Santa Fe Reporter*, a weekly newspaper published on Wednesday, or *Pasatiempo*, the weekly entertainment magazine of the *Santa Fe New Mexican*, the daily paper.

A particularly good deal is the New Mexico Culture Pass, which for $20 entitles you to a visit to each of the 14 state museums and monuments during a 12-month period. Contact www.newmexicoculture.org.

In addition to its arts scene, Santa Fe, which has always drawn health-seekers as well as quirky and eccentric people, is today a home of religious diversity, healing arts, and a great deal of spiritual searching. The town is by any measure very tolerant. Advocates for progressive causes seem to receive pretty unanimous support.

And of course, with its splendid location, it is a base for enjoying four seasons of recreation. Ski Santa Fe; the Dale Ball Trails, which may be accessed from town; hiking and cross-country skiing only minutes away from the Plaza are the beginning of the adventure. Appreciation for the outdoors is a way of life here.

A FEW TIPS AND CAUTIONS

As in the rest of New Mexico, smoking in public places is not permitted.

Pets must be leashed and picked up after.

Talking on a handheld cell phone while driving will get you a ticket.

Be especially careful of your safety and your property. Be aware of your surroundings and use caution at all times.

Drivers are impatient, so be very careful when on the road. Consult a map before you go out.

Look both ways before you cross the street. Do not expect traffic to yield.

While service in high-end restaurants and lodgings is generally quite good, in many establishments you may run in to staff that is new or not well trained. Exercise patience.

Santa Fe's history is wrapped up in its life as a destination—as the end point of the Camino Real, the Royal Road from Mexico City, and as the end of the Santa Fe Trail, a great 19th-century trade route across the plains from Independence, Missouri. And it is still a destination, one of those "must-see" places that never loses its appeal.

As arresting and as alluring as Santa Fe may be, it is unique in all New Mexico. The beating heart of the state lies in its small towns and villages. Santa Fe is very much the known world. If you are a real explorer, you will, on this trip or sometime in the future, want to venture outside the limits of the "City Different."

GUIDANCE Santa Fe Convention & Visitors Bureau (505-955-6200; www .santafe.org), 60 E. San Francisco St. Open Mon.–Fri. 8–5.

New Mexico Dept. of Tourism, Santa Fe Welcome Center (505-827-7400), Lamy Bldg., 491 Old Santa Fe Trail. Open daily, summer 8–7, winter 8–5.

Santa Fe Chamber of Commerce (505-983-7317), 8380 Cerrillos Rd., Ste. 302, Santa Fe Outlets. Open Mon.–Fri. 8–5. Business and relocation information and visitors guide. Mid-May–mid-Oct. the Bienvenidos booth at First National Bank on the Plaza provides tourist information.

Public Lands Information Center (505-438-7542), 1474 Rodeo Rd., Santa Fe. Open Mon.–Fri. 8:30–4:30. Information about recreation on public lands statewide, maps, camping permits, hunting, and fishing licenses.

GETTING THERE *By car:* I-25 north or south is the most direct route into Santa Fe.

By air: Santa Fe Municipal Airport (505-955-2908) has commercial flights to Denver on **Great Lakes Aviation.** The **Santa Fe Shuttle** (505-243-2300; 1-888-833-2300) operates a shuttle between Albuquerque International Sunport and Santa Fe, as does **Sandia Express Shuttle** (1-888-775-5696) and **Twin Hearts** (1-800-654-9456).

By train: The **Amtrak** Southwest Chief stops in Lamy, 18 miles south of Santa Fe. The **Lamy Shuttle** (505-982-8829) delivers passengers to Santa Fe.

By bus: **TNM&O** coaches link to **Greyhound** at Santa Fe Bus Station (505-471-0008), 858 St. Michael's Dr.

GETTING AROUND Capital City Cab (505-438-0000).

Santa Fe Trails (505-955-2001) provides public bus transportation around town weekdays 6:40 AM–9:50 PM, Sat. 8–8, Sun. 10–6. Pick up maps at the Public

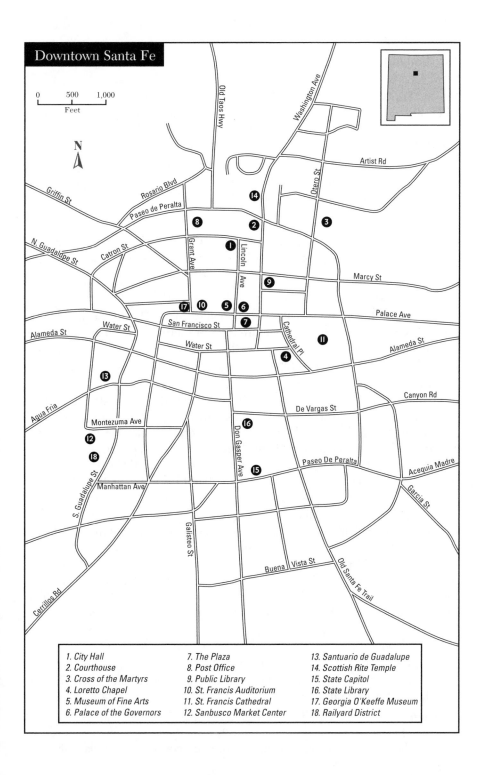

Downtown Santa Fe

0   500   1,000
Feet

N

Old Taos Hwy
Washington Ave
Artist Rd
Otero St
Griffin St
Rosario Blvd
Paseo de Peralta
⑭
⑧   ②   ③
Grant Ave
Lincoln Ave
①
Marcy St
N. Guadalupe St
Catron St
⑨
Palace Ave
⑰ ⑩ ⑤ ⑥
⑦
Alameda St
Water St
San Francisco St
Cathedral Pl
⑪
Water St
Alameda St
④
⑬
Canyon Rd
Agua Fria
De Vargas St
Montezuma Ave
⑯
⑫
Don Gasper Ave
Paseo De Peralta
Acequia Madre
⑱
⑮
Garcia St
S. Guadalupe St
Manhattan Ave
Galisteo St
Buena Vista St
Old Santa Fe Trail
Cerrillos Rd

1. City Hall
2. Courthouse
3. Cross of the Martyrs
4. Loretto Chapel
5. Museum of Fine Arts
6. Palace of the Governors
7. The Plaza
8. Post Office
9. Public Library
10. St. Francis Auditorium
11. St. Francis Cathedral
12. Sanbusco Market Center
13. Santuario de Guadalupe
14. Scottish Rite Temple
15. State Capitol
16. State Library
17. Georgia O'Keeffe Museum
18. Railyard District

Library, 145 Washington Ave., or City Hall, 200 Lincoln Ave. $1 adults, $.50 seniors and children under 18.

Greyhound Lines (505-471-0008) run buses between Santa Fe and Taos daily. Call for times and prices.

Faust's Transportation (505-758-3410) runs buses between Santa Fe and Taos and will pick you up and drop you off at almost any motel or hotel in Taos. The departure spot in Santa Fe is the Santa Fe Hilton, 100 Sandoval St.

Loretto Line City Tours (505-983-3701), Loretto Chapel, 207 Old Santa Fe Tr. Open daily, depending on weather. This open-air sight-seeing trolley ride covers an 8-mile loop and is a good way to get the lay of the land. The tour is approximately one and a quarter hour. $14 adult, $10 children under 12. Call for departure time.

MEDICAL EMERGENCY **St. Vincent's Regional Medical Center** (505-995-3934), 455 St. Michael's Dr. Fast-track emergency room open daily 8–midnight.

✳ To See

TOWNS **Santa Fe.** The "City Different," established in 1610, has been at the heart of New Mexico history and culture for over four centuries. The state capital and home of the Roundhouse, where the state legislature convenes each winter, is also the self-proclaimed capital of culture and tourism.

Tesuque (te-Sue-kay) is 3 miles north of Santa Fe on Bishop's Lodge Rd. Named for the nearby Indian pueblo, this community dates to 1740. An exquisite village of venerable adobes and architectural gems, cottonwoods, pastoral scenes, winding roadways, and architectural masterpieces that is a pretty, quiet suburb of Santa Fe. Oprah had a home here. Author Cormac McCarthy, author of the Oscar-winning book *No Country for Old Men,* currently lives here. You don't have to be rich and famous to live here, but it helps. Either that, or inherit one of these grand old places.

Los Alamos, 39 miles northwest of Santa Fe via US 84/285 and NM 502, is the secret "city on the hill" where J. Robert Oppenheimer assembled the cast that produced the bomb in the Manhattan Project. Today, the county has the highest concentration of PhDs than any other county in the United States, and the Los Alamos Laboratory is still the main employer around which most of the town revolves. The name means "the cottonwoods." In 1918, Ashley Pond established the Los Alamos Ranch School for boys. During the Manhattan Project era, after the school was taken over to house project scientists, Los Alamos was rumored to be a hideout for pregnant WACs. Thus was secrecy maintained.

La Cienega. Nine miles southwest of Santa Fe via I-25. The name means "the marsh." The winding streets maintain the feeling of the Hispanic agricultural village this once was—and still is.

Galisteo. Twenty-two miles south of Santa Fe via I-25, US 285, and NM 41. The site of an ancient Indian dwelling, this became a land of sheepherders and later ranchers, starting life as a Spanish colonial outpost in 1614. Today this funky, dusty village is home to artists, writers, healers, and the like, but its Spanish character remains predominant. It is drop-dead gorgeous.

HISTORIC PLACES, LANDMARKS, AND SITES **Miraculous Staircase/Loretto Chapel Museum** (505-922-0092), 207 Old Santa Fe Trail. Open Mon.–Sat. 9–6, Sun. 10:30–5, summer; Mon.–Sat. 9–5, Sun. 10:30–5, winter; closed Christmas. Loretto Chapel was begun in 1873 and designed to look like Sainte-Chappell in Paris. Stones came from the same quarry as those for St. Francis Cathedral, and the same French and Italian stonemasons worked on both structures. As the story goes, the sisters prayed for a staircase, and an unknown carpenter arrived and built them an amazing circular staircase, lacking both nails and visible means of support. When the job was complete, the mysterious carpenter vanished. $2, under seven free.

Santuario de Guadalupe (505-988-2027), 100 S. Guadalupe St., Santa Fe. Open Mon.–Fri. 9–4, Sat. 10–4, closed Sun. (summer). The Santuario is a Santa Fe landmark built by Franciscan missionaries in 1776–79 with 3- to 5-foot-thick adobe walls. It is the oldest shrine in the United States dedicated to Our Lady of Guadalupe, who revealed herself in a vision to Indian worshipper Juan Diego in Mexico in 1531.

Cross of the Martyrs Walkway. Enter on Paseo de Peralta, between Otero St. and Hillside Ave. Always open. Only a five-minute walk from the plaza, this

DOZENS OF GALLERIES MAKE CANYON ROAD ONE OF THE WORLD'S FINEST ART BOULEVARDS.

historic spot boasts the best view of downtown to those who brave the steep climb. A brick walkway winds up a small hill, and plaques highlight Santa Fe history. The white cross at the summit is a memorial to the 21 Franciscan monks killed in the 1980 Pueblo Revolt.

Sena Plaza, 125–137 E. Palace Ave., Santa Fe. A separate world that resonates with the flavor of colonial Santa Fe, Sena Plaza is reached by an adobe passage from busy Palace Ave. Now it holds private shops and a restaurant. You can stroll around and imagine the old days as you listen to the fountain, watch the birds, and enjoy the flowers and greenery.

The Plaza, center of town. Always open. Four hundred years of history speak from the Santa Fe Plaza. It was originally laid out according to the wishes of King Philip II in 1600. It is still one of the best people-watching spots in the city.

Canyon Road. One of Santa Fe's oldest and most colorful streets, Canyon Road was originally an Indian trail to the mountains. In the 1920s East Coast artists adopted it. Now the narrow, winding street is home to dozens of galleries, boutiques, and upscale restaurants. You are likely to find whatever type of art interests you represented here.

El Zaguan, 545 Canyon Rd., Santa Fe. The home of Historic Santa Fe, this 19th-century house sits next to a perfect Victorian garden where you can read or enjoy the flowers.

Fuller Lodge. Once the dining and recreation hall for Los Alamos Ranch School, after 1943 it was taken over by the U.S. government for the Manhattan Project. An impressive log building designed by John Gaw Meem, it is now a National Historic Landmark.

St. Francis Cathedral (505-982-5619), 131 Cathedral Place, Santa Fe. Open daily 7–6; use side doors. At the east end of San Francisco St. stands one of Santa Fe's most iconic and incongruous structures. Built in French-Romanesque style, it was the inspiration of Jean Baptiste Lamy, Santa Fe's first archbishop. The Hebrew inscription over the keystone is said to be a mark of Lamy's gratitude to the Jewish community for their contributions to the cathedral's building fund.

San Miguel Church (505-983-3947), 401 Old Santa Fe Trail, Santa Fe. Open daily 9–5:30 summer; 9–5 winter; Sun. 1–4:30 year-round. Mass 5 PM. The oldest church in the United States, San Miguel was built around 1626. It stands in the **Barrio de Analco,** Santa Fe's oldest neighborhood, next door to the Oldest House, 215 E. De Vargas St. $1, under six free.

Randall Davey Audubon Center (505-983-4609), end of Upper Canyon Rd. Open summer 9–4 for garden and trails; winter hours may vary; summer house tours Mon. 2–3. One of the few historic homes in Santa Fe open to the public, this center is a state office, an environmental education center, and National Audubon Society wildlife refuge. Set on 135 acres at the mouth of the Santa Fe River Canyon, it was the home of musician and artist Randall Davey. What is now the house was the original mill. An excellent bookshop is on the premises. $5 house tours, $2 trails, $1 children under 12.

MUSEUMS **El Museo Cultural de Santa Fe** (505-992-0591), 1615-B Paso de Peralta, Santa Fe. Open Tues.–Sat. 1–5. This young Hispanic museum showcases living contemporary and traditional artists of northern New Mexico through photography, weaving, tinwork, painting, and sculpture. Also here, find issue-oriented exhibits on subjects such as water and land use. The 200-seat theater features live performance with an emphasis on original work. Free for art, variable for performance.

Center for Contemporary Arts (505-982-1338), 1050 Old Pecos Trail. Open daily noon–7. Innovative, creative, challenging contemporary work shown here. The highlight is the small movie theater out back, which screens hard-to-find classic, indie, and world films. Gallery free. $8 films.

Site Santa Fe (505-989-1199), 1606 Paseo de Peralta, Santa Fe. Open Wed.–Sat. 10–5, Sun. noon–5. Closed Mon. and Tues. This innovative museum features contemporary art and cutting-edge exhibitions, including a challenging Biennial and works from Latin America. $10 adults, $5 students and seniors. Fridays free.

✍ **Museum of International Folk Art** (505-476-1200), 706 Camino Lejo, Museum Hill. Open Tues.–Sun. 10–5. Closed Mon., Thanksgiving, Christmas, Easter, and New Year's. Travel to all the continents and 100 countries through this amazing collection of folk art, including textiles, toys, masks, and clothing. The miniature Mexican village scenes delight children. The museum, established by Florence Dibell Bartlett in 1953, received the addition of Alexander Girard's collection in 1976. The Hispanic Heritage Wing, opened in 1989, showcases Spanish colonial and Hispanic folk art, emphasizing northern New Mexico. $5 adults. Sun. free to New Mexico residents. Wed. free to New Mexico seniors.

Museum of Indian Arts and Culture (505-476-1269), 710 Camino Lejo, Museum Hill. Open Tues.–Sun. 10–5. Closed Mon. This state museum brings together the past and present of Southwest Indian culture, including pottery, jewelry, basketry, and textile, over 50,000 artifacts assembled by the Laboratory of Anthropology. The continuing exhibit "From this Earth: Pottery of the Southwest" covers archaeological, historic, and contemporary Indian pottery. $5 New Mexico adults, $7 nonresidents, under 17 free. Sun. free to New Mexico residents, Wed. free to New Mexico seniors with ID.

Museum of Spanish Colonial Art (505-982-2226), 750 Camino Lego, Museum Hill. Open Tues.–Sun. 10–5. Closed Mon. A visit here is an excellent introduction to New Mexico history and will make any visit to Santa Fe more meaningful. An intimate museum, housed in a Pueblo Revival adobe structure created by architect John Gaw Meem, pioneer of "Santa Fe Style," it is home to the Spanish Colonial Arts Society's 3,000-piece collection, spanning 500 years. $6 adults, $3 New Mexico residents, under 16 free.

Wheelwright Museum of the American Indian (505-982-4636), Museum Hill. Open Mon.–Sat. 10–5, Sun. 1–5. Closed Thanksgiving, Christmas, New Year's. Founded by the unlikely combination of Boston blue-blood heiress Mary Cabot Wheelwright and Navajo medicine man Hosteen Klah, originally for the purpose of preserving Navajo customs and ceremonies, the 1927 museum to house their collections looks completely contemporary. The Case Trading Post, modeled after early-1900s southwestern trading posts, is a respected outlet of Navajo weaving and jewelry. Donation.

Bradbury Science Museum (505-667-4444), 15th and Central, Los Alamos. Open Tues.–Sat. 10–5, Sun.–Mon. 1–5. Photographs and documents provide in-depth education of the unfurling of "Project Y," the World War II code name for the laboratory that developed the first atomic bomb. Displays of the lab's weapons research program and models of accelerators as well as the latest research on solar, geothermal, laser, and magnetic fusion energy. A most interesting film on the history and personalities behind the Manhattan Project is screened regularly. Free.

Los Alamos Historical Museum (505-662-6272), 1921 Juniper, Los Alamos. Adjacent to Fuller Lodge, 35 miles northwest of Santa Fe via US 285 north and NM 502 west. Open Mon.–Sat. 10–4, Sun. 1–4. Housed in a log-and-stone building originally part of the Los Alamos Ranch School attended by J. Robert Oppenheimer, the museum covers a million years, beginning with the volcanic creation of the Pajarito Plateau. The exhibit "Life in the Secret City" details through vintage photographs and original accounts the story of Los Alamos during World War II. A booklet describing a Los Alamos walking tour is available. Free.

⚘ **Santa Fe Children's Museum** (505-989-8359), 1050 Old Pecos Tr., Santa Fe. Open Wed.–Sat. 10–5, Sun. noon–5. Closed Mon. and Tues. Hands-on exhibits encourage children to learn by touching, moving, experimenting, and playing. Lots of ongoing family programs, workshops, and performances keep things lively. $8 New Mexico residents, $4, Sun. $1.

⚘ **El Rancho de las Golondrinas** (575-471-2261), 15 miles south of Santa Fe, exit 276 off I-25 to La Cienega. Guided group tours Apr.–Oct., self-guided tours June–Sept., Wed.–Sun. 10–4. "The ranch of the swallows" has seen settlers and traders, bishops and Indian raiders in its 300-year history. It was the last stop before Santa Fe on the Camino Real. Caravans of traders, soldiers, and settlers made the six-month round-trip. The 18th-century house, defensive tower, water mills, blacksmith shop, and numerous farm animals are at their best at the spring and harvest festivals when costumed villagers portray life in Spanish colonial New Mexico. $5 adults, $4 seniors and teens, $2 age 5–12.

Georgia O'Keeffe Museum (505-946-1000), 217 Johnson St., Santa Fe. Open daily Nov.–June 10–5, 10–8 Fri., closed Wed. Open daily July–Oct. "In New Mexico, half your work is done for you," said the famous artist of the home she adopted permanently in the 1940s. Here she found the light and subject matter that built her reputation as "the most singularly original American artist before WWII." An iconoclast in life as well as her art, O'Keeffe's museum endeavors to show changing exhibits of the work and artists who impacted her life and art. To tour the O'Keeffe home in Abiquiu, contact the above number to arrange a tour Tues., Thurs., and Fri. at 9:30, 11, 2, or 3:30. Reservations must be made well in advance. Tours $25 adults, $20 students. Museum $8 adults, $7 seniors, free Fri. 5–8.

Palace of the Governors (505-476-5100), Plaza. Open Mon.–Sat. 10–5. Closed Mon. Dating to 1610, this is the oldest continuously occupied government building in the United States. While the building itself is interesting enough, the artifacts—textiles, carvings, and ceramics—displayed within eloquently speak the history of the area. The planned opening of the much-anticipated New Mexico History Museum behind the Palace is set for summer 2009. $6, free Fri. 5–8, Sun. free to New Mexico residents.

Museum of Fine Arts (505-476-5072), 107 W. Palace Ave. Open Tues.–Sun. 10–5. Closed Mon. This is the 1917 Pueblo Revival building that kicked off the architectural design known as Santa Fe style. On permanent exhibition are works by early-20th-century New Mexico artists such as Gustave Baumann, William Penhallow Henderson, and Jozef Bakos. The collection emphasizes 20th-century American art, particularly Southwestern. $5 New Mexico adults, $7 nonresidents, Fri. evening free, Sun. free for New Mexico residents.

Institute of American Indian Arts Museum (595-983-8900), 108 Cathedral Pl., Santa Fe. Open summer Mon.–Sat. 9–5, Sun. 10–5. Winter Mon.–Sat. 10–5, Sun. noon–5. Some of the best-known names in Indian art, including Allan Houser, Fritz Scholder, and T. C. Cannon, were students or teachers at IAIA. The museum houses a large collection of contemporary Indian art and demonstrates the vitality and innovation of these artists. $4 adults, $2 seniors and students, under 16 free.

THE ALTAR SCREEN AT EL RANCHO DE LAS GOLONDRINAS IS A FOLK ART CLASSIC.

MEET THE GROWERS AT THE SANTA FE FARMERS MARKET.

FARMERS' MARKETS **Santa Fe Farmers Market** (505-938-4098; www.santafe farmersmarket.com), 607 Cerrillos Rd., Ste. F, Santa Fe. Apr.–Nov. Sat. and Tues. 7–noon. The new 10,000-square-foot Market Hall with year-round vending plus summer outdoor sales adjacent is up and running in the Railyard.

GALLERIES **Shidoni Foundry and Galleries** (505-988-8001), Bishop's Lodge Rd., 5 miles north of Santa Fe. This 8-acre sculpture garden in the lush Tesuque River Valley is internationally known. Bronze pourings are on Sat. afternoons— call for times.

Gerald Peters (505-954-5700), 1011 Paseo de Peralta, Santa Fe. This international gallery, which is really a museum in its own right, contains classic Western and Taos Society artists plus contemporary realistic and minimalist work, as well as photography and sculpture. The gallery itself is worth a visit.

Victoria Price Art & Design (505-982-8632), 1512 Pacheco St., Bldg. B, Santa Fe. *Fresh* is the word here, with contemporary new art, home furnishings, and exhibitions on display.

Davis Mather Folk Art (505-983-1660), 141 Lincoln Ave., Santa Fe. One of the best collections of New Mexico animal woodcarvings and Mexican folk art resides in this small corner gallery.

Pachamama (505-983-4020), 223 Canyon Rd., Santa Fe. You can find something affordable here among this colorful collection of folk art from Latin America.

GOLF **Marty Sanchez Links de Santa Fe** (505-955-4400), 205 Caja Del Rio, Santa Fe. Open year-round, weather permitting, this public course offers a tremendous variety of golfing experiences, including an 18-hole championship course, driving range, and PGA-certified instructors. $43.

HIKING, CROSS-COUNTRY SKIING, SNOWSHOEING, AND MOUNTAIN BIKING An extensive system of trails that serve hikers and mountain bikers in warmer weather become cross-country trails when snow falls.

Dale Ball Trails (505-955-2103). This relatively new trail system, better than 14 miles round-trip, may be accessed most conveniently right in town at Canyon Rd. and Cerro Gordo as well as on NM 475 at Sierra del Norte. The bike trail is about 7 miles of single-track intermediate riding through the foothills of the Sangre de Cristos. The trail is generally easy but becomes more challenging as you go up the mountain.

Chamisa Trail. Six miles north from the Plaza on Ski Basin Rd. This is always a pleasant, as well as accessible and easy, 4.75-mile round-trip hike through rolling meadows.

Aspen Vista Trail. Easily the most popular trial in the Santa Fe area, the moderate 10-mile Aspen Vista is especially memorable in fall when the aspens are changing. It is at the top of Ski Basin Rd., 13 miles from town.

Borrego Trail. A 4-mile enjoyable, slightly more challenging, but still easy round-trip hike on only a few miles beyond the Chamisa Trail. It can be crowded on the weekend.

HORSEBACK RIDING **Bishop's Lodge** (505-983-6377), Bishop's Lodge Rd., Santa Fe. Two-hour guided trail rides within the lodge's 1,000-acre grounds start at 10:30 and 2 most days. Closed Sun. Call for reservations.

LECTURES **Lannan Foundation** (505-986-8160; www.lensic.com), 309 Read St., Santa Fe. The popular Lannan "Readings & Conversations" literary series on occasional Wed. evenings Sept.–May at the Lensic Theater brings in national and international literary stars to read and discuss their work. Tickets go fast. $6–15.

MUSIC **Santa Fe Chamber Music Festival** (505-982-1890; www.santafe chambermusic.org). Season: July–Aug. One of Santa Fe's biggest draws, the festival brings in foremost composers and musicians to play classical, jazz, folk, and world music.

Santa Fe Concert Association (505-984-8759; www.musicone.org). Season: Sept.–May. Since 1931 Santa Fe's oldest music organization has been bringing outstanding musicians from all over the world to perform a repertoire of classical and modern concert music.

Santa Fe Desert Chorale (505-988-2282; www.desertchorale.org). Season: July–Aug. and Christmas. One of the few professional choruses in the United States, the chorale performs a great many 20th-century works, as well as major music from all periods, particularly Renaissance and Baroque.

Santa Fe Opera (505-986-5900; www.santafeopera.org). Seven miles north of Santa Fe on US 285. Season: July 9 PM, Aug. 8:30 PM. Each season of the premier summer opera festival in the United States features an ambitious repertoire that usually includes unknown or new operas as well as popular standards and a revived masterpiece. The opera's mystique is amplified by its elegant amphitheater, now roofed, and the acoustics. Bring a warm coat and blankets; temperatures plummet after dark.

Santa Fe Pro Musica (505-988-4640; www.santafepromusica.com). Most special are the Christmas-season Baroque ensemble concerts played on period instruments.

Santa Fe Symphony Orchestra and Chorus (505-983-3530; www.sf-symphony .org). The symphony performs various concerts at the Lensic Theater.

RAILROADING **Santa Fe Southern Railway** (505-989-8600), 410 Guadalupe St., Santa Fe. Open year-round with excursions from two to four hours. Ride the rails to Lamy and enjoy scenic and holiday train events, including Friday Evening High Desert Highball and Saturday Evening BBQ trains that operate May–Oct.

THEATER **Greer Garson Theater** (505-473-6511), College of Santa Fe. Season: May–Sept. The Drama Department of the College of Santa Fe stages four plays each season in a theater named for the department's benefactor, who owned a ranch near Santa Fe. Each season usually includes a drama, comedy, musical, and a classic. The caliber of this student work is often up to professional standards.

Santa Fe Playhouse (505-988-4262), 142 E. De Vargas St., Santa Fe. Season: year-round. Founded in the 1920s by writer Mary Austin as the Santa Fe Community Theater, it remains the longest-running theater group in New Mexico, now at home in an intimate adobe theater in one of the city's oldest neighborhoods. A favorite each fall is the *Fiesta Melodrama*, a spoof staged the week of La Fiesta.

SPAS

Spaterre at Inn and Spa at Loretto (505-984-7997), 211 Old Santa Fe Trail, Santa Fe. Emphasizing the local indigenous herbs and minerals, this spa features exquisite cross-cultural modalities of Indonesian and Thai rituals, some to celebrate life passages. This is pampering to the max. $125–225.

RockResorts Spa, La Posada (505-986-0000), 330 E. Palace Ave., Santa Fe. Let's face it, Santa Fe is a city with some great, great spas. This one may not be the most aesthetically posh, but it sets the standard on service. You can choose from a menu that includes a Chocolate-Chile Wrap and a Rolling Thunder Massage; however, the River Stones hot rock treatment will, I promise, move you forward on the path of enlightenment. Pricey, but you get what you pay for. $125–200.

10,000 Waves Japanese Spa and Resort (505-982-9304), 3451 Hyde Park Rd., Santa Fe. Open daily 9:15–9:30. A 10-minute drive up Hyde Park Rd. is an exquisite Japanese bath-style spa that is a world of its own. It is considered a romantic, sensual date experience. There are public and private hot tubs and men's and women's scheduled tub hours, and patrons stroll about in fluffy white robes sipping herbal tea. Hourly tub rates are reduced for anyone with a New Mexico driver's license and for frequent users. It is a lovely experience but can be quite expensive, and, more to the point, the water temperature can be way too hot to allow for languorous soaking. Limited lodging is available in The Houses of the Moon by reservation. $32 hour basic tub rate.

Body (505-986-0362), 333 Cordova Rd., Santa Fe. Open daily 7 AM–9 PM. This place has it all: massage, movement, yoga, Pilates, organic and GMO-free café and spa, plus child care and children's and family classes.

Absolute Nirvana Spa, Tea Room, & Gardens (505-983-7942), 106 E. Faithway St., Santa Fe. Named one of the hot new spas by *Condé-Nast Traveler,* this is the place to purify and calm the body and mind with a range of Asian spa rituals. $90 on up.

SCHOOLS AND CLASSES Santa Fe School of Cooking & Market (505-983-4511), 116 W. San Francisco St., Santa Fe. Want to learn how to make a great salsa or serve an entire dinner of Southwestern cuisine? This is the place to learn from well-known chefs.

Santa Fe Photographic Workshops (505-983-1400). Workshops in all aspects of photography, taught by photographers of national and international repute, some abroad year-round.

Ghost Ranch at Santa Fe (505-982-8539), 401 Old Taos Hwy., Santa Fe. Classes and seminars, and Elderhostel programs, on history, arts, and New Mexicana are offered here year-round.

SKIING Ski Santa Fe (505-982-4429; 1-877-737-7366 for reservations), 16 miles northeast of Santa Fe on NM 475. Open Thanksgiving–early Apr. This is the reason why so many people love Santa Fe. With a base elevation of 10,350 feet and a 12,075-foot summit, this ski area is geared to appeal to every member of the family and is as fine a place to learn, as it can be thrilling. It also has packages for beginners, freestyle terrain, and multiday ticket bargains. Reservations are required for the adaptive ski program for both the physically and mentally challenged (505-995-9858; www.adaptiveski.org). $70–92.

WALKING TOURS Museum of Fine Arts (505-476-5072). Art walking tours of Santa Fe Apr.–Nov., Mon. at 10 AM. $10, under 18 free.

Palace of the Governors (505-476-5109). Daily at 10:15 except Sun. Two-hour historic walking tours conducted by the Friends of the Palace. Meet at the blue gate on Lincoln Ave. side of the Palace of the Governors. $10, under 17 free. No tipping.

Aboot About Santa Fe Walks (505-988-2774), various locations. This two-hour walking tour promises a total immersion with well-informed guides. No reservations required. $10, senior discount, under 12 free.

Historic Walks of Santa Fe (505-986-8388), La Fonda Hotel. Daily at 9:45 AM, 1:15 PM. No reservations required. Professional museum docent guides specialize in the history of Santa Fe landmarks. $12, senior discounts, under 12 free.

WINERIES Santa Fe Vineyards (505-753-8100), 20 miles north of Santa Fe on US 285. Since 1982, the Rosingana family has been producing award-winning vintages. Open daily. Closed major holidays.

Balagna Winery (505-672-3678), 223 Rio Bravo Dr., White Rock. Open Mon.–Sun. noon–6. Closed Mon. Sip fine wines above the clouds.

✳ Green Space

Bandelier National Monument (505-672-3861), 46 miles west of Santa Fe on US 285 north to Pojoaque, west on NM 502, south on NM 4. Open daily, year-round. Closed Christmas and New Year's. Summer 8–6, winter 8–4:30. Ruins trails open dawn 'til dusk. Tucked deep into a canyon on the Pajarito Plateau is the ancestral home of many Pueblo tribes that was occupied A.D. 1100–1550.

AT BANDELIER NATIONAL MONUMENT, YOU CAN CLIMB INTO AN ANCIENT CLIFF DWELLING.

You can climb among the cliff dwellings and view village ruins and ceremonial kivas. The loop trail of Frijoles Canyon ruins is an easy one-hour walk. Rangers offer "night walks" during the summer. There are more rigorous hikes out here, which you can learn about at the visitor center. $10 per car, $10 camping.

Valles Caldera National Preserve (1-866-382-5537), 40 miles northwest of Santa Fe. Continue on NM 4 past Bandelier about 15 miles. This vast, astonishing green basin—all that remains of what was once the world's largest volcano—is believed to be part of an 89,000-acre caldera, a basin formed during Pleistocene volcanic activity. Located on a 42-year-old land grant named Baca Location No. 1, it is also called the Valle Grande or Baca Location and is home to a herd of 45,000 elk. Since the area was named one of the country's newest national monuments, hiking, cross-country skiing, fly-fishing, mountain biking, night sky adventures, wildlife viewing, and hunting have become available for various fees on a reservations-only basis. It is managed with the goal of having it pay for itself. Variable fees.

Hyde Memorial State Park (505-983-7175), 8 miles northeast of Santa Fe via Hyde Park Rd. Open daily 8 AM–11 PM. Forested with aspens and evergreens, this easily accessed park is close enough for an afternoon hike or even a long lunchtime walk. In warm weather, the almost 4-mile Hyde Park Loop Trail provides stunning views of the Sangre de Cristo Mountains, although the first third of the trail is quite steep and attention must be paid to finding the correct return path. In winter, this is a close-in cross-country skiing, snowshoeing, and tubing area. Find the trailhead in back of the visitor center. $5 day use, $8–18 camping.

Ft. Marcy–Magers Field and Complex (505-955-2500), 490 Washington Ave., Santa Fe. Fitness complex including pool is open Mon.–Fri. 6 AM–8:30 PM, Sat. 8–6:30, Sun. 10–6. This facility has picnic tables, tennis court, baseball field, indoor swimming pool, fitness room, a parcourse, and well-used walking paths. Variable fees, quite reasonable.

Frank Ortiz Park, 160 Camino de las Crucitas, Santa Fe, is a popular dog park where pets can run free.

Santa Fe National Forest (505-753-7331), 1474 Rodeo Rd., Santa Fe. This truly vast national forest, measuring 16 million acres, includes much of the most beautiful scenery in northern New Mexico. It holds four wilderness areas: Pecos, San Pedro Parks, Dome, and Chama River Canyon, and three Wild and Scenic River areas: 11 miles of the East Fork of the Jemez (great for cross-country skiing), 24.6 miles of the Rio Chama, and 20.5 miles of the Pecos River, plus over 1,000 miles of trails accessible to horses, hikers, and mountain bikes, as well as four-wheel-drive vehicles. Close to Santa Fe is the Black Canyon Campground, northeast on NM 475 and convenient to the Borrego Trail.

✳ Lodging

BED AND BREAKFASTS, MOTELS, AND HOTELS ♿ **El Rey Inn** (505-982-1931), 1862 Cerrillos Rd., Santa Fe. This classic 1937 Route 66 motel gets high marks on several counts: convenient location, lovely landscaping, and classic Route-66-circa-1935, Southwest style; however, when I have stayed there, I found the antiquated heating system noisy enough to wake me at 3 AM. Many of the 87 rooms have flagstone floors and exposed vigas; 20 have fireplaces. There is a heated pool and indoor and outdoor hot tubs. Perhaps the passive-solar rooms might deliver a peaceful night. Or just bring your earplugs. This is an in-demand place, so book early. $84–140.

& "1" **La Fonda Hotel** (505-982-5511), 100 E. San Francisco St., Santa Fe. There's been an inn of some sort on the southeast corner of the Plaza for almost 400 years. La Fonda is still the only hotel on the Plaza, and no other can match its rich past. The dark, old-fashioned lobby with its INDIAN DETOURS sign, the clubby bar, the lovely La Plazuela restaurant with its colorful hand-painted glass, and the French Pastry Shop designed by Mary Elizabeth Jane Colter (designer for the Fred Harvey Hotels) all conspire to trick you into thinking you have time-traveled back into Santa Fe's past. Swimming pool, hot tubs, and spa are on-site, and La Fonda now features 14 "nontoxic" suites for environmentally sensitive guests. $219–319.

& "1" **Inn and Spa at Loretto** (505-988-5531), 211 Old Santa Fe Tr., Santa Fe. Built in 1975 on the site of Loretto Academy, a 19th-century girls' school, this inn's terraced architecture is modeled after Taos Pueblo. With 134 rooms, it includes a swimming pool, a bar with live entertainment, and a restaurant, Baleen. There is a deluxe spa on the premises, where you can reduce your stress pronto. An automatic $10 plus tax "hotel fee" is added to each day of your bill to pay for gratuities, newspaper, Wi-Fi, and the like. $249–340.

& "1" **Garrett's Desert Inn** (505-982-1851), 311 Old Santa Fe Tr., Santa Fe. Location, location, location. This place is pretty basic, not unpleasantly so, just not very imaginative in a city of romantic lodgings, but it is situated exactly where you want to be, in about two blocks' walking distance of the Plaza and other attractions. You will pay for the convenience of one of these plain 83 rooms. Note: there's an $8 a day parking fee. $67–149.

� **Santa Fe Motel** (505-982-1039), 510 Cerrillos Rd., Santa Fe. If you are looking for an attractive, affordable motel downtown, this one is set far enough off a busy intersection to have an air of seclusion. In addition to typical motel rooms, it includes 10 adobe casitas with refrigerator, microwave, and patio entrance. Across the street, kitchenettes are available. Many will find this an excellent value. Plus, a complimentary full breakfast is included. $79–134.

La Posada de Santa Fe (505-986-0000), 330 E. Palace Ave., Santa Fe. A 19th-century mansion, known as the Staab House and built by 19th-century pioneer merchant Abraham Staab, a complex of Pueblo-style casitas, and six acres of huge cottonwoods and fruit trees are some of the features of this unusual inn. The casitas have classic New Mexican décor: adobe fireplaces, hand-painted tiles, Indian rugs, and skylights. Guests enjoy a good-sized swimming pool and lovely courtyard for drinking and dining in nice weather. It is now a RockResort. The restaurant, Fuego, achieved a Four Diamond rating. $109–274.

Water Street Inn (505-984-1193), 427 Water St., Santa Fe. This handsomely restored adobe B&B has an air of romantic intimacy. It is hidden away on a side street within strolling distance of downtown. The 12 rooms are spacious with brick floors and four-poster beds. Most have a fireplace; some have private patios with fountains. Sunset views from the upstairs balcony are splendid, and hot hors d'oeuvres are served with New Mexican wines at cocktail hour. $150–185.

Inn of the Anasazi (505-988-3030), 113 Washington Ave., Santa Fe. This striking 57-room hotel is as close to the Plaza as you can get without landing on a bench there. It is done in classic Pueblo Revival style, with viga and latilla ceilings throughout, stone floors and walls, and a beautiful flagstone waterfall. Exquisite simplicity highlights the fine local artwork. Service is tops, as are on-site business services: staff will bring an exercise bike to your room or rent you a mountain bike. Offering the best sense of peace and privacy money can buy, this small luxury hotel continues to reign as the city's most chic address for visitors. It rates as Santa Fe's only Four Star, Four Diamond hotel, with a fine restaurant on-site. $239–349.

LODGES, INNS, AND RANCHES &

Galisteo Inn (505-466-4000), 9 La Vega, Galisteo. This exquisitely restored inn, at once so strong with its thick adobe walls, highly polished wood floors, and wooden beams, and so fragile, with its living legacy of history, is the ideal getaway, with a sparkling blue swimming pool, restaurant, and outside bar with kiva fireplace. There's also a sauna, bubbling jetted tub, massage, and exhilarating horseback rides and mountain bikes. $155–185.

☁ & Inn on the Alameda (505-984-2121), 303 E. Alameda, Santa Fe. This two-room inn across the street from the Santa Fe River feels a lot smaller than it is, due perhaps to the individual private courtyards surrounding rooms. (You will pay extra for a balcony.) It has two hot tubs, exercise room, full-service bar, and comfortable sitting rooms. The morning fare is a buffet breakfast feast. $125–215.

The Inn at Sunrise Springs (505-471-3600), 242 Los Pinos Rd., La Cienega. This lovely, secluded 70-acre resort a few miles south of Santa Fe in the old community of La Cienega features two spring-fed ponds, exquisite landscaping, two hot tubs, a pond, and a junior-Olympic-sized outdoor swimming pool, plus the Blue Heron restaurant. Each room has a balcony and patio—casitas have mini-kitchenette and fireplace—for a total of 60 accommodations. Classes and workshops in yoga, clay, and the Japanese tea ceremony make this a place to relax and retreat thoroughly. $90–145.

Bishop's Lodge (505-983-6377), Bishop's Lodge Rd., Santa Fe. Bishop Jean Baptiste Lamy, the model for Willa Cather's classic *Death Comes for the Archbishop*, chose this magnificent spot in the foothills of the Sangre de Cristo Range for his retirement and getaway home and garden a century ago. The lodge is activity- and family-oriented. Horseback riding, tennis, swimming, trap and skeet shooting, and fishing are available in-season on 1,000 acres. The rooms have a distinctly New Mexico flavor, and the restaurant offers a fine Sunday brunch. Best of all, there's still an air of serenity here, and Lamy's private chapel stands untouched. A new spa makes the place complete. $149–449.

CABINS AND CAMPING Rancheros de Santa Fe Campground (505-466-3482), 736 Old Las Vegas Hwy. Open Mar. 15–Oct. 31. Cabins, RV sites, full hookups, pool, tent sites—in short, whatever your travel style, it can be accommodated here. $20–30.

Santa Fe Skies RV Park (505-473-5946; www.santafeskiesrvpark.com), 14 Browncastle Ranch. One mile off I-25 at southeast end of NM 599 on the Turquoise Trail. Open year-round. A comfortable stop for RVers with modem hookups, too, this park boasts views of four mountain ranges. $30.

Santa Fe National Forest (505-438-7840). Open May 15–Sept. 30. Two campgrounds in the Santa Fe area are Aspen Basin and Big Tesuque, each about 12 miles northeast of Santa Fe on NM 475. Both grounds offer RV sites with no hookups and tent sites. $10.

Hyde Memorial State Park (505-983-7175), 740 Hyde Park Rd. Open year-round. Tent sites and RV hookups are available here. $8–18.

✳ Where to Eat

DINING OUT Café Pasqual's (505-983-9340), 121 Don Gaspar, Santa Fe. Open daily. Closed Thanksgiving, Christmas. Breakfast, lunch, dinner. Is it fair to have a favorite place to eat in Santa Fe, when there are so many great possibilities? I could well vote for Pasqual's, named for the saint of the kitchen, owned and operated by Kathy Kagel, organizer of a food distribution system that feeds the hun-

gry. Consistently on the list of "Ten Best Places to Have Breakfast in the United States," the huge, delicious, Mexican (from Mexico) breakfast is served all day. If you arrive in the off hours, you have a better chance of avoiding the line around Water St. Emphasis here is on flavorful organic and natural foods; Genovese omelet with sun-dried tomatoes and pine nuts, grilled salmon burrito, toasted piñon ice cream with caramel sauce. And it's fun to sit at the community table. Moderate–Expensive.

The Compound (505-982-4353; www.compoundrestaurant.com), 653 Canyon Rd., Santa Fe. Chef-owner Mark Kiffin revived this Canyon Rd. grande dame with its Alexander Girard–designed white interior. The art of service has been perfected here. Food as entertainment on the grand scale is to be expected. The beautiful people, dressed to the nines, nibbling designer Continental dishes concocted from ingredients air-freighted in from all over the world— it is truly to die for. Sweetbreads and foie gras, grilled lamb rib eye, blue corn dusted soft-shell crabs, and liquid chocolate cake for dessert. If you have one special splurge on your visit to Santa Fe, make your reservation here. Very Expensive.

Rio Chama Steakhouse (505-955-0765), 414 Old Santa Fe Tr., Santa Fe. Open daily. Closed Christmas. Lunch, dinner. Forget the cholesterol. Try this instead: prime dry-aged beef, succulent rib eyes and filets and Black Angus prime rib, house-made onion rings, rich creamed spinach, and shrimp cocktail. The blue cheese–green chile burgers are dripping with decadence and irresistible. Add in a full bar, and you've got a real meal going. Two can have lunch for under $30, but overall, expensive.

Coyote Café and Cantina (505-983-1615), 132 W. Water St., Santa Fe. The granddaddy of all nouvelle Southwestern cuisine, pioneered by anthropologist-turned-chef Mark Miller, still serves inspired dishes that blend native ingredients with sophisticated flavors. Miller has moved on, and famed Geronimo chef Eric de Stefano has taken the helm as chef-owner. In warm weather, the light-hearted rooftop patio serves reasonably priced simpler, but still delicious, fare, with Mexican beer, margaritas, and more. Very Expensive.

Geronimo (505-982-1500), 724 Canyon Rd., Santa Fe. Open daily. Lunch, dinner. Closed Mon. lunch. Housed in one of the city's finest historic adobes, this restaurant is the last word in minimalist Santa Fe elegance. The menu consists of American staples updated with Southwestern and other ethnic ingredients, but we aren't exactly sure where the place is headed without its former chef, who has moved on to the Coyote Café. Try lunch or Sun. brunch if you are trying to stay in budget. Very Expensive.

EATING OUT The Shed (505-982-9030), 113½ E. Palace Ave., Santa Fe. Open Mon.–Sat. Lunch dinner. Closed Sun. Located in an adobe dating from 1692 and tucked away in an enclosed patio, The Shed is a landmark where you can count on consistently delicious chile, ground on the premises. Colorful Southwestern décor adds to the fun of eating here. Selections of fish and beef are also available. Take a seat by a corner fireplace in winter, or on the patio on a summer night with a glass of wine,

and you know you can only be in one place, the capital of the Land of Enchantment. Moderate.

🍴 **Del Charro** (505-954-0320), 101 W. Alameda, at the Inn of the Governors. Open daily 11:30–midnight. They said it couldn't be done. However, at Del Charro you can find a very good, not gourmet, bargain lunch, in the $5 range, that might be a burger, enchilada, or cream of mushroom soup. Homemade fries, too. Choose from a bright, airy atmosphere or go directly to the bar. Inexpensive.

Maria's New Mexican Kitchen (505-983-7929), 555 W. Cordova Rd., Santa Fe. Open daily. Lunch, dinner. Closed Thanksgiving, Christmas. With over a half-century in the same location, Maria's is a Santa Fe classic that continues to draw crowds of all ages. You can watch the experts make fresh tortillas by hand. Sizzling fajitas, authentic green chile stew, and the classic blue corn–red chile enchiladas —you can't go wrong. Fresh guacamole on the side and scrumptious flan are a couple of other specialties. Owner Al Lucero has written a definitive book about margaritas, and his bartenders can concoct over 70 different kinds. You can order dinner in the bar. Moderate.

Plaza Café (505-982-1664), 54 Lincoln Ave., Santa Fe. Open daily for breakfast, lunch, and dinner. When you're out and about and looking for a bite, this is the place, with its black-and-white tile floor and old-timey counter service. You can count on excellent enchiladas, sopaipillas, diner food, salads, Greek food, and chicken fried steak, all served as consistently and efficiently as they have been since 1918, making this the oldest restaurant in town.

JOY! A DINNER OF ENCHILADAS AND SOPAIPILLAS IN SANTA FE.

San Francisco St. Bar & Grill: An American Bistro (505-982-2044), southwest corner of the Plaza at San Francisco St. and Don Gaspar. Open daily 11 AM–close. Lunch, dinner. Go upstairs to find a reasonably priced and well-varied menu of salads, sandwiches, and fresh fare that is bound to have something please any appetite. Moderate.

Santa Fe Bar & Grill (505-982-3033; www.santafebargrill.com), southwest corner DeVargas Center. Open daily. Lunch 11–5, dinner 5–10, Sun. brunch 11–3. Casual and warm, the place that comes to mind when you can't think where to go to meet a friend for dinner or have a business lunch where you can talk. The shopping center parking lot makes it a convenient stop. Love the fish tacos with black beans, but the menu has everything from swell burgers to enchiladas and lives up to the motto, "creative southwest cuisine." Inexpensive–Moderate.

Tia Sophia's (505-983-9880), 210 W. San Francisco St., Santa Fe. Open Mon.–Sat. 7:30–2. Closed. Sun. and major holidays. Breakfast, lunch. Located in the heart of San Francisco St., this is an unassuming little restaurant that serves consistently good New Mexican meals in a family atmosphere. The breakfast burritos and huevos rancheros, with red chile that has a kick, are worth ordering, and for lunch, try one of the homemade stuffed sopaipillas. Inexpensive.

Tecolote Café (505-988-1362), 1203 Cerrillos Rd., Santa Fe. Justifiably famous for breakfast, Tecolote serves delicious low-cholesterol alternatives to its heaping helping of French toast and fresh-baked muffins.

Counter Culture (505-995-1105), 930 Baca St., Santa Fe. The hip, the pierced, the tattooed, the artistic, and even their parents agree on the homemade fries and Asian soups of the eclectic menu served here. This little Baca St. neighborhood is sometimes called "the SoHo of Santa Fe" for its galleries, jewelry shops, and slightly edgy atmosphere. Inexpensive.

Pantry Restaurant (505-986-0022), 1820 Cerrillos Rd., Santa Fe. How about homemade corned beef hash (best in town), fresh-baked biscuits and gravy, pancakes stuffed with fruit and whipped cream, and endless cups of coffee, in a completely unpretentious spot that locals adore for good food and reasonable prices? Sit at the counter or grab a table. Inexpensive.

Guadalupe Café (505-982-9762), 422 Old Santa Fe Tr., Santa Fe. Open Mon.–Sat. Closed Mon. Breakfast, lunch, and dinner. Either arrive hungry or be prepared to split a main dish. New Mexican food, but don't ask for the chile on the side. The salads are humongous. Absolutely the best cinnamon rolls, too, big as pie plates. Moderate.

Tesuque Village Market (505-988-8848), junction of Bishop's Lodge Rd. and Tesuque Village Rd., Tesuque. Open daily 7–10. Wood-fired pizza, organic and all natural meats, fabulous blue corn pancakes, amazing homemade pies and decadent chocolate desserts, and boutique wine and rare tequila selections are all here at this neighborhood hangout with heated outdoor seating. Cowboys, artists, Hollywood types, and the president of the rose society are all at home here. Moderate.

Cowgirl Hall of Fame Bar-B-Que (505-982-2565), 319 S. Guadalupe, Santa Fe. Open daily. Closed Thanksgiving, Christmas. This place is known as much, if not more, as a hopping watering hole than as a restaurant. The décor is old-time cowgirl memorabilia. The specialty is the mesquite-smoked barbeque, but beside all the meat are vegetarian chile and butternut casserole. Try the the signature dessert, the Baked Potato, which is actually a chocolate sundae disguised as a spud, or just have the peach cobbler. Moderate.

Horseman's Haven Café (505-471-5420), 4354 Cerrillos Rd., Santa Fe. Despite spiffy new digs that make diners nostalgic for the old days in the gas station when the winter wind blew through every time the door opened, the Haven still serves what is probably the hottest chile in town.

Bobcat Bite (505-983-5317), 420 Old Las Vegas Hwy., Santa Fe. Open Tues.–Sat. Lunch, dinner. Closes by 7:50 PM. *Bon Appetit* named the burgers at Bobcat Bite the "best in America." But don't expect anything fancy at this teensy out-of-the-way lunch counter. Inexpensive.

COFFEE AND TEA HOUSES (Check the hours before you go—they can vary.)

Canyon Road Teahouse (505-992-0972), 821 Canyon Rd., Santa Fe. The aesthetic is Zen, the tea choices are in the dozens, and Tara's ice cream is creamy, organic, and comes in outrageous flavors like mango ginger, saffron, and chocolate tarragon. Many are fans of the serious porridge served here for breakfast. Inexpensive.

Downtown Subscription (505-983-3085), 376 Garcia St., Santa Fe. Good for browsing the shelves of magazines and newspapers, good for coffee, and good for hanging out on the informal patio. Inexpensive.

Ohori's Coffee & Tea (505-988-7026), 507 Old Santa Fe Tr., Santa Fe. For serious coffee drinkers, please. Coffee is what it's all about here. The beans are fresh roasted, and a different coffee is brewed every time the urn is emptied. Inexpensive.

❝❞ **Aztec Café** (505-820-0025), 317 Aztec St., Santa Fe. Here are homemade soups to warm a winter day and Sarah's homemade ice cream for a summer treat. Strong coffee, fresh baked goods, and substantial sandwiches, plus Wi-Fi, make this a longtime favorite hangout. The ambience is hip, but not tragically so. Inexpensive.

❝❞ **Santa Fe Baking Co. Cafe** (505-988-4294), 504 W. Cordova Rd., Santa Fe. Open Mon.–Sat. 6–8, Sun. 6–6. Breakfast, lunch, dinner. Read the paper; check your e-mail on the free Wi-Fi; go for a breakfast of bacon and eggs, served all day; or drool over the pastry counter. Everyone else does! Inexpensive.

French Pastry Shop (505-983-6697), 100 E. San Francisco St., Santa Fe. Just the place for a slice of quiche, fresh strawberry crêpe, or a chocolate éclair and a latte. 'Tis as French as a morning on the Rive Gauche. Inexpensive.

Chocolate Maven Bakery & Café (505-984-1980), 821 San Mateo, Unit C, Santa Fe. Monster chocolate croissants and unbelievable sandwiches make this one popular spot, but parking is hellacious, and you have to brave the crowds before you get to a tiny table. Inexpensive.

✳ Entertainment

You can hear live music on various nights at the Santa Fe hot spots below:

Second Street Brewery (505-982-3030), 1814 Second St. An award-winning microbrewery, this is a relaxed pub serving fish and chips, soups, and salads, with live weekend entertainment. **Eldorado Court & Lounge** (505-988-4455), 309 W. San Francisco St., has flamenco on weekends and a piano bar during the week. **Evangelo's** (505-982-9015), 200 W. San Francisco St., offers live country, jazz, and rock bands Fri.–Sat. nights. **La Café Sena Cantina** (505-988-9232), 125 E. Palace Ave., has waitstaff who belt out Broadway musical tunes. **Vanessie of Santa Fe** (505-982-9966), 434 W. San Francisco St., has a cocktail lounge atmosphere and live piano nightly. **La Fonda's La Fiesta Lounge** (505-982-5511), 100 E. San Francisco St., is a favorite of locals and visitors, with country dancing on the intimate dance floor plus jazz and flamenco on various evenings. **El Farol** (505-983-9912), 808 Canyon Rd., Santa Fe's oldest restaurant and cantina, also has nightly live entertainment in summer. In winter, there are salsa lessons followed by Cuban music on Wed. nights and world music Sun. evenings. **Green Onion** (505-983-5198), 1851 St. Michael's Dr. If you want to see what real locals look like, come on over to this sports bar with big-screen TVs that serves home cooking with plenty of meat, mashed potatoes, and gravy. **Tiny's Restaurant and Lounge** (505-983-9817), 1015 Pen Rd. Open daily. Closed Sun., except during football season. The lounge is the heart and soul of Tiny's, where you can get great carne adovada, chicken guacamole tacos, and posole. Here is where country and western meets Frank Sinatra. Live entertainment Thurs.–Sun. and dancing on weekends. It is a time capsule that never changes.

Lensic Performing Arts Center (505-988-1234; www.lensic.com; www.ticketssantafe.org), 211 W. San Francisco St., Santa Fe. Built originally as a grand motion picture palace, the 1930 Lensic is a fantastic creation in a faux Moorish-Renaissance style and boasts a silver chandelier from New York's Roxy in the lobby, along with the crests of Santa Fe's founding families. State-of-the-art sound equipment makes this a popular performing venue for an extraordinary variety of events, including Aspen Santa Fe Ballet, Big Screen Classics, and Live from the Met.

Maria Benitez Teatro Flamenco (505-982-1237), 750 N. St. Francis Dr., Santa Fe. June–Sept. No one who has seen diva Maria Benitez perform her passionate versions of flamenco can forget her powerful energy.

✳ Selective Shopping

Silver Sun (505-983-8743), 656 Canyon Rd., Santa Fe. Offering jewelry from 25 turquoise mines for over 30 years, Silver Sun promises that what is sold here is the finest quality, and you will receive reliable, informed guidance. Prices are fair (not cheap), and there are sales. Look in back.

Back at the Ranch Cowboy Boots (505-989-8110), 209 E. Marcy St., Santa Fe. You might actually go ga-ga when you look upon the fabulous selection of wild and fanciful cowboy boots. Expect to blow the budget on a lifetime purchase.

Lucille's (505-983-6331), 223 Galisteo St., Santa Fe. This store is hung from floor to ceiling with racks crammed full of soft, loose, ethnic-y dresses and separates in rayon, cotton, and other breathable fabrics. You can get a broomstick skirt here, for sure. It's moderately priced and has a good selection of roomy, larger sizes.

Palace of the Governors Portal (no phone), north block of the Plaza. Open daily. One of the best places in town to shop for traditional Indian jewelry is beneath the portal of the Governors' Palace. Here prices are reasonable for a huge array of guaranteed authentic handmade Indian wares.

Purple Sage (505-954-0600), 110 Don Gaspar, Santa Fe. When a Santa Fe woman wants to splurge on a special-occasion outfit, she is likely to go to the Purple Sage for an ensemble in their luscious hand-woven and hand-painted fabrics.

Santa Fe Flea Market (no phone), 10 miles north of Santa Fe on US 84/285. Open seasonally Fri.–Sun. 8–5. Although not the bargain-hunter's paradise this once was, the market, now operated by Tesuque Pueblo, still has a vast display of leather goods, jewelry, furniture, masks, and so much more. Buyer beware.

Santa Fe Design Center (no phone), 418 Cerrillos Rd., Santa Fe. Here is some great browsing turf, where you can stumble upon the unexpected piece of art, furniture, or antique that makes it all worthwhile. It's also the site of some interesting ethnic eateries.

Sanbusco Market Center Mall (505-989-9390), 500 Montezuma St., Santa Fe. Located in the Railyard area, this is an indoor arcade of high-end dress, accessory, and gift shops, plus a major chain bookstore.

Santa Fe Premium Outlets (505-474-4000), 8380 Cerrillos Rd., 8 miles south of Santa Fe. More than 40 outlet stores with bargain prices on many name brands.

Jackalope (505-471-8539), 2829 Cerrillos Rd., Santa Fe. "Folk art by the truckload" is the motto here. Whether you have a yen for handmade furniture from Mexico, chile lights, or a birdbath from the more than 2 acres of imported pottery, you will have fun shopping here. There's a patio restaurant, carousel, outdoors market, and plenty to amuse you for hours.

Keishi: The Zuni Connection (505-989-8728), 227 Don Gaspar, Santa Fe. For the best selection of guaranteed authentic Zuni fetishes, inlay and needlepoint jewelry, displayed brilliantly, with excellent advice, don't fool around, come here.

Doodlets Shop (505-983-3771), 120 Don Gaspar Ave., Santa Fe. A shop for kids of all ages, Doodlets stocks tin mermaids to chocolate sardines and all the postcards, stickers, Victoriana, and miniatures in between.

BOOKSTORES Ark Books (505-988-3709), 133 Romero St., Santa Fe. The New Age actually exists here, in these six rooms of books specializing in healing, world religions, magic, and mythology. Tapes, Tarot, jewelry, and incense make for a serene browse.

Collected Works (505-988-4226; www.collectedworksbookstore.com), 208-B W. San Francisco St., Santa Fe. This is the city's oldest and most complete independent bookstore. Check the calendar for readings and signings.

Photo-Eye Books & Prints (505-988-5152), 376 Garcia St., Santa Fe. Self-dubbed "the world's largest photography book store"; if you can't find it, they will order it.

Garcia Street Books (505-986-0151), 376 Garcia St., Santa Fe. With such an assortment of well-selected titles, you can't possibly walk out of here without a wonderful find.

✴ Special Events

July: **Pancake Breakfast** on the Plaza (505-982-2002), July 4. **Spanish Market** (505-982-2042), Santa Fe Plaza, last weekend. A juried show of traditional Spanish Colonial artwork created by artists of Spanish descent.

International Folk Art Market (505-476-1200), Milner Plaza, Museum Hill, second weekend. **Rodeo de Santa Fe** (505-471-4300), Rodeo Grounds, Rodeo Rd., second weekend.

August: **Indian Market** (505-983-5220), Plaza. Weekend closest to Aug. 19. The world's largest sale of Native American arts.

September: **La Fiesta de Santa Fe** (1-800-777-2489) is the oldest ongoing festival in the United States; second weekend. **Thirsty Ear Festival** (505-473-5723; www.thirstyearfestival .com), Eaves Movie Ranch, first weekend. **Santa Fe Wine and Chile Fiesta** (505-438-8069; www.santafe wineandchile.org), last week.

SO MANY BOOKSTORES, SO LITTLE TIME!

November: **Santa Fe Film Festival** (505-988-5225), various venues.

December: **Winter Spanish Market** (505-982-2226), first weekend. **Christmas at the Palace** (505-476-5100), hot cider and an old-fashioned celebration at the Palace of the Governors, midmonth. **Las Posadas,** midmonth, is a reenactment of a traditional holiday play around the Plaza. **Farolitos** tour, sunset–midnight, Dec. 24.

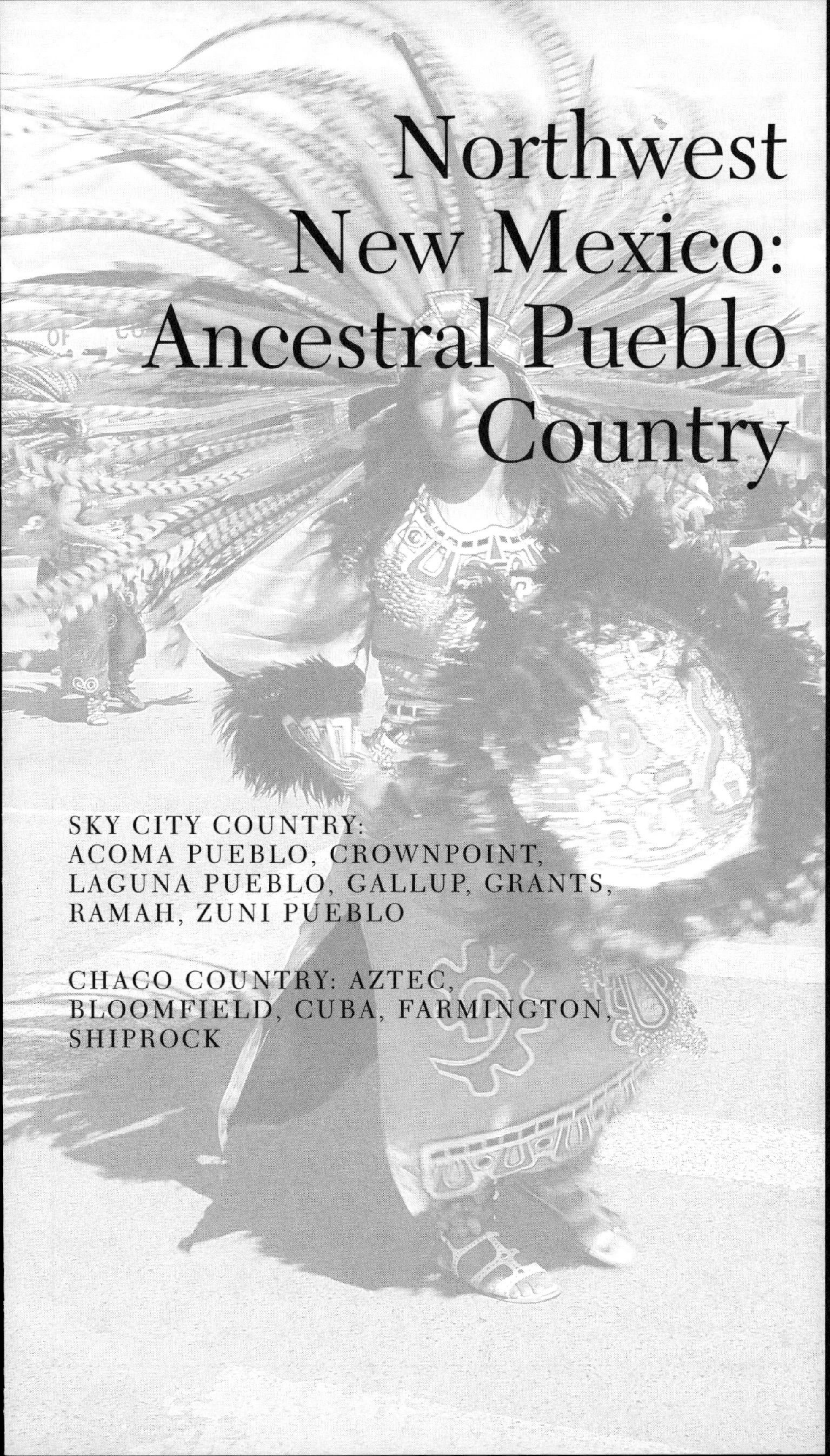

Northwest New Mexico: Ancestral Pueblo Country

5

SKY CITY COUNTRY:
ACOMA PUEBLO, CROWNPOINT,
LAGUNA PUEBLO, GALLUP, GRANTS,
RAMAH, ZUNI PUEBLO

CHACO COUNTRY: AZTEC,
BLOOMFIELD, CUBA, FARMINGTON,
SHIPROCK

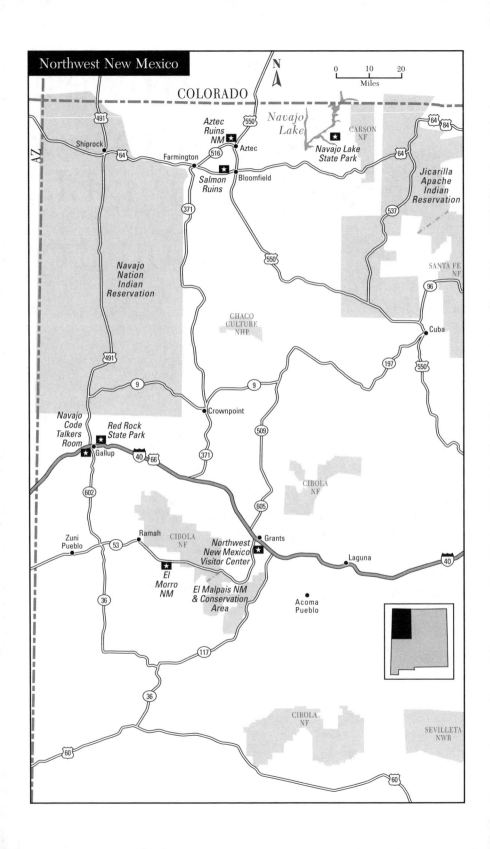

SKY CITY COUNTRY:
ACOMA PUEBLO, CROWNPOINT, LAGUNA PUEBLO, GALLUP, GRANTS, RAMAH, ZUNI PUEBLO

Taking a journey to northwest New Mexico is as close as a traveler can get to the mysteries of a civilization that thrived, then vanished, long before Europeans dreamed of setting foot on this continent. The monumental structures of Chaco Canyon, the restored Great Kiva at Aztec Ruins, and the solstice marker precise as a Swiss watch at Salmon Ruins provoke awe and wonderment in even the most worldly traveler.

The sight of these magnificent ruins raises more questions than we can answer. Was Chaco Canyon a trading or ceremonial center? Or the home of a priestly class? Were its arrow-straight roads, which lead to outliers throughout the Four Corners region, also related to religious traditions? How far did trading extend— to Mesoamerica, to the Andes? Did the inhabitants depart their homes because of drought, illness, or war? The best we can do is speculate and continue asking questions.

Once known as the Anasazi, now referred to as the Ancestral Pueblo, the people who lived here are now believed to be the forebears of contemporary New Mexico Pueblo Indians. Yet in this region one encounters, with the exceptions of Acoma, Laguna, and Zuni, not the Pueblos, but the Navajo, whose reservation extends throughout four states. For those who admire the fine weaving, silver and turquoise jewelry, and sand paintings of the Navajo, there are no better places to see these wares and shop for them than in the trading posts of Gallup and Farmington, or at the monthly Crownpoint Rug Auction.

To savvy fly-fishermen, the San Juan River outside Farmington is a holy grail, which is not to underestimate the attractions of the region for golfers, hikers, cavers, birders, and mountain bikers.

The rich, multilayered history of the exploration of the Southwest is vividly recorded on El Morro, or Inscription Rock, which bears the signs of those who passed by this water source. Petroglyphs, signatures of Spanish conquistadors, of U.S. Calvary, of homesteaders and miners, tell a centuries-old story. From the time Coronado passed through in 1540 on his search for the fabled "Seven Cities of Cibola" in his quest for gold, this harsh high-desert landscape, with its black lava, rich farming land, red buttes, and its resources of wood, coal uranium, natural gas, and oil, has held out the promise of fortunes to be made.

The name "Cibola" refers to a mythic city. In medieval Europe, a popular legend told of Seven Cities of Antilia located across the Atlantic Ocean. Spanish explorers came here searching for legendary cities, in hopes of discovering the same riches of gold as they had found in the southern hemisphere, among Mayan, Aztec, and Incan cities. In 1539, explorer Cabeza de Vaca first saw Zuni, and his report fueled Coronado's quest. Zuni was believed to be the smallest of the fabled cities.

In this region you can stand at the point where four states meet, cross the Continental Divide, witness the all-night winter ceremonial of Shalako at Zuni Pueblo, and travel long stretches of the Mother Road, Old Route 66. Many of the sights and experiences that make the West the West are found here. Best of all, these experiences can be had on a personal scale. These places remain true to themselves. They are not overwhelmed with or by tourism, but somehow manage to absorb visitors in a comfortable fashion, still moving at their own pace. While ample selections of amenities are available, this is not an area of high-end lodges, upscale boutiques, or fine-dining opportunities. Rather, it is a place to chat with old-timers in a local café, watch sunsets flame the sky, bask in the quiet of really

ZUNI OLLA MAIDENS IN THE GALLUP INTERTRIBAL CEREMONIAL PARADE.

wide open spaces, and, if you are lucky, see a mountain lion leap across the road. It is a place where adventure and discovery are still possible.

wide open spaces, and, if you are lucky, see a mountain lion leap across the road. It is a place where adventure and discovery are still possible.

By making a giant loop, it is possible to travel through Ancestral Pueblo country without going over the same territory twice. However, this country may also be traveled conveniently in two sections: Sky City Country, linked by I-40 and anchored by Acoma Pueblo with Gallup as a base destination; and Chaco Country, linked by US 550 and anchored by Chaco Canyon with Farmington and surrounds as a base.

GUIDANCE **Acoma Pueblo** (575-552-6604; 1-888-747-0181), Acoma.

Gallup Convention & Visitors Bureau (575-863-3841; 1-800-242-4282), 201 E. Historic Route 66, Gallup.

Gallup/McKinley Country Chamber of Commerce (575-722-2228), 103 W. Route 66, Gallup.

Grants/Cibola County Chamber of Commerce (575-287-4802; 1-800-748-2142), 100 N. Iron St., Grants.

Cibola National Forest, Mount Taylor Ranger District (575-287-8833).

Destination Acoma (575-552-1060; 1-888-759-2489).

Indian Country New Mexico (1-800-448-1240; www.indiancountrynm.org).

Laguna Pueblo (575-552-6654), Laguna Pueblo.

New Mexico Route 66 Association (www.rt66nm.org), 1415 Central Ave. NE, Albuquerque. Contact for events and guidance.

Northwest New Mexico Visitors Center (575-876-2783), off I-40 at exit 85, Grants. Open 8–5 MST, 9–6 MDS (summer). This stop is a must-do for trip planning to Chaco, El Morro, El Malpais, and all the area attractions, with an abundance of maps, books, and experience available.

Zuni Tourism (505-782-7238; www.experiencezuni.com), 1239 NM 53, Zuni.

GETTING THERE From Albuquerque, take I-40 west 221 miles to Gallup, passing Acoma Pueblo, Laguna Pueblo, and Grants, while following the direction of Route 66.

MEDICAL EMERGENCY **Rehobeth McKinley Christian Hospital** (575-863-7000), 1901 Redrock Dr., Gallup.

Cibola General Hospital (575-287-4446), 1016 Roosevelt Ave., Grants.

✳ To See

TOWNS AND PUEBLOS **Acoma Pueblo, or Sky City,** is said to be the oldest continuously inhabited community in North America. Acoma people have lived here for 2,000 years. After exiting I-40 at exit 102, 65 miles west of Albuquerque, follow Indian Route 23 south to Sky City Cultural Center. Tours with native tour guides take you by bus to the top of the 357-foot-high mesa, the original village site of 300 adobe structures, and the remarkable San Esteban del Rey Mission

Church. Acoma is especially well known for its fine pottery, which may sometimes be purchased from the makers on the pueblo tour and during feast days. Feast days and traditional observances open to the public are Dec. 24–28, Sept. 2, Aug. 10, and the first or second weekend in Feb.

Crownpoint (575-786-7386; 575-786-5302) is situated 24 miles north of the Thoreau exit off I-40 on NM 371 and is notable for its monthly Navajo rug auction. From here, it is about 40 rough miles farther on unpaved NM 57 to the south entrance of Chaco Canyon.

Laguna Pueblo (575-552-6654). Inhabited as early as 3000 B.C., this area has been occupied by Mesa Verde migrants since the 1300s. Laguna was named for a lake, which no longer exists and was first mentioned in accounts of Coronado's 1540 exploration party. Old Laguna Village is now the ceremonial center of several neighboring villages. Feast days are Mar. 19 and Sept. 19. The stone San Jose de la Laguna Mission Church and Convento is a landmark seen from the north side of I-40 about 35 miles west of Albuquerque.

Gallup claims title as "the Indian jewelry center of the world" with over 100 trading posts. It is the home of the annual Intertribal Ceremonial, held in late July or early August, as well as a noted Route 66 stop, and in its heyday, it was a coal mining and railroading center. The town is a gateway to the Navajo Reservation, a base for exploring Canyon de Chelley and Monument Valley, as well as a trading, shopping, medical, and educational center for the Navajo and Zuni.

Grants, a Route 66 stop and formerly "the uranium capital of the world" at the base of Mt. Taylor, is a good place to rest en route to Chaco Canyon and Crownpoint Rug Auction.

Ramah, chiefly a Mormon and Navajo town with one small museum, located along NM 53, is the home of Ramah Navajo Weavers Association, and Ramah Lake is 2.5 miles northeast of town. The Ramah Museum (575-783-4215), open Fri. 1–4, tells the story of the town.

Zuni Pueblo (575-782-5851), 32 miles south of Gallup on NM 53. The first Native American village encountered by Coronado on his search for the Seven Cities of Gold, it is believed Zuni was the inspiration for this conquistador legend. Shalako, the annual all-night winter ceremony held late Nov. or early Dec., is noted for the dancing of the 10-foot-tall Shalakos representing guiding spirits. Today's Zuni dwellers are known for fine inlay and turquoise needlepoint jewelry, their fetishes carved of semiprecious stones, and, of course, their hand-carved kachina figures. This is the largest of the pueblos, and the people speak their own language, Zuni, unrelated to any Pueblo languages. The restored mission church, Nuestra Senora de Guadalupe de Halona, originally established 1630–66, has life-sized restored murals.

MUSEUMS **Sky City Cultural Center and Haak'u Museum** (575-552-7869; 1-800-747-0181). Mesa tours are available daily on the hour May–Sept. 8–6 (last tour 5) and Oct.–Apr. 8–4:30. Please call ahead to confirm hours. The beautiful new cultural center displays pottery, jewelry, exhibits of history, and significant individuals of Acoma. Cultural center free. Tours $12 adults, $11 seniors, $9 children, $10 still camera permit.

Navajo Code Talkers Room (575-722-2228), 103 W. Historic Route 66, Gallup. Open Mon.–Fri. 8:30–5. During World War II, members of the Navajo Nation volunteered for a special mission. They translated intelligence into Navajo, and the Japanese never broke this code. Memorabilia and photos commemorate their contributions. Free.

Rex Museum (575-863-1363), 300 W. Historic Route 66, Gallup. Open Mon.–Fri. 8–3. Housed in a century-old stone building, the former home of the Rex Hotel, the museum displays memorabilia and history of this railroad and coal mining community. $2 adults, $1 seniors, $0.75 children.

Atchison, Topeka & Santa Fe Railway Depot/Gallup Cultural Center (575-722-3730), 201 E. Historic Route 66, Gallup. Open Mon.–Fri. 10–4. This restored depot contains exhibits and a gift shop, plus the Storyteller Museum and Gallery of the Masters. Indian dances are performed nightly at 7 in summer. Free.

New Mexico Mining Museum (575-287-4802; 1-800-748-2142), 100 N. Iron Ave., Grants. Open Mon.–Sat. 9–4. Visit the world's only underground uranium mining museum, learn about rocks of the region, and ride "the cage" down an actual mineshaft.

A:shiwi A:wan Museum and Heritage Center (575-782-4403), 02 E. Ojo Caliente Rd., Zuni. Open Mon.–Fri. 9–5. Closed during religious ceremonies. The heritage center displays artifacts retrieved when the ancient city of Hawikku was excavated in 1920. The center is located on the site of one of Zuni's first trading posts. Tours, exhibits, and programs about the village and the environment make this a sensible place to begin a visit. Free.

HISTORIC LANDMARKS, PLACES, AND SITES **Continental Divide.** Approximately 170 miles west of Albuquerque on I-40 is the pinnacle of a geological ridge that separates the nation's waterways. East of the Divide all waters flow east to the Atlantic Ocean, while those west of the Divide flow towards the Pacific.

El Morro National Monument (575-783-4226), 42 miles southeast on NM 53 from Grants. Closed Christmas and New Year's Day. Visitor center open daily Oct. 2–DST 9–5; trails open 9–4. Check for summer hours. El Morro is also known as Inscription Rock for its 2,000 inscriptions and prehistoric petroglyphs. In 1640, Francisco Coronado wrote "Paso por aqui" (I passed by here) in the sandstone formation. It is the pool, the reliable water source beneath the huge boulder, that caused travelers to stop here throughout history. There is a paved 0.5-mile loop trail from the visitor center to Inscription Rock and a two-hour round-trip moderate hike to the mesa-top, 13th- and 14th-century pueblo ruins. $3, under 16 free.

SCENIC DRIVES **Ancient Way** (575-287-4802), NM 53 as it parallels the ancient trade route between Acoma and Zuni pueblos and the route originally taken by Coronado. Take exit 81 off I-40 for a 73-mile scenic drive to Zuni Pueblo that leads en route to El Morro, or Inscription Rock. En route, pass the villages of San Rafael, San Mateo, and Cebolleta.

RIO PUERCO BRIDGE IS PRESERVED AS A ROUTE 66 LANDMARK.

Old Route 66. Driving east on I-40 between Albuquerque and Gallup affords many opportunities to get off the interstate and hop onto original stretches of Route 66, the Mother Road, as author John Steinbeck named it, with several Route 66 markers, such as the Rio Puerco Bridge, in evidence. The road from Chicago to Los Angeles was opened in 1926, then it was realigned in 1937 and subsequently made famous by songs and television shows that celebrated it as a road of freedom and discovery for postwar America.

Zuni Mountain Historic Auto Tour (575-287-4802). From Santa Fe Ave. in Grants, go west to NM 53, cross I-40, and go right on Zuni Canyon Rd. This tour leads 60 miles as it winds through Zuni Canyon to Agua Fria Valley to the historic town of Sawyer, and loops back to Grants via Bluewater Lake. It follows Forest Service dirt roads to trace the history of logging and railroading in Cibola National Forest with old railroad grades, town sites, and trestle remnants en route.

NATURAL WONDERS **Bandera Volcano and Ice Cave** (575-783-4303 or 1-888-ICE-CAVE), 25 miles southwest of Grants off NM 53. Open daily from 8 until one hour before sunset. The temperature in the ice cave is 31 degrees Fahrenheit year-round, kept that way by 20-foot-thick ice on the cave floor. Bandera is the largest of 29 extinct volcanoes in the region. It is a 40-minute hike to the volcano, and a 20-minute hike into the ice cave. Both are reasonably easy,

WEATHERED ADVERTISEMENTS SPEAK OF BYGONE DAYS ALONG ROUTE 66.

WILDER PLACES

Angel Peak Recreation Area (575-599-8900), 23 miles south of Aztec on US 550. Take the 6-mile gravel road northeast into the site. No water or services, but camping and picnic areas are available, as are hiking trails and wildlife viewing. Angel Peak is a striking 40-million-year-old geologic formation. This area is not recommended for RVs.

Bisti Badlands/De-Na-Zin Wilderness (575-599-8900; www.nm.blm.gov), 37 miles south of Farmington off NM 371, 2 miles down gravel road #7297. Forty-two thousand acres administered by the BLM. This wildly sculpted shale and sandstone formation with its fantastic, colorful landforms might well be a journey to the moon. The best formations may be reached by hiking 2 miles east from parking area. Primitive camping is possible, but there are no services. Free.

El Malpais National Monument and Conservation Area (575-783-4774; 575-783-4664), information centers at Mile Marker 62 on NM 53; 11000 Ice Cave Rd., Grants. Daily 8:30–4:30. Over eons, volcanic eruptions created this wild and rugged black landscape called El Malpais, or badlands, of over 100,000 acres of lava flows, lava tube caves, sandstone cliffs, and cinder cones. Lava flows from 2,000 years to over 300,000 years old may be seen here. Be sure to check out the Chain of Craters, two dozen craters stretched out over 20 miles along the Continental Divide accessible on Cibola County Road 42. Free.

Mount Taylor (575-287-8833). An ancient dormant volcano 11,301 feet high that is visible from Albuquerque, Mount Taylor is a sacred site known as Turquoise Mountain in Navajo culture. The mountain is part of the Cibola National Forest. The Mt. Taylor Quadrathlon is a grueling 44-mile race held every Presidents' Day weekend, starting from downtown Grants to the summit and back. The race includes biking, running, skiing, and snowshoeing. Trail 77 is a moderate 6-mile round-trip hike near the top—with amazing views. Go north on First St. in Grants to NM 547 (Lobo Canyon Rd.) for 13 miles, right on FR 193 for 5 miles to trailhead.

Ojito Wilderness (575-761-8700; www.nm.blm.gov), from Albquerque, go north on 1-25 for 16 miles, then exit on US 550 at second Bernalillo exit. Go 20 miles northwest toward Cuba. Two miles before San Ysidro, turn left onto Cabezon Road (CR 906), follow the left fork 10 miles to the Ojito Wilderness sign. This remote, austere, quiet place is a roadless area with no facilities, no services, and no water. The 11,000 acres are full of steep canyons and rugged cliffs to challenge experienced hikers. You can get into the wilderness only as far as a short distance from the road. You might see fossils, petroglyphs, petrified trees, and even seashells. Free.

BISTI BADLANDS SUGGESTS A REMOTE MOONSCAPE.

Cabezon Peak (575-761-8700; www.nm.blm.gov). West on US 550 onto CR 279, approximately 20 miles northwest of San Ysidro. Continue 12 miles past village of San Luis to Cabezon turnoff onto BLM road 1114. The pavement ends just beyond San Luis. At intersection of CR 279 and BLM Road 1114, pass the ghost town of Cabezon. Follow 1114 for 2.9 miles to a dirt road that leads to a trailhead. Check road conditions before attempting this journey. *Cabezon* translates as "Big head," and it is the most prominent volcanic neck in the Mt. Taylor lava fields, rising 8,000 feet above sea level. It is not recommended for children or pets. The trail, only for the fit and the adept, involves some Class 3 climbing and is accessible year-round. Caution: rattlesnakes are active in warmer weather. Primitive recreation. Camping for 14 days or less is okay. Free.

Morgan Lake (928-871-6451; www.navajofishandwildlife.org), 15 miles west of Farmington on US 64, on Navajo Reservation. Open year-round for bass and catfish fishing. A special license is needed. Contact number above. The lake is also known for windsurfing on 1,200 acres in water that remains 75 degrees Fahrenheit year-round.

Wild Spirit Wolf Sanctuary (575-775-3304), 2 miles past El Morro on NM 53 (approximately 50 miles southeast of Grants), left on BIA 125 for 8 miles, right on BIA 120 for 4 miles; on left. Open Tues.–Sun. Closed Mon. Guided tours at 11, 12:30, 2, 3:30. Meet wolf dog and wolf captive born in the Zuni Mountains. $5 adults, $4 seniors, $3 children, under seven free. $10 camping.

but the ice cave involves some intense stair climbing. There is an old-time trading post on the premises. $9 adults and teens, $7 seniors and military, $4 5–12.

La Ventana Natural Arch (575-287-4802). Access from NM 117. *La Ventana* means "the window," and that is exactly what this 165-foot-wide natural golden sandstone arch appears to be, a window onto the sky. Free.

✳ To Do

BICYCLING For trail maps and information on area races, call 1-800-448-1240.

Aztec Mountain Biking and Hiking Trails (575-334-9551) includes three main trails: Aztec Trails, Mountain View Trails, and Alien Run. The system starts near the city limits and leads to Hart Canyon, the site of the alleged 1948 UFO crash.

BOATING See the state parks under *Green Space*.

FISHING **Ramah Lake** (no phone), 2.5 miles northeast of Ramah. Fishing, boating, and picnicking.

San Juan River/Quality Waters (505-632-2278), 26 miles northeast of Aztec off NM 173 and NM 511. Year-round fishing in 12 miles of open water. Sought-after trophy trout fly-fishing in the waters west of Navajo Lake Dam brings fishermen to the San Juan to catch the big ones. But those big ones swimming around your waders are wily, as they have been caught and released so many times. Enormous rainbow trout that feed well makes this one of America's top 10 trout fishing waters. A section of the river for 6 miles south of the dam flows through a magical, scenic sandstone canyon. There are four wheelchair-accessible fishing piers along the river and an easy hiking trail that runs for 1.5 miles along the north side of the San Juan River. Quality waters have special restrictions. Free.

FLOATING AND KAYAKING See *Green Space*.

HIKING **Pyramid Rock,** in Red Rock Park. At the summit one can see 50 miles on a clear day. The 3-mile round-trip takes you through amazing rock formations, with a summit elevation of 7,487 feet. Church Rock Trail begins at Outlaw Trading Post parking lot, with great views of Church Rock Spires. From Gallup, go 6 miles east on Route 66/NM 118. Turn north onto NM 566 for 0.5 mile. Turn left into Red Rock Park, follow signs. Check with the visitor center for maps.

Zuni-Acoma Trail in El Malpais National Monument traverses the Continental Divide, which stretches from Canada to the southern border of the United States. You need strong shoes to hike from cairn to cairn across the lava of this ancient trade route, a segment of an old Indian trail connecting Acoma and Zuni pueblos. Bring lots of water for this lifetime hike. It will take five or six hours and is quite strenuous, ranging from easy to moderate to difficult.

MOUNTAIN BIKING **High Desert Trail System.** A new mountain bike trail on the high mesas northwest of Gallup has a stacked loop trail with trailheads near

Gamerco and Mentmore, former coal mines. To get to Gamerco, go 2 miles north of I-40 on US 491, and left at Chino Loop traffic signal; the trailhead is on the left just after the curve. The trail heads west for 2.25 miles around the mesa top with expansive viewpoints. Or turn right at Six Flags, continuing on to Second Mesa. The third mesa is higher to the south. Challenging.

Farmington Trails (575-326-7602) include: **Road Apple Trail,** behind San Juan College, with sandy washes and arroyos, hilly jumps, and steep climbs; **Kinsey's Ridge,** at the end of Foothills Drive, with 6 miles of rolling hills and great views; and **Pinon Mesa,** 3 miles north of Main St. on NM 170, with a trailhead marked by a large cottonwood on the west side of the highway.

Farmington Lake has many trails through all types of terrain that can be accessed off the Road Apple Trail.

See **Zuni Mountain Historic Auto Tour** under To See/*Scenic Drives.* Many of these old logging roads along the way are suitable for mountain biking.

SNOW SPORTS Best to check out opportunities at nearby **Durango Mountain Resort** (www.durangomountainresort.com) and **Wolf Creek Ski Area** (www .wolfcreekski.com).

WINERIES **Wines of the San Juan Tasting Room** (575-632-0879), 233 NM 551. Open Mon. and Wed.–Sat. 10–6, Sun. 2–6. Closed Tues. Find this rustic tasting room 6 miles below Navajo Lake State Park on NM 511 at Turley. The San Juan region is the ideal microclimate to produce these rich, fruity wines.

✳ Lodging

BED AND BREAKFASTS, INNS, AND MOTELS Ꮭ **Cimarron Rose, Zuni Mountain Bed & Breakfast** (575-783-4770; www.cimarronrose.com), 689 Oso Ridge Rd., 30 miles southwest of Grants on NM 53. To preserve your solitude and privacy, breakfast is delivered to your room. Local artists display their wares for sale in this true retreat and "green" lodging located on the Great Divide. Each of the three rooms has its own bath. $90–185.

The Inn at Halona (1-800-752-3278; www.halona.com), Zuni. Located in the middle Zuni Pueblo in the historic 1940 home of trader Bernard J. Vanden Wagen and operated by his granddaughter, Elaine, this eight-room bed and breakfast imparts a sense of a faraway adventure, in comfort. Several of the rooms are graced with comfortably furnished private patios. $79.

El Rancho Hotel (575-863-9311; 1-800-543-6351), 1000 E. Historic Route 66, Gallup. One block south of I-40 at exit 22. With 24 rooms, each named for a movie star, and the mezzanine decorated with black-and-white photos of all the stars that stayed here while shooting movies, this 1937 hotel is the epitome of Hollywood gone Western nostalgia. The hot pink neon beckons you to stop, and the pool, lounge, and quite decent restaurant serving breakfast, lunch, and dinner make this the top choice for a Gallup stay. Most of the rooms are on the small side; you can stay, however, for a not unreasonable price, in the Presidential Suite (aka the Ronald Reagan room). The open lobby with curving wooden staircases on either side, decorated in Navajo rugs and rustic Western furnishings, with a floor-to-ceiling stone fireplace, is one of the most welcoming sights along the road. $58–115.

Road Runner Motel (575-863-3004), 3012 E. Hwy. 66, Gallup. Sometimes you really do get what you pay for, and that's not a bad thing. Not here anyway. This small mom-and-pop stop is a budget traveler's joy, with its vintage Route 66 character, neon and all. It is dependably clean and well run, but expect nothing fancy, just a good night's rest. $40.

RANCHES AND LODGES **Zuni Mountain Lodge and Tours** (575-862-7616), 40 Perch Dr., Thoreau. Open year-round. Delicious breakfast and dinner are included with your stay here in this lovely cottagelike lodge that is a favorite of mountain bikers come to ride the old logging trails in the Cibola National Forest and of cross-country skiers in winter. All seven rooms have private baths. $60–95.

Stauder's Navajo Lodge (575-862-7553), Continental Divide, 20 miles east of Gallup. Seasoned innkeepers Sherwood and Roberta Stauder share their hospitality and love of this place in their quarters, filled with Indian arts and antiques. With only two rooms, each with private bath, guests are certain to feel catered to at this old-fashioned (in a good way), deeply Western lodge whether en route to Chaco Canyon or Crownpoint Rug Auction. There's a pretty courtyard and mind-blowing views of the red rock bluffs. Peach sauce from their own peach trees graces your scrumptious breakfast. Delightful! $75–95.

Apache Canyon Ranch B&B Country Inn (575-836-7220; 1-800-808-8310), 4 Canyon Dr., Laguna. Bordered by Indian lands, not far from Old Route 66, the ranch's views and the peace and quiet are unmatched. It's somewhat surprising to find an upscale lodging all the way out here, but there you are. The inn sits on several acres, and the main quarters has rooms and courtyards, a grand parlor for tea, a six-hole putting green, and a guest cottage with a whirlpool tub and kiva fireplace. Of course, the breakfast is gourmet quality, and dinner, should you choose to remain on the premises rather than zip over to the Route 66 Casino, may be prepared on request. $90–295.

☙ **Z Lazy B Guest Ranch** (1-888-488-2007), Ft. Wingate. Open year-round, weather permitting. The descendant of the original homesteaders on this land now lives here with her husband, and together they raise horses in this somewhat desolate and wild Zuni Mountain area that was formerly a busy logging territory. There are five comfortably and completely furnished log cabins, nothing shabby here, each sleeping 8–10, each with kitchen, bath, lounging, and private areas, and guests may choose to have the staff cook for them or prepare their own meals. A hearty meat and potatoes fresh-cooked breakfast is included, at any rate. The lodge is also known for horseback riding, offering trail, pony, and wagon rides May–Oct. $120 night double occupancy, $15 each extra person, under seven free.

CABINS AND CAMPING El Morro RV Park & Ancient Way Café (575-783-4612), NM 53, Ramah. Open year-round. Just down the way from El Morro National Monument are cozy cabins in the pines at the base of San Lorenzo Mesa with sleeping accommodations for four, and full hookup RV sites in a pet-friendly place with free Wi-Fi. The friendly café serves home-cooked breakfast, lunch, and dinner and is a gathering place where locals mingle with visitors for plenty of storytelling. Perfection! $65 cabin, $20 camping.

✳ Where to Eat

DINING OUT Chelle's (575-727-7698), 2201 W. Hwy. 66, Gallup. Dinner only. For a good steak or a special occasion night out, this intimate spot is a reliably fine place to celebrate and raise a toast with a glass of wine.

You do feel well cared for by the staff. It has a certain old-fashioned, or down-home, appeal. Moderate.

Don Diego's Restaurant and Lounge (575-722-5517), 801 W. Historic Route 66, Gallup. Open Mon.–Sat. 8–9. Closed Sun. Breakfast, lunch, dinner. Nightlife, such as it is, may be found here, along with pretty tasty New Mexican food and good hot red chile. Inexpensive.

EATING OUT Uranium Café (575-287-7540), 519 W. Santa Fe, Grants. Irregular hours. "Our food will blow your mine" is the motto at this Route 66–era café, where it's catch as catch can to find them open. The rear end of a Cadillac, with fins, serves as the salad bar. Inexpensive.

🦎 ♿ **Earl's Family Restaurant** (575-863-4201), 1400 E. Route 66, Gallup. Rightly called "Gallup's living room,"

RICHARDSON'S TRADING CO. IN GALLUP HAS AN UNMATCHED STOCK OF INDIAN WARES.

this is the place to eat reasonably priced green-chile-smothered enchiladas, but if you're not accustomed to the local cuisine, plenty of real mashed potatoes and gravy are served with delicious daily specials of fried chicken and meat loaf. Shop while you eat, as vendors circulate showing off their wares. If you don't care to be bothered, you can get a sign indicating so from the management. If you have time for only one meal in Gallup, by all means eat at this 30-plus-year-old family restaurant. Inexpensive.

Ranch Kitchen (575-722-2537), 3001 W. Hwy. 66, Gallup. Open daily. Closed Easter and Christmas. Breakfast, lunch, dinner. Here is Southwestern cooking, somewhat cowboy-style, in a place that comfortably accommodates the long-distance travelers who know it well. Love those big plates of smoky barbeque, and the Navajo tacos are mighty fine. The gift shop is a treasure chest of Route 66 memorabilia. For a feeling of road trip, come here. Inexpensive.

Virgie's Restaurant & Lounge (575-863-5152), 2720 W. Old Hwy. 66, Gallup. Closed Sun. Open Mon.– Sat. 7 AM–9 PM. Breakfast, lunch, dinner. In the glow of Virgie's neon, feast on enchiladas in true Old 66 splendor. Virgie's is at least as much a roadside institution as it is a restaurant serving steaks and Mexican food. Virgie's beef stew and the chico steak smothered in green chile and cheese are favorites. Or go for the crème de la crème, the crispy chicken taquitos. This fine family restaurant started serving its homemade pie around 1960. Inexpensive.

Eagle Café (575-722-3220), 220 W. Historic Hwy. 66, Gallup. Open Mon.–Sat. 7–7. Closed Sun. Breakfast, lunch, dinner. You can still hear the trains rolling in on the tracks across Old 66. Sink into one of the old-time booths and order mutton stew with local traders and Navajos. The Eagle has been here since 1904, and from the looks of the place, nothing much has changed. Inexpensive.

✳ Entertainment

Summer Theater Series in Lions Wilderness Amphitheater (575-599-1407; www.fmtn.org/sandstone). June 20–Aug. 2. Repertory Theater under the stars in a natural golden sandstone arena. Recent productions included *Cyrano de Bergerac* and a Gershwin revue. Optional Southwestern dinner is served before each performance. $7.

✳ Selective Shopping

Richardson's Trading Co. (575-722-4762; www.richardsontrading.com), 222 W. Historic Hwy. 66, Gallup. Open Mon.–Sat. 9–5. The selection of the best turquoise, coral, and silver Navajo and Zuni jewelry; Navajo rugs; sand paintings; pottery; and old pawn fills every nook and cranny of this creaky trading post established in 1913. As much a museum as a store, the store's staff is patient and knowledgeable, and Richardson's is as reliable a place (with fair prices) to make a purchase as you can find. There are treasures here at all price levels. Be prepared to take your time and look at all the wonderful things.

Old School Gallery (575-783-4710), NM 53. Open Thurs.–Sun. 11–5. An enterprise of the El Morro Area Arts Council, here you can find current exhibits and work of local artists in diverse media for sale. Lectures, workshops, and special events and celebration also go on at this gallery. Call for exact directions and schedule of events.

CHACO COUNTRY: AZTEC, BLOOMFIELD, CUBA, FARMINGTON, SHIPROCK

T wo activities of major interest dominate this region: visiting monumental ancient ruins and the opportunity to catch really big trout on the San Juan River. If your senses are truly open, you might catch a faint drum beat or a whiff of fry bread on the wind. There is a sense of being in uncharted territory, almost at the end of the world, which is highlighted in places like no other such as the Bisti Badlands or the area around Shiprock. The place is haunting and unforgettable.

GUIDANCE **Aztec Chamber of Commerce** (575-334-9551; 1-888-838-9551; www.aztecchamber.com), 110 N. Ash, Aztec.

Bloomfield Chamber of Commerce (575-632-0880; 1-800-461-1245; www .bloomfieldnm.info), 224 W. Broadway Ave., Bloomfield.

Cuba Chamber of Commerce (575-289-3514; 505-289-0302; www.cubanew mexico.com), Cuba.

Farmington Chamber of Commerce (575-325-0279; www.gofarmington .com), 100 W. Braodway, Farmington.

Farmington Field Office, BLM (575-599-8900), 1235 La Plata Hwy., Farmington.

Navajo Nation Tourism (928-810-8501; 928-871-6436; www.discovernavajo .com), Window Rock, Arizona.

Northwest New Mexico Visitor Center (575-876-2783), 1900 E. Santa Fe, Grants. Open daily 9–6 MDT, 8-5 MST.

MEDICAL EMERGENCY **San Juan Regional Medical Center** (505-325-5011 or 575-566-6100), 801 W. Maple, Farmington.

GETTING THERE From Albuquerque, go 180 miles northwest on 1-25 north to Bernalillo, then US 550 to Bloomfield, then US 64 to Farmington. Along the way pass Cuba, the road to Chaco Canyon, Bloomfield, and the Salmon Ruins.

✳ To See

TOWNS AND PUEBLOS **Aztec** is 14 miles northeast of Farmington on US 550. Supporting the early belief that the nearby Ancestral Pueblo ruins were of Aztec origin, the town's founders in 1890 named their village for them. Aztec maintains a sense of civic pride in its homesteading past. Main Street Historic District is charming and well preserved, as are the Victorian residences, which form the core of the town.

Bloomfield. Located on the San Juan River at the junction of US 550 and US 64, 11 miles east of Farmington, this oil and gas center is a convenient place to make a quick stop for gas and groceries.

Cuba is 102 miles southeast of Farmington on US 550. This little town was not named for the Caribbean country by veterans of the Spanish-American War, as is sometimes said. Rather, the name refers to a geographical feature and means "sink," or "draw" in Spanish. Several cafés and gas stations cater to travelers. The ranger station on the south end of town offers permits and information about hiking, camping, cross-country skiing, and fishing in the nearby Santa Fe National-al Forest (505-289-3264; P.O. Box 130, Cuba, NM 87103).

Farmington is 180 miles northwest of Albuquerque on US 550. Totah, "among the rivers," is the Navajo name for this gateway city where three rivers—the Animas, La Plata, and San Juan—come together. But English-speaking settlers named it for its fine agricultural produce, recognizing it as a "farming-town." The economy has gone boom and bust with the oil, gas, and uranium industries for the past 60 years, and today there are two Farmingtons—the nicely pre-served and still busy downtown, with its trading posts, cafés, and antiques shops, and the "parallel universe" of strip malls and shopping centers. In addition to making a great base for exploring the area, Farmington serves as the entertain-ment, shopping, and recreational center of the region, with summer theater, museums, an aquatic center, number-one-rated municipal golf course, and plen-ty of family activities.

Shiprock is 29 miles west of Farmington on US 64. Taking its name from its unforgettable landmark, the imposing "rock with wings," Shiprock is mainly a center of Navajo tribal business and services. The annual Northern Navajo Fair, held each fall, is an exceptional gathering of rugs, rodeo, and tradition.

MUSEUMS **Gateway Park Museum & Visitor Center** (575-599-1174; 1-800-448-1240), 3041 E. Main, Farmington. Open Mon.–Sat. 8–5. Closed Sun. Maps and trip planning; exhibits related to the history of the West and the Farmington area. Free.

Aztec Museum and Pioneer Village (575-334-9829), 125 N. Main Ave., Aztec. Open Apr.–Sept. 10–5; Oct.–May 10–4. Closed Sunday. Here find a wealth of pioneer Americana, plus oilfield, military, and farm equipment exhibits. $3 adults, $1 children 12–17, 11 and under free.

✐ ⅏ **Riverside Nature Center** (575-599-1425), off Browning Pkwy. in Animas Park, Farmington. Open Oct.–Mar. Tues.– Sat. 10–5, Sun. 1–4; Apr.–Sept. Tues.–Sat. 9–6, Sun. 1–5. Wildlife viewing; butterfly walks; hands-on exhibits of tracks, bones and seeds; xeriscape gardens; herb garden; history walks; and stargazing. Free.

☞ ᴕ **E-3 Children's Museum & Science Center** (575-599-1425), 302 N. Orchard, Farmington. Open Tues.–Sat. noon–5. Closed Mon. The kids will love the hands-on, science-related, and exploration exhibits found here. Free.

NATURAL WONDERS **Shiprock Pinnacle** (no phone; www.discovernavajo.com), 10 miles southwest of Shiprock off US 491. This signature Western landmark, a mass of igneous rock flanked by walls of solidified lava, was given its apt name by early area settlers. Known to the Navajo as "rock with wings," this volcanic rock formation rises 1,700 feet above the desert floor. Because it is a sacred site to the Dine, or Navajo, only viewing is permitted. There is no access.

Four Corners Monument (928-871-6647; www.navajonationparks.org), 30 miles northwest of Shiprock off US 64 and US 160. Open daily Oct.–May 8–5, June–Sept. 7 AM–8 PM. Erected in 1912, the Four Corners Monument is the only place in the United States where four states intersect: Arizona, New Mexico, Utah, and Colorado. You will find an Indian marketplace with handmade crafts as well. $3.

SHIPROCK, THE "ROCK WITH WINGS," IS A NAVAJO SACRED SITE.

ANCIENT RUINS

Chaco Culture National Historical Park (575-786-7014; www.nps.gov/chcu), Nageezi. The best access is off US 550 from the north at Nageezi, via County Rd. 7900. Or take Thoreau exit off I-40 for 25 miles to Crownpoint; 3 miles farther, turn east on Indian Highway 9. Continue to Pueblo Pintado. Go north on NM 46 to CR 7900/7950 to reach the visitor center. Visitor center open daily 8–5. Closed major holidays. Park open daily. Four-wheel drive is a necessity in difficult weather conditions. A word of caution: call the ranger number above if in the slightest doubt. There is no easy way to get to this World Heritage Site, this eternally monumental and mysterious center of ancient Indian civilization. Both dirt roads in are slow, rutted, and dangerously slippery when wet or icy. That said, a visit to this ancient trade and ceremonial center that linked over 100 communities in the Four Corners area is a must. There are no services, but there is a campground, and it is possible to make the moderate hike to the top of mesas where the entire complex of ruins that were deserted by A.D. 1200 may be viewed. A 9-mile self-guided paved road offers a tour of five major ruins, including massive great houses with hundreds of rooms. The Chacoan culture is believed to have been the ancestral origins of today's Pueblo Indians. While formerly known as "Anasazi," the current preferred term is "Ancestral Pueblo."

Just a few of the mysteries involve how these ancient people of this complex civilization created their remarkable astronomical alignments, their

CHACO CANYON IS ALWAYS WORTH THE JOURNEY.

AZTEC RUINS NATIONAL MONUMENT.

masonry construction, and the arrow-straight outliers, as the roads visible from the air leading to related settlements throughout the Four Corners region are known. Was this a dwelling place or a spiritual or trade center? We still do not know. $8 per vehicle (good for seven days); $10 camping.

Aztec Ruins National Monument (575-334-6174, ext. 30; www.nps/gov/azru), 84 CR 29, Aztec. Ruins Road, 0.75 mile north of NM 516. Open Memorial Day–Labor Day 8–6; remainder of year 8–5. Closed Thanksgiving, Christmas, New Year's Day. These dwellings, dating to A.D. 900 and abandoned by A.D. 1300, were inhabited as a Chaco outlier for 200 years. The inhabitants were related to Mesa Verde as well as Chaco. A 700-yard paved trail winds through the West Ruin, passing through several rooms with intact original roofs. The centerpiece is the reconstructed Great Kiva, the only one in the United States. $5 adults, under 16 free.

Salmon Ruins/Heritage Park, Archaeological Research Center and Library (575-632-2013; www.salmonruins.com), 10 miles east of Farmington on US 64. Open daily 8–5. Closed major holidays. Eleventh-century pueblo built in Chacoan style plus pioneer homestead. Ancestral Puebloan pottery, jewelry, tools, and hunting equipment are on display. $3 adults, $1 children 6–16.

NORTHWEST NEW MEXICO: ANCESTRAL PUEBLO COUNTRY

✳ To Do

GOLF Pinon Hills (575-326-6066), 2101 Sunrise Pkwy., Farmington. Open year-round, weather permitting. This Ken Dye–designed course is rated by a *Golf Digest* readers' poll as "America's best golf bargain . . . with large terraced greens, sculptured serpentine fairways and challenging sand bunkers. #1 municipal golf course in the nation." Special rates are available for those who live within a hundred-mile radius. $19–43.

SWIMMING ✐ Farmington Aquatic Center (575-599-1167), 1151 N. Sullivan, Farmington. Call for hours. This is a full-fledged 150-foot Olympic pool, open year-round, with a 150-foot double loop water slide. $5 adults; $4.50 13–18, $3.25 children 3–12, $2.50 lap swimming.

✳ Green Space

Riverside Park (575-334-9551), on the Animas River outside Farmington at US 550 and NM 574, west of the bridges on Light Plant Rd. into the park. There's excellent bird-watching year-round with wintering bald eagles fishing the Animas River, one of the last undimmed rivers in the West, and historical and wildlife interpretative signs lend depth to the experience.

River Corridor within the park, is 5 miles of multipurpose trails accessed off Browning Pkwy. south of Animas River, and at Scott Ave. and San Juan Blvd., behind the motels; **Woodland Trails,** found here, make excellent jogging and bicycling paths, with picnic areas with grills along the way.

Navajo Lake State Park (575-632-2278; www.nmstateparks.com or www .emnrd.state.nm.us/nmparks), 1448 NM 511 #1, Navajo Dam, 45 miles east of Farmington on NM 511. Boat slips, fishing and boating supplies, and houseboat and ski boat rentals supplement this year-round boating opportunity on the 15,590-surface-acre lake. In addition, find three recreation areas with fishing and camping, and directly below the dam is the famous San Juan River fishing area. Here see blue herons, bald and golden eagles, red-tailed hawks, a variety of ducks, and Canada geese. Altogether, there are 150 miles of shoreline fed by the San Juan, Pine, and Piedra rivers. Handicap accessible. $6 day use, $10–18 camping.

Red Rock State Park (575-722-3839; 575-863-9330), 7 miles east of Gallup, exit 31 north of I-40. A surprisingly interesting, tucked-away area of history may be found here in the Heritage Canyon display at the visitor center. High, wind-sculpted red sandstone formations frame this 640-acre park that is the site of the Gallup Intertribal Ceremonial on three sides. From the parking area, a hiking trails lead to views of Pyramid Rock and the spires of Church Rock. There's a welcome mat out for horses at the Horse Park. $6 day use, $10–18 camping.

Bluewater Lake State Park (505-876-2391) is a lovely oasis of rolling hills encircling a 7-mile lake stocked with trout and catfish year-round. Boating, wildlife watching, camping, and hiking are popular pastimes here, as well as ice fishing, waterskiing, swimming, and hiking. $6 day use, $10–18 camping.

1 mile east of Farmington on US 64. Go right. The 12,000-acre Bolack Ranch is a private wildlife preserve, an experimental farm, and a working farm and ranch. Two museums feature farm machinery, wildlife, and generating equipment. Tours by appointment.

✳ Lodging

BED AND BREAKFASTS, INNS, AND MOTELS 🐾 **Miss Gail's Inn Bed & Breakfast** (575-334-3452; 1-888-534-3452; www.missgailsinn.com), 300 S. Main, Aztec. A small 1905 registered historic landmark hotel with quiet country charm and an excellent central location, Miss Gail's has neither phone in room nor Internet connections, but both are available nearby. Originally built as a railroad hotel, then converted to a boardinghouse, Miss Gail's today is a model of nonintrusive B&B service. $58–88.

D's Bed & Breakfast at Navajo Dam (575-632-0044; www.dsbandb .com), Navajo Dam. You can walk right down to the river here, but you may have to share a bathroom. Only two of the six accommodations have a private bath at D's. It's a fishing delight, only 5 miles from Navajo Reservoir, a few hundred yards from San Juan River fishing. New as of 2004, the lodging has grand river views and a two-story wraparound porch. $85.

Casa Blanca (1-800-550-6503; www .4cornersbandb.com), 505 E. La Plata St., Farmington. This gracious, red-tiled Mediterranean-style home high on a bluff in town is the ideal spot for either the visitor or business traveler. It's quiet the way rich people might be quiet, and the gardens are well tended. When you taste the rich breakfasts of crepes Benedict, Belgian waffles with fresh raspberry sauce, or orange almond French toast, you might wish you could stay longer. $78–175.

Silver River Spa Retreat & Adobe B&B (575-325-8219; 1-800-382-9251; www.silveradobe.com), Farmington. Rustic yet elegant, the B&B perches on a sandstone cliff looking over the San Juan and the La Plata rivers. There's a nature reserve with hiking paths, so good birding and grandmother cottonwoods are part of your stay. Plus, enjoy the library and salon-style breakfast. You couldn't ask for a more serene getaway. The three rooms each have a private bath and entrance. $105–175.

Kokopelli's Cave (575-326-2461), 3204 Crestridge Dr., Farmington. Stay in a plush-carpeted, man-made cave inspired by the Cliff Dwellings at nearby Mesa Verde. Carved into 65-million-year-old sandstone, this single lodging is located 70 feet below the surface on a west-facing vertical cliff face granting you a 360-degree view of the Four Corners' outstanding geologic features. The bedroom balcony overlooks La Plata River Valley 250 feet below. What a sunset! Imagine, a waterfall-filled hot tub. You need to carry in your own food and supplies. This is an experience that can make your cocktail party talk for years to come! $240.

CABINS AND CAMPING **Ruins Road RV Park** (575-334-3160), 312 Ruins Rd., Aztec. This completely pleasant campground quite close to the Aztec

ABE'S FLY SHOP IS A MUST-DO WHEN FISHING THE SAN JUAN RIVER.

Ruins and the Animas River offers remote tent sites as well as 53 RV hookups. You will do well here. $10 tent, $20 hookup.

Abe's Motel & Fly Shop (575-632-2194), 1791 NM 173, Navajo Dam. Open year-round, daily, 7–7. Abe's, a landmark since 1958, is the fisherman's mecca on the San Juan. Over time, the fly shop has added RV parking and full hookups, a restaurant and lounge, grocery store, gas station, and boat storage facilities. Most rooms have two double beds and kitchenette, but it is easier to bring your own utensils. The motel rooms feel more like rustic cabins, but they are clean and within walking distance of the river. El Pescador Restaurant, which serves Mexican and American food, is closed during the winter. The fly shop is the place for all your needs on the river, and it's where you can book guided tours. Pets allowed. Motel $45–105, RV $18.95.

Cottonwood–Navajo Lake State Park Pine Site and Main Campground. See *Green Space*.

✳ Where to Eat

DINING OUT **K.B. Dillon's** (575-325-0222), 101 W. Broadway, Farmington. For a special night out, steaks, seafood, and spirits, especially if you like the lounge atmosphere, which here feels like it is suspended somewhere in the 1970s. It is more businesslike than romantic in atmosphere. Moderate–Expensive.

EATING OUT ✿ **Hiway Grill,** Aztec. Open Mon.–Sat. Breakfast, lunch, and dinner. Closed Sun. Cute 1950s–60s cruising theme for a restaurant and bar serving American fare of burgers, salads, and the like. The food is a standard, nothing adventurous, and a bit bland—don't expect anything but iceberg lettuce in your salad. It's a good family dining option. Inexpensive.

✿ **Three Rivers Brewery** (575-324-2187), 101 E. Main, Farmington. Open Mon.–Sat. Lunch, dinner. Closed Sun. A friendly family hangout serving microbrews, homemade sodas, huge menu, kid's menu; play area. In a 1912 building that housed the first newspaper in town. The original restaurant has expanded to practically the entire block and now includes a pool room. Investigate which atmosphere you prefer before you are seated. Plenty of good cooking goes on here, resulting in soups and big salads, and you can't go wrong with the burger that made them famous. It's a great place to cool off with a root beer float, made with house root beer, and the Friday night specials, like crab boil, are amazing. Inexpensive.

Spare Rib Bar-B-Queue (575-325-4800), 1700 E. Main, Farmington. Open Tues.–Sat. Lunch, dinner. Closed Mon. Order at the counter delicious hickory-smoked beef, ribs, sausage, chicken, homemade cole slaw, and cobbler. It's all served on picnic tables covered in red-checked cloths. You can be happy here. Very happy. Inexpensive.

Dad's Diner (575-564-2516), 4395 Largo St., Farmington. Open daily. Breakfast, lunch, dinner. A local, family-run place that serves decent milk shakes and French dip sandwiches. It looks just like a real, old-time gleaming silver diner. It is a fun place to hang out, and all you "diner experience" collectors won't be disappointed. Inexpensive.

Andrea Kristina's Bookstore & Kafe (575-327-3313), 218 Main St., Farmington. Open Mon.–Wed. and Sat. 7 AM–9 PM, Fri. 7 AM–10 PM, Thurs. 9–9. Closed Sun. Breakfast, lunch, and dinner. Generous breakfasts with fresh scones and muffins, hot sandwiches, pizza, fresh salads, lattes, and smoothies. Live music and poetry Fri–Sat. at 7. There is an excellent though not especially large book selection. This is the best café hangout in town. Inexpensive.

✳ **Special Events**

Monthly: **Crownpoint Rug Auction** (575-786-7386; www.crownpointrug auction.com), Crownpoint Elementary School, 72 miles south of Farmington on NM 371. Third Fri. of the month 4–6 PM rug viewing; auction at 7. This monthly auction of 300–400 hand-woven Navajo rugs sponsored by Crownpoint Rug Weavers Association affords an excellent opportunity to meet weavers and get great bargains, though you will be competing with collectors and dealers. The school carnival atmosphere, with Frito pies and fry bread, plus crafts such as jewelry, make this a bargain hunter's paradise.

March: **The Aztec UFO Symposium** (575-334-9890; www.aztecufo .com) is held annually to investigate the reported UFO crash in Hart

THREE RIVERS BREWERY IN FARMINGTON MAKES AN EXCELLENT STOP FOR A MICROBREW OR A ROOT BEER FLOAT.

Canyon, 12 miles outside Aztec, and is hosted by Friends of the Aztec Public Library.

June: **Aztec Fiesta Days** (575-334-9951; 1-888-838-9551; www.aztec chamber.org). During the first weekend in June, this "All-American City" bids summer welcome with a parade, crafts, a carnival, and the burning of Old Man Gloom.

August: **Connie Mack World Series** (575-327-9673; www.fmtn.org), Rickett's Park, Farmington. Aug. 4–11. Teams from the United States and Puerto Rico play in front of pro scouts and college officials at this world amateur baseball event. **Gallup Intertribal Ceremonial** (505-863-3896; 1-888-685-2564; www.indian ceremonial.com). Parade down Old Route 66, Gallup; Red Rock State Park All-Indian Rodeo; indoor and outdoor marketplace; contest powwow; ceremonial Indian dances; native foods. An enormous "gathering of nations" dating back over 80 years—not to be missed!

September: **Totah Festival** (1-800-448-1240), Farmington Civic Center, 200 W. Arrington. First weekend. Annual American Indian fine arts show, rug auction, and powwow.

October: **Northern Navajo Nation Shiprock Navajo Fair** (575-368-3727; www.swnf-inc.com), Shiprock Fairgrounds, Shiprock. Parade, fair, arts, crafts, rodeo, powwow, traditional food, song and dance, "the oldest and most traditional" Navajo fair.

November: **Aztec Fantasy of Lights** (www.aztecfantasyoflights.com), Fri. after Thanksgiving–New Year's Eve, six PM. A driving tour of two dozen lighted sculptures in Aztec's Riverside Park. $4 per vehicle.

December: **San Juan College Luminarias** (575-566-3403; 1-800-448-1240), San Juan College, 4601 College Blvd., Farmington. Dec. 1, sunset. The campus is illuminated with 50,000 luminarias for the largest nonprofit display in New Mexico. **Navajo Nativity** (505-325-0255), 2102 W. Main, Farmington. Dec. 23, 6–8 PM. This living nativity with native Navajo costumes and live animals is presented by children at the Four Corners Home for Children.

Southwest New Mexico: Ghost Town Country

CAMINO COUNTRY: SOCORRO,
TRUTH OR CONSEQUENCES,
ELEPHANT BUTTE, HATCH,
LAS CRUCES, MESILLA

OLD HIGHWAY 60 COUNTRY:
MAGDALENA, DATIL, PIE TOWN,
QUEMADO

GHOST TOWN COUNTRY:
HILLSBORO, GLENWOOD, RESERVE,
COLUMBUS, SILVER CITY, DEMING

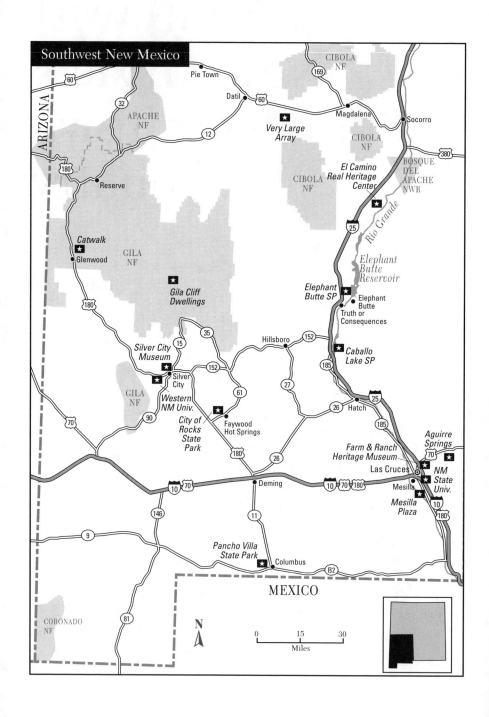

Southwest New Mexico

INTRODUCTION

Driving down I-25 past the green ponderosa pine mountain forests and the piñon-juniper covered hillsides of northern New Mexico into the creosote-covered landscape south of Albuquerque, you might think you have entered a dry, sparse land. You have. You are entering the northern edge of the Chihuahuan Desert. The south is not only very different physically, with a much hotter, drier climate, where the scarcity of water is a fact of life that historically has determined where and how people live and travel, it is culturally different as well.

The rural way of life is the predominant mode, and agriculture and ranching are the economic mainstays. Grapes, chile, alfalfa, and cotton grow abundantly in this fertile river valley, where farmers depend on water released from Elephant Butte Dam and cattle and horses graze in open fields.

There is less sense of urgency among people, who seem to make more time for visiting, baking, holding meetings of community concern, and caring for each other and their place. More leisure means a different sense of human values prevails in the small towns. Here folks either accept life and have made peace with it, or they are resigned to its limitations. Rushy-rushy is an unknown state here, you never do things in a "New York minute," and life moves slowly, people run late, and phone calls may not be answered in what is customarily considered a timely manner.

As this area is geographically closer to Mexico, the influence of that country south of the border—its language, food, religion, and strong family ties—has remained in force. Some believe the border itself is an artificial line drawn through the ancient kingdom of "Atzlan," and that the southern region of New Mexico and northern Mexico really belong together as one country.

Immigration is quite an issue here. You will see, and be required to pass through, Border Patrol stations along the way. There really is no way to travel through this area without experiencing these inspections, but they usually just consist of a quick look at you and your vehicle by an agent as you drive through the station.

Aside from the fast-growing urban area of Las Cruces, only 40 miles from the border at El Paso, Texas, and the retiree haven of Silver City, towns remain tiny, somewhat ingrown, and without any sense of change or impetus to adapt to the future. People are more inclined to do things the way their parents and grand-parents did them. New ways, and outsiders looking to bring them in, are some-what suspect.

And the past is well preserved in the hot, dry New Mexican desert. That goes for the 400-year-old trail markings of the Camino Real, the Royal Road, still visi-ble from the air. It once took oxcarts three years to make that round-trip between Mexico City and Santa Fe. This is the path taken by the conquistadors, by Juan de Oñate, in 1598, and it is the same path the Spanish and their follow-ers took when they fled back to El Paso in 1680 when the Pueblo Revolt drove them out. It is the road Don Diego de Vargas took when he returned with his followers at the Reconquest 12 years later and retook Santa Fe for the Spanish crown.

Like much of the rest of the state, southwest New Mexico includes a vast area that can be thought of in distinct regions, shaped by location and resources, and the history that resulted from the uses people made of those features. Probably each of them, depending on your personal pace, can be at least seen in a good long weekend. These three regions are the Camino Real Country, the Old High-way 60 Country, and the Ghost Town Country.

The new capital of the Camino Real Country is the International Camino

YOU CAN STILL GET A HORSE-DRAWN RIDE IN SOUTHWEST NEW MEXICO.

Real State Monument south of Truth or Consequences. This is the country that includes the towns accessible from I-25 from Socorro, Truth or Consequences, Elephant Butte, Las Cruces, and its next-door neighbor, Mesilla. It flows in more or less a straight line north to south, following the path of the ancient road along the river. Where it diverged from the river into the Journada de Muerto, the "dead man's journey," is a waterless stretch that tested the survival skills of those who dared cross it.

Travel is still the big story out here, particularly with the construction of the New Mexico Spaceport, designed to take private individuals for the ride of their lives. The Spaceport, which is anticipated to be a generator of jobs and visitors, is well within sight of the Camino Real.

Old US Highway 60, the Ocean-to-Ocean Highway, was the first paved transcontinental road, begun in 1912. It bisects southern New Mexico and remains the slow road from east to west, a two-lane with a 55 mph speed limit and no billboards, chain restaurants, or chain motels. Get on Highway 60, which still follows its original alignment through New Mexico, south of Socorro and travel to the Arizona border in a half-day passing through Magdalena, the old cattle railhead; seeing Kelly, the mining town up above it; on to Datil; Pie Town, with its remains of a 20th-century homesteading community; and Quemado; then on to Springerville, Arizona.

Let it be known that the residents of Catron County, along old US 60, object to two things in particular: environmentalists and wolves. This is an area of staunch independent thinkers, with strong Old West roots, and outsiders with nonlocal opinions are not favored. 'Nuff said.

It is possible, with any show of polite curiosity, to connect with the old-timers who still live along the road, who run the mom-and-pop shops, cafés, and motels. They have long memories and don't mind sharing their stories. There is not much going on, and days are fairly alike, so you yourself may provide the break in routine that is needed at the moment. This is where history still lives. With curiosity and a camera, you can experience the real West down to its bones. People are often willing to share information about historical characters, the legends of their place, their families, their special places, the best places to fish, those landmarks that aren't in the books, but where someone once lived, or where someone was once killed, or where a treasure is supposedly buried, and what ghosts haunt which buildings.

People out here are generally as friendly as their sharp ability to judge character instantly allows them to be. If they feel you are a decent person, they will literally give you the shirt off their back and the story of their lives. They will invite you to their home to look at their photos. The locals you encounter can be much better sources of information about a place than the initial pointers you will receive at the visitor center. This may be true for travelers in general, and it is especially true in rural New Mexico, where kindness is the currency.

Traveling west over NM 152 through the Black Range to Silver City, pass by Hillsboro and Kingston. Much of this area has gold, silver, and copper mining in its past. Some towns, like Silver City, have reinvented themselves as tourist towns with service economies. Others, like Winston, Chloride, and Kingston, have faded into true ghost town status. If you treasure the silence, the crumbling buildings of splintered wood and adobe, the ruins of former banks and jailhouses, and the spirit of place that evokes the past far more eloquently than any history book, you will find plenty to tempt you in Ghost Town Country.

Much of the country is still pretty wild, and it was among the last part of the United States to be taken from the Indians. This is the territory of Geronimo, Mangus Colorado, and the great woman warrior, Lozen, and other great Apache warriors, who fought hard for their homeland against the encroachment of the Americans. The vanished ancestors, the Mimbres, who made distinctive black-on-white pottery, and the people who built the Gila Cliff dwellings, left much to wonder about and be amazed at. They settled in the hospitable river country.

This is also the part of the world that inspired the first national wilderness area, named for the naturalist Aldo Leopold, who was inspired to push for the establishment of the Gila National Forest.

Another character who occupies a great deal of psychic space in our view of the West, Pancho Villa, made his foray over the border into the United States at Columbus, where old-timers continue to hold on to their versions of the raid. General Black Jack Pershing gave chase through Mexico, but he never managed to catch up with Villa. Pershing then went on to command the U.S. forces in Europe during World War I.

There is a sense in much of this place that life can still be hard. Folks' survival depends as much on their ability to trust as it does on their ability to read the rain clouds, and there's not much that escapes them.

If you like your history real, and you want to be immersed in it, and you don't mind the taste of grit or standing out in the wind, you will find much to appeal to you in southern New Mexico.

For convenience's sake, *Green Space* for all of southwest New Mexico is listed toward the end of the chapter, and all *Medical Emergency* information for the area is given at the beginning.

CAMINO COUNTRY: SOCORRO, TRUTH OR CONSEQUENCES, ELEPHANT BUTTE, HATCH, LAS CRUCES, MESILLA

B ig skies and wide open spaces define this area, as do the green chile fields of Hatch and the "six flags" that have flown over Mesilla Plaza. History is everywhere, in the faded advertisements painted on the sides of brick buildings, the thick adobe walls, and the WPA-era buildings. There is no forgetting that this is an area linked by road—yesterday's Camino Real, today's I-25. Beside the road, like a great ship, is the fantastic El Camino Real International Heritage Center. You will find a variety of experiences—starting with Bosque del Apache National Wildlife Refuge, to bustling Las Cruces, growing quickly with "amenities migrants," and the traditional small farming villages south of Mesilla. However, no matter how many Santa Fe and Albuquerque artists flee to quiet Truth or Consequences to open galleries and boutiques, and despite the construction of the Spaceport, a stronger sense of things continuing as they have always been remains. Refreshingly, Camino Country refuses to join the modern world completely.

GUIDANCE **Greater Las Cruces Chamber of Commerce** (575-524-1968), 760 W. Picacho, Las Cruces.

Elephant Butte Chamber of Commerce (575-744-4708), 608 NM 195, Elephant Butte. Open Mon.–Sat. 10–2.

Truth or Consequences/Sierra County Chamber of Commerce (575-894-3536), 400 W. Fourth St. at Civic Center, Truth or Consequences.

Socorro County Chamber of Commerce (575-835-0424), 101 Plaza, Socorro.

Socorro Heritage and Visitor Center (575-835-8927), 217 Fisher Ave., Socorro.

GETTING THERE Take I-25 south out of Albuquerque. Taking this road south to Las Cruces, you'll find all the towns and attractions listed in Camino Real

Country en route. To reach US Highway 60 country, take I-25 to exit 127 south to Socorro, then go west on US 60. To reach Ghost Town Country, take I-25 south to exit 63 onto NM 152.

MEDICAL EMERGENCY **Socorro General Hospital** (575-835-1140), 1202 Highway 60 West, Socorro.

Sierra Vista Hospital (575-894-2111), 800 E. 9th Ave., Truth or Consequences.

Memorial Medical Center (575-522-8641), 2450 S. Telshor Blvd., Las Cruces.

Mountain View Regional Medical Center (575-556-7600), 4311 E. Lohman Ave., Las Cruces.

Gila Regional Medical Center (575-538-4000), 1313 E. 32nd St., Silver City.

✳ To See

TOWNS **Socorro,** 72 miles south of Albuquerque on I-25, received its name from conquistador Juan de   in 1598 because he and his party were given much help and aid there by the native Piros. Today it is the home of a fine college, New Mexico Institute of Mining and Technology, a legacy from the days when it was the center of a rich mining district.

Truth or Consequences is 79 miles south of Socorro on I-25. When television host Ralph Edwards made the offer to bestow the name of his program, *Truth or Consequences,* to the American city that would change its name to that of the show, the little New Mexico town of Hot Springs jumped at the opportunity and became the town of Truth or Consequences, New Mexico. True to his word, Ralph Edwards returned every year for over 50 years to lead the parade in the annual May festival. Today the town is experiencing something of a renewal with the arrival of artists and artistically and community-minded folks from Albuquerque and Santa Fe looking for a cheaper place to live and express themselves. New Age–tinged paths of healing continue the older healing traditions of the place. The main street is now dotted with boutiques, health food stores, health-minded cafés, and a Black Cat bookstore as a result of the younger population's influence. T or C is still somewhat in transition, and it is an interesting and juicy transition, as the town reinvents itself and wakes up to find itself next door to the Spaceport. The town sits on a 110-degree hot spring aquifer and bills itself as the "Hot Springs Capital of the World," with many spa establishments. It also claims to be the most affordable spa town in the country.

Elephant Butte is 79 miles south of Socorro on I-25. With the construction of Elephant Butte Dam in 1912–16, a recreational area was born that today is home to marinas, vacationers, and year-rounders who enjoy the 40-mile lake and the 200 miles of shoreline that make it one of New Mexico's most popular state parks. If you look carefully—you may have to tilt your head or squint a bit—and use your imagination, you will see the silhouette of an elephant in a prominent butte.

Hatch is 34 miles south of Truth of Consequences on I-25. This agricultural town is known for three things: chile, chile, and chile! This is the home of the famous "Hatch chile," New Mexico's leading export and favorite food. Whether you favor red or green, this is the place to pull off the highway (I-25 at exit 41) and buy some. The best time to come here is August–October, when you can smell the aroma of roasting chiles and see the ripe red ones drying on rooftops and in strings of crimson chile ristras all over town.

Las Cruces is 223 miles south of Albuquerque on I-25. The unofficial capital of southern New Mexico, this rapidly expanding town near the border has been discovered by retirees and others seeking to relocate and is now a bona fide boomtown. It is home of New Mexico State University, and Aggies football and basketball are promoted and followed with much enthusiasm. With its climate, medical facilities, what has long been a reasonable real estate market, university, and a feeling of small town well-being and family-friendliness, the Las Cruces' attractions continue to grow. This is also the best place in the world to eat Mexican food. The only trouble is: so many cafés, so little time! This place is on a roll! (Or a tortilla!)

Mesilla. One mile south of Las Cruces on University Blvd. With Rio Grande *acequias* running through it, a historic plaza over which the flags of six nations have flown, and venerable adobe homes on streets wide enough for a burro cart to pass through, this sister city and next-door neighbor to the south of Las Cruces is the archetype of a historic village. The little town has plenty of

MESILLA VALLEY CHILE FIELDS.

galleries, cafés, and boutiques arrayed around the plaza, and it is fun to walk or jog along the ditch banks. The name "Mesilla" means "little table" and refers to the geographic spot where the town is located in the Mesilla Valley of the Rio Grande, a rich agricultural area where chile, cotton, onions, cotton, and pecans flourish.

MUSEUMS ♪ **Farm & Ranch Heritage Museum** (575-522-4100), 4100 Dripping Springs Rd., Las Cruces. Take the university exit 1 off I-25 and travel east, toward the Organ Mountains. Open Mon.–Sat. 9–5, Sun. noon–5. This is one place where the West is learned. This beautiful ranch-style museum maintains exhibits on agriculture in the West, and the best may be seen outside the galleries at daily blacksmithing demonstrations; the barns of sheep, cattle, and other animals; the Antique Equipment Park; and regular demonstrations of dowsing, milking, weaving, and quilting. There is ample vehicle access. A recent addition is the Green Bridge, New Mexico's second-oldest highway bridge, which was moved from the Rio Hondo and installed over Tortugas Arroyo. $5 adults; $3 seniors; $2 children 5–17; 4 and under free.

Geronimo Springs Museum (575-894-6600), 211 Main St., Truth or Consequences. Open Mon.–Sat. 9–5. Closed Sun. Located beside Las Palomas Plaza,

OLD-TIME MUSICIANS CELEBRATE THE INSTALLATION OF THE GREEN BRIDGE AT THE FARM & RANCH HERITAGE MUSEUM.

CHILDREN LEARN ABOUT QUILTING AT THE FARM & RANCH HERITAGE MUSEUM.

where Native Americans came to bathe in the hot springs, the museum has exhibits of each of Sierra County's cultures, from prehistoric times to the present day. Here get a good historical overview, from the mastodon and mammoth skulls to the Apache room; Hispanic Heritage Room, with a diorama of the Jornada del Muerto; to the exceptional pottery room; and best of all, the Ralph Edwards Room, with memorabilia on the Annual Fiesta. $2.

Mineral Museum (575-835-5420), southeast corner of Canyon Rd. and Olive Ln., on the New Mexico Tech campus, Socorro. Open Mon.–Fri. 8–5, Sat.–Sun. 10–3. Nicknamed "Coronado's Treasure Chest," this museum has an amazing display of gold, silver, fossils, mining artifacts, and precious gems, as well as top-quality mineral specimens found all over New Mexico. If you like rocks, this place will make you rock 'n roll. Free.

El Camino Real International Heritage Center (575-854-3600), 35 miles south of Socorro, I-25 exit 115. Open Wed.–Mon. 8:30–5. Closed Tues. This splendid state monument, just opened in 2005, sits on the Camino Real and tells the story of the road's 400-year history powerfully with state-of-the-art technology. Its magic conveys the story of the road as trade route, link between cultures, and lifeline from New Mexico to the rest of the world, to all ages. It sits like a magnificent ship out on the desert and must be seen by anyone who seeks to know this place. $5 adults, free 16 and under.

HISTORIC LANDMARKS, PLACES, AND SITES **Fort Craig** (575-835-0412), 32 miles south of Socorro, I-25 exit 124. A remote station on the Rio Grande, Fort Craig, commissioned 1854–85, was a base for U.S. Army campaigns against Native Americans and Confederates during the Civil War. Free.

Fort Selden State Monument (575-526-8911), Radium Springs. I-25 exit 19. Twelve miles north of Las Cruces. Open Wed–Mon. 8:30–5. Closed Tues. The second Sat. of every month 8:30–1 brings a living history program. The fort is so quiet now, the visitor would never imagine the activity it saw during the Civil War and the days of the Indian Wars. Perhaps its most famous resident was Captain Arthur MacArthur, its commanding officer in 1884, and his son, Douglas MacArthur, who became Supreme Commander of the Allied forces in the Pacific during World War II.

✹ To Do

BIRDING **Bosque del Apache National Wildlife Refuge** (575-835-1828), 9 miles south on I-25 to exit 139, east 0.25 mile on US 380 to flashing light at San Antonio, turn right onto NM 1, continue south 9 miles to visitor center. Visitor center open Mon.–Fri. 7:30–4, Sat.–Sun. 8–4:30. This premier winter day trip involves a drive to the bosque for the fly-in of thousands of cranes and geese at sunset. Winter is also the best time to spot bald eagles. Mid-Nov.–mid-Feb. is the peak time for viewing these migrants. Many varieties of birds winter here along the Rio Grande Flyway. Every season offers birding opportunities: summer is the time to see nesting songbirds, waders, shorebirds, and ducks; spring and fall warblers and flycatchers show up. Bring your bike for miles of level cycling along the ditches, lakes, and wetlands, and don't forget the binoculars. Fifteen-mile auto tour loop. $3 auto tour.

Mesilla Valley Bosque (575-524-4068), between Mesilla Dam and NM 538, is a brand-new day-use park state park on the banks of the southern Rio Grande, with a visitor center and interpretive programs highlighting birds and wildlife of the bosque, as well as beautiful trails for walking, jogging, and biking. $6.

CANOEING AND KAYAKING **Leasburg Dam State Park** (575-524-4068), 15 miles north of Las Cruces on I-25 or NM 185. Mar.–mid-Oct., enjoy canoeing and kayaking on the Rio Grande.

CLIMBING **Box Canyon** (no phone), I-25 exit 147 at Socorro, go west on US 60 for 6.8 miles, immediately after bridge go east. Second left is gravel road to parking area. This is a favorite red rock climbing and rappelling area west of Socorro.

FARMERS' MARKETS **Socorro Farmers Market** (575-835-8927), Socorro Plaza. July–Oct., Tues. 5 PM–7 PM, Sat. 8 AM–sellout. Fresh corn, watermelons, eggs, and all the glorious produce of the season sold in a neighborly, festive market.

Las Cruces Farmers & Crafts Market (575-541-2288), Downtown Mall, Las Cruces. Open-year round Wed. and Sat. 8–12:30. Several blocks of fresh produce and clever crafts, jewelry, handmade jams, soaps, and things you can't possibly find anywhere else make this one of the best farmers' markets.

Mesilla Mercado (575-524-3262), Mesilla Plaza. Thurs. and Sun. 11–4. Growers, artists, vendors, and street musicians bring the old plaza to life.

GOLF **New Mexico State University Golf Course** (575-646-3219), 3000 Herb Wimberly Dr., Las Cruces. Framed by the rugged Organ Mountains and the Mesilla Valley, the course challenges all skill levels by combining desert and traditional golf on this 18-hole course that is home to the Aggies' golf team. Very reasonable.

HIKING **Dripping Springs Natural Area** (575-525-4300), 10 miles east of Las Cruces. From exit 1 on I-25, take Dripping Springs Rd. to the end. At the base of the rugged Organ Mountains, this is the favorite hiking area of Las Cruces, with a 4.5-mile moderate-difficult hike. $3.

HOT SPRINGS **Truth or Consequences** (www.spa-town.com). The natural hot mineral springs here are geothermally heated with temperatures between

SUNDAY MORNING MARKET ON MESILLA PLAZA.

ORGAN MOUNTAINS, LAS CRUCES.

95–112 degrees Fahrenheit. With nine unique public bathhouses, ranging from funky to deluxe, mostly built in the 1920s, you have quite a choice of how you will experience getting into hot water here. Some have large tiled tubs, some have pebble-bottomed pools, and most have healing services such as massage, facials, aromatherapy, and hot rock treatments.

MOUNTAIN BIKING **Aguirre Springs** (575-525-4300), 22 miles east of Las Cruces on I-70. Mountain biking and camping, with a variety of trails that are part of the National Recreation Trail System. $3.

PARKS **Chihuahuan Desert Nature Park** (575-524-3334), east of Las Cruces on I-70, Mesa Grande exit to Jornada Rd. A 960-acre park with a 1.5-mile walking trail that has plant identification is a sweet education on the diverse ecosystems of the Chihuahuan Desert.

WINERIES **Blue Teal Winery** (575-524-0390), 1720 Avenida de Mesilla. Mon.–Sat. 11–6, Sun. noon–6. Hand-painted wine bottles and exhibits of local artists accompany tastings of award-winning reds.

La Vina (575-882-7632), 420 S. NM 28. Twenty miles south of Las Cruces.
Open Thurs.–Tues. noon–5. What a beautiful drive it is down south to the oldest
winery in the state, which hosts the oldest wine festival every October and a jazz
festival in April.

Wines of the Southwest (575-524-2408), next to the Fountain Theater in
Mesilla. Open Mon.–Thurs. 11–6, Fri.–Sat. 11–8., Sun. noon–6. When you need
(or want) to pick up a bottle of wine to enjoy, come here for the best selection of
New Mexico wine.

✷ Lodging

BED AND BREAKFASTS, MOTELS, AND INNS **Meson de Mesilla** (575-525-9212), 1803 Avenida de Mesilla, Mesilla. If you're looking for a small inn rather than a chain motel, this well-established 16-individually-decorated-room lodging will provide you with a fine breakfast cooked to order, full-service cocktail lounge, and a restaurant serving dinner on the premises. This is the nicest possible place to stay in the area. $129–189.

Sierra Grande Lodge and Spa (575-894-6976), 501 McAdoo St., Truth or Consequences. A rather upscale restored 1929 lodge with deluxe rooms featuring sunken tubs and well-chosen art, with complimentary outdoor tubs, as well as public facilities with massage and reflexology. The restaurant specializes in Mediterranean and Southwest fusion cuisine, featuring seasonal and vegetarian specialties. The restaurant is open for lodgers and the public Wed.–Sun. $99–129.

Dam Site Resort & Marina (575-894-2073), 5 miles east of stoplight on NM 52, Elephant Butte Lake State Park. An interesting conglomeration of legacies here: from the newly renovated Dam Site Lodge, built in 1911 to house dam construction engineers and now a comfortable lakeside resort; to the cozy, basic 1940-era tourist cabins built by the CCC; to

the Dam Site Restaurant and Lounge, which offers live music on the patio during warm weather; this is my favorite place to stay in the area. You can really see the elephant from here! This is the most interesting place to stay in the area. Out of the way, with a real sense of the expanse of the lake, as well as the feeling of a getaway, but not a fancy, resort. Rates vary. Moderate.

Elephant Butte Inn (575-744-5431), 401 NM 195, Elephant Butte. I-25, exit 83. From here, enjoy views of the lake and desert, spot wildlife, have a drink in the Ivory Tusk Tavern, and hike to Elephant Butte Lake. A deluxe continental breakfast is included. $80–90.

Riverbend Hot Springs (575-894-6183), 100 Austin, Truth or Consequences. Three outdoor soaking pools and one rock pool for $10 per person per hour. Open daily 8–7. Mineral soaks free with on-site lodging. $49–63.

CABINS AND CAMPING ⁗ᵀ⁗ **Caballo Lake RV Park** (575-743-0502), Caballo. Exit 59 off I-25, north 1 mile on NM 187 to Mile Marker 22. Wi-Fi, great fishing and birding, walking distance to the Caballo Lake beach, tours of remote ghost towns, and prospecting and gold panning are in easy reach here in this desert campground. $15 plus electric.

END

STOP

"♀" **Hacienda RV Resort** (1-888-686-9090), 740 Stern Dr., Mesilla. This is the life! Complimentary breakfast bar, concierge service, large patio, and hydrotherapy pool, plus Wi-Fi. Spacious, top of the line sites, cable TV. $34–39.

✳ Where to Eat

DINING OUT Double Eagle Restaurant (575-523-6700), Mesilla Plaza. daily 11–10. Within the oldest building on the plaza—and surely the most notoriously haunted; photos of the ghosts themselves are on the walls—is the most elegant dining in the area in Victorian splendor. Go for the opulent Sunday brunch, aged steaks (they claim the only dedicated beef aging room in the state) with fine wine from the extensive wine list, or just order a margarita at the long, ornate mirrored bar. **Peppers Café,** serving lighter, less expensive Southwestern fare, is located in the same venue. Expensive.

La Posta de Mesilla Restaurant, Cantina & Chile Shop (575-524-3524), Mesilla Plaza. Tues.–Thurs. and Sun. 11–9, Fri.–Sat. 11–9:30, in addition, open Mon. during summer. For a dedicated tourist restaurant, this place does a very good job of keeping up with the crowds. In fact, they serve my favorite chile rellenos plate, southern New Mexico style, just lightly sautéed in an egg batter, not breaded, so the taste and texture of the chiles stuffed with cheese sing forth. Located in the old Butterfield Stage Building, the place has a truly historic Southwest atmosphere. They boast of the largest tequila selection in the Southwest, and of course, the best margaritas. Moderate.

Los Arcos Steak & Lobster (575-894-6200), 1400 N. Date St., Truth or Consequences. Sun.–Thurs. 5–9 PM; Fri.–Sat. 5–10:30 PM. This is a dark, grown-up, scotch-and-steak sort of place, good for a date or a quiet conversation. A place with classic restaurant atmosphere, where service is as important, or more so, than the food, which is usually very good. Moderate.

EATING OUT Arrey Café (575-267-3822), Arrey. Daily 8–8. Is it the local beans and chile of this tattered homespun spot in the road, where chile growers are chowing down on the good stuff that makes this place such a find, or is it merely that it is so out of the way on a dusty deserted street that it could be the restaurant version of "the last picture show" that makes it so special? Drive the back road, NM 185, north of Hatch and find out. Inexpensive.

Pepper Pot (575-2678-3822), 207 W. Hall St., Hatch. Have a nice sit-down lunch, with tablecloths on the tables, where everyone seems to know each other, and you might even run into someone you graduated from college with, and order a big combination plate. Red or green, you can't lose. But this is green country, amigo. Inexpensive.

B&E Burritos (575-267-5191), 303 N. Franklin, Hatch. Are you going to eat green chile in the "Chile Capital of the World"? Aside from what religion the Pope is and what bears do in the woods, is that a silly question? Pull off the interstate and have a burrito, breakfast or otherwise, that you will remember the rest of your life. Inexpensive.

Owl Bar & Café (575-835-9946), US 380 and NM 1, San Antonio. Open Mon.–Sat. 8 AM–9 PM. Closed Sun. Home of the world-famous green chile cheeseburger, the Owl began when Manhattan Project scientists first came to the area to test the bomb on the nearby Trinity Site. The Owl is a New Mexico institution. The only thing to do is slide into a booth and order that burger with the homemade fries—the best. I am a fan of the moist, fresh-baked chocolate cake. Inexpensive.

Manny's Buckhorn Tavern (575-835-4423), 68 US 380, San Antonio. Closed Sun. Lunch, dinner. Located just across the street from the Owl, Manny's serves burgers superior to the Owl's, many say. Is the Owl just flying on its reputation? You be the judge. But locals' pickups jam this place every day at lunchtime.

Socorro Springs Brewing Co. (575-838-0650), 1012 N. California St., Socorro. Open daily. Lunch, dinner. This pleasant local brewpub serves good pizza, calzones, salads, sandwiches, and a menu with enough variety to please everyone in a relaxed atmosphere. Former New Mexico Tech grads started with a little place on the plaza, and it was so popular it grew into a main street attraction. Inexpensive–Moderate.

🍴 **Frank and Lupe's El Sombrero** (575-835-3945), 210 Mesquite, Socorro. Open daily. Lunch, dinner. Enjoy a wine margarita or imported beer with your delectable fajitas or chicken mole enchiladas. A friendly, long-established family-oriented local favorite. Inexpensive.

White Coyote Café (575-894-5160), 113 Main St., Truth or Consequences. Open daily. Breakfast, lunch. Organic,

vegetarian, and proud of it, this charming, sunny, corner 1920s-era building with the original red-oak floors have homemade baked goods that are well worth saving room for. Salads, omelets, and wraps make this a place to enjoy light, fresh fare. Go for the savory quiche. Inexpensive.

Andele Restaurant (575-526-9631), 2184 Avenida de Mesilla. Open daily. Breakfast, lunch, dinner. The fresh salsa bar is the attraction here, and the locals love it. This place could have the freshest, yummiest guacamole in town. Inexpensive.

🍴 **Dick's Café** (575-524-1360), 2305 S. Valley Dr., Las Cruces. Open daily 7 AM–8 PM. The college crowd mixes with bikers, truckers, and city employees to make this a classic casual stop with the locals. The chile cheeseburger is substantial and all-day sustaining. I love to wake up to the breakfast burrito doused in red, and the coffee has guts. There's a bit of turnover in the staff, and sometimes the service can be a little ditzy, but who cares? Relax, have another cup of coffee, and read the paper like the rest of the locals. A graduate of NMSU who confessed she got through school on the burgers, homemade fries, and delicious beans here introduced me to Dick's. Warning: the green chile is really hot. Inexpensive.

Chope's Bar & Café (575-233-3420), NM 28, La Mesa. Open Tues.–Sat. 11–2 and 5:30–8:30. Closed Sun.–Mon. Why are people standing in line out here in La Mesa, 12 miles south of Las Cruces, at lunchtime? While some maintain Chope's "isn't as good as it used to be," and truly, it has been uneven over the past few years, eating in this little old house where ladies are

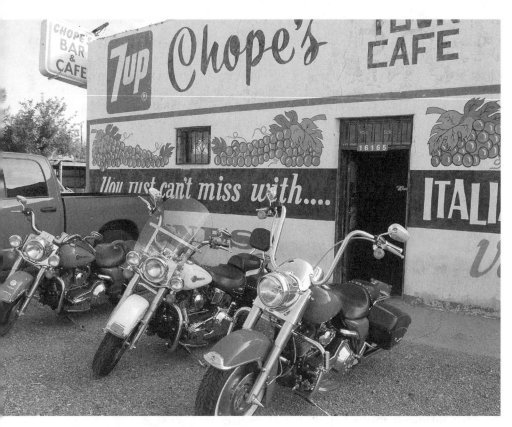

CHOPE'S HAS BEEN SERVING LA MESA SINCE BEFORE YOU WERE BORN.

rolling enchiladas in the kitchen is still a treat. The bar next door rocks with mariachis on a Friday evening. There's a good chance there was a Chope's before you were born, way back in 1940, and it is still in the founder's Benavidez family. It had a well-deserved reputation as a political hangout in the early days, and you can see several generations of families enjoying the red chile enchiladas and beef tacos together. Inexpensive.

Severino's (575-233-3534), across the street from Chope's in La Mesa. Open Wed.–Fri. 11–9, Sat. 10–9, Sun. 10–8. Don't overlook this place. The chips are fresh, the salsa is hot, the guacamole is fresh, and the food is authentic and made to order, then served by a waitress who actually cares about your enjoyment. You can avoid the overcrowding at Chope's and dine with more privacy, or just enjoy a cold one at the long mirrored bar. Inexpensive.

Caliche's (575-674-5066), 590 S. Valley Dr., Las Cruces. Open daily. If you haven't been to Las Cruces in a while, Scoopy's is now Caliche's. Good news—the frozen custard is still the best. Where else can you get a green chile pecan sundae? With a hot dog. If you can ever tear yourself away from the custard, try the mango Desert Ice to cool off. Better news—Caliche's now has locations in Alamogordo and Deming, in addition to the second Las Cruces location at Foothill and Roadrunner across from Mountain View Hospital. Free doggy cones! Inexpensive.

❝ɪ❞ **The Bean of Mesilla** (575-523-0560), 2011 Avenida de Mesilla, Mesilla. Open Mon.–Fri. 6:30–9, Sat. 7–9, Sun. 7–5. Breakfast, lunch, dinner. How pleasant it is to sip the fresh, strong coffee at a table on the sunny patio, munch a fresh-baked chocolate croissant, and leaf through the Sunday paper. This no-frills café has Wi-Fi, and you can catch performances of local musicians Thurs.–Sat. The Bean is a top-notch hangout or meetup café. Inexpensive.

Ranchway Bar-B-Que (575-523-7361), 601 N. Valley Dr., Las Cruces. Open Mon.–Sat. Lunch, dinner. Closed Sun. Las Cruces author and Border Book Festival founder Denise Chavez celebrates Ranchway in her memoirs, but that is only an indication of how dearly beloved this warm, chummy place is by those who grew up and live here. And how much they crave the meaty ribs slathered in that special sweet-spicy sauce. Mexican food is also served here, and the beef flautas are highly regarded, as is the caldo, the spicy stew. Inexpensive.

Nellie's Café (575-524-9982), 1226 W. Hadley Ave., Las Cruces. Open Tues.–Sat. 8–4. There is no better place to eat Mexican food than Las Cruces, and Nellie's is one of those local institutions that have helped the city establish and keep its reputation. Florescent-linoleum in feel, the minimal atmosphere only highlights the main attraction: the seriously delicious and seriously hot Mexican food of this "joint." It's all good! Nellie's started out as a burrito wagon in 1962. Inexpensive.

Cuchillo Café, Cuchillo. Fri. 4–7; Sat. 11–7; Sun. 11–7. It's not open often, and this simple whitewashed house is not exactly a four-star Michelin destination, but when it is, the stuffed sopaipillas are worth the drive off the interstate. Each entrée comes with a bottomless basket of hot, fluffy sopaipillas, and you can't resist eating more than your fill. Red chile over anything is the way to go here. And the fries are homemade, too. This would be a ghost town, but people actually live and work here. Nonetheless, you don't want to leave your camera home. Finding this place and eating here gives you bragging rights with those who think they know New Mexican food. Inexpensive.

✳ Entertainment

Fountain Theater & Mesilla Valley Film Society (575-524-8287), 2469 Calle de Guadalupe, half a block south of Mesilla Plaza. Screenings nightly 7:30 and Sun. matinees can catch you up and keep you current with cinema. This is virtually the only place south of Albuquerque where you can catch independent, foreign, and alternative films.

New Mexico Tech Performing Arts Series (575-835-5688), Macey Center, NM Tech, Socorro. Sept.–May. Live and symphonic and world music, dance, performance, and film brighten up the nights in southern New Mexico.

Capitol Bar (575-835-1193), 110 Plaza, Socorro. This 1896 watering hole presents live entertainment on the weekends. Bullet holes in the ceiling, shadows of jail cell bars, and surviving Prohibition, this is still the place to go in Socorro.

✳ Selective Shopping

Stahmann's Country Store (1-800-654-6887), 22505 NM 28 S., 6 miles south of Mesilla. Open daily 9–5.

Drive through the world's largest pecan orchard to this shop, where you can taste the products of the world's largest family-owned pecan business all produced right here. Over 128,000 trees produce from 8 to 10 million pounds of pecans a year. Candies, cookies, chile-flavored pecans, and chocolate-covered pecans, plus kitchenware and other goodies, are sold here. This is a great stop for gifts—who do you know who wouldn't love to receive a gift pack of chile pecans or chocolate pecan turtles? Tours may be scheduled to view the shelling process and candy plant.

Hatch Chile Express (575-267-3226), 622 N. Franklin, Hatch. Surprise your favorite chilehead with a gift from this well-stocked kitschy bazaar of chile-related and themed kitchenware, foodstuffs, and gifts, from a red chile spoon rest to chile-print boxers and ties. Jo Lytle, proprietor, holds the *Guinness Book of World Records* title for raising a 13.5-inch Big Jim chile.

Purple Lizard (575-523-1419), 1937 Calle de Parien, Mesilla. If your style tends to imports, funky or retro, or if you just want to pick up a unique handbag or accessory to punch up your look, this is a most enjoyable shop in which to hunt.

Del Sol (575-524-1418), 2322 Calle Principa, Mesilla. This Mesilla Plaza import shop is a treasure trove of lucky finds, in the way of wearables, household art, and décor. Casual, imports, natural fabrics, plenty of rayon and cotton for Southwest comfort, denim and hats, belts and jackets to accessorize, with good prices and good sales on styles that don't go out of style makes this one of my favorite places to shop.

La Vieja Antiques and Vintage (575-526-7875), 2230 N. NM 28, Mesilla. Ohmigosh! Vintage shopper alert! La Vieja, just off Mesilla Plaza, is absolutely crammed with one-of-a-kind wearables that, if paired properly, can make a memorable outfit for the opera or a potluck. My best find here: a fringed hot pink suede jacket for $20! My friend found an elegant embroidered green Chinese tunic she wears to the theater over black slacks with ballet flats.

Small Mall Antiques (575-647-0667), 810 W. Picacho Ave., Las Cruces. With over 20 dealers, this is a good place to kick off a tour of Las Cruces' Picacho antiques/second-hand district.

Rio Abajo Antiques (575-835-2872), one block south of Owl Bar on NM 1, San Antonio. Open Sun.–Wed. 10–4, June–July by appointment. A complete surprise en route to Bosque del Apache is this tiny shop packed with to-die-for classic silver and turquoise jewelry, maps, regional artifacts, religious items, books, postcards, and anything else worth collecting. The shop itself is a work of art to warm the heart of any true pack rat.

✳ Special Events

February: **Cuchillo Pecan Festival,** Cuchillo. **Festival of the Cranes** (575-835-1878), Bosque del Apache National Wildlife Refuge.

April: **La Vina Wine Festival** (575-882-7632).

May: **Ralph Edwards Day,** Truth or Consequences.

September: **Hatch Chile Festival,** Labor Day Weekend.

November: **Renaissance Fair,** Las Cruces. **El Dia de los Muertos** (575-526-7875), Mesilla.

THE PURPLE LIZARD IS A GREAT PLACE TO SHOP FOR THE OFFBEAT ITEMS YOU DIDN'T KNOW YOU NEEDED.

OLD HIGHWAY 60 COUNTRY: MAGDALENA, DATIL, PIE TOWN, QUEMADO

A long Old US Highway 60, nicknamed the "Pieway," you can find, in addition to many slices of fine homemade pie, sources of fascination from one end of the spectrum—cowboy country and wide open spaces—to the other, the very high-tech Very Large Array radiotelescope. In a sense, this slow road (55 mph), without chain stores or billboards, is a microcosm of New Mexico. The new and the old find the place big enough and accommodating enough to coexist and go their own distinct ways.

GUIDANCE **Magdalena Chamber of Commerce** (575-854-3092; 1-866-854-3217; www.magdalena-nm.com), P.O. Box 281, Magdalena, NM 87825.

✳ To See

TOWNS **Magdalena** is 27 miles west of Socorro on US 60. Supposedly the face of Mary Magdalene is visible on the mountainside at the eastern edge of town. The truth is, this was the cattle shipping railhead of the "Hoof Highway," or the "Beefsteak Trail," where cowboys rounded up and drove cattle in from ranches 125 miles west to Arizona and across the Plains of San Augustin and shipped them out on the railroad. The second weekend in July is "Old Timers Day," when the old storytellers return and the Queen, who must be over 70, is celebrated on a float in the parade.

Datil, 35 miles west of Magdalena on US 60, was named for the nearby Datil Mountains, which translates to "date" (perhaps a wild fruit that grew here). There's not too much to see here, but the Eagle Guest Ranch has been a convenient pit stop for travelers since folks first took to the road in automobiles. Gas, food, and lodging are still available.

Pie Town is 21 miles northwest of Datil on US 60. This 20th-century homesteader town baked its way out of the Depression by selling homemade pies to cowboys. Pies are still being baked here today, with a couple of cafés open, with

MAGDALENA, TRAIL'S END.

irregular hours, at what is largely a wide place in the road. Do get there early in the day if you want pie, because things tend to shut down by 3 PM.

Quemado is 43 miles west of Pie Town on US 60. Last chance! You're only 33 miles from the Arizona border here, so if you're heading west, you might think of gassing up and stopping for some home cooking in a local café before leaving. The name of the town means "burned" in Spanish, but no one is really certain how or why this name was given to the place.

MUSEUMS **Boxcar Museum** (575-854-2261), 108 N. Main St., Magdalena. A collection of vintage photos and artifacts of frontier life are housed here. Call for hours and fees.

HISTORIC LANDMARKS, PLACES, AND SITES **Very Large Array** (575-835-7243), 50 miles west of Socorro on US 60. Visitor center open 8:30–sunset. Closed major holidays. Did you see *Contact*, starring Jody Foster? If so, you will recognize the 27 giant dish antennas of the VLA, aka the National Radio Astronomy Observatory, out on the barren Plains of San Augustin. The visitor center shows a video and has exhibits explaining the VLA telescope and radio astronomy. An easy self-guided walking tour goes to the base of one of the antennas. Free.

Lightning Field, Quemado. An installation of 400 polished steel poles by American sculptor Walter De Maria that catches the changing light, and the lightning, of New Mexico's isolated high desert. You will be brought to the location, 45 miles outside Quemado, and permitted to stay overnight one night in a rustic cabin that sleeps six. You may be bunking with strangers. For reservations, contact: Dia Foundation, P.O. Box 2993, Corrales, NM 87048. $150 May–June, Sept.–Oct.; $250 July–Aug.

✳ To Do

CAMPING **Datil Well Campground** (575-835-0412), Datil. US 60 at Datil, south 1 mile on NM 12. You will find 1 mile of moderate hiking trails through piñon-juniper and ponderosa pine at this site of one of 15 wells that supplied water along the 1880s cattle driveway between Magdalena and Springerville, Arizona. Twenty-two campsites; firewood provided. $5 camping.

FISHING **Quemado Lake Recreation Area** (575-773-4678). From Quemado, west on US 60 for 0.5 mile, south on NM 32 for 16 miles to NM 103. Quiet and truly unspoiled, here are 800 acres of ponderosa pine that border a 131-acre man-made trout lake with three-season fishing. The area is regulated by the Quemado Ranger District of the Gila National Forest and contains seven campgrounds, two ADA fishing piers, and 7 miles of hiking trails. The Quemado Lake Overlook Trail is a moderate 1.5-mile hike one-way with about a 1,000-foot

VERY LARGE ARRAY RADIO TELESCOPE ON THE PLAINS OF SAN AUGUSTIN.

BACK ROAD REMNANT

elevation gain and is quite a photogenic trail with birding opportunities.

❋ Lodging

BED AND BREAKFASTS, MOTELS

The Western Bed & Breakfast, Motel and RV Park (575-854-2417/2412) offers three kinds of accommodations, including its 1956 knotty pine motel, or if you prefer, a Victorian room in old "Grandma Butter's" adobe home that served as a hospital during the 1920s. $41–60.

Rancho Magdalena Bed & Breakfast (1-800-462-5489), US 60, Mile Marker 109, west of Magdalena. "For Horses and their People," located right on the historic cattle driveway. Hunting and guide services are also available here. $105.

❋ Where to Eat

EATING OUT Pie-O-Neer (575-772-2711), US "Pieway" 60, Pie Town. Open Fri.–Mon. 10–3. Eat homemade pie on the Continental Divide. You have your choice of a dozen varieties. Homemade lunch as well. It's worth the trip!

Evetts Café & Fountain (575-854-2449), US 60 and N. Main, Magdalena. They can burn it, but they can't kill it. This old Magdalena Bank building has seen more fires and had more rising from the ashes than seems right, but it remains a necessary stop along the road, for nostalgia and for the real malts and milk shakes still served at a real lunch counter. The menu only lists the things that go best with such treats: burgers, fries, and hot dogs. So if you are seeking a

PIE-O-NEER CAFÉ, PIE TOWN.

return to those thrilling days of yesteryear, don't pass this place up. Inexpensive.

Daily Pie Café (575-722-2700), Pie Town. Open Tues.–Sat. 7–3. Closed Sun.–Mon. Order an entire pie with 48 hours advance notice. Home cooking on the Great Divide, and as they say, "It's all downhill from here." It's hard to say just who makes the best pie on this stretch of US 60, but this is an argument worth having. From the flaky crust to the flavorful fillings, the pies served here are absolutely divine. Join the "frequent pie-er" program. You can also get a very good home-cooked lunch. Inexpensive.

Eagle Guest Ranch (575-772-5612), US 60 and NM 12, Datil. This roadhouse began as a gas station and grocery shop and dates back to the early 20th century. It is still in the family. There is a competition on: many folks believe the pies baked here for the past 20 years by Loretta Kitchen are superior to those found up the road in Pie Town. You be the judge. Anything peach, lemon, or chocolate is worth tasting, and the towering coconut cream will send you to heaven. Steaks and burgers are the order of the day, and the Mexican food served Friday only will heat your bones. Expect to rub elbows with cowboys and hunters. Inexpensive.

MESILLA PLAZA.

❋ Entertainment

London Frontier Theatre Company (575-854-2519; www.london
frontiertheatre.com), Main at Fourth
St., Magdalena. Open select weekends Mar.–Dec. With over a dozen
seasons under its belt, and now
housed in its historic WPA theater,
the London Frontier Company regularly receives enthusiastic notices
from all who experience it. The season centers on plays related to the
West and its history, with the Christmas offering in December as a highlight. $3.50 adults; $2 children.

❋ Selective Shopping

Magdalena Arts, Inc. Gallery (575-
854-3318), 602 First St., Magdalena.
Find here an assortment of local art
by local artists in a wide range of
media.

Wild Horse Gallery (575-854-3388),
201 First St., Magdalena. This shop
features good Navajo rugs, jewelry,
gifts, and paintings.

Route 60 Trading Post and Gallery (575-854-3560), 400 First St.,
Magdalena. Authentic jewelry made
by Navajos living in nearby Alamo
is sold here, along with cowboy
art. You'll also find information on
US Highway 60 here.

GET YOUR DAILY PIE IN PIE TOWN.

❋ Special Events

July: **Magdalena Old Timers Day,**
Magdalena.

December: **Christmas Theater program,** Frontier Theater, Magdalena.

GHOST TOWN COUNTRY: HILLSBORO, GLENWOOD, RESERVE, COLUMBUS, SILVER CITY, DEMING

GUIDANCE **Old West Country** (1-800-290-833), 201 N. Hudson, Silver City.

Glenwood Area Chamber of Commerce (575-539-2711), P.O. Box 183, Glenwood, NM 88039.

Columbus Chamber of Commerce (575-531-3333), P.O. Box 350, Columbus, NM 88029.

Deming-Luna County Chamber of Commerce (575-546-2674), 800 E. Pine, Deming.

Silver City Chamber of Commerce (575-538-3785), 201 N. Hudson St., Silver City.

✳ To See

TOWNS **Hillsboro.** Once the center of gold mining activity, Hillsboro, 17 miles on NM 152 from the I-25 exit, was well on its way to becoming a true ghost town when it was discovered by a few urbanites who moved in and fixed up the old houses or built new ones to look just like the old ones. It's a pretty place with a decent café, and it really is the gateway to the Black Range. Cowboys drew from a hat for the honor of naming it, and it used to be the center of an apple-growing region. Alas! The Apple Festival is no more.

Glenwood. Sixty miles northwest of Silver City on US 180. Driving into Glenwood on a sun-dappled autumn day is like coasting into a lovely little piece of paradise, or a film set from the 1940s. Its proximity to the Catwalk has made it a pleasant stop for gas and a visit to any of the cafés you might happen to find open—usually one is.

Reserve is 36 miles north of Glenwood via US 180 and NM 12. Welcome to cowboy country, ma'am. A couple of bars, a gas station, and, if absolutely necessary, a motel, can provide for your immediate needs. This is not the place to

NO, PANCHO VILLA NEVER SLEPT HERE.

share your feelings with strangers. A retreat to your motel room with a good book is the best advice we can give.

Columbus is 32 miles south of Deming on NM 11. Not quite deserted enough to be classified as a true ghost town, Columbus still receives plenty of visitors seeking to learn more about Pancho Villa's Mar. 9, 1916, border raid as well as those touring Pancho Villa State Park. It is only 3 miles north of the Mexican border crossing at Palomas, and it is not a difficult matter to cross the border and do some shopping and dining "on the other side."

Silver City. Seventy-two slow miles across Emory Pass west of exit 63 off I-25, Silver City makes an excellent base for exploring the Gila Cliff Dwellings, attending any of the many annual area festivals, and enjoying the birdlife and wildlife, and it is a good enough stop on its own, with two museums, plenty of galleries, and some restaurants that will not disappoint you, plus an historic downtown. Founded in 1870 and named for the rich silver deposits west of town, its period architecture is marvelously well preserved. The place has, and still is having, a bit of a rough go as it transitions from being a mining town into tourism, or whatever comes next.

Deming, 61 miles west of Las Cruces on I-10, is convenient to both City of Rocks State Park and Rockhound State Park, and the town bills itself as

"Rockhound's Paradise." The big annual event is the annual Rockhound Round-up held in March. It is another small town you will generally spend time in because you are on your way to somewhere else, unless you are one of the many "snowbirds" who regularly winter here. There are over 30 restaurants, many of them chains, to serve the population. It has ample motel accommodations and low overhead, but there isn't much to do in the town itself, aside from touring the very worthwhile, recently remodeled Deming Lunas-Mimbres Museum.

MUSEUMS **Black Range Museum** (575-895-5233), NM 152, Hillsboro. Closed Jan.–Feb. Call for hours. This was once the home of British-born madam Sadie Orchard, the archetypal lady of the night with a heart of gold. She served the town during epidemics and donated to good works. Now it tells the story of the early days of Sierra County, with an emphasis on mining. Donation.

Percha Bank Museum (575-895-5032), Main St., Kingston. Open Sat.–Sun. 10–4 or by appointment. Hard as it is to believe, in 1890 this ghost town, population 30, was New Mexico's largest city, with 7,000 people. This museum offers an education on those days. Donation.

Deming Luna-Mimbres Museum (575-546-2382), 301 S. Silver, Deming. Open Mon.–Sat. 9–4; Sun. 1:30–4. Closed Thanksgiving, Christmas. Americana

A DELIGHTFUL COLLECTION OF ANTIQUE DOLLS AND DOLLHOUSES IS ON DISPLAY AT THE DEMING LUNA-MIMBRES MUSEUM.

SILVER CITY MUSEUM.

lovers, this is your new favorite place. Visit the Quilt Room; the Doll Room, with over 600 antique dolls; the ladies' fashion room; military room, with mementos of the Pancho Villa raid; and the Indian Kiva, with outstanding Mimbres pottery and native basketry. This newly remodeled 1916 armory now has 25,000 feet of exhibit space and a motorized chairlift. Contributions welcome.

Silver City Museum (575-538-5921), 312 W. Broadway, Silver City. Open Tues.–Fri. 9–4, Sat.–Sun. 10–4. Closed Mon. Open Memorial Day, Labor Day, and July 4. The museum, a brick Mansard-Italianate style home built by prospector Harry Ailman in 1880, showcases exhibits on local history and is not to be missed. This is one of the most beloved and best-curated and maintained museums in the Southwest. Free.

Western New Mexico University Museum (575-538-6386), Fleming Hall, 1000 W. College, Silver City. Open Mon.–Sat. This recently renovated hidden treasure of a museum houses the largest collection of prehistoric Mimbres black-on-white pottery in the nation. It will leave you breathless. Also on exhibit are Casas Grande pottery, mining artifacts, and prehistoric tools and jewelry. Call for hours. Free.

Columbus Historical Society Museum (575-531-2620), corner of NM 9 and NM 11, Columbus. Open daily 10–4. A restored 1902 Southern Pacific Railroad depot is the repository of collections on Columbus history, the Villa raid, and the railroad. Free.

HISTORIC LANDMARKS, PLACES, AND SITES **Poncho Villa State Park** (575-531-2711), 35 miles south of Deming via NM 11, Columbus. Open daily. Visitor center open daily 9–5. This is the only U.S. park named for a foreign invader! Here you can tour an extensive desert botanic garden; see the ruins of Camp Furlong, site of the attack; and view a display of early-20th-century military equipment. Birding is excellent, and camping is available. The new 7,000-square-foot exhibit hall showcases vehicles from the 1916 raid on Columbus in which 18 Americans were killed. This spot marks the site of the only ground invasion of American soil since 1812. The visitor center is housed in the 1902 Customs Service Building, and it is where you can learn from historic photos and exhibits all about Francisco "Pancho" Villa's attack, though many locals continue to tell their own versions of the event, if you show a bit of curiosity. $5 day use; $18 camping.

Gila Cliff Dwellings National Monument (575-536-2250), 44 miles north of Silver City on NM 15. Memorial Day–Labor Day 8–6, visitor center 8–5; the rest of the year 9–4, visitor center 8–4:30. Closed Christmas and New Year's Day. Contact the visitor center for information on guided tours. A short drive from the visitor center along the West Fork of the Gila River, a 1-mile loop trail leads through the dwellings, natural caves that were made into 40 rooms with stone quarried by these indigenous people. They were farmers who raised squash, corn, and beans on the mesa tops and along the river. We know them by these dwellings and for their exquisite black-and-white pottery. We do not know why they abandoned their homes and can only speculate that they may have joined other pueblos. They were the home of the Mogollon people who lived here from the 1280s until the early 1300s. The trail is steep in places, as there is a 180-foot elevation gain. For camping information, inquire at the visitor center. $3 individual; $10 family.

WILDER PLACES **Catwalk,** Glenwood. Take US 180 from Silver City to Glenwood; go right at NM 174 for 5 miles. Originally constructed by miners in 1889, this high walkway and suspension bridge leads to a waterfall through narrow Whitewater Canyon and over the Whitewater River in the Gila National Forest. You can easily imagine the ancient people who lived here, as well as Geronimo and Butch Cassidy hiding out here. The sycamore trees and rock walls make this place special any time of year, though especially in fall. The Catwalk follows the path of a pipeline built in the 1890s to deliver water to the mining town of Graham. The trail itself is easy, though there is some mild up and down. Free.

✳ To Do

FARMERS' MARKETS **Silver City Farmers' Market** (575-388-9441), 1400 US 180 E., Silver City. Open May–Oct., Sat. 8:30–noon.

PICNICKING NEAR THE CATWALK IN GLENWOOD.

SCENIC DRIVES

Geronimo Trail Scenic Byway (575-894-6600), 211 Main St., Truth or Consequences, is the site of the trail's interpretive and visitor center. Open Mon.–Sat. 9–5. The geology, flora and fauna, history, and events of the area are available here. Travel a loop starting from Truth or Consequences up the Mimbres across Emory Pass of the Black Range, passing through geological and cultural eons, and certainly, traveling in Geronimo's footsteps. The trail loops back at San Lorenzo on NM 152. This is an all-day trip for sure at 220 miles, and you might want to choose a place, like Kingston or Hillsboro, to spend the night.

NM 185 Back Road. North from Las Cruces or Dona Ana to San Antonio through pecan groves and chile fields for a view of the wilder side of the Rio Grande you can't get any other way. You can avoid the interstate all the way along this scenic two-lane. Glorious!

Lake Valley Back Country Byway. East from Deming to Truth or Consequences via Hillsboro. Take NM 1521 and 27 for 47 miles. Slow going and well worth the trip. You'll see ghost towns and unparalleled views of the mountains south of Truth or Consequences.

Gila Cliff Dwellings/ Trail of the Mountain Spirits Scenic Byway. NM 15 north from Silver City into the Gila National Forest to the Cliff Dwellings for 110 miles, through Pinos Altos, Lake Roberts, the Mimbres River, and the Santa Rita open pit copper mine to the Cliff Dwellings. Allow plenty of time, as the road is slow and there is much to see.

FISHING **Lake Roberts** (575-536-3663), US 180 north from Deming to City of Rocks turnoff. Continue on NM 61, then NM 35 for 66 miles to the intersection of NM 15 and NM 35. Or take NM 35 north from Silver City. Open year-round. This sweet trout fishing lake, which appears like a surprise on the side of the road in the Gila National Forest, has three campgrounds. $7 camping.

GOLF **Rio Mimbres Country Club and Golf Course,** Deming. Eighteen-hole public golf course, east end of Deming with views of Cooke's Peak and the Floridas, with pleasant lakes and paths. Inexpensive.

Silver City Golf Course (575-538-5041), NM 90 west from downtown, left on Ridge Road. Open year-round, weather permitting. A challenging 18-hole championship public course with high desert vistas, natural vistas, and mild weather. $16–21.

HORSEBACK RIDING **Gila Wilderness Ventures** (575-539-2800; www.gila wildernessventures.com). Take US 180 for 3 miles north of Glenwood, then go 3 miles east on NM 159. Leah Jones is a well-seasoned veteran outfitter on the

GHOST TOWNS

Kelly. While the rumor is that Monsieur Gustav Eiffel, of Eiffel Tower fame, constructed the mining head frame here, it turns out to be a colorful story only. Once a booming mining town of 3,000 located 2 miles north of Magdalena where zinc, copper, then silver were mined, Kelly is a ghost town made for exploring. Artists come here to retrieve materials, and care must be taken because not all the old buildings or mine shafts are well protected. However, even if you don't actually see the ghosts said to roam here, you can certainly feel their presence.

Bayard Historical Mining District (575-537-3327). Now owned by the Phelps Dodge Mining Co., the six underground shafts with head frames of this once-busy mining district, which produced more gold, silver, copper, lead, zinc, iron, manganese, and molybdenum than all the other mining districts in New Mexico combined, may be toured by automobile. This area is popular with mountain bikers, horseback riders, and birders. The Buffalo Soldiers, the African-American unit of the Ninth Cavalry, was stationed here 1866–99. Get tour information at the Bayard City Hall.

Winston (no phone) is so close to Chloride that the two towns are generally visited on the same trip. Both towns are at the base of the Black Range.

Chloride (575-743-2736), Main St., Chloride. California retirees Don and Dona Edmonds were inspired to purchase the entire town of Chloride, and they have, through the saintly labor of their own hands, been restoring it building by building. The general store has become the Pioneer Store Museum, open daily 8–5. Open for tours. All the original stock is still in place. You have to really want to come here, and it is an effort to reach this place, but you won't soon forget it, either.

Mogollon (mo-go-yone). Two hours north of Silver City on US 180, right on NM 159 between Glenwood and Alma. Calling all hardcore explorers: what is termed New Mexico's most remote ghost town, and, I must say, one of its most haunting, is accessible only by a 9-mile road that climbs 2,080 feet via switchbacks, without guardrails. The last 5 miles become a one-lane road. Founded in 1895, this gold rush boomtown was the state's leading mining district by 1915. While accommodations and attractions (aside from exploring and photographing on your own) come and go, at last moment before press time, the **Silver Creek Inn** (1-866-276-4882) was a functioning bed and breakfast, and the **Mogollon Prehistoric Native Museum** (575-539-2016) was open during summer weekends. Do check road conditions carefully before you go.

Kingston. Nine miles west of Hillsboro on NM 152. The home base of Sadie Orchard, the British madam with a heart of gold who made her fortune here, Kingston was a rip-snorting place with dozens of brothels and saloons and banks during the silver mining heyday. Hard to believe now, but it was once home to 7,000. Today, population 30. The old Victorio Hotel and Percha Bank still stand. Now it is quiet, picturesque, and the home of one delightful Black Range Lodge (see *Lodging*), and where javalinas roam Percha Creek.

Pinos Altos. Six miles north of Silver City on NM 15, this town sits directly on the Continental Divide. The Old West lives on here in a mining town where the Hearst Mine supplied the gold for the Hearst Castle. It is fun to photograph the splintering, wooden buildings, some housing the occasional gallery or ice cream parlor, at sunset in their splendid decay; perhaps spot an elk wandering across the road; and order a steak at the Buckhorn Café.

San Antonio. Fourteen miles south of Socorro at the junction of NM 1 and US 380 off I-25 exit 139 east, San Antonio is known as the hometown of hotelier Conrad Hilton, whose father ran a boardinghouse here. It is also the gateway to Bosque del Apache National Wildlife Refuge and on the main road east to Lincoln and Billy the Kid country. Today it is the home of two famous burger houses: the Owl Café and, coming up quick in the polls, Manny's Buckhorn.

Shakespeare (575-542-9034), 2.5 miles southwest of Lordsburg. I-10 from Lordsburg at Main St. exit 22, go south and follow the signs. Open a few days each month. Guided tours available. Shakespeare, which bills itself as "the West's most authentic ghost town," might well call itself Phoenix. Owned and operated since 1935 by the Hill family, it has recovered from the ashes of a terrible fire in 1997 and is again offering 90-minute guided tours by Janaloo Hill as well as shootouts and special events for slightly high admission. Shakespeare, named for the mining company that held silver claims, was a stagecoach and mining town in its day, and here you can see the assay office, old mail station, saloon, general store, and much more. $4 adults; $3 children 6–12.

Gila Wilderness. Whether you prefer a day ride, pack trip, custom trip, or drop camp, it can all be arranged to your liking. Leah's talents include Dutch oven cooking.

WolfHorse Outfitters (575-534-1379), Santa Clara. Within the Gila National Forest, create a horseback adventure with this Native American guide service. Rides through the wilderness, lodge to lodge, to the ruins, and in the moonlight.

HOT SPRINGS **Faywood Hot Springs** (575-536-9663; www.faywood.com), next to City of Rocks State Park on NM 61, halfway between Silver City and Deming. Open daily 10–10. There are over a dozen shaded, outdoor, natural, geothermal mineral water soaking pools, some public, some private, and some for overnight guests, who may use the public pools all night. "Limp in, leap out" is the motto here. Cabins, RV, and tent sites are available.

PARKS **Big Ditch Park**, behind Bullard St., Silver City. The flood of 1895 roared through Silver City with 12-foot-high waters, leaving behind a ditch 35 feet below street level. The subsequent flood of 1903 lowered the "Big Ditch" 20 feet more. It is now a pleasant town park for strolling and picnicking, directly behind downtown.

Happy Flats Iris Garden (575-895-5635), NM 152 and Ninth St., Hillsboro. Blooming April and May. Ellen Tow has cultivated a stunning display of iris varieties on her property; she sells bulbs as well as homegrown and homemade apple butter and peach jam. A find!

WILDLIFE REFUGES **Wolfsong Ranch** (575-557-2354), Rodeo. Sitting near the New Mexico–Arizona border in the San Simon Valley, on 440 acres in the "boot heel" country of Hidalgo County. Habitat preservation, education, and experimental learning opportunities abound, and many of these animals have been injured or orphaned. This is a refuge for unwanted and abandoned wolves, wolf dogs, and other wild animals. Horseback tours are available. Donations recommended.

WINERIES **St. Clair Winery** (1-877-366-4637; www.stclairvineyards.com), 1325 De Baca Rd., Deming. I-10 west from Las Cruces about 60 miles. Open Mon.– Sat. 9–6, Sun. noon–5. No appointments are needed for the tours offered Sat. and Sun. Grapes grown in the vineyards right here produce lovely Cabernet, Chardonnay, and Zinfandel. St. Clair also operates a restaurant and tasting room in Albuquerque's Old Town.

✳ Green Space

Elephant Butte State Park, Caballo Lake State Park, and Percha Dam lie like three separate but neighboring versions of a similar geography, all fed by the Rio Grande, arrayed from north to south.

Elephant Butte State Park (575-744-5923), I-25 exit 83, 5 miles north of Truth or Consequences. Open daily, 24 hours a day. It is huge, with 200 miles of shoreline and hundreds of campsites. This is a place for water sports of all kinds: wind surfing, fishing, and waterskiing, in addition to fishing, birding, and rock-hounding. Elephant Butte Lake is the largest body of water in New Mexico, and it is well known for trophy fish, including striper, bass, and walleye. There are no elephants, only the eroded core of a volcano in the middle of the lake that some-how reminded someone of an elephant. The park hosts close to 1.7 million visi-tors annually. Be forewarned, Memorial Day, Fourth of July, and Labor Day can draw between 80,000–100,000 visitors. The U.S. Bureau of Reclamation built the dam from 1912 to 1916, primarily for irrigation purposes; the reservoir capacity is 2.2 million acre feet. Boats and Jet Skis are available for rental at the two marinas. Public tours of the power plant are available. $5 day use; $10–18 camping. Houseboat, pontoon, ski boat rentals (1-888-736-8240).

Caballo Lake State Park (575-743-3942), 16 miles south of Truth or Conse-quences at exit 59 off I-25. Named for the wild horses descended from the horses brought here in the 1540s by the Spanish, at Caballo find a recreation area and lake against the background of the Caballo Mountains just south of Ele-phant Butte, and it is much, much quieter, with excellent bass and walleye fish-ing. The champion striper from Caballo Lake weighed 51 pounds. There is plenty of camping available here. This is just about your best bet to see migrat-ing bald and golden eagles. We have spotted a few during the winter, and about 50 are known to reside in the area. $5 day use; $10–18 camping.

Percha Dam State Park (575-743-3942). Just south of Caballo Dam. Known for its ADA-accessible playground and spectacular bird-watching, this park, with

GILA NATIONAL FOREST

3005 E. Camino del Bosque, Silver City (575-388-8201). Ranger office open Mon.–Fri. 8–4:30. Measuring over 3.3 million acres—the nation's sixth-largest national forest—the vast Gila is incomparable in its diversity and the opportunities it offers for outdoor recreation. Its varied terrain ranges from high desert at 4,200 feet to rugged mountain and canyon lands at 10,900, and four of the six life zones of planet Earth are found here. Your best bet is to contact the number above to plan your trip around your specific interests. The forest, named for the Spanish corruption of a Yuma Indian word mean-ing "running water that is salty," is accessible from many of the small towns in southwest New Mexico, including Quemado, Glenwood, and Reserve. Whether your interests include birding, hiking, camping—which is mostly primitive, but does include RV hookups—ATV-ing, fishing, rafting, mountain biking—it is all here, at all levels of challenge. Nearly 400 species of birds make this their home or nesting area. The forest includes the Gila Wilder-ness and the Aldo Leopold Wilderness, the nation's first, founded in 1924. A section of the Continental Divide Trail lies within the forest. You could spend a week here, a summer, or a lifetime.

CITY OF ROCKS STATE PARK.

its huge cottonwoods, usually remains quiet, as it is still somewhat undiscovered.
There are no developed hiking trails, only paths to the river, and walking along
the dirt roads is a fine way to go. $5 day use; $10–18 camping.

City of Rocks State Park (575-536-2800), US 80 24 miles from Deming west
toward Silver City, then 4 miles northwest on NM 61. Open daily 7 AM–9 PM.
With the feel of a natural Stonehenge, this state park is an astounding array of
pillars of 34.9-million-year-old wind-sculpted volcanic ashes, some up to 40 feet
tall. Paths run between the rock columns like the streets of a "city." There's an
astronomy observatory and starry-night programs. This could be the state's premier dark-skies opportunity. $5 day use; $10–18 camping.

Rockhound State Park/Spring Canyon (575-546-6182). From Deming, go
south 5 miles on NM 11, then east on NM 141 for 9 miles. Open daily 7:30–sunset. Set on the western slope of the Little Florida Mountains, the visitor center
here has displays pertaining to the geology and history of the area. Known as a
rockhounder's paradise; every visitor is permitted to take 150 pounds of rocks
home. There are good pickings in jasper and perlite, and you can find some geo-
des or thunder eggs, as they are known. $5 day use; $10–18 camping.

✳ Lodging

**BED AND BREAKFASTS, MOTELS,
AND INNS** 🏠 **Black Range Lodge**
(575-895-5652; www.blackrangelodge
.com), 119 Main St., Kingston. When
Kathryn Wanek and her new husband
drove out from Los Angeles on their
honeymoon, they spotted this old mining hotel, fell in love with it, and
decided to buy it on the spot. Since
that fortuitous day, this rather dark,
massive lodge has turned into a merry
B&B. Massive stone walls and log-
beamed ceilings date to 1940, but the
original dates to the 1880s, when it
was built to house miners and cavalry.
Despite improvements in the seven
guest rooms, the original character of
the place has not been tinkered with.
Cyclists and tourists come from all
over the world to stay and enjoy the
informality of the buffet breakfast with
homemade bread, waffles, and fruit. It
has the feeling of a hostel, with shared
claw-foot tubs. The new luxury guest
house has a jetted hot tub and complete kitchen and wraparound deck
($139). The new Percha Creek House

has five bedrooms, kitchen, dining, living room, and large deck ($250).
Kathryn has since become an expert
on straw bale construction. $69–89.

Palace Hotel (575-388-811), 106 W.
Broadway, Silver City. Every town has
a grand old hotel, and the 1900 Palace
is Silver City's. Though rather more
diminutive than grand, it is where to
stay if you collect historic hotel experiences. The 22 rooms are small, and,
facing directly on a busy street corner,
it is not the quietest place in the
world. The continental breakfast will
get you going, but you won't find anything out of the ordinary. But it is
comfortable, it has been restored, and
if you are not expecting the Holiday
Inn and don't mind carrying your lug-
gage up and down a couple flights of
stairs, all will be well. And all of
downtown is in walking distance. $49.

⁗¡⁗ **Casitas de Gila Guesthouses**
(575-923-4827), 310 Hooker Loop,
Gila. Five private guest houses in perfect Southwest style and comfort are
perched on a ledge overlooking Bear

BLACK RANGE LODGE, IN THE BLACK RANGE GHOST TOWN OF KINGSTON.

Creek and the Gila Wilderness. The experienced innkeepers, Becky and Michael O'Connor, used to run a bed and breakfast in Ireland, and privacy and peace and quiet are what you can expect here. The gallery displays a good selection of folk art, icons, and jewelry. Bring your binoculars to spot the bighorn sheep across the river. Also, bring your own food to cook in the fully equipped kitchens. Wi-Fi, too, but no TV. Great stargazing, though. This spot frequently makes the list of "most romantic spots in New Mexico." $125–200.

Inn on Broadway (575-388-5485), 411 W. Broadway, Silver City. Three guest rooms and a Garden Suite conjure the glories of this 1883 mer-

chant's home with marble fireplaces and hand-carved imports from Germany. There's a shady front veranda in this grand home. $90–140.

RANCHES AND LODGES **Bear Mountain Lodge** (575-538-2538), 2251 Cottage San Rd., Silver City. Now owned and operated by the Nature Conservancy, this 11-room lodge is a birder's dream come true, especially during hummingbird season in July–Aug., when numerous varieties descend on Silver City. $115–185.

WS Land & Cattle Co. (575-539-2513), Glenwood. Saddle up and giddy up at this multigeneration working ranch in Alma just outside

Silver City. Rest up in the rustic yet elegant bunkhouse. Ask about rates.

CABINS AND CAMPING Continental Divide RV Park (575-388-3005), 6 miles north of Silver City on NM 15, Pinos Altos. Smack in the middle of an apple orchard with views of the Gila National Forest, this site accommodates RVs. Cabins and tent sites available, too.

Bear Creek Motel and Cabins (575-388-4501). Bordering Bear Creek at the gateway to the Gila National Forest are some comfortable furnished cabins with porches and balconies among the tall pines. $99–119.

Lake Roberts General Store (575-536-9929), Lake Roberts, Silver City. The cabins are fully furnished with kitchens or kitchenettes, so you can catch it and cook it.

Gila Hot Springs Ranch & Doc Campbell's Post (575-536-9551), Gila Hot Springs. Enjoy a real kickback time in a motel-like room; bring your RV or camp by the river. Natural hot pools and jetted tub, horseback riding, and fishing make this a real vacation. $50–75.

✳ Where to Eat

DINING OUT ❧ **Diane's Restaurant and Bakery** (575-538-8722), 510 N. Bullard St., Silver City. Lunch Tues.–Sun. 11–2, brunch Sat.–Sun. 9–2, dinner Tues.–Sat. 5:30–9. No matter how many times you eat at this lovely downtown bistro, the food and service are impeccable. Fish, chicken, steak, and more light, harmonious, sophisticated fare, thoughtfully prepared, with just the right spicing and saucing, at a reasonable price—what more

could you ask? Try the roast Asian duck with sweet sesame glaze, juicy meat loaf with garlic mashers, or pesto pasta. Moderate.

❧ **Shevek and Mi** (575-534-9168), 602 N. Bullard St., Silver City. Open Thurs.–Tues. Lunch, dinner weekdays; breakfast, lunch, dinner weekends. Closed Wed. One special feature of this excellent restaurant is that you may order the same dish in one of three sizes: tapa, mezze, or entrée, depending on your appetite or your desire to sample several tastes. This is a vegetarian-friendly place: feta stuffed roasted pepper, Cabrales blue cheese and apple crostini are served along with orange and coriander duck, lobster mousse, and tournedos of beef with sautéed wild mushrooms and lemon-mint roasted potatoes. You find a level of sophisticated and authentic Mediterranean taste, along with an extensive wine list, that you would expect in a big city. Moderate–Expensive.

❧ **Buckhorn Saloon & Opera House** (575-538-9911), NM 15, Pinos Altos. Open daily 6–10 PM, dinner only. Saloon opens at 3. Closed Sun. Open-mic night Mon.; live music Wed.–Sat. This 1860s establishment is really a necessary New Mexico experience. The Old West saturates the foot-and-a-half thick adobe walls, and the Buckhorn radiates real romance in its dimmed lights. In fact, this place may have invented "character." You're guaranteed to meet memorable characters at the bar, if that is your choice. The steaks are excellent, prepared perfectly, and served with fresh baked sourdough bread and all the trimmings, including house-made dressings for your salad. Love that filet mignon! Reservations are a very

WHIMSICAL SILVER CITY DOORWAY.

good idea here, especially on weekend nights. Moderate–Expensive.

EATING OUT ☙ **Jalisco Café** (575-388-2060), 103 S. Bullard St., Silver City. When I first ate here about 20 years ago, there were lace curtains on the windows of a one-room establishment. When Silver City rancher friends brought me here last summer, the place had expanded to three colorful rooms of folks enjoying the hot fluffy sopaipillas, green chile chicken enchiladas, and zippy salsa on the warm, house-made chips. Inexpensive.

La Fonda (575-546-0465), 601 E. Pine St., Deming. Enjoy the fresh warm chips, deliciously spicy salsa, fluffy sopaipillas, and delicious enchiladas at this very friendly and welcoming local spot. The Mexican food served here ranks with the best. Inexpensive.

✳ Entertainment

Pinos Altos Melodrama Theatre (575-388-3848), Opera House, Pinos Altos. Fri.–Sat. at 8 most of the year. Reservations are usually necessary for this slapstick melodrama. Enter through the Buckhorn Saloon.

Copper Creek Ranch (575-538-2971), 20 Flury Ln., Silver City. Four and a half miles east of Silver City on US 180 east. Open daily, rain or shine, late May–early Sept., Fri.–Sat., 6–closing. This particular chuckwagon BBQ supper and Western show gets good reviews even from locals. Live music is provided by Silver City's Copper Creek Wranglers.

✳ Selective Shopping

Gila Hike & Bike (575-388-3222), 103 E. College, Silver City. This is the place to come when preparing a bike trip of any kind, to get equipment, service, maps, and rentals.

Yankie Street Artist Studios (575-313-1032), 103 W. Yankie, Silver City. Various local artists display their pottery and paintings here.

Southwest Women's Fiber Arts Collective (575-538-5733), 107 Broadway, Silver City. This grassroots cottage industry markets the work of fiber artists in the rural Southwest.

✳ Special Events

February: **Cuchillo Pecan Festival** (575-894-0707), 211 Main St., Cuchillo. Last Sat. I-25 exit 83, west on NM 54 for 15 miles. This tiny family-owned pecan orchard puts on a great big party with orchard tours, homemade chocolates, food, and crafts booths; evokes the old days.

March: **Border Book Festival** (575-524-1499). Comprehensive celebration of Southwest literature, including children's and Spanish literature, with authors, book signings, music, special events all over town, and a book fair on Mesilla Plaza. **Rockhound Roundup** (575-267-4399), Southwestern New Mexico Fairgrounds, 4750 Raymond Reed Blvd., Deming. Second weekend.

May: **Tour of the Gila Bike Race** (1-800-548-9378), Silver City, first week. This event is billed as America's most popular five-day stage race. **Southern New Mexico Wine Festival** (575-522-1232), Southern New Mexico State Fairgrounds. Live entertainment and sampling of New Mexico wines. Last weekend.

July: **Magdalena Old Timers' Reunion,** weekend after Fourth of July. Cattle drive, parade, rodeo, barbeque, fiddlers' contest; and a good time is had by all.

August: **Great American Duck Race** (575-544-0469), 202 S. Diamond, Deming. Fourth weekend. Has it come to this? It sure has.

September: **Hatch Chile Fiesta,** Labor Day Weekend, despite its popularity and longevity, retains its down home authenticity with food and craft booths, live music, and, of course, lots of fresh-roasted chile to sample and buy. **Whole Enchilada Festival** (575-526-1938), Meerscheidt Recreation Center, Las Cruces. Having set the Guinness world record for the biggest enchilada, this festival has evolved into one for-sure big old street party. **New Mexico Wine**

Harvest Festival (575-522-1232), Southern New Mexico State Fairgrounds, Labor Day weekend.

October: **Geronimo Days** (575-894-6600), Truth or Consequences, second week, is a celebration of the many cultures that have sought the healing waters. **Whole X Prize Cup** (310-587-3355), Las Cruces International Airport, is billed as "the greatest space exposition on earth" with demo flights and a spaceflight symposium. Third weekend.

November: **Festival of the Cranes** (575-35-1828), Bosque del Apache National Wildlife Refuge, weekend before Thanksgiving. Workshops, tours, special birding events. **Dia de los Muertos,** Day of the Dead,

THE AUTHOR CAN'T RESIST THE HATCH CHILE FIESTA.

Mesilla Plaza, Mesilla. First weekend. Following the Mexican custom of building altars and feasting on the graves of departed family members, Mesilla Plaza is now filled with altars and craft booths at this time, and the custom has been revived here during the past 10 years to include a procession to the cemetery. **Renaissance**

Craftfaire, Young Park, Las Cruces. Second weekend. Joust on, all ye lords and ladies, knights and maidens, in costume, please.

December: Most towns and many state parks and monuments have luminaria tours during the month. Please check individual listings.

Southeast New Mexico: Billy the Kid Country

BILLY'S STOMPING GROUNDS:
CAPITAN, FORT SUMNER, LINCOLN,
CARRIZOZO, TULAROSA,
ALAMOGORDO, RUIDOSO, ROSWELL,
CLOUDCROFT, CLOVIS

CAVERN COUNTRY: CARLSBAD,
WHITE'S CITY

OIL PATCH COUNTRY: ARTESIA,
HOBBS, LOVINGTON, PORTALES

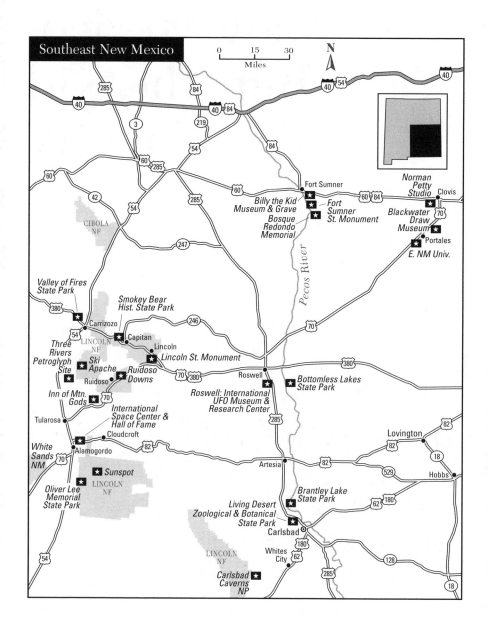

Southeast New Mexico

0   15   30
Miles

N

Norman Petty Studio
Clovis
Blackwater Draw Museum
Portales
E. NM Univ.

Fort Sumner
Billy the Kid Museum & Grave
Fort Sumner St. Monument
Bosque Redondo Memorial

Pecos River

CIBOLA NF

Valley of Fires State Park
Smokey Bear Hist. State Park
Carrizozo
Capitan
LINCOLN NF
Lincoln
Lincoln St. Monument
Three Rivers Petroglyph Site
Ski Apache
Ruidoso Downs
Ruidoso
Roswell
Bottomless Lakes State Park
Inn of Mtn. Gods
Roswell: International UFO Museum & Research Center
Tularosa
International Space Center & Hall of Fame
Cloudcroft
Lovington
White Sands NM
Alamogordo
Artesia
Hobbs
Sunspot
LINCOLN NF
Oliver Lee Memorial State Park
Living Desert Zoological & Botanical State Park
Brantley Lake State Park
Carlsbad
LINCOLN NF
Whites City
Carlsbad Caverns NP

INTRODUCTION

Like a hidden canyon where exposed walls reveal the earth's turbulent formation, southeast New Mexico tells the tumultuous story of the West's natural and social history. In this easily accessible region, it is possible to experience within a few days the history of the West, from the prehistoric petroglyphs of Three Rivers to one of the West's most notorious battles, the Lincoln County War, starring one William H. Bonney, aka, Billy the Kid. In addition, southeast New Mexico holds the beginnings of the Atomic Age at the Trinity Site and the visual record of space travel at the New Mexico Museum of Space History in Alamogordo. Along the way are enduring legends and unsolved mysteries, agricultural festivals and Apache ceremonials, all highlighted by eye-popping natural beauty around almost every turn in the road.

Entering southeast New Mexico off I-25 south of Socorro and heading east, the visitor traverses the Valley of Fires State Park, a stunning black rock landscape, known as *malpais* (badlands), created by a lava flow as recently as 1,000 to 1,500 years ago, a landscape relieved by the 10-foot-high yucca stalks.

As extraordinary microcosms of evolution, critters living on the black lava flows have evolved to blend in, as creatures that dwell in the White Sands have evolved to white.

A user-friendly, well-maintained road system links towns and sites efficiently while granting the traveler continuous access to the area's varied natural beauty. Getting on and off the more traveled highways onto two-lane and scenic byways is easy.

As in other areas of New Mexico, it is always wise to be aware of rapid changes in weather, particularly afternoon thunderstorms that may cause flash floods. Temperatures may vary by as much as 40 degrees from day to night, so it is advisable to dress in layers and travel with warm jackets and rainwear, even if the sun is shining and the thermometer reads 80 when you set out. Good hiking boots or sturdy walking shoes are essential. Sunscreen, ample water, and a solid spare tire with the tools to install it are a must.

In this region, the mysterious vastness of the White Sands National Monument and the World Heritage Site of Carlsbad Caverns, with its fantastic crystal formations, coexists with the stomping grounds of the West's most famous outlaw, Billy the Kid. Vibrant Apache initiation ceremonials still take place in

ANOTHER THEFT OF BILLY THE KID'S GRAVESTONE IN FORT SUMNER SEEMS UNLIKELY.

Mescalero, and the *acequias* (irrigation ditches) hand-dug by pioneers still flow with water from the snow-capped 12,000-foot peak of Sierra Blanca through the streets of Tularosa's historic district.

Memories are long here, and it is possible to run into Lincoln County old-timers who grew up hearing versions of the Lincoln County War and its participants that never appeared in history books. To many natives, Billy the Kid is regarded more as a likeable Robin Hood than a violent thug. Questions about "the Kid" still evoke passionate debate: Did he really kill one man for each of his 21 years? Or was he simply doing what was just, at least according to the "law west of the Pecos," avenging the honor of his comrades, resulting in no more than three murders by his own hand?

The disappearance of attorney Albert Fountain and his son Henry in the White Sands more than a century ago, to this day New Mexico's most famous "unsolved mystery," still evokes strong opinions about "who done it" among locals. And somewhere out there, supposedly, is a cache of Spanish gold waiting to be discovered.

In addition, southeast New Mexico beckons with family fun, with downhill skiing at Ski Apache, cross-country skiing and tubing in Cloudcroft, picnicking and playing in the dunes at White Sands National Monument, and camping, fishing, and hiking in the Lincoln National Forest. Other highlights include Smokey Bear Historical Park in Capitan and Alamogordo's Kid's Kingdom with the Toy Train Depot and the Southwest's first zoo, as well as the comprehensive New Mexico Museum of Space History. The warm-weather bat flights out of Carlsbad Caverns are another family favorite.

The forested green Mescalero Apache Reservation, home of the elegant yet comfortable Inn of the Mountain Gods, with its Las Vegas–style casino, champion golf course, and possibly the state's best buffet, is but a fraction of the land formerly occupied by this nomadic tribe of hunters and warriors. Today, efforts are under way to preserve, record, and teach the Apache language and cultures.

For those intrigued by the phenomenon of UFOs, Roswell is the certified capital of speculation about extraterrestrial life, and Fourth of July weekend is the great gathering of UFO believers, many in costume.

As the area is large, when navigating or planning your tour, it may be best to think of it in three separate, broadly defined areas: Billy's Stomping Grounds, Cavern Country, and Oil Patch Country. Each is described below.

The *Green Space* listing is found near the end of the chapter, before the *Special Events* calendar.

Whether or not you believe in UFOs, and whether or not you believe Sheriff Pat Garrett really shot and killed Billy the Kid in cold blood one night in 1881 at Pete Maxwell's ranch, and that Billy actually is the individual interred in Fort Sumner, one thing is sure: southeast New Mexico is the place where you will certainly encounter both the grand beauty and great legends of the American West.

BILLY'S STOMPING GROUNDS: CAPITAN, FORT SUMNER, LINCOLN, CARRIZOZO, TULAROSA, ALAMOGORDO, RUIDOSO, ROSWELL, CLOUDCROFT, CLOVIS

Where else can you time-travel between the eras of the notorious Billy the Kid and the Roswell crash of 1947? This is the one and only place. There is a relaxed pace and lots of space between attractions, which you will need as there are so many interesting sights, and so much information, to take in. It is hot and dry year-round, with few exceptions, such as the marvelous historic district known as the "49 blocks" of Tularosa. The green mountains of Mescalero, Ruidoso, and Cloudcroft also provide a refreshing break from the desert. Flash floods and forest fires do occur here, so be sure to keep tuned in to weather conditions. Rich in history and natural marvels, this part of New Mexico is an essential tour for the dedicated roadmeister.

GUIDANCE **Alamogordo Chamber of Commerce** (575-437-6120; www .alamogordo.com), 1301 N. White Sands Blvd., Alamogordo.

Capitan Chamber of Commerce (575-354-2273; www.villageofcapitan.com; www.smokeybearpark.com), Capitan.

Carrizozo Chamber of Commerce (575-648-2732; www.townofcarrizozo.org), Carrrizozo.

Cloudcroft Chamber of Commerce (575-682-2733; www.cloudcroft.net), Cloudcroft.

Clovis/Curry County Chamber of Commerce (575-763-3435; www.clovisnm .org), 105 E. Grant St., Clovis.

Fort Sumner/DeBaca County Chamber of Commerce (575-355-7705; www .ftsumnerchamber.com), 707 N. Fourth St., Fort Sumner.

Roswell Chamber of Commerce (575-623-5695; www.roswellnm.com), 131 W. Second St., Roswell.

Roswell Visitors Center (575-624-7704), 426 N. Main, Roswell.

Ruidoso Valley Chamber of Commerce/Visitor Center (575-257-7395; www.ruidosonow.com), 720 Sudderth, Ruidoso.

GETTING THERE To get to southeast New Mexico, take US 380 east off I-25 at San Antonio, 13 miles south of Socorro. Continue east on US 380 through Carrizozo to Capitan and Lincoln and on to the Hondo Valley to Roswell; or south on US 54/70 past Three Rivers into Tularosa, Alamogordo, and White Sands. From Tularosa, follow US 70 north to Mescalero, Ruidoso, and San Patricio, then east to Roswell. From Roswell, go south on US 285 through Artesia to Carlsbad.

MEDICAL EMERGENCY **De Baca Family Practice Clinic** (575-355-2414), 500 N. 10th St., Fort Sumner.

Eastern New Mexico Medical Center (575-622-8170), 405 W. Country Club Rd., Roswell.

Gerald Champion Regional Medical Center (575-439-6100), 2669 N. Scenic Dr., Alamogordo.

Lincoln County Medical Center (575-257-8200), 211 Sudderth St., Ruidoso.

Plains Regional Medical Center (575-769-2141), 2100 Martin Luther King Jr. Blvd., Clovis.

Presbyterian Healthcare Services Healthcare Clinic (575-648-2317), 710 Avenue E., Carrizozo.

Presbyterian Healthcare Services Healthcare Clinic (575-354-0057), 330 Smokey Bear Blvd., Capitan.

Sacramento Mountain Medical Center (Presbyterian Medical Services) (575-682-2542), 102 Hwy. 82, Cloudcroft.

✷ To See

TOWNS **Capitan,** where US 380 meets NM 246 and NM 48, makes an attractive lunch stop where kids will love the Smokey Bear Café, and grown-ups can dine splendidly in the Greenhouse across the street, either before or after a tour of the Smokey the Bear Historical Park. The several small shops downtown make for pleasant browsing.

Fort Sumner, 41 miles southeast of Santa Rosa on US 84, holds the legendary gravesite of Billy the Kid. The pleasant little town, which feels like a step back in time, also has museums and plenty of opportunities to purchase Kid souvenirs and memorabilia. It is also the site of the Fort Sumner State Monument, where Navajo and Apache people were confined during the 1860s, with the Bosque Redondo Memorial to that epoch.

Lincoln, 46 miles southeast of Carrizozo on US 380, is the now-quiet, well-preserved site of the Lincoln County War, essentially a rivalry between mercantile factions that indelibly marked New Mexico and Western history. Step into that history here at the Lincoln County Courthouse, where Billy the Kid slipped

IF ONLY THE FORTIFIED WALLS OF LINCOLN'S TORREON COULD SPEAK.

through handcuffs to make his daring escape, and learn the entire story, which is well documented at the Lincoln State Monument museum.

Carrizozo, at the junction of US 380 and US 54, at the gateway to the Valley of Fires State Park, has one of New Mexico's beloved burger stops, the Outpost.

Tularosa, at the junction of US 54 and US 70, is as charming an oasis as exists in New Mexico. Giant pomegranates, poplars, and sycamores sink deep roots into the ditch banks that run throughout the historic district. This district, known as "the 49," was the original town site established by 19th-century pioneers who moved here from Mesilla after their farmlands got flooded out. Following the Civil War, Union soldiers of the California Column settled here, married local women, and built homes, many of which have been restored. The variety of vernacular architecture is well worth a stroll. Tularosa has several delightful eateries but lacks lodgings.

Alamogordo lies at the junction of US 54/70 and US 82. The home of Holloman Air Force Base and one of the region's larger towns, with a variety of restaurants, chain motel lodgings, and shopping mall, Alamogordo makes a good overnight stop or a base for exploring White Sands. Here find New Mexico International Space Museum, IMAX Theater, and plenty of activities to interest children, as well as the Flickinger Center for the Performing Arts.

OUTPOST CAFÉ IN CARRIZOZO HAS ONE OF THE STATE'S BEST BURGERS.

Ruidoso, 32 miles northeast of Tularosa on US 70, famous for Ruidoso Downs, home of the richest Quarter horse race in the country, and a lively, bustling community filled with shops, restaurants, and condominiums. In addition to tourists, the town, whose name translates to "noisy water," for the stream, which runs through town, attracts retirees and vacation homeowners. There's plenty to do here, with abundant golfing, art activities, hiking, shopping, horseback riding, and fishing opportunities.

Roswell, at the crossroads of US 285, US 70, and US 380, a major stop on the Goodnight-Loving and Chisum cattle trails of the Old West, has reinvented itself several times. After losing Walker Air Force Base in 1967, the town diversified into a thriving hub of business, education, and tourism. Dairies have largely replaced cattle operations, and the old downtown is filled with UFO museums and shops marketing UFO-themed curiosities and trinkets. Best of all, the Roswell Museum exhibits a must-see collection of Southwestern artists, in particular Roswell native Peter Hurd and his wife, Henriette Wyeth, whose landscapes and portraits of their Hondo Valley neighbors are seldom seen elsewhere.

Cloudcroft, 26 miles east of Alamogordo on US 82, is high in the Sacramento Mountains at 9,100 feet. Originally founded as a railroad town, early on it became a cool vacation escape for El Pasoans. With its superb Lodge at Cloudcroft, unique shops, and galleries on Burro St. and other accommodations, tiny Cloudcroft is a the perfect base for hiking the Lincoln National Forest and enjoying winter snow sports, with the outdoor James Sewell Ice Rink downtown.

Clovis, 67 miles east of Fort Sumner on US 60, named for the French king who converted to Christianity, has roots deep in railroading and agriculture. It is today a superb place for antiquing and for appreciating Pueblo Deco architecture. Joe's Boots is a well-stocked warehouse of discounted cowboy boots, hats, Western regalia, and décor. The home of Cannon Air Force Base, Clovis has ample modern amenities, shopping malls, and motels.

MUSEUMS **Billy the Kid Museum** (575-355-2380), 1435 E. Sumner Ave., Fort Sumner. Open May 15–Sept. daily 8:30–5, Oct.–May 15 Mon.–Sat. 8:30–5, closed Sun. Learn about the Old West, including a variety of Billy the Kid memorabilia. $5 adults, $4 seniors 62+, $3 children 7–15, children under 6 free.

Hubbard Museum of the American West (575-378-4142; www.hubbard museum.org), 841 Hwy. 70 W., Ruidoso Downs. Open daily 9–5. Closed Thanksgiving and Christmas. An affiliate of the Smithsonian Institution. Collection of over 10,000 Western items. Exhibits of Western and cowboy artifacts, saddles, wagons, Pony Express rig, Kid's Corral, and the Anne C. Stradling collection of antiques, horse equipment, and memorabilia. Includes the Racehorse Hall of Fame, with exhibits dedicated to Triple Crown Champions, All American Futurity winners, women in racing, as well as memorabilia from world champions. $6 adults, $5 seniors and military, $2 children 6–16,children under 6 free.

International UFO Museum & Research Center (575-625-9495; 1-800-822-3545), 114 N. Main, Roswell. Open daily 9–5. Closed Thanksgiving, Christmas and New Year's Day. Expanded hours during Roswell UFO Festival, first week of July. Find in this vast warehouselike space the Roswell Incident Timeline, witness testimonies, photographs, maps, and newspaper and radio reports that endeavor to give a complete account of the purported UFO incident that occurred here in July 1947. This center also contains the largest and most comprehensive collection of UFO-related information in the world, as well as records of those who have experienced sightings, abductions, or contact. $5 adults, $3 military and seniors, $2 children 5–15, 4 and under free.

Lincoln State Monument (575-653-4372), 12 miles east of Capitan on US 380, Lincoln. Open daily 8:30–4:30. Old Lincoln Town's main street—actually, its only street—is lined with 11 buildings of stone and adobe that make up this National Historic Landmark. Here history seems very close at hand, because this site looks as it did during the heyday of Billy the Kid and Pat Garrett, and just as it did when the Lincoln County War raged during 1878–1881. The Old Lincoln County Courthouse Museum gives the context of the era, with information on Hispanic settlers, Buffalo soldiers, major players in the Lincoln County War, and the politics of the time. $5 ticket includes four museums open Nov.–Mar. and six museums open Apr.–Oct., under 16 free. Sun. free to New Mexico residents, Wed. free to New Mexico seniors.

AIRCRAFT AND SPACE EXPLORATION ENTHUSIASTS WILL RAVE OVER THE ALAMOGORDO NEW MEXICO MUSEUM OF SPACE HISTORY DEDICATED TO THEIR PASSION.

New Mexico Museum of Space History (1-877-333-6589; 575-437-2840). Located at the top of NM 2001, Alamogordo. Open daily 9–5. Closed Thanksgiving and Christmas. Five stories of space history include artifacts, models, and exhibits celebrating space voyage. The Stapp Air and Space Park displays actual rockets; the International Space Hall of Fame and the Tombaugh IMAX Dome Theater (closed Mon.) and Planetarium create a total experience intriguing to children and adults. $3 adults; $2.75 seniors and military; $2.50 children 4–12; under 4 free.

Old Fort Sumner Museum (575-355-2942), adjacent to Billy the Kid's grave, 7 miles southeast of Fort Sumner on NM 272. Historical items from the 1880s give depth to the Billy the Kid era. Open daily 8:30–5, Wed.–Thurs. 9–5. $3.50 adults; $2.50 children; children under seven free.

Roswell Museum/Art Center (575-624-6744), 100 W. 11th St., Roswell. Open Mon.–Sat. 9–5; Sun., holidays 1–5. Closed Thanksgiving, Christmas, New Year's Day. The term "regional" in no way diminishes the fine exhibits of contemporary and classic artists of the West shown here. Permanent exhibits of native Peter Hurd and wife Henriette Wyeth are stunning, while works of renowned artists such as Fritz Scholder and Georgia O'Keeffe appear regularly. The Goddard Rocket Museum is included. Free.

Robert H. Goddard Planetarium (575-624-6744), 912 N. Main, Roswell, has science exhibits, including Goddard's rockets. Open Tues.–Sat. 1:30–5, Fri. until 7:30. $3 planetarium; $5 laser light shows.

Clovis Depot Model Train Museum (575-762-0066; 1-888-762-0064), 221 W. First St., Clovis. Open Wed.–Sun. noon–5. Closed major holidays and February and September. Set in restored Clovis Santa Fe Passenger Depot, with nine working model train layouts and displays of U.S. and British toy trains, this is a great place to share fun between the generations. From the second floor, you have a bird's-eye view of the working Burlington Northern train yard below. $4 adults; $3 children; $2 seniors.

Carrizozo Heritage Museum (575-648-1105), 103 12th St., Carrizozo. Open Tues.–Sat. 10–2. Closed Sun.–Mon., major holidays. Emphasis here is on the town's railroad history and local ranching. Free.

HISTORIC LANDMARKS, PLACES, AND SITES **Fort Stanton** (no phone; www .museumofnewmexico.org). East on US 380 from Capitan, right on NM 220. Check for hours. Established in 1855, abandoned during the Civil War, and reoccupied after the Civil War by Kit Carson, this was the base of the Buffalo Soldiers of the Ninth Cavalry. After it was decommissioned in 1896, it served as a TB hospital, later on as an internment camp for WWII German POWs and Japanese. A Merchant Marine cemetery is on the site. The fort was recently made a state monument. $5.

Trinity Site (575-835-9424), 12 miles east of San Antonio on US 380, 5 miles south through Stallion Range Center. Open the first Sat. in Apr. and Oct. only, 8–2. At the north end of White Sands Missile Range is ground zero, where the first atomic bomb was detonated on July 16, 1945. Free.

THE FIGURE OF SUSAN MCSWEEN RECALLS THE LINCOLN COUNTY WAR.

Three Rivers Petroglyph National Recreation Site (575-585-3457), 28 miles south of Carrizozo off US 54. East 5 miles from US 54 at Three Rivers on County Road B30. Open daily 8–6. Closed Christmas. The half-mile gently inclining trail contains outstanding examples of 21,000 petroglyphs, or rock carvings, carved by the vanished Mogollon people 1,000 years ago. Another short trail leads to a partially excavated prehistoric village. Caution: stay on the path as rattlesnakes really do live here. Beware. $2 per vehicle.

Bosque Redondo Memorial at Fort Sumner State Monument (575-355-2573), 3 miles east of Fort Sumner, NM 60/84, 3.5 miles south on Billy the Kid Rd. Open daily 8:30–5. Closed Tues. and major holidays. This moving memorial commemorates and honors Navajos and Apaches forced from their homelands in 1864. Cultural and historic programs are presented throughout the year. A new museum designed by Navajo architect David Sloan and an interpretive trail cast light on this tragic period in U.S. history. $5 adults; children 16 and under free; New Mexico residents with ID free Sun.; New Mexico seniors with ID free Wed.

Goodnight Loving Trail. Originally spanning 2,000 miles between Texas and Wyoming, this cattle trail was blazed in 1866 by Charles Goodnight and Oliver Loving. The New Mexico portion follows the Pecos River to Fort Sumner.

Blackdom (no phone), 18 miles south of Roswell, 8 miles west of Dexter. This all-black homesteading town founded in 1911 by 20 families was led by Francis Marion Boyer, who walked from Georgia to New Mexico hoping to establish a self-sustaining community. Blackdom was abandoned in the 1920s. Very little remains on the site. Free.

🏷 **Smokey Bear Historical Park** (575-354-2748), 118 Smokey Bear Blvd., Capitan. Open daily 9–5. Closed Thanksgiving, Christmas, and New Year's Day. Opened in 1979 in honor of the bear cub found with burned paws after a disastrous 1950 forest fire in the Capitan Mountains who became the symbol of forest fire prevention. After living at the National Zoo in Washington, D.C., Smokey was returned to his home and buried here. Presentations and exhibits on ecology, forest health, and fire prevention, plus a playground, picnic area, and the original Capitan train depot highlight the park. Smokey Bear Days are held the first weekend in May. $2 adults; $1 children under 6 free.

Toy Train Depot (575-437-2855), 1991 N. White Sands Blvd., Alamogordo. Open Wed.–Sun. noon–5. Closed Christmas and New Year's Day. Ride the toy train 2.5 miles around Alameda Park (departures every 30 minutes) and visit the century-old depot with a gift and model train shop. Hundreds of model and toy trains on display, plus historic railroad artifacts to intrigue train buffs. Adjacent Kid's Kingdom Park is a great place for children to play and let off steam. Admission $4; train rides $4.

THE SITE OF THE FIRST ATOM BOMB DETONATION IS OPEN TO THE PUBLIC TWICE A YEAR.

Alameda Park Zoo (575-439-4290), 1321 N. White Sands Blvd., Alamogordo. Open Wed.–Sun. noon–5. Closed Christmas and New Year's Day. Established in 1898, this is the oldest zoo in the Southwest, with 300 animals of 90 species. $2.20 adults and children over 12; $1.10 seniors, children under 12; under 3 free.

GHOST TOWNS **White Oaks.** Three miles north of Carrizozo on US 54, 9 miles east on NM 349. A full-fledged ghost town, the quiet remains of an 1880s gold mining boomtown has a historic cemetery, the School House Museum and Miners Museum that are catch as catch can for being open, and the No Scum Allowed Saloon, the place most likely to be open, with a shuttle that runs to Carrizozo. The town has been for some time experiencing a slow-motion revival, with artists occupying the old houses.

SCENIC DRIVES **Billy the Kid National Scenic Byway** (575-378-5318; www .billybyway.com). Follows NM 48; NM 220; US 70/380 for 84.2 miles. The Billy the Kid National Scenic Byway Visitors Center, next to the Hubbard Museum of the American West in Ruidoso Downs, is the best place to orient the trip and make the most of it with maps and brochures. The byway links Ruidoso, Lincoln, Fort Stanton, and the pleasant green Hondo Valley. The entire area was the stomping ground of Billy the Kid.

ROCK ART IS EVERYWHERE AT THE THREE RIVERS PETROGLYPH SITE.

THE MONUMENT AT BOSQUE REDONDO COMMEMORATES THE LONG WALK OF THE NAVAJO PEOPLE.

Sunspot Scenic Byway (1-800-733-6396, ext. 24371). Eighteen miles on NM 6563 that wind through the tall pines of the Lincoln National Forest along the front rim of the Sacramento Mountains, south of Cloudcroft, leading to the National Solar Observatory on Sacramento Peak. From here view the Tularosa Basin and White Sands National Monument, as well as the space shuttle spaceport.

WINERIES **Tularosa Vineyards** (575-585-2260), 2 miles north of Tularosa on US 54 at 23 Coyote Canyon Rd. Open daily 9–5. Taste award-winning wines made from grapes specially acclimated to New Mexico. This winery specializes in premium reds and highly drinkable whites and blushes. Tours by appointment.

Arena Blanca Winery (1-800-368-3081), 6 miles north of Alamogordo on US 54. In combination with McGinn's Country Store at the Pistachio Tree Ranch, Arena Blanca offers free wine tastings plus free pistachio samples. Located on a 111-acre pistachio orchard.

NATURAL WONDERS **Sierra Blanca.** At just under 12,000 feet, this imposing mountain is a snow-capped beacon throughout most of southeast New Mexico.

BILLY THE KID SLIPPED HIS WRISTS OUT OF HIS HANDCUFFS AND SHOT HIS WAY OUT OF THE LINCOLN COUNTY JAIL.

White Sands National Monument (575-679-2599; www.nps.gov/whsa), 15 miles west of Alamogordo on US 70. Closed Christmas Day. Open daily Memorial Day–Sept. 2, 7 AM–9 PM; winter hours 7–sunset. Dunes Drive is 17 paved miles of the 300 miles of pure white gypsum dunes. This place's vastness and beauty make it seem like a moonscape here on Earth. You can get out of the car, hike, and play in the dunes. Reservations required for monthly Full Moon Nights and accompanying programs. Call 575-679-2599. The gift shop is vast, and the bookstore has a grand selection of Southwest and nature reading. $3 per person over 15; under 15 free. Good for seven days.

✳ To Do

BICYCLING AND WALKING **Spring River Hike & Bike Trail** (575-624-6720), Spring River Park, 1101 W. Fourth St., Roswell, offers 5.5 miles of paved, gentle, and scenic hiking and biking.

BIRDING See the state parks under *Green Space*.

BOATING See the state parks under *Green Space*.

FISHING Bonito Lake. Left off NM 48 onto NM 37, 1.5 miles to "Y," left to Bonito Dam to a man-made lake, well stocked during fishing season, with easy to moderate hiking trails and camping areas. Free.

Rio Peñasco (505-687-3352), 37 miles east of Cloudcroft on US 82, is the southernmost spring creek in United States.

Lake Van is 15 miles southeast of Roswell on NM 256/NM 2, in the hamlet of Dexter. Cool, pleasant Lake Van has lazy fishing, some camping, and swimming, or just picnicking. Free.

GOLF The Lodge at Cloudcroft (575-682-2089), 1 Corona Pl., Cloudcroft. Open Mar.–Oct. High-altitude, mountain bluegrass fairways and Scottish rules of play make a memorable nine holes. $14–30.

Desert Lakes Golf Course (575-437-0290), south end of Alamogordo on US 54. Open year-round. This is an attractive suburban municipal course in the Sacramento foothills with elevated greens and water hazards. Very affordable.

Clovis Municipal Golf Course (575-769-7871), 1200 N. Norris St., Clovis. nine-hole public course. Very affordable.

Inn of the Mountain Gods (1-800-446-2963), Carrizo Canyon Rd., Mescalero. Elegant 18-hole public course. Affordable.

THE LODGE AT CLOUDCROFT IS A FAVORITE SMALL INN, WITH AN EXCELLENT RESTAURANT AND GOLF COURSE.

THE MESCALERO APACHE–OWNED INN OF THE MOUNTAIN GODS IS THE LAST WORD IN LAS VEGAS–STYLE LODGING.

The Links at Sierra Blanca (575-258-5330), 105 Sierra Blanca Dr., Ruidoso Downs. Open year-round, weather permitting. This challenging, highly rated 18-hole spikeless Scottish-style course was designed by PGA Seniors Tour player Jim Colbert. $35–80.

HIKING Sacramento Rim National Recreation Trail, south of Cloudcroft. Follows rim of Sacramento Mountains 14 miles. Moderate hike. Spectacular views of Tularosa Basin 5,000 feet below.

Dog Canyon National Recreational Trail (575-437-8284), Oliver Lee Memorial State Park. A 5.5-mile strenuous hike, with panoramic views of Tularosa Basin, Lincoln National Forest, and White Sands, was an ancient Native American Trail. The trail rises about 3,100 feet. $6.

Trestle Area Loop Trails (Cloud-Climbing Rail Trail) (575-682-2551; 575-682-2733). The Rails-to-Trails Association has created all levels of hiking paths out of the overgrown railroad beds out of use since trains toted logs out of the Sacramento Mountains last, in 1947. Call to arrange a tour of the historic railroad trestles.

HORSE RACING Ruidoso Downs Race Track and Casino (575-378-4431), 2 miles north of Ruidoso on US 70. Open Memorial Day–Labor Day. This track has the reputation as top Quarter horse racetrack in United States, and the richest Quarter horse race, the All American Futurity, where instant millionaires are made, runs Labor Day Weekend.

HORSEBACK RIDING Chippeway Riding Stables (575-682-2565; 1-800-471-2384), 602 Cox Canyon Hwy., Cloudcroft. Call for prices and hours.

ICE SKATING James Sewell Ice Rink (505-682-4585), Zenith Park, downtown Cloudcroft. Open daily during the season, weather permitting. Skate rentals, and later on warm up with hot cocoa by the inside fireplace.

MOUNTAIN BIKING Rim Trail (575-682-1229), Cloudcroft. Access this steep, difficult 13.5-mile trail, T105, which parallels Sunspot Scenic Byway part of the way for views of the Tularosa Basin.

SNOW SPORTS Ski Apache (575-336-4356; 575-464-3600), 6 miles north of Ruidoso on NM 48. Left on Ski Run Rd. Owned and operated by the Mescalero Apache Tribe on the Lincoln National Forest; the stated goal is to "provide the best ski experience for all ages and abilities." Both skiers and snowboarders of all levels find terrain variety on 55 trails served by 11 lifts. Lines are rare; elevations between 9,600–11,500 feet provide abundant snow that makes for a 180-inch annual average. Free lift ticket for a first-timer with a lesson purchase; children's programs, rentals, and lessons. Moderate.

✦ **Ski Cloudcroft** (575-682-2333), 1 Corona Pl., Cloudcroft. With 21 trails at all levels, three lifts, tubing, snowboarding, and a ski school on 68 acres at 9,000 feet, this tiny area could be just right for the whole family. $17–35.

✦ **Triple M Snowplay Area** (575-682-2205), south of Cloudcroft on Sunspot Scenic Byway, NM 6563. Snowmobile rentals, tubing with a lift.

✦ **Ruidoso Winter Park** (575-336-7079), Ruidoso. One-quarter mile west of NM 48 at the bottom of Ski Run Rd. Inner tubes provided, with a conveyor lift, for those who love winter but aren't skiers, or for the little ones. Call for prices and hours.

✳ Lodging

BED & BREAKFASTS, INNS, AND MOTELS ♿ **Smokey Bear Motel** (1-800-766-5392), US 380, Capitan. The convenient Smokey Bear Motel has been operating here for 40 years in this, the final resting place of the original Smokey Bear. The clean, comfortable ersatz-rustic motel has some rooms that include refrigerator and microwave. The Smokey Bear Restaurant, with vintage photos of Smokey, on the premises serves hearty breakfast, lunch, and dinner, with specials like chicken fried steak and beef stew seven days a week. The motel is located 13 miles from Ski Apache. $52–83.

Fite Ranch B&B (575-838-0958; www.fiteranchbedandbreakfast.com), 7.5 miles east of San Antonio exit off I-25 on US 380. The Fite Ranch B&B

is located on a working ranch that has been in existence since the 1930s. In 2002, ranchers Dewey and Linda Brown purchased it from original owner Evelyn Fite and the place is now run with love and care by their family. A home-cooked full and filling breakfast is served every day. The B&B is furnished with antique Western décor with a touch of the Southwest. Each of the five lodgings includes at least one bedroom, a kitchen, a personal living area, and a private bath. The ranch borders the Bosque del Apache National Wildlife Refuge and is a favorite of birders. Weekly and monthly rates available. $90–175.

&. **Ellis Store Country Inn** (1-800-653-6460), US 380 at Mile Marker 98, Lincoln. To become enveloped in the charm of the past, Ellis Store Country Inn, where Billy the Kid was held captive for two weeks during the Lincoln County War in the late 1800s, cannot be beat. This inn is reputedly the oldest building in Old Lincoln Town. It is located in the Rio Bonito Valley and has been in operation since the mid-1800s. The adobe Main House, built in the 1850s, and the Mill House, built in the 1880s, hold eight guest rooms, filled with antiques, wood-burning stoves, and hand-made quilts. The Ellis Store restaurant, Isaac's Table, features an extensive wine list and serves dinner by prearrangement. Innkeepers are David and Jinny Vigil, one of New Mexico's finest chefs. $89–119.

&. **Casa de Patrón B&B Inn** (575-653-4676), US 380, Midtown Lincoln. Hosts Cleis and Jeremy Jordan welcome guests to the original home of Juan Patrón, a legend in the New Mexico territory in the late 1800s.

The inn is made up of four separate buildings. The traditional adobe-style main historic house, built around 1860, includes three rooms with an extensive collection of antique washboards. The Old Trail House has two bedrooms rooms plus a conference room, where the full, delicious breakfast is served daily. Two casitas are available and are especially comfortable for families. $82–112.

LODGES AND RANCHES Inn of the Mountain Gods Resort and Casino (575-464-7777; 1-800-545-9011), 287 Carrizo Canyon Rd., Mescalero. Four miles south of Ruidoso on NM 48. The 273-room stunning, exciting Inn of the Mountain Gods Resort and Casino is set in the picturesque Sacramento Mountains next to shimmering Lake Mescalero. Recreational activities include the Inn of the Mountain Gods Resort Championship Golf Course, a fully equipped workout facility, indoor pool, fishing, horseback riding, and sport clay shooting. Ski Apache is approximately 45 miles away. Las Vegas–style casino gaming at the resort offers everything from penny slots to high roller games. Dining options include steak-and-seafood fine dining at Wendell's, casual barbeque meals including breakfast at Apache Summit BBQ Co., Gathering of Nations Buffet—possibly the best buffet in the state—and burgers, sandwiches, and beer at the casual Big Game Sports Bar and Grill. No need to leave the resort, once you check in. Rates vary dramatically, depending on weeknight versus weekend and time of year. $99–389.

☺ **The Lodge Resort & Spa** (1-800-395-6343), 1 Corona Pl., Cloudcroft. The Lodge Resort & Spa is located in Cloudcroft at 9,000 feet elevation in the Sacramento Mountains, surrounded by the Lincoln National Forest. The resort offers 59 rooms and suites. The original resort was destroyed by fire, and the current property is said to be haunted by characters from its past, in particular a wronged maid named Rebecca. Every New Mexico governor has slept in the elegant Governor's Suite. Amenities include a heated outdoor pool, year-round sauna and outdoor hot tub, fitness room, nine-hole traditional Scottish format golf course, and hiking trails. A variety of treatments are available at the Spirit of the Mountain Spa. Rebecca's, named after the resident ghost, serves breakfast, lunch, and dinner, plus an elaborate Sunday brunch. Rebecca's Lounge, which was once owned by Al Capone, serves drinks throughout the day as well as light lunch fare. The Lodge has had several famous guests: Judy Garland, Clark Gable, and Pancho Villa. If you climb to the top of the bell tower, you can see where Clark Gable inscribed his name. In the 1930s, the resort was managed by Conrad Hilton, who was born and raised in San Antonio, New Mexico. According to reports, Hilton was familiar with The Lodge and wanted to be closer to his family while his hotel chain took off. Words cannot do this delightful and beautifully well-managed place justice. It is simply divine, one of my favorite New Mexico escapes, where you can truly make the world go away. It is especially lovely at Christmas time and Valentine's Day. Murder Mystery weekends are a hoot. $115–350.

Hurd–La Rinconada Gallery and Guest Homes (575-653-4331), 105

La Rinconada Ln., San Patricio. Twenty miles east of Ruidoso on US 70 at Mile Marker 281. The exquisite gallery and guest homes are located on the historic and splendid Sentinel Ranch, home of the first family of American art, the Hurd-Wyeth family. Located among quiet rolling hills near the Rio Ruidoso River, the original ranch-hand quarters on Sentinel Ranch have become utterly romantic guest houses with modern conveniences. They are filled with antiques and designer furnishings and art created by the Hurd-Wyeth family. Each of the houses has a private patio. On the southeast corner of the family polo field is an impressive gallery of original works by members of the Hurd-Wyeth family. Rates are based on the number of people in your party, ranging from $125 for two to $355 for six; two-night minimum. Additional fees for single-night stay.

Burnt Well Guest Ranch (575-347-2668; 1-866-729-0974; www.burnt wellguestranch.com), 399 Chesser Rd., Roswell. Thirty-five miles southwest of Roswell. Call for exact directions. If you're looking for a "ranch vacation," this may be the place. This hacienda-style inn with Old West rustic décor has only two rooms. Three generations of the Chesser family live on the property and run a working cattle and sheep ranch. The hacienda includes an inviting covered porch, and a great room with a checkerboard table, hobbyhorse, and piano. Guests have access to a kitchenette and laundry facilities. Capacity is 10 people with some bunk beds. Guests are invited to join in the daily workings of the ranch, including cattle drives. Dutch oven suppers, old-time story-

THE HURD FAMILY RANCH IN SAN PATRICIO IS NOW A LOVELY GUEST RANCH.

telling, and riding the range to your heart's content are all part of the deal. $117 children, $245 adults; three-night minimum Mar.–Apr.

CABINS AND CAMPING For camping, see the state parks listed under *Green Space*.

Cabins at Cloudcroft (575-682-2396; 1-800 248-7967), 1000 Coyote Ave., Cloudcroft. The 16 delightful cabins at Cloudcroft are open year-round in the aspens and pines, yet still within village limits. Cabins include full kitchens, baths, and firewood, and a coin-operated laundry is on the premises. Guests may choose between a wood-burning stove or a fireplace. Propane grills and picnic areas are available during the summer months. Two night minimum; one-night stay negotiable. Small pets allowed. $75–315.

Story Book Cabins (575-257-2115; 1-888-257-2115), 410 Main Rd., Ruidoso. Located amid the tall pines of Ruidoso's Upper Canyon along the "noisy" Ruidoso River, these "upscale rustic" cabins feature hot tubs, Jacuzzis, fully equipped kitchens, fireplaces, grills, private porches, and patios, as well as cable TV and DVD. The knotty-pine cabins have between one and six bedrooms. Secluded, yet close to in-town dining, galleries, and shops. $119–189.

❋ Where to Eat

DINING OUT Wendell's Steak & Seafood Restaurant (575-464-7777), Inn of the Mountain Gods Casino & Resort, Mescalero. Open dinner only Mon.–Thurs. 5–9; breakfast, lunch, Fri.–Sat. 8–2, dinner 5–9; Sun.

brunch 11–2, dinner 5–9. Steaks galore, with a $66 Kobe-style filet mignon in truffle sauce headlining the menu, plus pan-seared fresh halibut, New Mexico elk tenderloin in apple brandy reduction, and other delights. Expensive. The adjacent Wendell's Lounge serves soup, burgers, sandwiches, and salads daily 11–10. Inexpensive.

Rebecca's (575-682-2566; 1-800-395-6343), The Lodge, 1 Corona Pl., Cloudcroft. Serves breakfast, lunch, or a very special dinner. Try the Chateaubriand for two. Famous for its deluxe Sunday brunch buffet and panoramic view of the Tularosa Valley. The finest restaurant in the area. Moderate–Expensive.

Memories Fine Dining (575-437-0077), 1223 New York Ave., Alamogordo. Mon.–Sat. 11–9. Closed Sun. Lunch and dinner. Within this two-story 1906 Victorian-style, antiques-filled home may be found delectable food served in style in what must be the area's most popular, well-established "evening out" restaurant. Think pork loin in port wine sauce, fresh tuna grilled to perfection, homemade creamy mushroom soup, and house-baked rolls. Beer and wine, too. Moderate.

Greenhouse Café (575-354-0373), 103 S. Lincoln, Capitan. Closed Mon.–Tues. Dinner Wed.–Sat. 5–9; Sun. brunch 10–2. Lunch summer only, approximately mid-June–mid-Oct. 11–2. Yes, it really is a greenhouse, as the monster-sized, just-picked crunchy lettuce leaves of your salad testify. Located in the old Hotel Chango, this is a definite must-do. The menu changes every two months but always includes steak, chicken, pork, and fresh fish. Chef Tom's specialties include rack of lamb with mint leaves in Dijon mustard volute and fresh tilapia with wild mushrooms. Moderate.

Tinnie's Silver Dollar Restaurant & Saloon (575-653-4425), Hondo. Twenty-eight miles east of Ruidoso on US 70. Dinner Tues.–Sat., Sun. champagne brunch 10–3. If you like elegant atmosphere, history, and ghosts with your steak, or a margarita served up at a 100-year-old bar, head for Tinnie's. Classic fare, steaks, rack of lamb, roast chicken, prawns and lobster, fresh oysters, filet Oscar, beautifully served. Wine flights are a reasonable way to sample the wine list. Suites and a general store are also on the premises. Worth the drive, and the cost. Moderate–Expensive.

EATING OUT Wortley Pat Garrett Hotel (575-653-4300), US 380, midtown Lincoln. Open Easter–Thanksgiving, Thurs.–Sun., breakfast 8–10, lunch 11–3. Your basic "bacon and egg" breakfast and cheeseburger lunch, but in Lincoln, where it is difficult to find anything to eat, you may be very hungry. Here they claim the kitchen is "mostly open" Mon.–Wed., which may depend on how hard you beg. Service can be slow. No kidding, this is a fun place to hang out, and you're likely to meet some real characters, both local and out of state. Rooms in this 1874 hotel rent for $89, and breakfast is included. Inexpensive.

Can't Stop Smokin' BBQ (575-630-0000), 418 Mechem Dr., Ruidoso. Open Tues.–Sun. 10–7. Lunch, dinner, delivery. Wow! Head over here when the big BBQ craving hits. The

slow-smoked brisket, ribs, and chicken are fall-off-the-fork tender, and the place can be a tad rowdy and a lot of fun. The "secret spice" mixture is MSG- and preservative-free. Inexpensive.

Yum Yum's Donut Shop (575-585-2529), 460 Central Ave., Tularosa. It is worth going out of your way to stop at this tiny, modest-looking café that is so much more than a donut shop. Although you won't want to pass up a fresh daily "wildcat paw" or maple donut, do not, repeat, do not miss the brisket burrito with green chile. Mrs. Abeyta, who has lunch here every day, says the brisket is so tender she can "take her teeth out to eat it." Tell Helen I sent you! Erratic hours, so call first. Inexpensive.

Atticus Books & Teahouse (575-257-2665), 413 Mechem Dr., Ruidoso. Open daily. Savor a delectable homemade scone with your latte, or choose from among 30 varieties of tea in this comfy, cozy, well-stocked new and used indie bookstore, named for the owner's cat. Inexpensive.

Smokey Bear Restaurant (575-354-2253), 310 Smokey Bear Blvd., Capitan. See Smokey Bear Motel listing. Inexpensive.

The Nut House (575-437-6889), 32 Ivy Ln., La Luz. The best pecan pie you ever tasted, fixed from the harvest of pecan trees in the orchard next door. Fine local art, nuts galore, wholesome sandwiches, and strong coffee. What a find! Inexpensive.

Phat Phil's Barbecue (575-430-8090), 213 12th St., Alamogordo. Open Mon.–Sat. Lunch, dinner. Closed Sun. Why are people lined up outside this hole in the wall in Alamogordo's historic district? Locals are addicted to the lunchtime BBQ Phil dishes up. Big plates for small dough. Inexpensive.

Martin's Capitol Café (575-624-2111), 110 W. Fourth St., Roswell. Mon.–Sat. 6 AM–8:30 PM. Breakfast, lunch, and dinner. Martin's has been downtown so long, it must be doing something right—and it is! Absolutely authentic, tasty New Mexican red and green chile, just hot enough to be serious, served in a warm, Mexican-style dining room. Martin's has been discovered so is usually busy. Try for the off-hours. Inexpensive.

🍴 **Gathering of Nations Buffet** (575-464-7777), Inn of the Mountain Gods Resort and Casino, Mescalero. Open daily. Breakfast 7–10; lunch 11–3:30; dinner Sat. 4:30–10, Sun.–Thurs. 4:30–9. This is quite possibly the best, biggest, tastiest, freshest of the casino buffets. Watch out for holiday specialties, T-bone Tuesdays, and Seafood Extravaganza Wednesdays. The food, plus the warmly lit atmosphere, makes it my favorite, for sure. It's a terrific value. Moderate.

Old Road Restaurant (575-644-4674), 692 Old Road, Mescalero. Open daily. Hours may vary. Guaranteed some of the most delicious New Mexican food you will ever put in your mouth. Go for the red combination, or just the red enchiladas. Chef-owner Henry Prelo Jr. makes his chile rellenos fresh every morning. A comfortable log cabin atmosphere with local art and stellar service. Inexpensive.

✳ Entertainment

Spencer Theater for the Performing Arts (575-336-4800; 1-888-818-7872), 108 Spencer Rd., Alto.

Presenting a full season of outstanding theater, dance, and music Sept.–May. Headliners have included Moscow Festival Ballet, violinist Natalie MacMaster, and Mel Torme. The theater itself, with Dale Chihuly glass décor, is worth seeing.

Flickinger Center for the Performing Arts (575-437-2202), 1110 New York Ave., Alamogordo. Here is a newly remodeled venue for a lively season of music, theater, and dance.

Ruidoso Downs Race Track and Casino (575-378-4431), 2 miles north of Ruidoso on US 70. Open Memorial Day–Labor Day. Summer country music stars.

Le Cave at Le Bistro (575-257-0132), 2800 Sudderth St., Ruidoso. This is a special place for a glass of wine of an evening.

✳ Selective Shopping

Burro Street, Cloudcroft. Find here a worthwhile row of local craft shops, boutiques, antiques stores, galleries. You can create a teddy bear or get a gelato.

Sudderth Street, Ruidoso's premier shopping street. The place to find stylish household décor, Western wear, women's clothing—at Rebekah's —and lunch and a cold one.

Eagle Ranch Pistachio Groves (575-434-0035), 7288 US 54/70, Alamogordo. Open Mon.–Sat. 8–6, Sun. 9–6. Hop on a free tour of these family-run pistachio groves, munch red and green chile flavored nuts, shop for New Mexico gifts, and splurge on homemade pistachio ice cream.

Joe's Boot Shop (575-763-3764; 1-800-658-6378; www.joesbootshop

com), 2600 Mabry Dr., Clovis. With 16,000 pairs of boots and 10,000 hats to choose from, why shop for Western wear anyplace but Joe's? My closet is full of deeply discounted Luccheses I never could have otherwise afforded but for Joe's. This is one of the grandest shopping experiences you will ever know, and it is completely worth the drive to Clovis!

JOE'S BOOT SHOP IN CLOVIS STOCKS 16,000 PAIRS OF COWBOY AND COWGIRL BOOTS.

CAVERN COUNTRY: CARLSBAD, WHITE'S CITY

What's great here are the caverns. That's the reason to come. Carlsbad Caverns are one of the three World Heritage Sites in New Mexico, the others being Taos Pueblo and Chaco Canyon. You can easily spend days exploring the underground formations, sure to instill a sense of wonder in anyone who views them. It can be very hot in the summer, but it's always cool in the caverns. Bat flights and the water slide at White's City make this an excellent family vacation spot.

GUIDANCE **Carlsbad Chamber of Commerce/Convention and Visitors Bureau** (575-887-6516; www.carlsbadchamber.com), 302 S. Canal, Carlsbad. **White's City** (575-785-2291; www.whitescity.com), 17 Carlsbad Caverns Hwy., White's City.

MEDICAL EMERGENCY **Carlsbad Medical Center** (575-887-4100), 2430 W. Pierce St., Carlsbad. **Lea Regional Medical Center** (575-492-5000), 5419 N. Lovington Hwy., Hobbs.

✳ To See

TOWNS **Carlsbad,** at the junction of US 285 and US 62/180, while known for its underground caverns, has made the most of its location on the Pecos River with its annual "Christmas on the Pecos" boat rides to see the lights along the banks. Make time for a visit to the Living Desert Zoological and Botanical State Park north of the city off US 285, a showcase of flora and fauna native to the Chihuahuan Desert. Also along the Pecos, stroll 2.5 miles of winding pathways. Boating, fishing, swimming, and waterskiing are all available here.

White's City, 13 miles south of Carlsbad on US 62/180, White's City is at the entrance to Carlsbad Caverns National Park. Named for Jim White, the discoverer of Carlsbad Caverns, White's City also has the Million Dollar Museum, which displays antique dollhouses and such oddities as a two-headed rattlesnake.

Numerous motels, RV park, dining, water park just outside Carlsbad Caverns National Park.

MUSEUMS Million Dollar Museum, White's City. Sixteen rooms of antique dollhouses and dolls, Victoriana, Western Americana to browse and get lost in. $3 adults; $2.50 seniors; $2 children 6–12; children under 6 free.

HISTORIC LANDMARKS, PLACES, AND SITES ✒ **Living Desert Zoo and Gardens State Park** (575-887-5516; www.nmparks.com), Carlsbad, northwest end of town, off US 285. Open daily summer 8–8, winter 9–5. Closed Christmas. This marvelous indoor/outdoor attraction highlights native plants and animals of the Chihuahuan Desert. An easy 1.3-mile trail leads through desert habitat. A chief attraction is Maggie, the painting black bear. Yes, she really paints. Another is the superb greenhouse packed with succulents and cacti. Over 40 species of critters, including mountain lion, endangered Mexican grey wolf, bobcats, javelina, and bear, call this zoo home. $6 per vehicle.

SCENIC BYWAYS Guadalupe Back Country Scenic Byway (575-887-6544). NM 137/US 285, 30 miles. Twelve miles north of Carlsbad or 23 miles south of Artesia, enter at junction of NM 137 and US 285 near Brantley Lake State Park. Travel 30 miles to the southwest for dramatic views of the East Guadalupe Escarpment along a winding road with waterfalls, rugged limestone hills, and canyons. There are many possibilities for discovery here, with jeep trails and opportunities for hiking, caving, and mountain biking.

NATURAL WONDERS Carlsbad Caverns National Park (575-785-2232), Memorial Day weekend–Labor Day weekend daily 8–7, last entry into cave 3:30. Cave tours begin 8:30. Labor Day–Memorial Day weekend 8–5, last entry into cave 2. Cave tours begin 8:30. Year-round temperature of 56 degrees Fahrenheit is constant throughout this phenomenal underground display of stalactites and stalagmites that were formed drop by drop over millions of years. An elevator is available for those who prefer to ride the 750-foot descent. Ranger-guided tours available for the Hall of the White Giant and Spider Cave. Pet kennels are available, and portions are wheelchair accessible. The park also has over 50 miles of primitive backcountry hiking, with trailheads located along park roads. $6 adults; $3 children 6–15; children under 6 free. Entrance fee is good for three days.

OIL PATCH COUNTRY: ARTESIA, HOBBS, LOVINGTON, PORTALES

T his is the land that oil built. Aside from ranching, the fossil fuel business is what keeps folks in beans here, and some families do both oil and cows. Some New Mexicans think this section of the state actually belongs in Texas.

GUIDANCE **Artesia Chamber of Commerce** (575-746-2744; www.artesia chamber.com), 107 N. First St., Artesia.

Hobbs Chamber of Commerce (575-397-3202; www.hobbschamber.org), 400 N. Marland, Hobbs.

Portales/Roosevelt County Chamber of Commerce (575-356-8541; www .portales.com), 100 S. Ave. A., Portales.

MEDICAL EMERGENCY **Artesia General Hospital** (575-748-3333), 702 N. 13th St., Artesia.

✳ To See

TOWNS **Artesia** is located on US 285 midway between Roswell and Carlsbad. This little town built on oil refining has a restored railroad station and an excellent small museum featuring local history.

Hobbs, 63 miles northeast of Carlsbad on US 62/180, lies just across the Texas state line. Plenty of parks and swimming pools; fishing in Maddox Lake and Green Meadows Lake; and RV hookups, camping, and fishing in Harry McAdams Park make this friendly town a convenient stop.

Lovington, 44 miles east of Artesia on US 82, is the site of the Western Heritage Museum and Lea County Cowboy Hall of Fame, housed in a historic hotel building. With homesteading roots, the town boomed from oil and remains a center of an agricultural and ranching economy. Chaparral Park offers lake fishing.

Portales, 18 miles south of Clovis on US 70, is famous for its peanut industry. It is also the site of Eastern New Mexico University, and north of town on US 70 is the Blackwater Draw Museum, where artifacts representing the oldest habitations in North America are displayed. Also nearby is the Blackwater Draw site, where the Clovis points were unearthed in 1928, along with remains of ancient bison and mammoth.

MUSEUMS Artesia Historical Museum & Art Center (575-748-2390), 505 W. Richardson Ave., Artesia. Open Tues.–Fri. 9–noon, Sat. 1–5. Closed Sun., Mon., major holidays. Exhibits of regional material culture and social history in a 1904 cobblestone-façade home. Free.

Blackwater Draw Archaeological Site & Museum (museum 575-562-2202; site 575-356-5235; www.enmu.edu/services/museums/blackwater-draw). Museum open daily Memorial Day–Labor Day Mon.–Sat. 10–5, Sun. noon–5. Closed Mon. remainder of year. Site open Memorial Day—Labor Day 9–5 daily; Apr.–May, Sept.–October 9–5 weekends only. May be closed major holidays. Museum is 5 miles east of Portales on US 70. Site is 5 miles north of Portales on NM 467. This museum displays and explains the finds made at Blackwater Draw, recognized since 1929 as one of the most significant archaeological sites in North America due to 13,000-year-old remains of Clovis Man's era. In addition to the finely carved "fluted" stone points of Clovis Man, other weapons and tools, as well as the remains of ancient bison, mammoth, and other creatures of the Late Pleistocene era, were found preserved here. $3 adults, $2 seniors, $1 children 6–13 and students with ID, children 5 and under free.

Western Heritage Museum & Lea County Cowboy Hall of Fame (575-492-2676; www.nmjc.edu), 5317 Lovington Hwy., Hobbs. Closed major holidays. Open Tues.–Sat. 10–5. Located on the campus of New Mexico Junior College, this museum features exhibits of ranchers and rodeo performers while sharing history from the perspective of Indians, homesteaders, buffalo hunters, and soldiers. $3 adults; $2 seniors, children 6–18; children under 5 free.

✳ To Do

BICYCLING AND WALKING Pecos River Walk (575-887-1455), Carlsbad. Six and a half miles of paved bike trails and walkways along the Pecos River are a pleasant way to explore the area.

HIKING Rattlesnake Canyon, Carlsbad Caverns National Park. Features a 670-foot descent into the canyon on an easy 2.2-mile hike. Trailhead #9 on Desert Loop Dr.

MOUNTAIN BIKING Cueva Escarpment Mountain Bike Trail (575-887-6516), Carlsbad. Fifteen miles of single-track riding at all levels of challenge await.

✳ Green Space

MOUNTAINS AND DESERTS Lincoln National Forest (575-434-7200), 1101 New York Ave., Alamogordo. A million acres of hiking, backpacking, trail riding, camping. A 20-mile drive goes through terrain from desert, hills, and valleys filled with orchards to high mountain meadows and peaks covered in tall evergreens. A haven for alpine sports in winter, with good cross-country skiing through the Sacramento Mountains near Cloudcroft. Many camping facilities are located within a 4-mile radius of Cloudcroft, accessible by Highways 82, 130, 244, and 6563 in the **Sacramento Ranger District.** Contact listed number or drop by the office for maps and permits. Near Carlsbad, the **Guadalupe Ranger District** of the forest includes 285,000 acres and Sitting Bull Falls Recreation Area, open Oct.–Mar. 8–5 and Apr.–Sept. 8–6, with a 150-foot waterfall. $5 per vehicle.

Valley of Fires State Park (575-648-2241), 5 miles west of Carrizozo on US 380. The park is 426 acres, with picnic and camping areas and a playground. The nature trail has a 0.75-mile wheelchair-accessible portion. The entire Malpais, or badlands, of the lava flow covers 125 square miles. Here are archetypal, dramatic landscapes photographers will love. $6 per vehicle; $18 camping.

Oliver Lee Memorial State Park (575-437-8284), 12 miles south of Alamogordo via US 54 at the western base of the Sacramento Mountains. Open year-round. Tour Oliver Lee's restored ranch headquarters and picnic, plus camping at one of 44 developed sites. $6 per vehicle day use; $18 camping.

DESERTED CALIFORNIA MISSION-STYLE RAILROAD STATIONS PUNCTUATE US 60.

RIVERS AND LAKES Bottomless Lakes State Park (575-624-6058), 16 miles southeast of Roswell via US 30 and NM 409. Open year-round. Hang out among eight small lakes bordered by high red bluffs with walking trails, plus pleasant swimming, fishing, and rental paddleboats. $4 per vehicle day use, $10–18 camping.

Brantley Lake (575-457-2384), 16.5 miles northeast of Carlsbad via US 285 and County Road 30. Find here boating, waterskiing, and fishing, with lakeside camping on 3,800-acre Brantley Lake. $6 per vehicle day use, $18 camping.

Oasis State Park (575-356-5331), 6.5 miles north of Portales via NM 467. Truly an oasis in the high plains, with tall cottonwoods and a fishing pond stocked with catfish and trout. Plenty of wildlife and over 80 species of birds to spot. There's camping, easy hiking, and a playground. $6 per vehicle day use, $18 camping.

Sumner Lake State Park (575-355-2541). Calling all water sports lovers: powerboats, canoes, sailboats, and windsurfers abound here. This park makes a great camping base to explore nearby Billy the Kid sites, with sites for large RVs

---

UNIQUE ADVENTURES

Norman Petty Studio (575-356-6422), 1313 W. Seventh St., Clovis. Tours by appointment. See the original 1950s recording studio where Petty produced the "Clovis sound" that made stars of Buddy Holly, Roy Orbison, and the Fireballs. It is unchanged from those days, and the studio is in perfect condition. $7.

Sunspot Astronomy & Visitor's Center (575-434-7190), National Solar Observatory, Sacramento Peak, Sunspot, 16 miles from Cloudcroft on NM 30 then NM 6563. Open daily Apr.–Dec. 10–6. Guided tours daily 2. Self-guided tours sunrise–sunset. Fascinating interactive exhibits on the work of this telescope that tracks solar activity in the visitor center. $2.

Dalley Windmill Collection (575-356-6263; 1-800-635-8036), 1506 S. Kilgore, Portales. Call for hours. Begun in 1981 when Bill Dalley obtained a Standard brand windmill, this collection numbers 85 restored, working windmills from around the world, creaking and spinning on 20 acres.

Peanut Processing (1-800-635-8036), Portales. By appointment, have a peanut-processing tour and see how everything peanut is made, from candy to peanut butter.

Bat Flights, Carlsbad Caverns National Park (575-785-3012), sundown, late May–mid-Oct. Witness an awesome living swarm of thousands of bats as they leave the caverns. Amphitheater seating is available. Free.

WILDER PLACES

Hondo Iris Farm and Gallery (575-653-4062), US 70 and Mile Marker 284, Hondo. Perhaps not exactly wilder, but definitely off the beaten path, this exquisite display of hundreds of varieties of iris, a botanical garden of sorts, is at its height during mid–late May. Wonderful picnic site, outstanding gallery of imported clothing and home fashions, and Alice Seely's afford-able, fine original silver jewelry. Free.

Lake Lucero (575-679-2599), White Sands National Monument. Monthly three-hour guided tour of the dry lake that is the source of the White Sands. Drive 18 miles and hike 0.75 mile to Lake Lucero. $3.

Slaughter Canyon Cave (1-800-967-CAVE), Carlsbad Caverns National Park, Carlsbad. Summer tours daily 10 and 1, winter tours Sat.–Sun. 10. Strictly for the adventurous, this challenging two-hour tour explores an undeveloped cave 23 miles from the visitor center. Access is by a half-hour hike from Slaughter Canyon Cave parking lot. Children under six not allowed. $15.

Mescalero Apache Reservation (575-464-4473; 575-464-4494), 16 miles east of Tularosa on US 70. A magnificent forested place in the Sierra Blanca mountains, recognized in 1874 as the Mescalero homeland, it is now home to 3,100 Native Americans. Famed for its fierce warriors, the tribe is now known for its tradition of the Apache Maidens' Puberty Rites, with dances of the Mountain Gods, celebrated in annual July 4 festivities at Inn of the Mountain Gods, Ski Apache, and St. Joseph Mission. You can find fishing in Eagle Creek Lakes, which also offer camping, and Mescalero Lake.

to simple tenting alongside the lake. Gently rolling juniper-covered hillsides frame the rocky shoreline. $6 per vehicle day use, $10–18 camping.

✍ **White's City Water Park** (575-785-2291), at Carlsbad Caverns National Park. Open seasonally. This is the only resort water park in the state, with two ample pools, two spas, and two 150-foot water slides. Free to resort guests.

WILDLIFE REFUGES **Bitter Lake National Wildlife Refuge** (575-622-6755), Roswell. North on US 285, east on Pine Lodge Rd., 9 miles to headquarters. Open daily year-round, dawn to dusk. This Pecos River wetlands is home to over 90 species of dragonflies, and 357 bird species visit or live here, plus some endangered species. Several short, easy hikes feature native plants and butter-flies. Bike riding is available on the 8-mile gravel drive of the paved 4-mile round-trip trail. Tours available with reservations. The best viewing is available one-half hour before sunrise to one-half hour after sunset. Free.

✳ Lodging and Dining

Chain motels and eateries are your best bet out here.

✳ Special Events

April: **Trinity Site Tour** (575-437-6120).

May: **Smokey Bear Days** (575-354-2748), Smokey Bear Historical Park, Capitan, first weekend, with parade, crafts marketplace, chainsaw carving, music. **Lincoln Fiber Festival** (575-653-4372), Lincoln State Monument, Lincoln, midmonth. Textile artists, sheep-shearers, basket makers, spinners, and more.

June: **White Oaks Miners Day** (no phone), White Oaks, first Sat. **Mountain Blues Festival** (575-257-9535), Ruidoso, early June. **Mountain Park Cherry Festival** (575-652-3445), High Rolls, midmonth. **Art in the Pines** (575-257-7395), Ruidoso, midmonth. Tour area artists' studios. **Old Fort Days** (575-355-2573), Fort Sumner, midmonth. Storytelling and book signing featuring Navajo literature.

July: **Roswell UFO Festival** (575-623-5695), Roswell, first week in July. **Art Festival,** Ruidoso. **Fourth of July Celebration** (575-464-4473), Mescalero; Apache Maidens Puberty Rites, powwow, rodeo. **Smokey Bear Stampede** (575-354-2748), Capitan, Fourth of July week; more contestants than any other U.S. amateur rodeo. **Art Loop Tour** (575-378-8273; www.artloop.org), Lincoln County, first weekend. Tour of diverse artists' studios for some of the most original jewelry, pottery, fiber art, and fine art to be seen anywhere. **Bluegrass Festival** (575-746-9619), Weed.

August: **Lincoln County Fair** (575-354-2748), Smokey Bear Historical Park, Capitan, second week. **Old Lincoln Days, Billy the Kid Pageant** (575-653-4372), Lincoln Pony Express Race, Capitan Gap to White Oaks. **Lea County Fair and Rodeo** (575-492-2676), largest county fair in state. **Bat Flight Breakfast** (575-785-2232), Carlsbad Caverns, second Thurs. in Aug.; nominal fee.

September: **Chile and Cheese Festival** (575-623-5695), Roswell. **All American Futurity** (575-378-7262), Ruidoso Downs, the world's richest quarter-horse race. **White Sands Star Party** (575-679-3599), White Sands. **Clovis Music Festival** (575-763-3435) Clovis. Rock 'n roll like back in the day.

October: **Lincoln County Cowboy Symposium** (575-378-7262), Glencoe. Second weekend in Oct. Chuckwagon cook-off, cowboy poetry, swing dancing, Western art, crafts, cowboy

MESCAL ROAST AND MOUNTAIN SPIRIT DANCE

Living Desert Zoo and Garden State Park (505-887-5516), second full weekend in May. Mescal is harvested in the traditional way and then cooked in an underground pit. Traditional Apache Feast dinner. Pit is opened at 11 AM on Sunday, and all are invited to taste the roasted mescal. Bonfire; Native American dancers in ceremonial dress perform Dance of the Mountain Spirit to honor coming of age of young women. Tickets go on sale Apr. 1. $15 for feast and dances; $10 for dances only.

gear, rodeo, roping for kids, country music concert. **Peanut Festival** (575-356-8541), Portales, first weekend.

November: **Trinity Site Tour** (575-437-6120). **Christmas on the Pecos** (505-628-0952; www.christmason thepecos.com), Nov. 23–Dec. 31. Closed Christmas Eve. Twelve departures nightly view; over 100 homes decorated with holiday lights along the banks of the Pecos River.

December: **Christmas Eve Luminarias** (575-653-4372), Historic Lincoln. **Santa Land** (575-682-2733), Zenith Park, Cloudcroft. Santa and Mrs. Claus arrive with candy and cookies, hot cider, and holiday music.

Northeast New Mexico: Santa Fe Trail Country

SANTA FE TRAIL REGION: CAPULIN, CIMARRON, CLAYTON, DES MOINES, EAGLE NEST, FOLSOM, RATON, ROY, SPRINGER, WAGON MOUND

LAND GRANT COUNTRY: LAS VEGAS, MAXWELL, MORA, OCATE, PECOS

ROUTE 66 COUNTRY: SANTA ROSA, TUCUMCARI

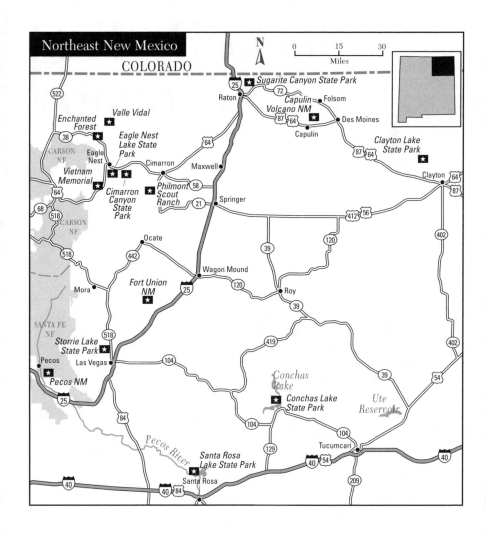

Northeast New Mexico

COLORADO

Sugarite Canyon State Park
Raton
Capulin Volcano NM
Folsom
Des Moines
Capulin
Clayton Lake State Park
Clayton

Enchanted Forest
Valle Vidal
Eagle Nest Lake State Park
CARSON NF
Eagle Nest
Cimarron
Maxwell
Vietnam Memorial
Cimarron Canyon State Park
Philmont Scout Ranch
Springer
CARSON NF

Ocate
Wagon Mound
Mora
Fort Union NM
Roy

SANTA FE NF
Storrie Lake State Park
Pecos
Las Vegas
Pecos NM

Conchas Lake
Conchas Lake State Park
Ute Reservoir

Pecos River
Santa Rosa Lake State Park
Santa Rosa
Tucumcari

0   15   30
Miles

INTRODUCTION

Northeast New Mexico is an explorer's delight as much as for what it lacks as what it offers. If you like clear turquoise skies and 360-degree views; back roads beckoning onward to the horizon; miles of fields and meadows with few people, billboards, or sign of human habitation save an occasional tumbledown, abandoned cabin; wildflowers galore . . . a place so big it can make you feel small, this could become your new favorite place. Encounters with antelope, elk, deer, wild turkey, and, occasionally, bear and bobcat are part of the journey, and at night, spangled ink-black skies unfurl to dazzle the stargazer. Best of all, the outdoors is easily accessible, right up the road, just about any road.

Still, the visitor is not without familiar diversions. In Clayton you can see a movie in the 1916 Luna Theater, where the same person sells you your ticket, makes the popcorn, and screens the film. You may feel like you've found the best "last picture show." You can see first-rate theater at the Shuler Theater in Raton and hear the very best live classical music at Music from Angel Fire.

In the great northeast, you can also be the only person hiking a trail for miles; fish for trout in transparent mountain streams, with enough quiet to really hear that stream babbling; and experience a wonderland of butterflies, wildflowers, and birds at Sugared Canyon State Park; or stop the car for a herd of elk crossing the road in Cimarron Canyon.

This place will take you in and wrap you up in its natural warmth and lack of pretension.

Here you can follow the heart line of Western history—the Santa Fe Trail, where wagon ruts still trace the path westward, and the place is changed so little it is easy to imagine the sights and sounds of the pioneer experience.

And if you enjoy odd, funky little out-of-the-way museums where history has not yet been gift-wrapped, and where the volunteer at the front desk knows everyone in town, you will be in heaven.

Still, despite the similarities of people, customs, and economies, the place is just so big and diverse, it's best to think of it by breaking it into three main geographic areas: the Santa Fe Trail Region of the northeast corner, where the small towns of northeast New Mexico—Clayton, Raton, Cimarron, and Springer still run on the Western mainstays of ranching, railroading, and mining (though coal mining has given way to oil and gas exploration); Land Grant Country, with

Las Vegas as the central and largest town; and Route 66 Country veering off I-40 to the east.

The population of northeast New Mexico is a mixture of descendants who immigrated here to work the mines—from Italy, the Slavic countries, Greece, and Mexico; the descendants of homesteaders; ranchers and ranching families; those who count as their ancestors the original Spanish settlers; and those who somehow found their way here by way of an escape from the bigger cities.

Increasingly, those who grew up here are returning, fixing up the old family house, or building a new one, or fixing up another old one, and joining the retirees from colder and more urban climates who feel like the peace and quiet, the recreational opportunities right out the front door, and the clean air and water are just what their hearts desire. The unspoiled beauty of the place draws artists and celebrations of the arts as well.

The simple, authentic delights of the small town abound here: the ease with which you can get around; the smiles, waves, and hellos you can count on when you go to the post office or the grocery store; the genuine sense of community, a community that still knows and cares about its neighbors; and the joyous, simple American traditions of high school football, the annual lighting of the Christmas tree, Fourth of July fireworks, the county fair, and the rodeo. And if you enjoy

DUTCH OVEN COOKING IS STILL THE FAVORITE WAY TO FEED COWBOYS.

the flavor of historic hotels, with the resident ghost or two, northeast New
Mexico can charm you with its legendary lodgings.

As much as the world has changed during recent decades, as computer-savvy as we have become, and as susceptible to anxiety and danger, there remains a pervading sense of something else more enduring—a sense of values, of old-fashioned courtesy and respect, of bonds, of deals still done on a handshake, of shared memories and the assumed importance of community. Somehow, this part of the world still seems to have escaped, or been protected from, the stresses, prejudices, angers, and shocking violence seen on the evening news.

Yet these small towns are not immune. Many of the current social problems—domestic violence, drugs, degraded quality of schools, health care, lack of jobs, gangs, and welfare dependence—also exist here. And there is not much to do at night. But for all that, it is possible to live comfortably outside of the compulsion for conspicuous consumption, and thus to have a very relaxed visit. You will be judged on the reliability of your word, not on the model of your vehicle, and you will be respected according to your generosity to friends and the community, not according to the size of your house or the designer labels on your clothes.

Consequently, time takes on a different quality here. There is time to drop in and visit with a friend, to take a neighbor to the doctor, and the lake is close enough to take a child fishing. Hard work is valued, and there is a holdover from blue-collar days when people worked mainly with their hands. It is a good place to kick back, whether for a weekend, a week, or who knows? Maybe much longer.

Much of this land, including Colfax County, Union County, and San Miguel County—once the hunting grounds and dwelling place of Utes, Apaches, and Comanches—has seen mountain men, like Kit Carson, and giants, like Lucien Maxwell, whose Maxwell Land Grant, at 1.7 million acres, stood as the largest land holding in the hemisphere. It has seen the wagons of the military and merchants cross the Santa Fe Trail via both the Mountain Route, over difficult Raton Pass, and the more dangerous Cimarron Cutoff—wagon traffic so heavy and frequent that the ruts those wagons left on the landscape are visible to this day. This route of commerce, over which merchants transported goods between Missouri and New Mexico, was used between 1821 and 1880 and died out with the coming of the railroad.

Approximately 19 miles north of Clayton, off NM 406, a portion of the Cimarron Route crosses the Kiowa National Grassland. It is a 2-mile section of trail, with an interpretive site. It has seen those who built the railroads and those who worked a living out of the land with every bit of their strength and ingenuity, and who built the towns and ranches that many of their families still inhabit, three and four generations down the line.

And it has seen the Colfax County War of the 1870s. There is much history to be learned here, and here it can be seen and felt and touched, because it is still remembered. The war pitted the settlers on the Maxwell Land Grant against the big company that claimed the land. And it tore the region apart.

At the Dawson Cemetery, the results of tragic early-20th-century coal mining accidents are visible in the hundreds of crosses marked with the same dates of death, plain crosses standing over the graves of dozens of nationalities.

From the mile Rim Walk around Capulin Volcano, it is still possible to see four states—New Mexico, Colorado, Texas, and Oklahoma. And in Las Vegas, you can visit the Montefiore Cemetery, where the German Jewish merchants of the 1800s lie.

This is where the Great Plains meets the Rockies. Beginning with the Homestead Act of 1862, settlers began to pour in. By the end of the 1870s, the Plains Indian tribes had lost their historic use of the lands. Cattle and sheep replaced the bison, and following their path came soldiers, prospectors, and railroad builders.

Las Vegas, New Mexico, has over 900 buildings listed on the National Register of Historic Places, as well as nine historic districts, each worthy of a walking tour. Brochures are available at the visitor center.

By way of contrast, you can scuba dive in Santa Rosa's 67-foot deep artesian Blue Hole as well as pet and feed the prize alpacas at the Victory Ranch outside Mora.

Colfax County has at least 284 farms and ranches. A wonderful place to experience this culture is at the annual Colfax County Fair, held the second weekend in August at the Springer Armory. Pie sale, junior livestock sale, steer show—all the treasured customs of rural Americana can be experienced here, and the annual cakewalk.

At the annual Fourth of July Santa Fe Trail Balloon Rally, dozens of brilliant hot-air balloons fly aloft over Raton.

So, if you like having the trail to yourself during an early-morning hike, the peace of a glass-smooth alpine lake with trout jumping a foot in the air, going eyeball to eyeball with deer and antelope, poking around and antiquing in little towns without stoplights, and historic hotels loaded with legend and lore aplenty, plus a few hardy ghosts—have we got the place for you!

GETTING THERE *By car:* Private automobile is the only realistic way to travel and see the sights up here. From Albuquerque, drive north on I-25 for 123 miles to Las Vegas. Continue north on I-25 another 102 miles to Raton. Cimarron is 41 miles from Raton via I-25 south to US 64. Clayton is 90 miles east of Raton on US 64. Or, at Springer, exit I-25 and travel US 53 to Gladstone, then on to Clayton.

By train: Amtrak stops once daily, both north and southbound, in Raton and Las Vegas.

GUIDANCE Please be aware that in small towns, chambers of commerce are often staffed by volunteers and may be closed during posted hours of operation, which may also be irregular. Patience and some advance planning will help cut down on frustration. In general, they are open during the week—generally 10–2 is the safest times to find them in—and tend to be closed weekends in the smaller towns (or at best, open a half-day on Saturday). Some do not have a physical location, and others may just ask you to call back.

SANTA FE TRAIL REGION: CAPULIN, CIMARRON, CLAYTON, DES MOINES, EAGLE NEST, FOLSOM, RATON, ROY, SPRINGER, WAGON MOUND

The Old West is alive and well out here, where the code of the West still rules and the economy traditionally runs on ranching, railroading, and mining. It's pretty quiet, quiet enough to hear a meadowlark warbling. This is an excellent area to take your own wildlife photo safari. Springtime is windy, so you'll likely be dodging tumbleweeds, and there's a good chance you'll get snowed in during winter. If you are sincere, and down to earth, Colfax County folk will be friendly; if you're not, don't expect them to be real sociable. Some of the oldest ranches in the country are located here, and many are run by the third and fourth generation. The Santa Fe Trail winds through the country, and the ruts left by wagons that traveled that trail are still visible. Memories are long with history, and there's probably a cowboy with a good story ready to tell sitting next to you at the bar in the St. James Hotel.

GETTING THERE *By car:* Private automobile is the only realistic way to travel and see the sights up here. From Albuquerque, drive north on I-25 for 123 miles to Las Vegas. Continue north on I-25 another 102 miles to Raton. Cimarron is 41 miles from Raton via I-25 south to US 64. Clayton is 90 miles east of Raton on US 64. Or, at Springer, exit I-25 and travel US 53 to Gladstone, then on to Clayton.

By train: Amtrak stops once daily, both north and southbound, in Raton and Las Vegas.

GUIDANCE Cimarron Chamber of Commerce (575-376-2417), 104 N. Lincoln Ave. A tiny wooden office in the town's central park off US 64 beside a statue of Lucien B. Maxwell is the place to find out about local happenings.

Clayton/Union County Chamber of Commerce (575-374-9253; 1-800-390-7858), 1103 S. First St., Clayton, is professional and will return phone calls in a timely manner. It's good to make contact here for specific directions and drive time to more remote locations.

Eagle Nest Chamber of Commerce (575-377-2420; 1-800-494-9117), 54 Therma Dr., Eagle Nest. Hours are catch as catch can.

Raton Chamber & Economic Development Council Inc. (575-445-3689; 1-800-638-6161), 100 Clayton Rd., Raton.

Raton Visitor Information Center (575-445-2761), 100 Clayton Rd., Raton, is a spacious, comfortable place offering an abundance of regional literature, weather information, and free Wi-Fi.

Springer Chamber of Commerce (575-483-2998), Springer. Good luck!

MEDICAL EMERGENCY **Miners Colfax Medical Center** (575-445-7700), 200 Hospital Dr., Raton.

Union County General Hospital (575-374-2585), 301 Harding St., Clayton.

✳ To See

SANTA FE TRAIL COUNTRY TOWNS **Capulin.** A place name frequently encountered in New Mexico, the word is Spanish for "chokecherry," or "wild cherry." Here it refers to the little village 28 miles southeast of Raton on US 64/87 near the border of Colfax and Union counties. The main attraction is the dormant volcano that is the centerpiece of Mount Capulin National Monument. It was originally a settlement of Hispanic farmers founded sometime after the Civil War.

Cimarron. Four miles southwest of Raton. South on I-25 to exit 419, then US 64 west. Cimarron is located at the junction of US 64 and NM 58 and 21. While the exact meaning of this word is not certain, as it may refer either to wild Rocky Mountain bighorn sheep or the wild plum or wild rose that once grew here abundantly; the word *wild* is applied with accuracy to the town, which still exudes a Wild West flavor. Founded in 1841 as the headquarters for the Maxwell Land Grant and home of land baron Lucien Maxwell, it became known as a hideout for desperados as well as a gathering spot for traders, miners, and travelers on the Santa Fe Trail. The Las Vegas *Optic* once reported, "It was a quiet week in Cimarron. Only three shootings took place." Nearby are the Philmont Scout Ranch and the home of Kit Carson. Cimarron is a pleasant stop for exploring Santa Fe Trail history, browsing the unpretentious shops and galleries, and absorbing the energy of a place still inhabited largely by cowboys, ranchers, old-timers, and artists. The saloon of the St. James Hotel, with 27 bullet holes in the ceiling, is a good place to meet up with as many characters as you deserve to.

Clayton. Ninety miles east of Raton on US 64/87. Dating to 1888, Clayton was born with the arrival of the railroad, when it became a major cattle-shipping point. It remains to this day a center of ranching activity that pioneer descendants still call home. Among its historic treasures are WPA murals of the New Deal, the 1916 Luna Theater, the Herzstein Memorial Museum, and the recently restored 125-year-old Eklund Hotel. Nearby are Clayton Lake State Park and the Dinosaur Trackway, the second-largest preserved field of dinosaur tracks in the western hemisphere. The town was named for Sen. Stephen Dorsey's son, Clayton. Dorsey was a crony of Albert Fall of Teapot Dome notoriety. Originally home to Indians, then a resting point for Santa Fe Trail settlers, it grew from a campground for cattle drovers. The railroad came through in 1888, and Clayton subsequently became a prosperous shipping and supply station, as well as a target for Black Jack Ketchum, a notorious train robber. Clayton High School has a WPA museum, but appointments must be made in advance to see it. Check with the chamber of commerce.

Des Moines. Thirty-eight miles southeast of Raton on US 64/87 at the junction of US 64/87 and NM 325. Originally a village of homesteaders founded in 1887 when the railroad came through, Des Moines is named for the town of the same name in Iowa and pronounced with an audible *s* at the end of *Moines*. It supposedly got its name when two cowboys, wondering what to call the place, noticed a railroad car and saw the words *Des Moines* painted on the side. Today it remains a proud, small community of ranching folk and, if you are an artist or photographer, is a gold mine of opportunities for making images of weathered barns, windmills, and tumbledown houses. Recently, some folks from Santa Fe have

WINDMILLS ADORN WINTER LANDSCAPES.

moved in and opened the interesting Gallery C on the main street, US 64/87, which features live poetry and music from time to time.

Eagle Nest. Sixty-four miles southwest of Raton, at the junction of US 64/87 and NM 38. The hamlet, in the shadow of 13,161-foot-high Wheeler Peak, the state's highest, is the gateway to Cimarron Canyon. Originally called Therma, for the daughter of the postal inspector, Eagle Nest is a lovely mountain village on the shore of Eagle Nest Lake State Park, a haven for fishermen, ice fishermen, and RV campers. Back in the day, Eagle Nest was known as a wide-open gambling town patronized by politicians traveling across the state. Now it is a quiet, restful place to kick back and enjoy the clear mountain air and excellent fly-fishing. Fourth of July is celebrated with a mighty fireworks display over Eagle Nest Lake.

Folsom. Across scenic Johnson Mesa, which may be closed in winter on account of snow, 38 miles east of Raton off NM 72, lies sleepy Folsom. When President Grover Cleveland's wife, Frances Folsom, came through on the train in 1888, the little railroad settlement known as Ragtown changed its name to Folsom in her honor. Today the tiny town is known as the place where George McJunkin, the observant African-American foreman for the Crowfoot Ranch, in 1926 made a remarkable discovery. He found large bones in an arroyo containing ancient Pleistocene bison skeletons and 19 chipped stone spear points that revised how long man had inhabited this area—at least 10,000 and as much as 15,000 years. The originals are housed in the Denver Museum of Natural History, and the Folsom site is designated a National Historic Landmark. Folsom was proclaimed a State Monument in 1951. It is also the site of Folsom Falls, a spring-fed waterfall on the Dry Cimarron River, 4 miles northeast of Folsom on NM 456. But beware of rattlesnakes if you go there! Folsom Museum is housed in the historic 1896 Doherty Building. The Folsom Hotel was built in 1888 and was originally the Drew & Phillips General Mercantile Store.

Raton is 225 miles north of Albuquerque on I-25. Originally called Willow Springs, this town on the edge of Raton Pass into Colorado was a watering stop for military and Santa Fe Trail travelers coming over the Mountain Route. The town came to life in 1880 as a support stop for the Santa Fe Railway roundhouse and shops. Yet earlier, following the Civil War, the government mail stage carrying passengers descended challenging Raton Pass and stopped at the Clifton House Stage Station below Red River Peak for dinner, then galloped into Cimarron on the way to Fort Union. Raton has plenty of motels and eateries left over from the era of La Mesa Racetrack, a well-preserved historic walking district alongside the railroad tracks, and a museum packed with coal mining history, and it makes a good base for exploring the area.

Roy. Nine miles east of the Canadian River. Originally a homesteading community that found its reason for existence when the railroad came through, founded by Frank Roy and three brothers from Canada, Roy became a ranching center that was decimated by the Dust Bowl. Today it is a sleepy village in the middle of Harding County, the biggest county in New Mexico by area, but with only 900 inhabitants.

Springer is 131 miles north of Santa Fe on I-25, at the junction of US 56. Formerly the capital of Colfax County, today Springer is the site of the Colfax County Fair and Rodeo held in early August, and the Santa Fe Trail Interpretive Center and Museum. Not too much to see here.

Wagon Mound. Twenty-five miles southwest of Springer on I-25. A stop of the Santa Fe Trail, the town is named after the butte on its eastern edge that resembles a covered wagon, a Santa Fe Trail landmark. Its previous name was Santa Clara. You can get gas here, but not much else.

MUSEUMS **Folsom Museum** (575-278-2122), Folsom. Open weekends Memorial Day–Labor Day, weekends only May and Sept. 10–5, winter by appointment only. Displays of Folsom Man, whose points (arrows) were first found in this area by black cowboy George McJunkin. It has been a long time since this museum was updated, and the crowded walls recall a bygone, nostalgic perspective on the world. $1 adults, $.50 children 6–12 , 5 and under free.

Herzstein Memorial Museum (575-374-2977), corner Second and Walnut St., Clayton. Open Tues.–Sat. 10–5. The museum, donated by the pioneer Herzstein family, is home of the Union County Historical Society, which lovingly tends the collections housed in a former 1919 church. Collections include a wealth of homesteader artifacts, memorabilia, furniture, and art, and the museum makes for a surprisingly refreshing experience. Free.

Kit Carson Museum (575-376-2281), Philmont Scout Ranch, Rayado. Eleven miles south of Cimarron on NM 21. Open June–Aug. daily 8–5; Sept. and May

THE KIT CARSON MUSEUM IN RAYADO IS RESTORED TO HISTORIC ACCURACY.

Mon.–Fri. 8–5. This hacienda, and home of Indian scout and mountain man Kit Carson, was actually the original Fort Union, protecting the frontier from Indian raids, built before the fort now bearing that name was constructed. As histori- cally accurate as it can possibly be, down to the flour sacks in the storehouse, this museum is an excellent way to get a true feel of the Santa Fe Trail day, the fur trade, and the early settlement of New Mexico. A really special experience is the Wed. 7 PM candlelight and storytelling tour, June–Aug., $3. Reservations are necessary. Free.

R.W. Cowan Livery Stable (575-483-2825). Corner of Third St. and Maxwell Ave., Springer. By appointment only. Built in 1880 of native stone, this museum houses one of the largest collections of period and post-period antiques in the Southwest. Free.

Old Pass Gallery (575-445-2052; 1-877-278-248), 145 S. First St., Raton. Closed major holidays. Open Tues.–Sat. 10–4. Here you will find exhibitions of local watercolorists and photographers, as well as art of regional interest and a nicely renovated Wells Fargo freight office. Free.

Raton Museum (575-445-8979), 216 S. First St., Raton. Open Wed.–Sat. 10–4. While it is rumored this museum is moving to a larger space on S. Second St., it remains as of this writing in the historic district as a stunningly crammed collec- tion of mining, railroad, Santa Fe Trail, and ranching artifacts. In fact, it is a must-do history lesson for all who want to understand this place. Free.

Old Mill Museum (575-376-2417), 220 W. 17th St., Cimarron. In May and Sept., open weekends: Sat. 9–5, Sun. 1–5. In summer (Memorial Day–Labor Day), open Sun. 1–5, Mon.–Sat. 9–5, closed Thurs. Originally known as the Aztec Mill, it was built by land baron Lucien Maxwell in 1864 to grind wheat and corn flour for nearby Apaches and Utes, as well as Fort Union, with whom he had contracts to supply provisions. You can easily spend half a day wandering the three floors that tell the history of the Maxwell Land Grant, Native Ameri- cans, ranchers of the area, and scouting. $3 suggested donation.

Villa Philmonte (575-376-2281), Philmont Scout Ranch, Rayado. Ten miles south of Cimarron on NM 21. Open daily June–Aug. 10–4. This grand, elegant Mediterranean summer home of oilman Waite Phillips and his wife, Genevieve, is now the property of the Philmont Scout Ranch, of which Phillips is the bene- factor. Built 1926–27; all art and furnishings remain intact, as does the splendid original tile work. $4.

Santa Fe Trail Museum and Interpretive Center (no phone), 606 Maxwell Ave, Springer. Open Memorial Day–Labor Day 9–5. This hodgepodge, quaint collection is housed in the former Colfax County Courthouse (built 1882). Here you will find a complicated jumble of Santa Fe Trail exhibits, historic photos, artifacts, old letters and maps, and information on the New Mexico Territorial period in northeast New Mexico. For dedicated funky museum goers only. Free.

HISTORIC LANDMARKS, PLACES, AND SITES **Black Jack Ketchum's Grave** (575-374-9253), Clayton Cemetery, Princeton Ave., Clayton. This is the final resting place of the notorious train robber who was hanged in 1901 at Union

County Courthouse. His last words were reputedly, "I had breakfast in Clayton,
but I'll have dinner in hell!" Free.

Dawson is a ghost town 5 miles northwest of Colfax, formerly a prosperous Phelps-Dodge mining town. In its heyday it was one of the liveliest towns in northeast New Mexico, known for its many winning teams, particularly baseball. Here miners from all over the world, of various ethnic backgrounds, and their families lived, worked, and played together. While the town has been dismantled, the Dawson Cemetery, where hundreds of miners killed in tragic accidents in 1913 and 1923 are buried beneath simple white crosses, remains a moving sight and an important, if often overlooked, chapter in the history of the West. Free.

Historic First St., Raton. Paralleling the railroad tracks, this four-block historic district includes the Old Pass Gallery, occupying a former Wells Fargo freight office; the classic California Mission Atchison; Topeka & Santa Fe Railway station, antiques shops; and well-preserved late-19th to early-20th-century buildings.

Mandala Center (575-278-3002), 35 miles east of Raton on US 64/87, Des Moines. An ecumenical spiritual retreat center open to all, the Mandala Center on Sierra Grande Mountain offers workshops year-round as well as opportunities for private retreats and workshops for leadership, spiritual development, writing skills, and health and wholeness, as well as personal renewal. Based on Christian religious principles, it is indeed welcoming to people of all faiths. And the food is wonderful!

Mills Mansion (575-483-2428), 804 First St., Springer. This three-story adobe, built in 1877, was the home of one of the most powerful, if lesser known, figures in New Mexico history, Melvin Mills. He created a fruit empire in the Canadian River Canyon, was a colorful lawyer who ran a stage line between Kansas and Fort Union, served in the territorial legislature, and turned up in the Colfax County War as an attorney for the Maxwell Land Grant. Call for information on tours.

Santa Fe Trail (SFT) Sites: **Point of Rocks** (575-485-2473), 23 miles east of Springer on US 56, north on County Road 52. Seven miles from rest area, 2 miles east, then 1 mile north, look for SFT sign-in box at ranch house, which is on the Santa Fe National Historic Trail. Wagon ruts, graves, Indian campsites. **McNees Crossing** (575-374-9652), 25 miles north of Clayton on NM 402. Santa Fe Trail site named for trader killed there in 1828. Nearby are trail ruts.

Shuler Theater (505-445-2052; 1-877-278-2489), 131 N. Second St., Raton. Completed in 1915, this European Rococo jewel box of a theater, with WPA murals depicting the history of the area, continues to host a variety of outstanding theater and music productions year-round, from ballroom dance to mariachi, Neil Simon to Brazilian dance. Tours available by appointment.

Philmont Scout Ranch (575-376-2281), 137,000 acres 10 miles southwest of Cimarron on NM 21, Rayado. Oklahoma oilman Waite Phillips donated this lush property to the Boy Scouts of America. Each summer, it is used by scouts from all over the world for backcountry camping.

NATURAL WONDERS Capulin Volcano National Monument (575-278-2201), Capulin. North of Capulin 5.5 miles on NM 456. Closed major holidays. Open Memorial Day–Labor Day 7:30–6:30, Labor Day–Memorial Day 8–4. This natural cone of a relatively young volcano, only 7,000 years old, is one of the few places in the world where you can hike inside a cinder cone. Visitors may walk 2 miles round-trip into the 415-foot-deep crater and hike along the 1-mile rim trail overlooking much of the Raton-Clayton volcanic fields. From the rim trail, you can see four states, and to the west, view the snowcapped Sangre de Cristo Mountains. $5 per vehicle.

Sierra Grande. Ten miles southeast of Folsom, off US 64/85, is the largest single mountain in the United States, measuring 40 miles around the base, covering 50 square miles, at an altitude of 8,720 feet.

Tooth of Time is a prominent, toothlike rock formation visible from Cimarron that was significant to Santa Fe Trail travelers. When trail pioneers saw the Tooth of Time, they knew they only had seven more days to reach Santa Fe.

SCENIC DRIVES For information on New Mexico's Scenic Byways, visit www.newmexicoscenicbyways.org or call 1-800-733-6396, ext. 24371.

SIGHTING THE TOOTH OF TIME MEANT ONLY SEVEN MORE DAYS TO SANTA FE FOR THE PIONEERS.

Dry Cimarron Scenic Byway. NM 406 north to NM 456, it extends 40 miles north of Clayton. The Dry Cimarron River ran mainly underground but would surface occasionally. This mostly deserted scenic road runs through Union and Colfax counties, and it has served as an alternate route between Clayton and Raton. There is much history in the way of Santa Fe Trail wagon ruts, old mining camps, and many landmark features. The drive brings the traveler through high prairie, national grasslands, nature preserves, volcanoes, mesas, and colorful geologic formations.

Santa Fe Trail Scenic Byway (www.newmexico.com/tours/santafe_trail.htm). Follow the actual path of the Santa Fe Trail wagons and see wagons and abandoned forts in the rugged landscape of mountain canyons. The byway extends 480 miles altogether. If you are following the route, you can go to Santa Fe via Clayton, Raton, Cimarron, and Springer, to Las Vegas. In New Mexico, highlights include Fort Union National Monument in Watrous, Kiowa National Grasslands in Clayton, Pecos National Historical Park, Pecos, and the Santa Fe National Forest.

Johnson Mesa is 41 miles from Raton to Folsom along NM 72. Spectacular views of the Sangre de Cristo Mountains are yours here above Raton, and there is no better place for stargazing in the entire state. Settlers believed this was a paradise of rich grasslands. Many of the early settlers worked in the coal mines. When winter came, survival became difficult. The little stone church on the mesa is always open. This is truly a scenic byway, but it's not passable for much of the winter. Summertime, the mesa is covered with white flowers and herds of antelope gallop, while the land serves as summer pasture for local ranchers. Homesteader cabins and dugouts are visible still, and a few hardy souls continue to live up here.

✳ To Do

FISHING **Charette Lakes** (575-483-2998), 35 miles southwest of Springer. I-25 exit 404 and west on NM 569. Boating and fishing as well as primitive camping are yours on the shores of this deep natural volcanic lake, which can be windy in the evening.

Cimarron Canyon State Park (575-377-6271), US 64 east of Eagle Nest. One of the state's prime German brown trout fisheries, with 9 miles of fly-casting along the Cimarron River. $6 day use; $10–18 camping.

Eagle Nest Lake State Park (575-377-6271), NM 64 north of Eagle Nest. Boating, fishing, and ice fishing are popular on this 2,400-acre lake that yields some of the finest trout and Konkani salmon fishing in the state. The patient wildlife watcher will see elk, deer, bears, and eagles. This is a beloved lakeside summer picnic area. $6 per vehicle.

Springer Lake (575-483-2998), 4 miles northwest of Springer on CR 17. Picnicking, camping, and fishing for northern pike and catfish make this small lake a favorite with locals. Free.

GOLFING **Raton Country Club and Municipal Golf Course** (505-445-8113), 510 Country Club Rd., Raton. Voted "Best Nine Hole Course in New Mexico," this lovely 6,500-foot-high course, with plenty of hazards, was built in 1922 by a coal baron. Greens fee for nine holes around $20.

MOUNTAIN BIKING See **Sugarite Canyon State Park** under *Green Space*. You can just about choose your own level of terrain here, with this uncrowded, premium area that is pretty much an insider's secret. Here are challenging up and down trails and sweet flats packed with greenery, wildflowers, meadows, forests, and lake views. It's a fairly easy ride through ride former coal camp, around Lake Maloya, to the Colorado border. The visitor center provides trail maps. $6.

SNOW SPORTS **Enchanted Forest Cross-Country Ski and Snowshoe Area** (575-754-2374; 1-800-966-9381). At the summit of Bobcat Pass, just north of Red River, the Enchanted Forest is the state's premier cross-country and snowshoeing venue, offering everything you could want or need, including rentals and lessons. There are almost 20 miles of groomed Nordic ski trails for varied skill levels, and close to 10 miles of snowshoe trails, plus designated dog trails, though you may use the trails if you are pet-free, all amid heart-stopping alpine scenery. Under $20.

✳ Lodging

BED & BREAKFASTS, INNS, AND MOTELS ⚱ & **Heart's Desire** (575-445-1000; 1-866-488-1028), 301 S. Third St., Raton. This sweet three-story, 1885 Victorian home in comfortable walking distance of downtown, the historic district, and train station happens to be run by an antiques lover. This bed and breakfast reflects the charm and cozy clutter of her love. Plus, if you feel like doing a little shopping, many of the collectibles are for sale. You will feel cared for and catered to here, with evening snacks, chocolates, and eggs Benedict for breakfast. The third-floor Hunting and Fishing room, with its views of nearby mountains, is truly a getaway, and the Blue Willow room will romance the heart of any lady. An evening at this retreat into the past would make a darling Valentine's Day surprise. $125–195.

🐾 & **Best Western Kokopelli Lodge** (575-374-2589), 702 S. First St., Clayton. Clean, light, very spacious rooms with Southwest décor and all conveniences make this a most pleasant stop. A café serving a better-than-average complimentary hot buffet breakfast, swimming pool, and a swell gift shop are on the premises. $95–180.

🐾 **Oasis Motel** (575-445-3681), 445 S. Second St, Raton. With a popular café on the premises, and 14 clean and serviceable rooms in classic motel décor, this locally owned and operated motel is a good choice. $75.

Moore's Rest/Econo Lodge (575-377-6813), 715 Hwy. 64 East, Eagle Nest. With balcony rooms overlooking Eagle Nest Lake, this contemporary lodging can accommodate all size groups with apartments, suites, and rooms, and is all conveniently located near Angel Fire, Red River, and Taos. $76.

HEART'S DESIRE B&B IN RATON IS AN ANTIQUES LOVER'S DELIGHT.

&. **Casa de Gavilan** (575-376-2246),
10 miles south of Cimarron on
NM 21. Still very much the gracious
home it was, originally built with 18-
inch-thick walls and stout wooden
vigas (ceiling beams) for Jack and
Gertrude Nairn, this 1910 Pueblo
Revival white adobe villa perched
directly below the Santa Fe Trail
landmark known as the Tooth of Time
retains the essence of traditional New
Mexico. Remingtons and Russells
adorn the patio, and comfortable sitting rooms furnished with plump,
cushy sofas call you to curl up with a
book or enjoy a relaxing conversation.
The inn is located beside the
Philmont Scout Ranch. Stargazing is
superb, as is the wildlife viewing on

the 225 acres of pine forests. There's
more cowboy than chichi in the
hearty, wholesome breakfasts that
provide the fuel you'll need to spend
the morning exploring. $80–140.

**LODGES AND RANCHES Vermejo
Park Ranch** (575-445-2059), Raton.
Once part of the Maxwell Land
Grant, later the private getaway of
Mary Pickford and Douglas Fair-
banks, this piece of grand history is
today the property of media mogul
Ted Turner. Former guests include
presidents, industrialists, and celebrity
movers and shakers from Hollywood
to Washington, D.C. An exclusive
hunting and fishing lodge for the priv-
ileged, it is possible, for a price, to

visit and enjoy the Vermejo, with its 21 stocked lakes, legendary trout streams, and abundant herds of elk and bison. Since Turner purchased the property in 1996, the Vermejo has actively sought to restore the ecology and bring back native animals, including black-footed ferrets and wild wolves. Two-night minimum required, guide services extra. Gourmet meals, served in the clubby dining room overlooking the Sangre de Cristo Mountains, are included. Fishing season is May–Sept. Starts at $450 per night; $225 children.

CABINS AND CAMPING

¶¹ ♂ ♿ **SummerLan RV Park** (575-445-9536), 1900 Cedar St., Raton. With 42 full hookups, tent camping, cabins, a playground, laundry, store, free Wi-Fi, and even minor RV repairs available, this pet-friendly, handicap-accessible park has a reputation for friendliness and service. It's at 7,000 feet, so nights can be chilly, but it's a great place for stargazing and wildlife watching. Located on a frontage road off 1-25, it somehow manages to be a quiet spot. $23.

✳ Where to Eat

DINING OUT **Pappas Sweet Shop Restaurant** (575-445-9811), 1201 S. Second St., Raton. Closed Sun. A place for a nice lunch or dinner out, especially if there is business to be conducted, with decent prime rib, home-cooked stews, homemade soup daily, and a sense of itself as a bastion of gentility in a fast-food world. It's still in the family, generations after the original Mr. Pappas started out selling candy to the coal miners. Moderate.

Eklund Hotel & Bar (575-734-2551; 777-355-8631), 15 Main St., Clayton.

This grand dame, century-plus-old railroad hotel has recently received a million-dollar-plus meticulous restoration, bringing it back as close to the original as possible. Originally built by Swedish entrepreneur Carl Eklund, the rock hotel was long considered "the only first-class hotel between Trinidad, Colorado and Fort Worth, Texas, and has long had a reputation for fine food and drink." Whether eating a burger in the old saloon, complete with brass-rail bar, or a steak in the chandeliered dining room with velvet settees, the history of the Eklund captures the imagination. The chile, while mild, is tasty. Try the smothered stuffed sopaipillas. Inexpensive–Moderate.

⊚ **Carson-Maxwell Dining Room, St. James Hotel** (575-376-2664), 167 S. Collinson, Cimarron. Dinner only. Delectable house-baked rolls, chocolate pecan pie, falling-off-the-fork bison pot roast, and more, much more, are served in the faded elegance of the St. James dining room, with bullet holes in the tin ceiling, and a recently rediscovered original mural along the walls. If you seek memorable dining experiences, do not miss this opportunity to taste and touch the romance of the Old West. Originating in 1873 as a saloon operated by Lincoln's chef, Charles Lambert, this fine establishment offers a convivial full bar and café in addition to the dining room. Moderate.

EATING OUT **Colfax Tavern, Cold Beer, New Mexico** (575-376-2229), 11 miles east of Cimarron on US 64. You can see the tall white letters on the red-painted building from a mile out. The only establishment in the ghost town of Colfax, this bar has been here since Prohibition, so they say. It is by far the best cowboy bar in New Mexico, with live music and lots of locals who'd never let the truth stand in the way of a good story. Here you can hang out with the cowboys, or you might even run into Ted Turner, who is reportedly seen here in the vicinity of his Vermejo Ranch. It's friendly and comfortable, with live music and dancing on weekends in summer on the outdoor dance floor. Spaghetti night is every Monday, and burgers and pizza are served the rest of the time. The highly competitive summer Jeopardy tournament, for real money, held each July, is a social highlight. Mardi Gras is also celebrated in high style. Do definitely wear your boots. The slogan here is: "Where there's not much going on, you'd better be there when it is." Inexpensive.

Park Ave. Café (575-445-9090), 240 Park Ave., Raton. Really wonderful homemade soups, desserts, and breakfast specials are served here, adjacent to the historic El Portal Hotel. Anything chocolate is worth ordering. Their version of eggs Florentine smothered with cheese sauce, served with café potatoes, is my favorite. Inexpensive.

Piper's (575-445-3660), 215 Clayton Rd., Raton. This family-run establishment quickly established itself in town as a popular New Mexican eatery. The service is quite good, and ice cream treats are available as well. Get your breakfast smothered in red chile, and, on weekends, the local specialty, menudo (a hearty tripe stew that is a traditional hangover cure), is served. Those who crave their menudo approve. Piper's is the number one dining choice while in Raton. Inexpensive.

✐ **All Seasons Family Restaurant** (575-445-9889), 1616 Cedar St. (just off Clayton Road), Raton. It's fun to browse this ample curio emporium, which has joke gifts as well as country preserves and candles. The weekend breakfast buffet is a good deal, and there's always the salad bar and kids' menu, which can solve a lot of problems. Breakfast is served all day, and daily specials highlight the big variety of American and New Mexican offerings. There's something for everyone, for sure, and it continues to feel delightfully nonfranchise here. Inexpensive.

St. James Café (575-376-2664), 617 S. Collison Ave., Cimarron. This light and bright, friendly café, located in the historic St. James Hotel, is well worth a stop for lunch or breakfast, as it serves up excellent homemade soups, fresh salads, New Mexican fare, and tasty burgers, all at a fair price. Inexpensive.

Elida's Café (575-483-2985), 801 Railroad Ave., Springer. With plastic tablecloths, fluorescent lighting, and a menu tilted toward south of the border, Elida's couldn't be a more real, down-to-earth stop for homemade, from scratch, every day, sopaipillas, Frito pie, or a torta—a "Mexican sub." Try the gorditas, a homey, hard-to-find specialty of fried masa (cornmeal) stuffed with ground beef and served with beans and rice. The service is caring and thorough. A three-item combo will set you back $7.50. Inexpensive.

The Brown Hotel & Café (575-483-2269), 302 Maxwell Ave., Springer. Imagine homemade cinnamon rolls big as pie plates in granny's parlor, more than respectable huevos rancheros, counter stools that spin, and

IF YOU KNOW WHERE TO LOOK, YOU CAN FIND VINTAGE WEAR THROUGHOUT NORTHEAST NEW MEXICO.

furniture covered with lace doilies. Time stands refreshingly still at the Brown, a favorite meeting site of the Silver Spur CowBelles and a lunch stop for locals and visitors alike. Inexpensive.

✍ **Minnie's Dairy Delite** (575-483-2813), 42 US 56, Springer. Open summer only. Wash down those cheeseburgers and fries with a chocolate malt or a thick, creamy milk shake at this old-fashioned, down-home favorite roadside stop. You'll have trouble spending more than $7 on lunch or dinner. Inexpensive.

Gladstone Mercantile (575-485-2467), 4618 US 56, Gladstone. Just when you thought there was nothing out there but the high lonesome sky and the wind, along comes the quintessential stop in the road, where you can find a welcome with fresh hot coffee, hot soup, yummy barbeque brisket sandwiches, gifts to warm the heart of any cowgirl, and books by local authors. The place also doubles as a local grocery store. You'll love it! Inexpensive.

✴ Selective Shopping

Heirloom Shop (575-445-8876), 132 S. First St., Raton. Run by antiques maven Hattie Sloan and her daughter, Cathy Naylor, the items in this shop are well selected and in excellent condition. This is just the place to find those missing pieces in your grandmother's china set. Hattie's enthusiasm extends to the historic restoration she undertook when she acquired this

old Abrouzak Building and kicked off the restoration and preservation of many of the fine railroad-era buildings in the First Street Historic District across from the railroad tracks. If you're lucky enough to find her in, ask her about her nursing service during WWII.

Santa Fe Trail Traders (575-445-2888), 100 S. Second St., Raton. This is a well-established, reputable place to shop for high-end Indian-made wares, including jewelry, pottery, baskets, storytellers, and sand paintings, with the work of many well-known artists on the shelves.

Jespersen's Cache (575-843-2349), 403 Maxwell Ave., Springer. Extraordinary hodgepodge warehouse collection of secondhand collectibles, from Depression glass and boxed Barbies to an electrified antique British puppet theater. Be alert, as contemporary items that may appear vintage are mixed in with the rest. It's easy to spend a good chunk of an afternoon browsing here, and you have a good chance of making a real find. If they are closed, don't be shy about calling the number on the door. The owner will be right down to let you in.

The Outfitter (575-376-9128), 129 E. 12th St., Cimarron. Here find handmade leather goods and Whitney blanket coats, plus a mind-boggling array of vintage boots, hats, quilts, and whatever you need for a Rendezvous or Western Reenactment outfit. But do check it out, even if you are just a wannabe.

LAND GRANT COUNTRY: LAS VEGAS, MAXWELL, MORA, OCATE, PECOS

GUIDANCE **Las Vegas/San Miguel County Chamber of Commerce** (575-425-8631), 701 Grand Ave., Las Vegas, housed in the newly renovated Santa Fe Railway Depot, is professionally staffed and well stocked with information about local attractions.

Mora Valley Chamber of Commerce (575-387-6072), NM 518, Mora, is the place to learn about the work of local artists and small town festivals that feel like family gatherings.

MEDICAL EMERGENCY **Alta Vista Regional Hospital** (575-426-3500), 104 Legion Dr., Las Vegas.

✳ To See

TOWNS **Las Vegas.** Sixty-four miles northeast of Santa Fe on I-25. Named "the meadows," part of an original Spanish land grant, Las Vegas has 900 buildings listed on the National Register of Historic Places and a rough-and-tumble past. The historic structures may best be appreciated in individual self-guided walking tours described in chamber of commerce brochures. The "hanging tree" still stands on the Plaza, which is dominated by the venerable 1880s Plaza Hotel, and a revived Bridge Street radiating out from that Plaza is a pleasure to stroll and browse, with bookshops, cafés, and antiques shops. An up-and-coming area of interest is the recently restored Santa Fe train depot, which houses the visitor center, next to the old Hotel Casteneda, an original Fred Harvey hotel that stands vacant, except for the bar, in disrepair. A major Santa Fe Trail stop, then railroad town, Las Vegas was once the dominant city in New Mexico. Now home of New Mexico Highlands University and Armand Hammer's College of the American West, the town is an interesting mixture of descendants of old families, college students, and recent retirees. There is much history, including that of the German Jewish merchant pioneers, and much of the outdoors to explore here. West Las Vegas was originally called Nuestra Senora do los Dolores de las Vegas

Grandes, begun in 1835 as a land grant community of Spanish sheepherders. After the Santa Fe Trail days, when it was an important trail destination 650 miles from Missouri, the Plaza area thrived. Later, as a result of the AT & SF Railroad line, Las Vegas split into a whole separate city to the east, and it remained so until the 1970s. Locals referred to these separate towns as Old Town and New Town. Most of the adobe structures, both residential and commercial, are west of the Gallinas River in Old Town. Plentiful lodging and a variety of restaurants make Las Vegas a reasonable travel base.

Maxwell, 30 miles south of Raton on I-25, is important chiefly as the site of the Maxwell National Wildlife Refuge, a superb birding locale. It was formerly the shipping center for the Maxwell Land and Irrigation Company, and a significant site for the Maxwell Land Grant.

Mora. Thirty-one miles north of Las Vegas on NM 518. A town remaining on the huge Mora Land Grant of 1835, located in the Mora Valley, that was inhabited since ancient times by Pueblo and Plains Indians, as well as the migrating Jicarilla Apaches. Subsequently, Mora became rich territory of French Canadian mountain men and beaver trappers. Small farms and ranches populate the delightful valley, which offers excellent camping in lovely mountain campgrounds. Here may be found tiny, well-weathered Hispanic villages, churches, fishing, and wildflowers, and a feeling of the long ago as well as the faraway. The place and its people prefer their old ways and remain more or less isolated and somewhat off the grid. Expect to encounter the old wood carvers, santeros, weavers, farmers, and remnants of the Penitente brotherhood. This is not an easy area for an outsider to penetrate, and strangers may be regarded with more suspicion than friendliness.

Ocate. Twenty-three miles northwest of Wagon Mound on NM 120. A largely abandoned, scantly populated village that was home to Hispanic settlers about 150 years ago, and before that, was a hunting ground for Indians. Today, it makes appealing inspiration for photographers and artists.

Pecos. The gateway to the Pecos Wilderness, a popular fishing, hiking, and backpacking area, this little town on the Pecos River was once a mining center.

✳ To Do

MUSEUMS **City of Las Vegas Museum/Rough Riders Memorial Collection** (575-454-1401, ext. 283), 727 Grand Ave., Las Vegas. Open Tues.–Sat. (in summer, Sun.) 10–4. This museum houses extensive displays of city history, particularly around ranching and railroading, and Santa Fe Trail history, with maps, photos, ranching gear, household items, and Native American pottery. The distinctive feature is memorabilia of the Rough Riders who fought in the Spanish-American War, which was fought by the United States and Cuba in 1898, and who held their first reunion, led by Theodore Roosevelt, here. New Mexico contributed over one-quarter of the troops that fought. The Rough Rider Museum began as a private memorial. Between 1899 and 1968, reunions were held in Las Vegas. The museum is housed in a New Deal–era building. Free.

Cleveland Roller Mill Historical Museum (575-387-2645), NM 518. Open

weekends Memorial Day–Labor Day, 10–3. Two miles south of Mora in Cleveland, the mill operates once a year, only during the Cleveland Roller Mill Festival, Labor Day weekend. The Mora Valley was once a significant wheat-growing region, hence the need for the mill. The Cleveland Roller Mill was one of several in the area, opened in 1901. This adobe mill was the last to be built in northern New Mexico and was one of the largest mills in the Southwest in its day. $2 adults, $1.50 children 7–16, and under 7 free.

HISTORIC LANDMARKS, PLACES, AND SITES Bridge St. The restored Plaza Hotel on the Las Vegas Plaza anchors Las Vegas, and this is a neighborhood of interesting cafés, bookstores, restaurants, and shops that appeal to locals and visitors alike. A stroll down the three-block area, with its imposing late-19th-century architecture, suggests the powerful position Las Vegas once enjoyed as a major stop and trading center on the Santa Fe Trail and later on the Atchison, Topeka, & Santa Fe Railway. Free.

ADELE ILFELD AUDITORIUM IS THE PRIDE AND JOY OF THE NEW MEXICO HIGHLANDS CAMPUS.

LAS VEGAS' HISTORIC BRIDGE ST. OFFERS GALLERIES, CAFÉS, AND SHOPS.

La Cueva National Historic Site (575-387-2900), 25 miles north of Las Vegas via NM 518, Buena Vista. The mill, built by Vicente Romero, is the centerpiece of this historic site, along with the San Rafael Mission Church, known for its restored French Gothic windows and the mercantile, now the Salman Ranch Store. It is part of the Mora Land Grant of 1835, and Romero is believed to have been an original grantee. Much horse and ox wagon traffic between here and Fort Union took place, as La Cueva was a major shipping center for livestock and agricultural produce. Today, from Labor Day into the fall, depending on weather and harvest, visitors flock to purchase the fresh raspberries and raspberry sundaes sold in season on the Salman Raspberry Ranch located here (505-387-2900). Free.

Casteneda Hotel (575-425-8631), 524 Railroad Ave., Las Vegas. Falling into increasing disrepair, the once-proud Casteneda, an original Harvey House railroad hotel built in 1898, is closed. Only the bar, a dark, tiny place (worth a visit mainly to say you have been there), remains in operation. Free.

Montezuma Castle (575-454-4221), 5 miles northwest of Las Vegas on NM 65, Montezuma. This recently restored 1882 grand hotel is now part of Armand

Hammer United World College of the American West. Originally known as the Montezuma Hotel, it was designed for the AT & SF Railroad in Queen Anne style. After a series of fires, in 1886, the final Montezuma Castle opened. In its heyday, it was a popular destination with casino, bowling alley, stage, dance floor, stained glass from Europe, and a staff from the finest hotels in New York, Chicago, and St. Louis. Guests included Theodore Roosevelt, Rutherford B. Hayes, Ulysses S. Grant, and Jesse James. Closed in 1903, it was from 1937 to 1972 a seminary for Mexican priests. In 2001, the landmark underwent a $10.5-million renovation, transforming it into an international center. Call for public tour information. Free.

Pecos National Historical Park (575-757-6414; 505-757-6032), 2 miles south of Pecos on NM 63. Closed Christmas Day. Open daily Memorial Day–Labor Day 8–5, Labor Day–Memorial Day 8–6. This abandoned site of pueblo ruins and 18th-century mission church ruins reveal 12,000 years of history. The ruins are all that remain of the ancient pueblo of Pecos. Additional historic and cultural layering is present in two Spanish colonial churches and plentiful Santa Fe Trail sites, while the museum in the visitor center tells of the history of the Forked Lightning Ranch (previously owned by actress Greer Garson, now the property of Jane Fonda) and the Civil War Battle of Glorieta Pass. A 1.25-mile self-guided trail through Pecos pueblo and mission ruins is the best way to see the park. Guided tours of the ruins and Glorieta Battlefield are available to groups booking in advance. The trails are 80 percent wheelchair accessible. An essential stop. $3, 16 and under free.

Fort Union National Monument (575-425-8025), Watrous. Take I-25 for 12 miles north of Las Vegas, exit 366, then 8 miles on NM 161.Open daily Memorial Day–Labor Day 8–6, Labor Day–Memorial Day 8–4. Built in 1851 of adobe near the Mountain and Cimarron branches of the Santa Fe Trail, Fort Union became the largest fort in the Southwest, serving as defense and supply depot. It became a longed-for destination of Santa Fe Trail travelers. When they arrived here safely, they were as good as home. Living history programs, candlelight tours, and cultural demonstrations take place during summer months. An interpretive trail of 1.6 miles takes you through the ruins of the fort, and nearby, 1.1 miles east of the visitor center on Utah State Highway 24, are Native American petroglyphs. $3, 16 and under free.

NATURAL WONDERS **Hermit's Peak** is a massive boulderlike butte of pink granite, north of Las Vegas and visible from I-25, that is believed by some local folk to have been the home of a hermit who would care for all who were lost by rescuing them, taking them to his cave, and feeding them bread.

✳ To Do

BIRDING **Maxwell National Wildlife Area** (575-375-2331), Maxwell, just off I-25. Winter wildlife viewing includes mule deer and much birdlife, with golden and bald eagles, owls, herons, cranes, and Canada geese. Established in 1966 at an altitude of 6,050 feet, the refuge includes over 3,000 acres of rolling prairie and prairie lakes and farmland. This untouristed refuge is capable of providing a truly thrilling birding experience, with numbers that can top 990,000 migratory birds, including snow geese and numerous varieties of ducks. Free.

Las Vegas National Wildlife Refuge (575-425-3581; 505-375-2331; www .fws.gov/southwest), Route 1, Las Vegas. Six miles southeast of Las Vegas off I-25. Providing wintering and migration habitat for ducks and geese of the Central Flyway, plus some 250 migratory bird species. With 14 species of raptors, this is a great place to see eagles. There is an 8-mile auto loop through the heart of the refuge with interpretive panels and observation decks. The Gallinas Nature Trail Walk is a half-mile round-trip into a beautiful canyon, but open only on weekdays. Free.

FISHING **Pecos River,** Pecos Wilderness, Santa Fe National Forest (575-438-7840), Pecos. Apr.–late Sept. To escape the crowds and find the native browns and Rio Grande Cutthroats, it is necessary to hike into the high country of the wilderness area. If you want to cast your line without the effort required, seek the streams below Cowles.

HIKING **El Porvenir Canyon** (575-435-3534), 17 miles northwest of Las Vegas on NM 65, past Montezuma. Take Hot Springs Blvd. northwest out of Las Vegas to where it dead-ends. The Skyline Trail, accessible out of El Porvenir Campground, is a 13-mile moderate hike with altitude that ranges from 7,520 to 11,280 feet. Wildflowers are abundant, particularly wild iris in late May–early June. Once the summer resort of Las Vegas families, this canyon is now a favorite locals' place to hunt and fish. There are two creekside campgrounds close to Hermit's Peak, in the Santa Fe National Forest. $2 hiking permit, $8 camping.

Pecos Wilderness, Santa Fe National Forest (575-438-7840), Pecos. While there are dozens of trails through this stunning landscape, Jack's Creek and Baldy and Beatty's Trail among the most traveled, there are not really any easy ones. Most are difficult or moderate to difficult. Be prepared for weather changes and afternoon rains, and remember, altitudes are from 9,000 to 12,000 feet. Tread carefully.

HORSEBACK RIDING **Tererro General Store and Riding Stables** (575-757-6193), 14 miles north of Pecos via NM 63, Terrero. Open May 31–Sept. 30. Started in 1940, this remains a family-run business where you can outfit for an overnight camping trip with a wrangler to hoist your gear and make camp at 10,500 feet in the Pecos Wilderness, or just take a leisurely ride into the Santa Fe National Forest for an hour or two. Reservations a must. $30 per hour, $185 per person overnight.

Circle S Riding Stables (575-757-8440; www.circlesridingstables.com), Pecos Wilderness. Call for directions. Closed Nov.–Apr. Take one of their two-hour or overnight trips, or personalize your own journey for a half-day, a day, or longer. $55 two-hour rides.

HOT SPRINGS **Montezuma Hot Springs** (no phone), 5 miles west of Las Vegas on Hot Springs Blvd. at NM 65. Here find a very rustic, rather undeveloped hot natural spring in outdoor baths, adjacent to the Montezuma Castle. The setting is not secluded, and you need to bring your own towels. Free.

GOLFING **Pendaries Village Golf & Country Club** (1-800-733-526), Rociada. Open Apr. 15–Oct. 15. A stunning 18-hole mountain golf course perched at 7,500 feet, with, naturally, mind-blowing mountain views. Greens fees for nine holes under $30.

SNOW SPORTS ✍ **Sipapu Ski & Summer Resort** (575-587-2240), 11 miles east of Peñasco on NM 75 and NM 518 or 20 miles southeast of Taos on NM 518. With 33 trails, four chairlifts, snowboarding, a variety of trails, and terrain for all skill levels, with skilled, patient instructors, Sipapu has a well-earned reputation as a moderately priced family-friendly resort. The base elevation is 8,200 feet. It has become over the years a year-round resort, with fly-fishing in a private pond and the rainbow-stocked Rio Pueblo River. Fall is a grand time for mountain biking on the over 300 miles of trails, and bike rentals are provided. You can kick back quite happily here, in the midst of the Carson National Forest. The River Café serves homemade favorites. Tent campsites and RV hookups are also available.

WINERIES **Madison Vineyards & Winery** (575-421-8028), Ribera. Twenty-six miles south of Las Vegas on I-25, exit on NM 3. Starting with 80 French hybrid vines in the village of El Barranca on the Pecos River, Bill and Elise Madison have been making wine here since 1980. They have kept their operation small and family-run, crafting only 5,000 gallons per year. Come enjoy a beautiful operation in an exquisite setting. Wines include European-style dry and semi-sweet. Tasting room open Mon.–Fri. noon–6; Sat. 10–5; Sun. noon–5. Closed Wed. Irregular winter hours; call ahead.

✳ Lodging

BED & BREAKFASTS, INNS, AND MOTELS ⁼ʇ⁼ **Inn on the Santa Fe Trail** (1-888-448-8438; www.innon thesantafetrail.com), 1133 Grand Ave., Las Vegas. There is no more pleasant or professionally run motel in Las Vegas. When you land in one of the 28 rooms arranged hacienda-style, amid bright flower gardens, with pool and hot tub, you will relax in style. Two casitas are also available. The breakfast buffet is adequate. Blackjack's Restaurant is located on the premises. Innkeepers Lavinia and David Fenzi are excellent sources of information about the area. Book

early! This is a popular spot and a good value. $71–83.

Pecos Paradise Inn (575-757-3669), 14 Main St., Pecos. How perfect! Only 21 miles from Santa Fe, the village of Pecos is near ancient ruins and the Pecos Wilderness. If you stay at this four-room, beautifully restored 1908 home in the middle of town, you can walk to a nearby old Route 66 restaurant, and enjoy the fireplace and the services of a concierge. This lovely place is a bargain, but note, breakfast is not included, although it may be ordered at extra cost. $100.

Star Hill Inn (575-425-5605; www .starhillinn.com), Sapello. Ten miles north of Las Vegas on NM 518. An outstanding astronomy resort with eight private guest houses, each with fully furnished kitchen—BYOB (breakfast). Well stocked with telescopes and digital photo equipment, Star Hill encourages closer encounters with the heavens. Informative star tours by the owner are provided on request. $170–245.

RANCHES AND LODGES **Pendaries Lodge** (505-425-3561; 1-800-733-5267), Rociada. Twelve miles north of Las Vegas on NM 518, then left at Sapello onto NM 94/105 for 12.5 miles. Go left into Pendaries Village and follow the signs. Justifiably well known for its golf course, Pendaries is a secluded, quiet, unpretentious lodge with 18 rooms plus additional accommodations in summer homes. The restaurant serves dinner daily, and breakfast and lunch are available in the Club House. The Moosehead Saloon must be seen to be appreciated and is certainly the place for a drink. Golf packages are available at this challenging high mountain golf course tucked away in the Sangre de Cristo Mountains. $74–84.

✎ ♞ **Cow Creek Ranch** (575-757-2107, summer; 575-471-9120, winter; www.cowcreekranch.com), Pecos. If you choose to visit this well-weathered and well-loved mountain guest ranch in the Santa Fe National Forest, you will have a vacation to remember all year long. Cow Creek is an Orvis-approved historic fly-fishing guest ranch about 40 miles from Santa Fe off I-25 (please see Web site for driving instructions). Open May 21–Sept. 20, it has 20 guest rooms,

each with a kiva fireplace. The ranch bell chimes when it's time to dine. All meals are included, and there are enough outdoor activities to keep you busy all day, including riding, mountain biking, and children's programs, so you can enjoy a deeply restful slumber. Minimum three-night stay $900; children over four only, $825.

♞ **Los Pinos Ranch** (575-757-6213), 45 miles from Santa Fe, 20 miles north of Pecos via NM 63, Terrero. Since the 1920s, this small family-run guest ranch on the Pecos River in Cowles, with only 12 aspen log rooms, has been delighting guests with its superb birding, fly-fishing on the Upper Pecos River, hiking from trailheads right on the property, wildflowers, riding, and fine dining on home cooking prepared by dedicated owner Alice McSweeney. Breakfast and dinner are served in the lodge. The rooms have neither phones nor televisions. This is a perfect place to be cared for, and to renew and retreat. Open June 1–Sept. 30. $125 per day; children over six only $75.

CABINS AND CAMPING **Mark Rents Cabins** (575-988-7517). Offering nine fully furnished, renovated log cabins overlooking the Pecos River a mile from Tererro, near Pecos, this is a place that can comfortably accommodate families and larger groups. Rustic comfort is the word. There is a three-night minimum, and reservations are required. $110–190.

Pendaries RV Resort (575-454-8304), 22 miles north of Las Vegas, Park Place #3, NM 105, Rociada. Open May 1–Nov. 1. With 50 RV units and six comfortable, two-bedroom, two-bath cottages. Jean Pendaries (Pan-da-rey) moved from

France to build the Plaza Hotel in Las Vegas, then in 1875 moved to the Rociada area, still a gorgeous, quiet hideaway deep in the northern New Mexico mountains. There he built a sawmill and gristmill, which can still be seen near Pendaries Village. And today those visiting here can enjoy the high mountain golfing as well as serenity you dream about. Cottage $125, RV pad $26.

✴ Where to Eat

DINING OUT **Renate's** (575-757-2626), Pecos Rd., Pecos. Dinner only. Discover a diminutive, intimate European inn with lace curtains just off I-25 exit 299 near Pecos, under the pines. Here, Renate herself, with her daughter, make and serve authentic, delicious, homemade German food and pastries. The upright comes to life on weekend evenings as diners eat their fill of lovingly prepared sauerbraten and poppy seed cake, spaetzle, and red cabbage. Divine! Moderate.

Blackjack's Grill (575-425-6791), 1133 Grand Ave., Las Vegas. Steaks, pasta, seafood. *Gourmet* magazine called Blackjack's "One of the best restaurants in the Southwest," but methinks this sentiment is a bit over the top, perhaps because there are so few places in town that serve wine with dinner. Decent steaks, trout, New Mexican food. While certainly a pleasant place to have dinner, in most other contexts it would appear somewhat ordinary. Moderate.

EATING OUT **Hatcha's Café** (505-387-9299), 10 Hwy. 518, Mora. This place, which is actually on the main drag and easy to find, is one of the very best New Mexican restaurants in existence. Here are fabulous red chile and light, yeasty homemade sopapillas worth a drive from just about anywhere. Everything is made from scratch, the locals know the real thing, and this is where to find them. Enjoy your enchiladas with wine, beer, or a margarita. Call ahead, as hours can be irregular. Inexpensive.

Frankie's at the Casanova (575-757-3322), on the corner of NM 50 and NM 63, Pecos. Closed Mon. Breakfast, lunch, and dinner. Housed in the old Casanova Bar dating to the 1920s, Frankie's is an authentic Southwestern grill with a spiffy new outdoor patio bar serving a good selection of beer and wine. Go for the piñon pancakes for Sunday brunch. The chile, red or green, is hot and flavorful, and the fajitas practically sizzle off the plate. Live music Fri., Sat., Sun. nights. Moderate.

Estella's Café (575-454-0048), 148 Bridge St., Las Vegas. Breakfast, lunch, dinner weekends. Would you like to eat in your New Mexican *abuelita* (grandma's) kitchen, right down to the oilcloth on the table? Of course you would. And at Estella's Café, you can. This food is as authentic as New Mexican cooking gets, and this restaurant goes high on any "Top Ten" list. In business almost 60 years, it is now run by the third generation, Estella's granddaughter. The green chile is tastier than it is hot, and the sopaipillas are divine when slathered with honey. Order the combination plate for the best deal. Hours may be irregular, but they can be counted on for lunch and, sometimes, dinner Thurs.–Sat., but be sure to get there before 8 PM. If in doubt, call ahead. Inexpensive.

Charlie's Bakery & Café (575-426-1921), 715 Douglas Ave. Open daily.

CHARLIE'S SPIC 'N SPAN IN LAS VEGAS IS A MUST-STOP FOR MEXICAN-FOOD LOVERS.

Breakfast, lunch, dinner. Excellent green chile, tortillas so fresh you can watch them being made, a showcase of pastry delights, and Starbucks coffee. This is a local hangout for college students, professors, and old-timers, where everyone knows each other by their first name. It is a clean, pleasant, spacious place that is a sentimental longtime favorite frequently referred to by its former name, the "Spic 'n Span." Charlie's is just about always open. Inexpensive.

✳ Selective Shopping

Tapetes de Lana (575-426-8638), 1814 Plaza, Las Vegas (on the northwest corner of the Plaza). Watch weavers at work, and check out the handmade rugs, table runners, and shawls, in beautiful, natural colors at reasonable prices. This is a wonderful place to find gifts. In Mora, you'll find their second shop at NM 518 Junction 434, or Main St. Tours of the mill are available here during the week. This is a nonprofit organization that is an important local employer.

Rough Rider Antiques (575-454-8963), 501 Railroad Ave., Las Vegas, across the street from the restored Train Depot and Visitor Center. This spacious, freshly restored historic building holds the premier collection of antiques, sold by assorted consigners, in a town jam-packed with antiques shops. Whatever your interest—vintage postcard collecting, finding that embroidered Mexican felt jacket from the 1950s, a Fiesta skirt, or a Fiesta pitcher—your chances of finding it here are quite good. Prices are fair, and fun is guaranteed.

ROUTE 66 COUNTRY: SANTA ROSA, TUCUMCARI

Getting your kicks is no problem out here. You'll find plenty of vintage neon and a culture that celebrates the Route 66 era. In addition, Santa Rosa and Conchas Dam have swimming and boating and a way to stay cool. It's hundreds of miles of nostalgia.

GUIDANCE **Santa Rosa Visitor Information Center** (575-472-3763), 486 Historic Route 66, Santa Rosa, is a sophisticated stop with all the information and contacts you could want to experience the area fully.

Tucumcari/Quay County Chamber of Commerce (575-461-1694), 404 W. Route 66 Blvd. Open Mon.–Sat. 9–5; closed Sun. Tucumcari is a traveler-friendly, professional road stop.

MEDICAL EMERGENCY **Dan C. Trigg Memorial Hospital** (575-461-7000), 301 E. Miel De Luna, Tucumcari.

Guadalupe County Hospital (505-472-3246), 535 Lake Dr., Santa Rosa.

✳ To See

TOWNS **Santa Rosa**, 114 miles east of Albuquerque on I-40. This railroad-era Fourth Street Business District with its Ilfield Warehouse and many old storefronts has been known as a Route 66 stop since 1926, when the Mother Road first came through. Many landmarks are still visible in Santa Rosa, where part of the film *Grapes of Wrath* was shot. Plenty of colorful Route 66 establishments are still going strong in Santa Rosa, and it is, unexpectedly, known for its lakes and water sports, in particular, the Blue Hole of scuba diving fame.

Tucumcari, 173 miles east of Albquerque on I-40. With probably the most and best-preserved vintage Route 66–era neon, including several that have recently been refurbished, Tucumcari is the largest town closest to the eastern border of the state. Nostalgia rules when the Blue Swallow Motel lights up at twilight. There is good access here to Conchas Lake State Park, Ute Lake State Park, and the Mesalands Scenic Byway, with plenty of wildlife viewing and excellent birding. Tucumcari has, in addition to marvelous Route 66–era architecture, with a restaurant shaped like a sombrero and a curio shop shaped like a teepee, the longest mural devoted to Route 66 in the United States at its convention center. Two museums of note are here—the Mesalands Dinosaur Museum and the Tucumcari Historical Museum. The name of the town is possibly derived from a Comanche term meaning "lookout point" or "signal peak." Tucumcari Mountain was, in fact, used as a lookout for Comanche war parties. The town's original name was "Six Shooter Siding."

MUSEUMS ✐ **Mesalands Dinosaur Museum** (575-461-3466), 211 E. Laughlin, Tucumcari. Open Labor Day–Feb. Tues.–Fri. 10–6, Sat. noon–5. A surpris-

UNIQUE ADVENTURES

✐ **Victory Ranch Alpacas** (575-387-2254), MM 1, 1 mile north of Mora on NM 434, Mora. Open daily 10–4. Visit, pet, and feed the alpacas, gentle small cousins of llamas, grown for their wool. The Victory Ranch herd is one of the largest and finest in the United States. A 3,000-square-foot clothing and gift store stocks rugs, jackets, sweaters, toys, yarn, and fiber on this magnificent 1,100-acre ranch. $3 adults, $2 children 12 and under.

✐ ♿ **Dinosaur Trackway** (575-374-8808), Clayton Lake State Park. (See Clayton Lake State Park under *Green Space*.) More than 100 million years ago, this area was an inland sea extending from the Gulf of Mexico to Canada. The creatures that roamed here left their footprints, and at least eight different kinds have been identified among the 500 dinosaur tracks that have been preserved, including some of the winged pterodactyl. The tracks are located on the dam spillway, at the end of a gentle 0.25-mile trail. The best times to view the tracks, when they are most clearly visible, are in morning and late-afternoon light.

NRA Whittington Center (575-445-3615), 10 miles southwest of Raton on US 64. Amid these 30,000 acres are Santa Fe Trail ruts. Shooting ranges and lessons in all sorts of weaponry are offered. Lodging, camping, and RV hookups are available, too. Many of the world's top competitions are played here. A variety of ranges available—skeet, sporting clays, black powder pistol, and more.

Santa Rosa Blue Hole (575-472-3370), Will Rogers Hwy., Santa Rosa. A unique geological phenomenon—a natural bell-shaped artesian pool 81 feet deep with a constant water temperature of 62 degrees Fahrenheit year-round and visibility of 80 feet, making it ideal for training. It is in the high

ingly in-depth collection of dinosaur skeletons, fossils, sculptures, and exhibits are shown at Mesalands College. $6 adults, $5 seniors 65+, $3.50 children and teens, under 5 free.

Route 66 Auto Museum and Malt Shop (575-472-1966), 2866 Will Rogers Dr., Santa Rosa. Open Nov.–Mar. Mon.–Sat. 7:30–6, Sun. 10–5; Apr.–Oct. Mon.–Sat. 8–5, Sun. 10–5. If you love vintage autos, this is the place for you. While dedicated to the preservation of Route 66 custom cars and memorabilia, this museum serves darn fine chocolate malts. $5.

Tucumcari Historical Museum (575-461-4201), 416 S. Adams St., Tucumcari. Sept.–May Mon.–Fri. 8–5; June–Aug. Mon.–Sat. 8–5. If you like looking into the

desert at 4,600 feet above sea level, making the bottom equivalent to over 100 feet of ocean depth. Winter is actually the busiest season. The Santa Rosa Dive Center is open weekends to rent gear and fill tanks, and midweek by appointment. Go to the visitor center to purchase permits, 8–5 Mon.–Fri. Permits $8 weekly; $25 annually. To dive in the Blue Hole, you must have PADI or NAUI or other certification papers.

FEEDING THE ALPACAS IS ENCOURAGED AT VICTORY RANCH.

way people lived in the past, from their parlors to their kitchens, you will enjoy this sentimental collection of furniture, farm and ranch exhibits, Indian artifacts, and early town memorabilia. Free.

SCENIC DRIVES **Mesalands Scenic Byway,** 320 miles total, in Quay and Guadalupe counties. *Mesa,* meaning "table" in Spanish, is the term used to describe high, flat plateaus. This is the country of high lonesome, a dry, dramatic and evocative landscape. On the southern edge of this scenic byway is the El Llano, Estacado, or the Staked Plains, a 32,000-mile mesa. The estacado refers to the cap rock, a geologic feature throughout this area. The habitat of prong-horn antelope and sandhill cranes, this byway encompasses Santa Rosa in Guadalupe County and Tucumcari in Quay County.

✳ To Do

BOATING See the state parks listed under *Green Space.*

Santa Rosa Park Lake (575-472-3763). Open for swimming Memorial Day–mid-Sept. Certified lifeguards are in attendance, and Park Lake is the South-west's largest swimming pool featuring a free water slide. Kids and seniors can fish in two stocked ponds. You can rent a pedal boat for $1 each half-hour. No overnight camping. Free.

GOLFING **Tucumcari Municipal Golf Course** (575-461-1849), 4465 Route 66. Five miles west of Tucumcari. Closed Mon. This pleasant, tree-lined nine-hole golf course with the greens located between high mesas will satisfy your need to putt while in town. Greens fees for nine holes $10.

✳ Green Space

WILDLIFE REFUGES AND AREAS **Colin Neblett Wildlife Area** (575-445-2311). These 36,000 acres between Eagle Nest and Cimarron along US 64 include Cimarron Canyon State Park, making it the largest state-run wildlife area for deer, elk, and other forest critters. The Cimarron River, a great German brown fishery, runs through it. Bring binoculars and cameras, and try your luck with a Rio Grande King.

Elliott S. Barker Wildlife Area (575-445-2311), 14 miles northwest of Cimarron. Here, in the heart of the northeast, find over 5,000 acres of hiking, hunting, wildlife viewing, and, should you choose, horseback riding. High-clearance vehicles are strongly recommended, as the roads can be rocky and the streams can swell in this pristine and primitive area. There's a good chance you'll spot bear up here. I have.

Valle Vidal (575-586-0520), 27 miles north of Cimarron off US 64. This unit of the Carson National Forest means "Valley of Life." If you've ever longed to see herds of magnificent, noble elk in their natural setting, this is your best bet, par-ticularly at twilight. The Valle Vidal is 100,000 acres of specially managed prime elk habitat, home to a herd of 1,700 elk, in the Carson National Forest. Also, in season, find fishing and backcountry camping. A word of warning: be sure your spare tire is in good working order. Perhaps it is our karma, perhaps it is the loose rocks in the road, but we get a flat every time we come up here. If you drive the entirety, from north of Cimarron across to Costilla, you'll put 64 miles on your vehicle.

MOUNTAINS Villanueva State Park (575-421-2957),Villanueva. I-25 exit 323, go south 23 miles, then 15 miles south on NM 3. Nestled between 400-foot-high red and gold sandstone bluffs along the Pecos River near the Spanish colonial village of Villanueva is a picturesque campground shaded by giant cottonwoods along the Pecos River. This park is a haven with fishing, hiking trails within views of old ranching ruins, and one trail that leads to a prehistoric Indian ruin. The 2.5-mile Canyon Trail loops from the river to the top of the canyon and back. Kayaking and canoeing are enjoyed when the water level is high enough, from early May–mid-June, usually. Day use $6, overnight camping $8–18.

Sugarite Canyon State Park (575-445-5607), northeast of Raton on NM 72 for 11 miles. During the height of summer, this is a busy place, with coal camp tours, kids' programs, and occasional evening talks by local historians and naturalists. From the wild iris of late May to wild rose, bluebell, larkspur, scarlet penstemon, blue flax, and sunflowers and aster, Sugarite is unbeatable for wildflowers. Butterflies love it here, too. Find showers, camping, hiking, and a fine exhibit of coal mine camp. There is year-round trout fishing on Lake Maloya, one of three alpine jewel lakes surrounded by an extended cliff of basaltic rock. The lake has recently been stocked with trophy trout. Hikers and mountain bikers have access to more than 12 miles of trails. This is the only place in New Mexico where you can explore the ruins of a coal mining camp. The former camp post office is the colorful visitor center. The first mine in the canyon opened in 1901, with full-scale mining beginning in 1912 with the building of the Sugarite Coal Camp. In its prime, 500 people lived, worked, shopped, worshipped, and went to school here. It was a melting pot of Italians, Slavs, Japanese, Mexican, and British. The coal camp ended in 1941 when oil replaced coal. $6 day use per vehicle, $8–18 overnight camping.

RIVERS AND LAKES Cimarron Canyon State Park (575-377-6271), 3 miles east of Eagle Nest on US 64. Open year-round. The clear Cimarron River runs through the 8 miles of forested land on both sides of US 64, with abundant elk, deer, turkey, grouse, and bear for the sighting. Two billion years of complex geology are visible here, notably, the 400-foot-high crenellated granite Palisades. But the Cimarron is best known for its excellent fly-fishing for German brown and rainbow in a variety of waters: gravel pits, beaver ponds, and running streams. For peace, wildflower viewing, and getting away from it all, whether for a day or a longer stay, the Cimarron can't be beat. Many campers make long stays; make reservations early. The 96 sites in several campgrounds—Maverick and Tolby are favorites—offer good river access. $5 day use, $10–18 overnight camping.

Conchas Lake State Park (575-868-2270), New Mexico State Park and Recreation Division, Conchas Dam. Thirty-two miles northeast of Tucumcari on NM 104. This is an outstanding getaway and prime recreation spot for fishing,

IT'S FUN TO COOL OFF IN THE CIMARRON RIVER.

boating, waterskiing, wind surfing, and swimming, with 60 miles of shoreline and plenty of coves, canyons, and sandy beaches to explore. Both north and south recreation areas have well-developed marinas, stores, cafés, camping, and picnic areas. South Conchas Lodge (505-868-2988) has cozy rooms as well, plus 110 RV units. Completed in 1939 by the Army Corps of Engineers, Conchas Dam rises 200 feet above the Canadian River. The lake covers about 15 square miles, extending 4 miles up the Canadian River and 11 miles up the Conchas River. Open year-round for fishing. Abundant walleye, catfish, and largemouth bass swim the waters. Have fun! $6 day, $8–18 overnight camping.

Santa Rosa Lake State Park (575-472-3111), Santa Rosa. The lake is actually a high plains Pecos River reservoir 7 miles from Santa Rosa on NM 91, with waterskiing, wind surfing, and excellent fishing. Canoeing, too! Stay a while with 76 developed camping sites and 25 electric sites, restrooms, showers, and a visitor center. The easy to moderate hiking trails offer wildlife viewing through 500 acres of parkland. Here also is one of the state's few designated equestrian trails and all necessary accommodations for horses. There are two short paved wheelchair-accessible trails as well.

Ute Lake State Park (575-487-2284), 30 miles northeast of Tucumcari via US 54, then 3 miles west of Logan via NM 540. This 13-mile-long, narrow lake, producer of many state record fish, is a happy local camping destination with boating, welcome swimming in the summer heat, hiking, wildlife viewing, and fishing for walleye, bass, and catfish. $6 day use, $8–18 overnight camping.

Clayton Lake State Park (575-374-8808; reservations 1-877-664-7787), 141 Clayton Lake Rd., Clayton. Twelve miles northwest of Clayton on NM 370. Fishing and boating Mar.–Oct.; hiking, camping, Dinosaur Trackway. One-hundred-seventy-acre lake, a blue jewel in the desert. Boats are restricted to trolling speeds (no whitewater). During winter, the lake is a migration point for waterfowl. It's an excellent place to spot bald eagles. The Dinosaur Trackway and boardwalk along the gentle half-mile trail provide extensive information. Among rolling grasslands near Santa Fe Trail, the lake is a waterfowl resting area in winter. $6 day, $8–18 overnight camping.

Storrie Lake State Park (575-425-7278). North of Las Vegas on NM 518. Wind surfing, fishing, boating, waterskiing, picnicking. Camping and RVs. The park is open to all boating, with no horsepower restrictions, so it is geared for wind surfers and water-skiers. Kayaks and canoes are also popular here. There is year-round trout fishing as well. $6 day, $8–18 overnight camping.

Coyote Creek State Park (575-387-2328), 17 miles north of Mora on NM 434. At 7,700 feet in the eastern foothills of the Sangre de Cristo Mountains, find in this off-the-beaten-path park mountain trout fishing in the most densely stocked fishing area of the state, lovely solitude, camping, picnicking, and a 1.5-mile, easy trail through ponderosa pine. $6 day use, $8–18 overnight camping.

WILDER PLACES

Canadian River Canyon runs 13 miles through the Kiowa National Grasslands, approximately 10 miles northwest of Roy. The 800-foot canyon is a natural wildlife refuge in the prairie for mountain lion, wild turkey, eagles, and waterfowl. Mills Canyon Campground, offering primitive overnight camping, is located at the bottom of the gorge. A remnant herd of Barbary sheep roams through this stark, remote, and unforgettable place.

Kiowa and Rita Blanca National Grasslands (575-374-9652), 15 miles south of Clayton via NM 402 or east via US 87. Rita Blanca is 17 miles east of Clayton via US 64/56. For those who want to put their feet on the trail, here are 2 miles of Santa Fe Trail ruts, plus grasslands. In their entirety, these grasslands stretch through New Mexico, Texas, and Oklahoma. The New Mexico section of the Kiowa National Grassland covers 136,562 acres near Roy and Clayton, with plenty of habitat for wildlife. This land was purchased by the Federal government during the Great Depression following the Dust Bowl, removed from farm cultivation, planted, and maintained as grasslands.

✳ Lodging

BED & BREAKFASTS, INNS, AND MOTELS **Blue Swallow Motel** (575-461-9849), 815 E. Route 66, Tucumcari. Closed Oct.–Mar. Owned and operated by Lillian Redman, a former Harvey Girl, for over 40 years; current owners Bill and Terri keep the tradition of this Route 66 beacon alive. With its classic Route 66 neon, the 1939 humble stucco motel, with eight rooms, preserves its comfy, vintage character. $45.

CABINS AND CAMPING **¹ɪ¹ Santa Rosa Campground** (575-472-3126), 2136 Will Rogers Dr., Santa Rosa. Open year-round. With the extra added attractions of the Western Bar-B-Q (served each evening 5–8), homemade peach cobbler (in the restaurant with an outdoor patio), beer and wine, plus free Wi-Fi, you can enjoy all manner of camping. There are 70 pull-thru RV sites, tent sites, and a cabin where you can get out of the camper and stretch out for a while. There's a gift shop, playground, heated swimming pool, laundry facilities and 50-amp services, groceries, and supplies here as well. $30.

HISTORIC HOTELS
Plaza Hotel (505-425-3591; 1-800-328-1882; www.plazahotel-nm.com), on the Old Town Plaza at 230 Plaza, Las Vegas. Built in 1882, when it was known as "The Belle of the Southwest," this is a great Victorian hotel renovated to preserve a clean, not fussy, 19th-century atmosphere. The Landmark Grill restaurant has never been known for its cuisine, but the Old West Byron T's Saloon (named for the resident ghost), high-speed wireless Internet, room service, on-site masseur, and the fun of returning to those glorious days of yesteryear makes this an excellent choice for travelers. You can even stay in one of four suites overlooking the Plaza. The Plaza is currently undergoing a large expansion. $69–149.
St. James Hotel (575-376-2664; 1-866-472-5019), 617 S. Collinson, Cimarron. Every outlaw who was any outlaw stayed at the St. James, as did Buffalo Bill Cody, Annie Oakley, Kit Carson, and Wyatt Earp. Photos of desperados and heroes line the downstairs hallway, decked with an antique roulette wheel. Mounted trophy heads adorn the period lobby. The beds are quilt-covered, the curtains draped in lace, and the rooms of the old hotel are not very soundproof. Twenty-seven bullet holes may be seen in the ceiling of the Lambert Saloon. Fourteen restored rooms with 19th-century furnishings occupy the main hotel; a two-story annex adjacent provides an additional 10 rooms. The St. James is located smack dab on the Old Santa Fe Trail. Murder Mystery Weekends here are very popular. Begun as a saloon in 1873, established by Lincoln's chef, Henri Lambert, this place became a haven for

Where to Eat

DINING OUT Lake City Diner (575-472-5253), 101 S. Fourth St., Santa Rosa. Dinner only. Unexpectedly located in the midst of Route 66 land, this place is one of those small, cozily elegant establishments where each dish is freshly made by hand and served in a lovingly restored tin-ceiling building with white linen tablecloths. The beautiful salads, fresh pasta, and steaks will leave you feeling well dined, indeed. It's a pleasant change from ubiquitous roadside burgers!

EATING OUT Silver Moon Café (575-472-3162), 3501 Will Rogers Dr., Santa Rosa. Open daily. Breakfast, lunch, dinner. Serving travelers since 1959, with that cool Route 66 neon lighting up the night and home-cooked meals lighting up smiles. Tasty Mexican and American food served here.

Del's Restaurant & Gift Shop (575-461-1740), 1202 E. Route 66, Tucumcari. Closed Sun. If you are actually eating a meal in Tucumcari, Del's is your best bet. This place, a standard roadside family diner that retains its original 1956 flavor

Santa Fe Trail traders and mountain men. It has been featured on *Unsolved Mysteries* and is reportedly highly haunted. There are an elegant restaurant serving dinner, a comfortable café, and a legendary bar on the premises, though "dancing naked on the bar is no longer permitted." $80–120.

Eklund Hotel (575-374-2551), 15 Main St., Clayton. This is a lovely, recently restored 19th-century railroad hotel built by immigrant-entrepreneur Carl Eklund. For many years it has been owned and operated by a consortium of local residents. The rooms are not large, but they are clean and comfortable. Both the bar and the restaurant are memorable; the same menu is served in each. This hotel has been lovingly, painstakingly brought back to its original, authentic self. For a true taste of the Old West in modern comfort, do not miss! $83–133.

El Portal Hotel (575-445-3631), 101 N. Third St., Raton. Built by immigrant entrepreneur Hugo Seaberg in 1903, this downtown hotel with café next door boasts WPA-era murals in a lobby crammed with overstuffed Victorian furniture, and it is indisputably a place with character. For those who prefer to stay away from chain motels and want a more colorful experience, here is your place. With 18 private rooms furnished with antiques and claw-foot tubs, it has a dusty elegance you can write home about. You can easily walk to the train station from here. $45.

Historic El Fidel Hotel (575-425-6761), 500 Douglas Ave., Las Vegas. Built in 1923 in Spanish colonial revival style, this is another place loaded with local color and offers its 18 rooms at bargain prices. D-Vino's Italian Restaurant next door serves wine and beer. $45–85

(courtesy of the owners, sisters Yvonne and Yvette), serves reliably good homemade American cooking, the kind you long to find on a cross-country drive, as popular with locals as with travelers. The burgers are juicy, and the chicken fried steak with mashed potatoes and cream gravy is a triumph, as good as the best on the road. Even liver is on the menu! Yummy beef taquitas, too. The salad bar is more than respectable, and two homemade soups are included. Inexpensive–Moderate.

Pow Wow Restaurant & Lizard Lounge (575-461-0500), 801 Route 66, Tucumcari. This place is dark and would be smoky, if smoking were allowed. It is, and always has been, the premier town hangout, the place where visiting politicians rub elbows with the locals, the cowboys, the Indian traders, and the Route 66 tourists from Germany. It is also a good place to order a steak. Moderate.

La Cita (575-461-7866), 812 S. First St., Tucumcari. You'll want to have your picture taken here, for sure, so you can show the world you dined in a sombrero. The Mexican food isn't the greatest, and some think the portions are too small for the price, but it's not bad, either, and you'll have so much fun you probably won't notice. Inexpensive.

✳ Entertainment

Aside from occasional live performance events at the Shuler Theater in Raton, the best we are likely to come up with in the way of nightlife is a drink at the bar of the historic hotel or the chance to catch a movie at a vintage theater like the recently reopened El Raton. Mostly, folks go to bed early here, so it's a good place

to catch up on your reading or do some stargazing.

✳ Selective Shopping

Tee Pee Curios (575-471-3773), 924 E. Tucumcari Blvd., Tucumcari. Not only is this a classic Route 66 photo op, with the front of the shop a white concrete teepee painted in bright turquoise lettering, but inside you can find every T-shirt, shot glass, and travel souvenir of your road trip that you could ever imagine. I recently purchased a Route 66 print overnight bag here for $10. A highly amusing must-do.

✳ Special Events

January: **Ice Fishing Tournament and Chile Dinner** (575-758-3873), Eagle Nest. Look for this event mid-month, all you frozen fish lovers.

February: **Moonlight Ski Tours and Headlamp Snowshoe Tours** (575-754-2374), Enchanted Forest XC Ski and Snowshoe Area, Red River.

May: **Guided ruins tours and cultural demonstrations,** Pecos National Historical Park, weekends, Memorial Day–Labor Day.

June: **Mule Days** (1-888-376-2417), Maverick Rodeo Grounds, Cimarron. **Shortgrass Music Festival** (575-376-9040), Cimarron. **Raton Rodeo** (575-445-3689), York Canyon Rodeo Grounds, Raton. **Las Vegas Celebrates the Arts** (575-425-8631), Las Vegas, tours of artist studios. **Fort Union Days** (575-425-8025), Fort Union National Monument, Watrous. **Santa Fe Trail Rendezvous** (575-445-3615), Raton, mountain man gathering, NRA Whittington Center.

July: **International Santa Fe Trail Balloon Rally** (575-445-3689; www.raton.info.com), Fourth of July

TEE PEE CURIOS IN TUCUMCARI IS WHERE TO GET YOUR SOUVENIRS OF THE MOTHER ROAD.

weekend, La Mesa Airfield, Raton, with pancake breakfast to accompany the liftoff of rainbows of hot-air balloons. **Maverick Club Parade and Rodeo** (1-888-376-2417), Fourth of July, Maverick Arena, NM 64, Cimarron. Longest running open rodeo in the West. **Fourth of July Parade and Fireworks** (575-377-2420), Eagle Nest. **Route 66 Celebration** (505-461-1694), Convention Center, 1500 W. Route 66, Tucumcari.

August: **Las Vegas Historic Home Tour** (575-425-8803; www.lasvegasnm .org), Las Vegas, first Sat. **Colfax County Fair** (575-445-8071), Springer Armory, Springer. Cakewalk, parade, pie contest, barbeque dinner;

second weekend. **Music From Angel Fire** (1-888-377-3300; www.music fromangelfire.org). Outstanding classical music performances throughout northern New Mexico in Raton, Las Vegas, Angel Fire, late Aug.–early Sept.

September: **Cimarron Days Festival** (1-888-376-2417), Village Park, NM 64, Cimarron, Labor Day weekend. **Raspberry Roundup,** Salman Ranch, Labor Day weekend into Sept., generally the first three weeks of the month. Fresh raspberries and raspberry treats abound in country store at La Cueva Historic District. **Cleveland Roller Mill Festival** (575-387-2645), Cleveland, Labor

Day weekend. This is the only weekend of the year when the creaky old mill operates, and it is a true festival of northern New Mexico dance, food, and crafts. **Wagon Mound Bean Days** (575-666-2410), Wagon Mound, celebrates the days when Wagon Mound was the bean capital of the world, with barbeque worth waiting in line for, crafts, parade, and politicians aboard floats. **Nara Visa Cowboy Poetry Gathering** (575-633-2220), Nara Visa, third weekend. As much local color, with music and rhyme, as you can find anywhere. **Annual Route 66 Festival** (575-472-3763). Come on out and get your kicks here in Santa Rosa.

October: **Clayton Arts Festival** (575-374-9253; 1-800-390-7858), Clayton, first weekend. A long-established, much-anticipated, profuse display of Western art. **Artesanos del Valle Tour,** Las Vegas area, first weekend. Diverse and wonderful artists' studio tour.

November–December: **City of Bethlehem** (575-445-3689), Raton. Thanksgiving weekend through Christmas holidays, enjoy a nostalgic tour of life-sized cartoon characters that guide the way up into Climax Canyon, where the Christmas story is presented high in the rocky hills, accompanied by seasonal music. This free event is an annual family favorite.

INDEX